THE DAEMON

IN THE WOOD

THE
DÆMON

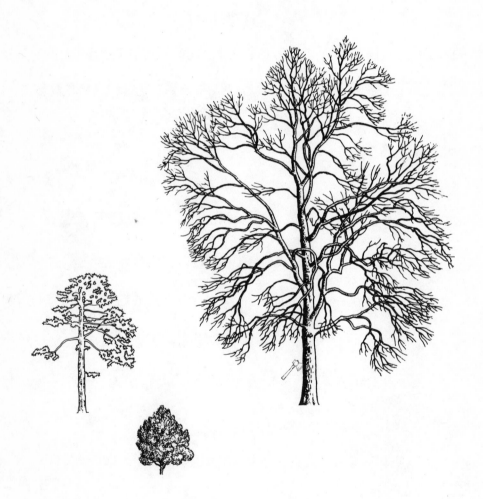

PUBLICATIONS
OF THE
MILMAN PARRY COLLECTION

GENERAL EDITOR

ALBERT B. LORD

MANAGING EDITOR

DAVID E. BYNUM

MONOGRAPH SERIES

NUMBER ONE

HARVARD UNIVERSITY
CAMBRIDGE, MASSACHUSETTS

PUBLICATIONS OF THE MILMAN PARRY COLLECTION

Documentation and Planning Series

1. The Haymes Bibliography of the Oral Theory. Compiled by Edward R. Haymes.
2. Oral Literature at Harvard since 1856. By David E. Bynum.

Texts and Translations Series

1. The Wedding of Smailagić Meho. Translated with Introduction and Commentary by Albert B. Lord.
2. Ženidba hadži-Smailagina sina. Edited by David E. Bynum.

Monograph Series

1. The Daemon in the Wood; a Study of Oral Narrative Patterns. By David E. Bynum.

in
the WOOD

A Study
of Oral Narrative
by
Patterns
David E.

Bynum

with a Foreword by ALBERT B. LORD

published by
the center for study of
oral literature

Harvard University
Cambridge, Massachusetts
1978

Copyright © 1978 by David E. Bynum.
All rights reserved.

Library of Congress catalog card number: 78-20294.
International Standard Book Number (ISBN): 0-674-18031-3.

Designed and set in Bodoni type by the author.
Printed in the United States of America by
Thomson-Shore, Inc., Dexter, Michigan.

Distributed by Harvard University Press,
Cambridge, Massachusetts.
Harvard University Press bookcode: BYNDAE.

Library of Congress Cataloging in Publication Data:

Bynum, David E
    The daemon in the wood

    (Publications of the Milman Parry Collection : Monograph
series ; no. 1)
    Includes bibliographical references and index.
    1. Folk literature—Themes, motives. 2. Oral tradition.
3. Parry, Milman. I. Title. II. Series: Milman Parry Collection.
Publications. Monograph series ; no. 1.
GR74.4.B96   398'.042   78-20294
ISBN 0-674-18031-3

To Grace

Tolerant Friend
and Gentle Wife

εἰ δ' ἄγε τοι καὶ δένδρε' ἐϋκτιμένην κατ' ἀλωὴν
εἴπω, ἅ μοί ποτ' ἔδωκας, ἐγὼ δ' ᾔτεόν σε ἕκαστα
παιδνὸς ἐών, κατὰ κῆπον ἐπισπόμενος· διὰ δ' αὐτῶν
ἱκνεύμεσθα, σὺ δ' ὠνόμασας καὶ ἔειπες ἕκαστα.
ὄγχνας μοι δῶκας τρισκαίδεκα καὶ δέκα μηλέας,
συκέας τεσσαράκοντ'· ὄρχους δέ μοι ὧδ' ὀνόμηνας
δώσειν πεντήκοντα, διατρύγιος δὲ ἕκαστος
ἤην· ἔνθα δ' ἀνὰ σταφυλαὶ παντοῖαι ἔασιν,
ὁππότε δὴ Διὸς ὧραι ἐπιβρίσειαν ὕπερθεν.

    Ὣς φάτο, τοῦ δ' αὐτοῦ λύτο γούνατα καὶ φίλον ἦτορ,
σήματ' ἀναγνόντος τά οἱ ἔμπεδα πέφραδ' Ὀδυσσεύς·
ἀμφὶ δὲ παιδὶ φίλῳ βάλε πήχεε· τὸν δὲ ποτὶ οἷ
εἷλεν ἀποψύχοντα πολύτλας δῖος Ὀδυσσεύς.

– ΟΔΥΣΣΕΙΑΣ Ω 336-348

Contents

Acknowledgment and List of Illustrations   xi

FOREWORD *by Albert B. Lord*   xvii

PREFACE   3

Chapter One: HIDE AND SEEK   35

Chapter Two: TREES AND TRICKSTERS   55

Chapter Three: INTER DVOS ARBORES   85

Chapter Four: THE RITUAL FALLACY   149

Chapter Five: UP, DOWN, ALL AROUND, AND
WHO MADE THE WORLD   257

EPILOGUE   *Some Observations Concerning*
Method and Rationale   293

APPENDIX   *OGRES AND COSMOTACTS:*
Further examples and notes
on the Two Trees' Pattern   331

NOTES   439

INDEX   449

ACKNOWLEDGMENT

The author gratefully acknowledges the help given during the preparation, writing, and composition of this book by the Clark Fund and the Canaday Humanities Fund in the Faculty of Arts and Sciences at Harvard University; by the Harvard College Library and its staff; and by the National Endowment for the Humanities. Professor Mary Louise Lord of Connecticut College read and astutely criticized both the typescript of this book and also its unpublished sequel, a herculean parergon to her busy professional life by which she made this book both better and easier to read. Rick Stafford helped generously with the photography and photographic apparatus. The students in the General Education program at Harvard and Radcliffe Colleges stimulated and compelled whatever clarity this work can be said to bring to its subject.

Special thanks are due to the Trustees of the Pierpont Morgan Library for permission to publish the photographs of the objects in their collection reproduced here in Figures 36, 37, 38, 39, 40, 41, 42, 43, 44, 47, 48, 56, 57, 60, 63, 64, 65, and 66.

LIST OF ILLUSTRATIONS

A typical stand of grass on the Central African Plateau. *Photograph by the author.* page 40

Figure 1. Women pounding grain. *Photograph by the author.* page 101

Figure 2. A 'milk tree.' *Photograph by the author.* page 111

Figure 3. A fresh cut in a milk tree. *Photograph by the author.* page 112

Figure 4. A fresh cut and an old 'scab' on a blood-wood tree. *Photograph by the author.* page 113

The author's source of a Central African Flood story. *Photograph by the author.* page 118

Figure 5. A general view of a Baobab tree. *Photograph by the author.* page 129

Figure 6. Detail of a Baobab tree. *Photograph by the author.*   page 130

Figure 7. Fragment of a steatite pyxis from Knossos.   page 166

Figure 8. A gold signet ring from Mycenae.   page 167

Figure 9. Intaglio on a steatite lentoid from Ligortino, Crete.   page 168

Figure 10a. A young fruit tree fenced against goats. *Photo-
graph by the author.*   page 169

Figure 10b. A fence that failed. *Photograph by the author.*   page 170

Figure 11. A gold signet ring from Knossos. *Photograph by
the author.*   page 172

Figure 12. A gold signet ring from Crete. *Photograph by the
author.*   page 173

Figure 13. A gold signet ring from Asia Minor.   page 173

Figure 14. A gold signet ring from Mochlos. *After Seager,*
Explorations in the Island of Mochlos, *fig. 52; the
original ring is lost.*   page 174

Figure 15. A gold signet ring from Mycenae. *Photograph by
the author.*   page 174

Figure 16. A gold signet ring from Mycenae.   page 175

Figure 17. Impression of a gold signet ring. *After Martin P.
Nilsson,* The Minoan-Mycenaean Religion, *plate I, 2.
Some consider this ring a forgery.*   page 176

Figure 18. A gold signet ring from Mycenae. *Photograph by
the author.*   page 177

Figure 19. A gold signet ring.   page 177

Figure 20. A gold signet ring from the Vapheio tomb at
Mycenae. *Photograph by the author.*   page 178

Figure 21. A gold signet ring from Mycenae. *Photograph by
the author.*   page 179

Figure 22. Shard of a vase from Cyprus.   page 180

Figure 23. Intaglio on a lentoid gem from Goulas, Crete.   page 181

Figure 24. Impression of a crystal signet ring from Mycenae.   page 182

Figure 25. Impression of a lentoid gem from Mycenae.   page 182

Figure 26. The Lion Gate of Mycenae. *Photograph by the author.*   page 183

Figure 27. The pillar-and-lion relief over the gate at Mycenae. *Photograph by the author.*   page 184

Figure 28. Intaglio on a lentoid gem from Zero, Crete.   page 185

Figure 29. A gold signet ring from Mycenae.   page 186

Figure 30. Impression of a lentoid gem from Mycenae. *Photograph by the author.*   page 187

Figure 31. A gold signet ring from Mycenae. *Photograph by the author.*   page 187

Figure 32. Intaglio on a lentoid gem from Kydonia, Crete.   page 188

Figure 33. A signet ring of electron from Mycenae. *Photograph by the author.*   page 189

Figure 34. Fresco on a sarcophagus from Hagia Triada. *Photograph by the author.*   page 191

Figure 35. A relief of Gilgamesh. *Photograph by the author.*   page 193

Figure 36. Impression of a carnelian cylinder seal.   page 194

Figure 37. Impression of a cylinder seal of white calcedony.   page 194

Figure 38. Impression from a cylinder seal of green and white siliceous stone.   page 196

Figure 39. Impression from a cylinder seal of yellowish chert.   page 198

Figure 40. Impression from a cylinder seal of brown and grey jasper breccia.   page 198

Figure 41. Impression from a cylinder seal of greenish calcedony.   page 199

Figure 42. Impression from a cylinder seal of bluish calcedony.   page 200

Figure 43. Impression from a cylinder seal of black serpentine.   page 201

Figure 44. Impression from a damaged cylinder seal of pink chert.   page 202

Figure 45. Impression from a cylinder seal showing a hero with griffins and a tree.   page 202

Figure 46a. A women's mural painting from Moravia. *After H. Th. Bossert*, Ornamente der Folkskunst (Neue Folge).   page 204

Figures 46b-e. Views of the painted mosque in Travnik, Yugo-slavia. *Photographs by the author.*   pages 204-6

Figure 47. Impression from a cylinder seal of greenish black and olive buff serpentine.   page 207

Figure 48. Impression from a concave shell cylinder seal.   page 207

Figure 49. Impression of a cylinder seal from Tell Asmar.   page 208

Figure 50. Impression from a cylinder seal in the British Museum.   page 208

Figure 51. Impression from a cylinder seal showing a scene of offertory.   page 211

Figure 52. Impression of a cylinder seal showing an offertorial procession.   page 212

Figure 53. Impression of a cylinder seal showing the feeding of cattle.   page 213

Figure 54. Impression from a cylinder seal showing the feeding of small livestock.   page 215

Figure 55. Impression from a cylinder seal showing green tree and herbivores.   page 216

Figure 56. A cylinder seal.   page 218

Figure 57. Impression from the cylinder seal shown in Fig. 56.   page 219

Figure 58. Impression from a cylinder seal.   page 221

Figure 59. Impression from a cylinder seal.   page 221

Figure 60. Impression from a cylinder seal of whitish calcedony.   page 222

Figure 61. Impression from a cylinder seal in Geneva.   page 223

Figure 62. Impression from a cylinder seal in East Berlin.   page 224

Figure 63. Impression from a cylinder seal of black serpentine.   page 224

Figure 64. Impression from a cylinder seal of black serpentine.   page 225

Figure 65. Impression from a cylinder seal of orange chert.   page 226

Figure 66. Impression from a cylinder seal of black serpentine.   page 233

"The Horn-Snake," a drawing by John McLenan for the frontispiece in Harden E. Taliaferro, *Fisher's River (North Carolina): Scenes and Characters*, New York, 1859.   page 328

Figure 67. A detail (impalement) from a prospect of Papa (Hungary).   page 355

Detail from a drawing by Grandville (Jean I.I. Gérard) from his published collection *Un Autre Monde*, Paris, 1844.   page 447

Foreword

This book is about oral traditional stories and their meanings. Dr. Bynum takes the concept of tradition very seriously. Many people, however, in their thinking about tradition go no further back than two generations. To them the common phrase "handed down from generation to generation" stops with grandparents. If one does not restrict the process in that way but carries it back very literally to time immemorial, then there is a distinct possibility that the story one heard from one's grandfather might be very, very old. This is not only sound logical reasoning, it is also common sense. Not every tale told will be primeval, of course. There are late entries into the body of traditional narratives. But there is a group of narratives, probably the most significant of man's stories, which contains basic symbols of vital importance to storytellers and to their audience since times beyond history.

Dr. Bynum in this book concentrates on such stories and reports on his exploration of one of the richest and most significant motifs in the vast tracts of traditional narrative. He has searched widely in the world for the "daemon in the wood" and has caught glimpses of him in far-flung places and in ancient as well as in modern times. For trees are found nearly everywhere, and they live and die and are useful to man in hundreds of ways, not least of all as symbols in his stories. In the various contexts of mythic and other narrative they grow and flourish and are in full leaf in groves and forests; or as wood cut, smoothed, and polished, they serve the needs of man.

Much of great value has been written on the formulaic and thematic style of oral traditional literature and on the characteristic techniques of composition and transmission of those literatures which help scholars to determine whether a text from the past belongs to an oral tradition or not. There is still a large amount of extremely important and crucial research yet to be undertaken in those areas. But it is time that more attention should be paid than heretofore to discovering the meanings to be found locked in oral traditional literatures. This book is, therefore, refreshing in that it leaves aside other considerations for the moment and turns to identifying the kernels of meaning to which the traditional formulas have given shape. It is devoted to exploring Parry's proposition of "*how* [any poetry] should be understood if it was oral." In so doing it takes the reader on exciting adventures, but it must be read slowly and carefully in order that one should not miss any closely thought-out point.

One of the many extraordinary features of this book is that all its elements—chapter titles, the quotations at the head of each chapter, the illustrations, and the text—work together to form an artistic and intellectual whole. Take, for example, the little story on the title page of chapter four, "The Ritual Fallacy," and its illustration on the page preceding the Appendix. In that tale and drawing can be found the essence of the "daemon in the wood," who lurks throughout this work in other traditional multiforms both narrative and graphic. Dr. Bynum's study of the motif of trees in oral traditional stories emphasizes the way in which man has expressed in them, and still continues to do so, some of his most profound feelings and comments on life and its values. The art of story with its astonishingly ancient use of symbols is the crowning achievement of man's gift of speech.

Cambridge, Massachusetts   Albert B. Lord
July, 1978

PREFACE

This is the green tree; what then shall be done in the dry?

- Samuel Butler

The 'Parry Test' and the primacy of 'essential ideas.'   p.   3

The clustering of essential ideas: a Yugoslav example from
        the Parry Collection.   p. 13

The 'solution from the text,' and the distraction of other
        methods.   p. 18

The Two Trees: an example of oral narrative tradition's
        universal adaptability.   p. 26

Milman Parry's brief career of scholarly achievement had two parts. He studied Homeric style, and he collected South Slavic oral poetry, in that order. The genius of his accomplishment lay in his perception of a necessary nexus between those two activities.

Two passages have most often been recited from Parry's writings as encapsulations of his doctrine regarding oral tradition and the oral traditional style of poetic composition. The first passage is strictly descriptive, pertains to style, and stems from the study of Homer. It is Parry's definition of the oral traditional poetic 'formula' as *"a group of words which is regularly employed under the same metrical conditions to express a given essential idea."** The second passage is narrative, pertains to interpretative criticism, and stems from Parry's experimental research as a field-collector of South Slavic oral poetry. He wrote about his own field collection:

> . . .the present collection of oral texts has. . .been made. . .with the thought. . .of obtaining evidence on the basis of which could be drawn a series of generalities applicable to all oral poetries; which would allow me, in the case of a poetry for which there was not enough evidence outside the poems themselves of the way in which they were made, to say whether that poetry was oral or was not, and *how* it should be understood if it was oral.
>
> A method is here involved, that which consists in *defining the characteristics of oral style.* . . .Style, as I understand the word and use it, is the form of thought. . . .†

As the central mechanism of oral style, the 'formula' in Parry's definition was no theoretical end in itself. It was the key that would give him access through the doorway of his field experience in Yugoslavia to a whole new interpretative technique, and open to him a new understanding of early and primal poetries quite beyond the reach of any understanding that existing literary theory could offer. The needfulness and the possibility of such an innovation in interpretative criti-

---

*Adam Parry, ed., *The Making of Homeric Verse; the Collected Papers of Milman Parry*, Oxford (Clarendon Press), 1971, p. 272. The italics are Parry's own.

† Ibid., p. 440.

cism presented themselves to Parry's mind because of the distinctive way oral traditional poets made their poems. Parry observed, and demonstrated in his early writings, how the oral traditional poet's manner of composition was utterly different and apart from the literary poet's in any age. That radical difference sprang not from the divergence of intrinsically verbal, prosodic, or other merely *expressive procedures* between the oral and the literary poet, but rather from the fact that the oral and the literary poet were fundamentally, necessarily, and irreconcilably different in *how and what they thought,* and were obliged *by the force of their divergent ideas* to use distinctively different diction and compose poetry in characteristically different styles.* Oral traditional poetry differs in style from belletristic poetry not because literary poets generally do not or have not ever wished to imitate poetry in oral tradition, but more compellingly, because they *cannot.* Thus did Milman Parry deny the pertinence of literary theory to Europe's first and oldest poetry.

But Parry also discriminated rigorously between his proposition and its proof. He understood clearly, as his followers in later decades have too often not understood or remembered, that the proof of exactly how and what oral traditional poets think has to come in the first instance from poetic traditions known to be oral, not merely conjectured to be so on the written evidence of dead poetries—i. e., from poetry that was oral traditional *de facto* and not merely *de jure.*† Hence his own Yugoslav collection, and the others, forestalled by his death, which he expected to make.

The shortness of Parry's life and of his scholarly career robbed us in later years of little that those who knew him while he yet lived could not extract and develop for us from suggestions in his writings or in his remembered talk concerning formula and oral traditional style. What he did not live to give us, which we have most needed and too

---

*The dominant idea in Parry's *L'Épithète traditionelle dans Homère,* the least read and most basic of his writings. See especially part IV of that work (Parry, op.cit., pps. 118-172). Parry chose Homeric epithets as material for beginning the delineation between oral traditional and belletristic poetic styles just because the epithets most immediately disclosed the 'unconscious' and conventional thinking of oral bards; but see also the discussion of "The Art of Traditional Poetry" in Parry, op.cit., pps. 333-337.

† Parry, op.cit., pps. 439-440.

long hesitated to evolve for ourselves, was instruction about just those ideational fundaments which he said underpinned and accounted for the stylistic peculiarities of oral tradition. In the four decades since his death, other scholars in all manner of fields have welcomed Parry's Oral Theory with its inherent promise of new interpretative insights.‡ Yet almost to a man they have behaved as though they thought the kernel of Parry's Oral Theory lay in his formal observations about the oral style of composition; that is, in the formulaic rhetoric of oral traditional poets. Much has been ventured, and some gains registered in the forty years of formula studies since Parry, but a palpable *ennui* has also emerged among scholars who were once attracted to the Oral Theory as the practice of formula-counting has become more common, lost its first blush of novelty, and for the most part failed to deliver the innovations in the substantive understanding of oral traditions which were expected of it from the first.

This disappointment springs, however, not from any weakness of the Oral Theory or of Parry's demonstrations of it in his own writings. It is rather the work since Parry that has too often been disappointing in its inexact, mechanistic, and ideologically timid utilization of the Theory.

I have said that Parry's theory was welcomed by scholars in many fields. The commonest way of welcoming it has been an act of almost ritual devotion, repeating the basic gesture of what may be fairly called the Parry Test of Orality. Having previously established at great length what he conceived oral formularism to be, and how that differed from mere repetition of poetic phrases in the belletristic manner, § Parry first demonstrated his now famous Test in part 5 of his "Studies in the Epic Technique of Oral Verse-Making. I. Homer and Homeric Style." * The most dramatic and easily imitated part of his Test consisted in noting in an arbitrarily selected passage of twenty-five lines (first in the *Iliad* and then in the *Odyssey*) all "the expressions. . .which are found elsewhere. . .in Homer." The mechanical procedure was to "put a solid line beneath those word-groups which are found elsewhere in

---

‡ Many of these are catalogued in: Edward R. Haymes, *A Bibliography of Studies Relating to Parry's and Lord's Oral Theory*, Cambridge (Publications of the Milman Parry Collection), 1973.

§ Parry, op.cit., pps. 24-36; 280-301; *et passim*.

* Ibid., pps. 301-314.

the poems unchanged, and a broken line under phrases which are of the same type as others."†

In its first, classic demonstration by Parry himself, the Parry Test was, however, carefully circumscribed and controlled by several prior and posterior considerations. First, Parry applied his Test only to Homer, that is to say, to long, metrical, and presumably sung, fabulous narrative—in a word, to epos. The Test was, furthermore, applied only to texts in which oral formula (as distinct from mere phrasal repetitions or repetends) had *already previously been shown to exist.*‡ And then, when within those two prior restrictions the mechanical work of noting and underlining repetitions in twenty-five selected verses had been done, there remained to complete the Parry Test the further steps of proving both the *length* and *thrift* of the formulaic systems to which the repetitions and repetends noted in the twenty-five-line samples belonged. For as Parry himself insisted immediately after presenting his own charts of solid and broken underlining in samples of the *Iliad* and *Odyssey*, ". . .the difference between the repetitions in Homer and those in the works of later poets is very great; . . .we are looking for the difference not in repeated phrases but in formulas. It is important at this point to remember that the formula in Homer is not necessarily a repetition. . . ."§

Those who, following Parry, have welcomed the prospect of a new criticism for oral traditions to be evolved through the investigation of oral style have widely embraced the Parry Test as a kind of touchstone or litmus test for oral tradition in poetry of unknown or uncertain provenience, especially when that poetry belonged to an early age in literary history. This has been true especially as awareness of the Oral Theory spread outward from its point of origin in Homeric studies to find application in other language traditions. As that diffusion took place, the procedures and controls of the Parry Test should, if anything, have been even more strictly observed and more refined by experience than they were in Parry's own work. But such has rarely been the case. Instead of increasing precision, increasing imprecision

† Ibid., p. 301.

‡ By the method employed in both *L'Épithète traditionelle* and before the Test in the same paper where Parry introduced it: see Parry, op.cit., pps. 266-301.

§ Parry, op. cit., p. 304.

and a growth of downright confusion has accompanied wider application of the Parry Test. For the mere observation and underlining of
repetitions in sample lines of poetry never was and never will be anything but an empty gesture unless it is attended by at least those same
restraints and procedural concomitants which Parry himself found
necessary, prescribed, and obeyed in devising his famous Test:

1. The Test represents a theory applicable only to texts
    from traditions of long, metrical, presumably sung,
    fabulous narrative, or *epos.*

2. It is applicable only to texts in which the presence of
    formula (as distinct from repetition) has already been
    shown.*

3. Both the formulary (solidly underlined) and the formulaic
    (brokenly underlined) language found by means of the Test
    must further be shown to adhere to "formulaic systems."

4. The "formulaic system" must further be tested for its
    distinctive *length.*

5. Having been demonstrated to be long, formulaic systems
    require further to be tested for their distinctive *thrift.*

---

*From this point the acute reader will appreciate that in reality the Parry Test
never was, nor was it intended to be, a proof of the *fact* of oral formularity in
given texts, but only of its *extent.* Parry's method of testing for the *fact* of formula (i. e., the difference between formula and mere poetic repetition) turned
rather upon the oral traditional Singer's evident want of awareness in his use of
a formulaic system as to that system's meaning. For whereas a formulaic system
might have a deep or complex sense as seen by a critic studying oral tradition,
the oral poet himself must, like Homer, use the system in such a way as to betray that he often gave no consideration to the exact sense or rightness of the
juxtapositions he gave to formulas in his composition, but only to the conventional appropriateness or *expectedness* of their occurrence under given metrical
conditions. In this connection Parry most emphatically discerned that the essence
of the oral formulaic style was not formal but ideational. Not the poet or Singer
himself, even when he was so great as Homer, but rather the tradition as it evolved
and survived over great spans of time kept the ideas found in it; and just as no
"single man or even a whole group of men who set out in the most careful way
could. . .make even a beginning at such an oral diction. It must be the work of
many poets over many generations," so too no single Singer, not even great Homer, could in himself personally grasp in a conscious manner more than a small
part of all the ideas in the tradition he bore. The Singer's diction in betraying
that fact gave the tell-tale stamp of orality to his use of formulaic systems, and
so makes it possible for us as critics to distinguish oral formulas from literarily
repeated phrases.

Oversimplification of the Parry Test leads to spurious results and needlessly confuses scholars who want to know what literarily preserved monuments of the past might be oral compositions. Such confusion has been felt most acutely in the field of Old English. Perhaps because Parry was an American, and because in America Old English studies are carried on by a more numerous professional cadre than any other language field affords (including Parry's own field of Homeric studies), more attempts at application of the Parry Test have been made upon Old English poetry than upon any other. But Parry's example was from the first imperfectly understood in this field, and the effects of that misapprehension, compounded over decades of research and controversy, have latterly brought the subject to so serious an impasse that many now feel helpless to proceed with the subject in any way at all. The movement began with Francis P. Magoun's paper on the "Oral-Formulaic Character of Anglo-Saxon Narrative Poetry" where Magoun dutifully performed the convert-to-Oral-Theory's initiatory ritual of the twenty-five-line Parry Test not just once but twice over.* He did so, however, without regard to the vital distinction between epos and other kinds of poetry; from the outset he strove to bring *into* the compass of hypothetically oral traditional poetry the very genres which Parry had in the case of ancient Greek been obliged by his understanding of formulaic style specifically to *exclude* despite the considerable incidence in those genres of phrasal repetition, namely 'lyrical-elegaic' and 'encomiastic' ('praise') poetry,† riddles, and such manifestly non-epic poems as *Christ and Satan*. Whereas Magoun diligently quoted Parry's warning that "usefulness rather than mere repetition is what makes a formula," he nevertheless made his twenty-five-line Parry Test of *Beowulf* without any preliminary consideration as to whether the *fact* of oral formula could be shown in *Beowulf* as Parry had done for Homer before he even tried to appraise the *extent* of the formulary language there. Instead, Magoun presented a twenty-five-line chart of repetitions he had found in *Beowulf* as though the chart itself were somehow proof of oral formulaic style, and innocently commented, "The formulaic character of the verse is demonstrated by Chart I . . . ." Satisfied with this supposed proof that *Beowulf* was an oral traditional composition, he further omitted entirely to consider

---

* *Speculum*, XXVIII, 3, (July, 1953), 446-467.

† Hence the recently touted expansion of the search for oralism to include praise poetries such as those found in Africa, Ceylon (Sri Lanka), and the Indian subcontinent, which, if it has any merit in its own right, has nevertheless nothing to do with the application, proof, or disproof of Parry's theory.

whether the repetitions in *Beowulf* were assimilable to formulaic systems, much less whether any such systems if they could be found might display the identifying traits of *length* and *thrift*.

Magoun's mechanical imitation of Parry without regard to the controls Parry set upon his own procedure set a precedent for a whole generation of younger scholars to elaborate in the same vein. Soon there was hardly any poetry in Old English for which someone had not mooted oral origins, and always with as much reliance as possible on the merely mechanical part of the Parry Test, and as little reliance as possible on any ideational factors, including the crucial ideational test for the *fact* of formula that Milman Parry had devised years before his invention of the twenty-five-line chart.

In the same doggedly formalistic fashion, those who did not welcome the critical separation of Old English poetry from the historical continuum of English literary tradition fought back against the Oralists with technical questions about how the Parry Test was carried out, and whether the tallies and percentages resulting from it were fairly computed. For a time it seemed that no opinion for or against orality could be defended in the Old English field without the advocacy of a statistician. Finally in 1966 the growing corps of opponents of the Magoun school found a spokesman who was willing to combine competence in the tabulation of repetitions and repetends with some regard for the ideational values that had fallen into disregard so long as the controversy remained preoccupied with wrangling over the statistical aspects of the Parry Test. The spokesman was L. D. Benson, who parodied the title of Magoun's original article in the title of his own paper, "The Literary Character of Anglo-Saxon Formulaic Poetry."*

But in the event, Benson's criticism of the Magoun school was not more disciplined from the point of view of Parry's original hypothesis and procedure than Magoun's own work had been. However inattentive to it he was in practice, Magoun had at least once known and quoted Parry's warning that repetition was no proof of oral formularism. But Benson gave no sign of ever having known the distinction between *repetition* and *formula* in the first place. To him that consideration carried just the weight that it had actually had in Magoun's practice, where in truth it was only a distinction without a difference.

---

*PMLA, LXXXI, 5, (October, 1966), 334-341.

The difference was real and essential to Parry, but Benson had before him the powerful example of ignoring that difference as set not only by Magoun but also by the numerous other intermediaries subsequent to Magoun who had intervened in the Old English field between Benson's time and Parry's. Benson's aim being only to disallow his predecessors' dubious proofs of oral formularism in Old English poetry, not himself to investigate whether any works in that poetry were reliques of oral tradition or not, he did not return to the Homerist's own work to learn what the Homerist had taught.

Benson wrote in his challenge to the Magoun school,

> Perhaps the most fruitful and exciting development in Old English studies in recent years has followed from F.P. Magoun's discovery that the Parry-Lord theory of oral verse-making can be applied to Old English poetry. This theory has caught the imagination of critics and has produced a "kind of revolution in scholarly opinion" not simply because it shows us that the style of this poetry is traditional—that has been known for many years —but because it offers a new and useful way of approaching the problems raised by this style, because it provides a new way of considering some of the relationships between these poems, and because it casts light on an area that we thought was forever darkened, the pre-literary history of Germanic and Old English verse.

Considering the rest of his comment in the same paper, it is plain that Benson meant this bit of praise to be an epitaph for the Parry theory in the Old English field. He went on to write:

> So useful has the theory proved and so widely has it been accepted that it is not surprising to find it already hardening into a doctrine that threatens to narrow rather than broaden our approach to Old English poetry.

It may be true that Parry's theory affords little license for the kinds of "approach to Old English poetry" that Benson referred to. But neither he nor we are presently in any position to evaluate that matter. For viewed from the pristine and still valid position of Parry's own writings, it was not at all the "Parry-Lord theory" but only Magoun's loose and mistaken construction of that theory that was in 1966 "already hardening into a doctrine that threatens to narrow" both the interpretative and the technical criticism of Old English poetry. Even a moderately strict constructionist of Parry's method

must admit that the work in Anglo-Saxon *has yet to be begun* in a
mode acceptably faithful to the original model. And until Parry's own
method (rather than the mechanistically imitative, unreasoning one
devised by Magoun) has actually been applied to the *one* text in Anglo-
Saxon that is by its genre clearly appropriate to the Parry Test, namely
Beowulf, and the results of that application are carefully compared
with Parry's results for Homer, there can be no basis for speculation
about the orality of any other texts in Anglo-Saxon within the framework of the Parry theory.

More than a decade has passed since Benson published his chastis-
ing paper, and nothing has so demonstrated the inadequacy of the
repetition-tabulating school as its evident inability to correct even those
most fundamental misconstructions of Parry's thought in Benson's
critique of the work on Old English. It is, for example, absurd in
Parry's terms to speak as Benson did of Anglo-Saxon poetry in the
mass as "obviously formulaic even when lettered;" for to Parry phrasal
repetition (which of course occurs to some extent in all kinds of poetry) was *formula* only when it occurs in oral traditional epos where it
conveys ideas that are basically unavailable to poets who write. But
nothing has yet been shown by Parry's own method to be both oral
and traditional in the surviving corpus of Anglo-Saxon poetry, and so
no justification yet exists for calling any repetitions or repetends in
that poetry formulas or formulaic. Reflecting as he did only upon
the work of Magoun and his successors, and hence confused by Magoun
on this central point, Benson could hardly escape thinking that in Old
English "some of the poems that survive may indeed be oral compositions, but we can never be sure which they are." Indeed no other conclusion was ever possible by Magoun's method.

If someday an Anglo-Saxonist will examine at first hand how
Parry analyzed Homer, and then follow *that* method with *Beowulf,*
we may yet very reasonably hope for real knowledge as to what is
or is not a relique of oral tradition in Old English. *Mutatis mutandis,*
much the same must be said also about other language-fields where
short-cuts and abbreviations of the full Parry Test have been relied
upon to prove oral composition. If the progress of studies in those
other fields has not yet brought them to the impasse seen in Old
English, it is only a matter of time until the fewer hands laboring in
those fields also find themselves obliged by similarly equivocal results
to begin again what they too should have more conscientiously done

from the outset in applying Parry's method. For nothing in that
method was redundant or superfluous. Time and sound experience
may show us that we need further refinements or extensions of
Parry's method, but that conclusion must likewise wait upon the
full and faithful use of what we already have at hand as example
in Parry's study of Homer.

One may reduce the distinction Parry drew between poetic repetition and oral formula in parts 2 and 3 of his article on "Homer and
Homeric Style"* to a simple contrast. For the oral poet who sings
long, traditional, fabulous narrative, the ideas prescribed in the tradition summon certain conventional phrases to mind according to the
metrical moment; and when the Singer repeats those phrases, as he
must, in a system with other phrases which have the same metrical
value and which are enough alike in thought and words to leave no
doubt that the poet who used them knew them not only as single
phrases but also as phrases of a certain type,† then we have to do
with the formulas of oral composition. For the literary poet, however,
it is the phrase that brings an idea to mind, both to him and to his
readers. I am strongly reminded of H. A. Wolfson's metaphor for words
as 'floating buoys' that mark the place of submerged thoughts—as nice
a statement of the literary poet's typical attitude as I know. Without
the buoy, the thought is lost. But for the oral poet the ideas in tradition are ever present, and it is only the words that need be summoned to mind to fill the meter. While the literary poet is free as the Singer in oral tradition never is to invoke any idea he pleases, he is also
obliged at some time consciously to inspect and appreciate the sense
of all his phrases no matter how often he may later routinely repeat
them. Thus his diction is *particulate* rather than *systematic* as the oral
traditional Singer's is, and while freer in its conscious gamut of ideational reference, it is nevertheless far more confined in the richness of
ideational reference it may unconsciously achieve.

To see the truth of this essential proposition, one must leave for
a time, as Parry left, the contemplation of a dead tradition's fossil-texts
(like the texts of Homer or of *Beowulf)* to see formula and formulaic
systems at work in the living dynamics of actual Singers' poetic practice. There and only there are the hypotheses about what oral poets

---

*Parry, *The Making of Homeric Verse*, pps. 272-279.

† Here I paraphrase Parry's own description, op. cit., p. 275.

'might do' in traditions of metrical epos finally demonstrable. Therein will be found too the fulfillment of that necessary nexus between Parry's definition of formula and his collection of Yugoslav oral poetry that made Parry's short career so enduring an example. The aim of this book is further to elaborate that nexus. For upon the strength of that nexus depends, as Parry said it did, the certainty of anything we may subsequently be able to say about the oral character of texts whose provenience, like that of *Beowulf,* we do not more directly know.

THE CLUSTERING OF ESSENTIAL IDEAS: A YUGOSLAV EXAMPLE FROM THE MILMAN PARRY COLLECTION

The formula is *"a group of words which is regularly employed under the same metrical conditions to express a given essential idea.* The essential part of the idea is that which remains after one has counted out everything in the expression which is purely for the sake of style."* But Parry's 'essential ideas' are seldom altogether so simple as the shortness of Parry's definition or the usual brevity of formulas themselves, the conventionality of the epic style, or the banality of most formulas' lexical reference may superficially suggest. The essential ideas in tradition which the formulaic language of the oral style serves—the ideational fundaments of the Singer's art which Parry said existed but did not himself live to elucidate—these are at one and the same time the basic denominators of Parry's 'formulaic systems' and the premises of the innovation in interpretative criticism which his approach promises for our understanding of oral traditions. The mechanical formality of formula-counting and formula-parsing which has for forty years since Parry preoccupied the Oralists has brought some benefits, but it has also contributed disappointingly little to our ability to understand what formulas are really about—the essential ideas of oral tradition.

Any arbitrarily selected passage by an ordinary Yugoslav Singer represented in the Parry Collection will show many 'essential ideas' of the tradition of a simple kind. The following two passages represent the same segment in a tale which Parry obtained by dictation twice— with an interval of four months—from the same Singer in Novi Pazar in 1934. The narrative concerns a pause in a journey by an inexperi-

---

*Parry, op. cit., p. 272.

enced youth who gives up old associations and gains new ones by chance encounters in the wilderness.*

Nesta polja, pridje planinama.	Nesta polja, pridje planinama,
Dvije redom prolazi planine,	Dokljen dvije prolazi planine,
Bukovika i Orahovika,	Bukovicu i Orahovicu, 150
A kad dodje u Kunar planinu, 145	Pa ispade na Kunar planinu,
Ode šljeći niz lazinu belu.	Na planinu na vel'ku lazinu.
Jelje rjetke do neba su takle.†	
A kad stiže na dno od lazine,	Uze djadu pravo niz lazinu.
Pa udari niz tvrdu klisuru.	Kad laz prodje, nad klisurom dodje,
Ode mu se nešto poslušati. 150	Ode mu se nešto poslušati. 155
Ozdol tutanj, sve se zemlja trese.	Ide tutanj ozdolj uz planinu.
Sam beg beše, pa se prepanuo,	Sam bijaše, pa se prepanuo,
Koje li su halje uz planinu.	
Pa se skide sa konja dorata,	Pa se skide sa konja dorata.
Pa se maće z desna na lijevo,‡	
Pa se sakri pod jelu zelenu.	Uvede ga u jelovo granje.§

The flatlands vanished; he came to the mountains.	The flatlands vanished; he came to the mountains.
Two mountains he crossed, one after the other,	After he had crossed the two mountains,
Mount Beech and Mount Walnut,	Beech Mountain and Walnut Mountain,
And when he came into Mount Kunar,	He came out onto Mount Kunar,
He descended by way of a broad, bare clearing.	And a great clearing upon the mountain.
Fir trees here and there grew up to the very heavens.	
When he came to the foot of the clearing,	He made his way directly down the clearing.
He went on by way of a close glen.	When he had passed the clearing, he emerged above a glen.
A sound caught his attention, and 150 he fell to listening:	A sound caught his attention, and he fell 155 to listening:
It was a thunderous sound from below, making the earth quake.	A thunderous sound was moving up the mountain.
The bey was alone, and took fright,	The bey was alone, and took fright,

---

* For the larger framework of this traditional tale, see my "Themes of the Young Hero in Serbocroatian Oral Epic Tradition," *PMLA* 83 (1968) 1296-1303.

† Cf. verse 458, 'Vitke jelje do neba su rasle,' in: Albert B. Lord, ed., *Serbocroatian Heroic Songs*, II (Novi Pazar: Slavic Texts), Cambridge and Belgrade (Serbian Academy of Sciences and Harvard University Press), 1953, p. 60.

‡ Cf. verse 195, ' " 'Ajde ovde," kaže, "z desna na lijevo," ' again followed in the next verse by direction to a fir tree, op. cit., p. 110.

§ Both of these Serbocroatian passages are drawn from Lord, op.cit., pps. 173 and 159 respectively.

Fearing what terrible beings might be
   ascending the mountain.
So he got down from his white horse, .   So he got down from his white horse,
And turning smartly withershins,
He hid himself beneath a green fir tree.   And led him into a thicket of fir branches.

The repetitions and repetends seen in the two parallel passages above (both performed by the same *de facto* oral traditional poet) meet two of Parry's criteria for formulas. They display their performer's sometimes conventional use of phrases whose necessity or pertinency to his themes he evidently does not consciously reflect upon. We see here the ideas prescribed in tradition finding words in the poetic habits of the Singer without his contemplative volition. Salih Ugljanin, the Singer before us, can in no wise explain just why fir trees (and not any others) are the right 'decorations' for this scene, while we as critics can see—as I have tried to show in the body of this book—that the fir trees he knows consciously only as 'decorations' are in their meanings both essential and extraordinarily ancient in the tradition which this Singer only unconsciously (but no less effectively for that) bears witness to for us. In Parry's method, however, even this is not enough evidence of orality. The repetitions and repetends in these passages must also display membership in formulaic systems whose *length* and *thrift* we may further examine at our leisure in the extensive corpus of texts which Parry collected from this same Yugoslav Singer. Now it follows from the nature of *systemic length* that in short passages of oral traditional poetry such as the two adduced here (or those in any typical 25-line Parry Test if the text analyzed is oral and traditional) that a higher incidence of *formulaic* than of strictly *formulary* (exactly repeated) phrases should be expected. This is in fact what we see in Salih Ugljanin's performances.

How typical of his tradition were Salih Ugljanin's performances? A second Singer who was palpably even more able than Ugljanin, and who belonged to the tradition in another district of the same region, sang in a style no less demonstrably oral by Parry's criteria than Ugljanin's. But while the essential ideas of the second, better Singer's formulas correspond neatly to those of the first Singer, the phrases which the 'essential ideas' found for their expression in the second Singer's mind more often than not reflect a discontinuity of formulaic systems between the two oral poets. The two performances by Ugljanin from which I extracted the two passages quoted above totalled 1,297 and

1,195 verses respectively, while the second Singer's text on the same themes, which I shall quote below, ran to 3,738 verses and remained unfinished with only about a quarter of the whole narrative told. Correspondingly, the verses I quote from the second Singer were interspersed with other lines from verse 1,267 through verse 1,393 of his performance. One may begin in such examples to understand the relationship between formulas and thematic length; for whereas the proportion of overall length of performance between the two Singers is almost 1:3 and would have been twice that or more had the second Singer finished his performance (judging from the average length of the twelve other performances which this Singer did finish for Parry), the 'essential ideas' we are now examining in the two Singers' disparate performances and disparate formulaic systems are nevertheless clustered in sections of verse having lengths with the same proportional relationship to each other as the whole performances from which they are extracted also do. In the following chart I use Parry's technique of defining essential ideas as "that which remains after one has counted out everything in the expression which is purely for the sake of style." I give the essential ideas in italics with sequential numbers, and under the italics the oral poets' own diction, that of the first Singer (Salih Ugljanin) in the first column, and that of the second Singer (Avdo Medjedović) in the second column.

1. *Leaving the plains, and reaching*
   the mountains.

Nesta polja, pridje planinama

Kad Kladuško polje pregazijo,
Udbinskog se polja nafatijo.
Kad je hemen polje pregazijo   1269

Na Kunaru kad su iskočili   1329

2. *Traversing Mount Kunar.*

A kad dodje u Kunar planinu
/ Pa ispade na Kunar planinu

Na Kunaru kad su iskočili

3. *Other mountain(s) traversed (named*
   according to the dominant species of
   trees in the covering forest).

Dvije redom prolazi planine,
Bukovika i Orahovika
/ Dokljen dvije prolazi planine,
  Bukovicu i Orahovicu

Pod Brešljen hi mrki akšam nadje 1339

4. Four places traversed.

Nesta polja [1], pridje planinama.
Dvije redom prolazi planine,
Bukovika [2] i Orahovika [3],
A kad dodje u Kunar planinu [4],

/ Nesta polja [1], pridje planinama,
Dokljen dvije prolazi planine,
Bukovicu [2] i Orahovicu [3],
Pa ispade na Kunar planinu [4]

Kad Kladuško polje [1] pregazijo,
Udbinskog se polja [2] nafatijo.

Cijel Kunar goru prijedjoše [3]   1338
Pod Brešljen *h*i mrki akšam nadje [4]

5. A glade entered.

Ode šlje*c*i niz lazinu belu.
A kad stiže na dno od lazine
/ Na planinu na vel'ku lazinu.
Uze djadu pravo niz lazinu.
Kad laz prodje, . . .

U mrki *h*i homar zavedoše   1341

6. High trees.

Jelje rjetke do neba su takle.

Pokraj puta prevelike jele
Preko klanca preplešu grane   1350

7. A narrow mountain pass.

Pa udari niz tvrdu klisuru
/ . . . nad klisurom dodje

Tjesni klanci, dugi karamani   1351

8. Commotion of a terrific warrior's approach.

Ozdol tutanj, sve se zemlja trese.
/ Ide tutanj ozdol uz planinu

Tutanj velik ide uz bogaze   1353

9. Listening.

Ode mu se nešto poslušati

Dok se Halka dade poslušati   1352

10. Dismounting.

Pa se skide sa konja dorata
/ Pa se skide sa konja dorata

Oba momka konje odsjedoše   1340

11. Concealment in trees.

Pa se sakri pod jelu zelenu
/ Uvede ga u jelovo granje

U mrki *h*i homar zavedoše   1341

12. Movement withershins

Pa se ma*c*e z desna na lijevo

"Z desna, brate, na lijevo zadji."   1393

Reviewing these dozen 'essential ideas' in two Yugoslav oral epic Singers' tradition, one is hard put to say that there is any ideational content in them severally that would dictate however unconsciously to the Singers the habit of singing just these formulae together in the same place in their songs. What necessity is there, after all, that just four places should be traversed, or that *leaving the plains and reaching the mountains* should be associated with just those four places; and why must *high trees* attend the *commotion of a terrific warrior's approach*? Yet manifestly there is some such necessity, even if its cause is not apparent in the several formulaic systems themselves, since *the Singers do not sing these formulas otherwise than in these clusters.* And these clusters denote another, larger, and temporally even deeper kind of 'essential idea' in the history of oral epic tradition, an idea from which all the subsidiary ideas of the specific formulas in the cluster gain both their importance and their stability in the Singers' diction. Of all his essential ideas, the kind underlying such formulary clusters as that just seen above is also most unconscious in the traditional Singer's mind and most inscrutable to any form of his active contemplation. More than any other, this kind of 'essential idea' characterizes the conventionality of oral tradition. I begin in this book the task of describing such ideas, and I conceive of this description as the necessary preliminary to showing in a subsequent volume how the concatenation of such ideas forms the web of whole tales in tradition, and so defines the whole tradition in both its ideational and its stylistic aspects simultaneously.

THE 'SOLUTION FROM THE TEXT' AND THE DISTRACTION OF OTHER METHODS

Again following Parry, I hold "to the principle of getting 'the solution from the text,'"for I agree with him that "it is here, rather than in the study of religious, or cultural, or social, or historical details that we must look for the answer to the question of how the poems were made. . . ."* But I also recognize, as Parry did, the manifold or *polymorphic* nature of text in an oral narrative tradition. For if the text of Salih Ugljanin's tale as he told it in November of 1934 was no less the text of that tale than the other text of it he dictated

---

*Parry, *The Making of Homeric Verse*, pps. 268-269.

the previous July, then the text follows the tale in an oral epic tradition just as the formulas for its telling follow the 'essential ideas' laid up in the unconscious intellectual habit of the Singer. The attestation of the essential ideas will accordingly be bounded only by their historical influence on all Singers' intellectual habits, however much more narrowly they may be defined in their concatenations and formulations in the formulaic systems of particular language traditions and individual Singers.

The subject of this book is therefore oral traditional story-telling —as found in oral epic in the first instance, but also as witnessed in folktales, ballads, myths, legends, and the like. In particular, I have written here about certain elemental fictions which story-telling in oral tradition seems habitually to produce in any human population and in every historical period where it has been recorded. A number of other subjects are naturally touched upon in the course of this study, including some aspects of art, literature, and religion that are not necessarily directly derived from oral traditions; but all such excursions are solely for the purpose of illuminating oral narrative tradition, which is this book's only proper subject.

A very old tendency in Western learning that goes back at least to the time of Saint Paul and his famous stricture upon "godless myths and old wives' tales" (1 Timothy 4, 7) permits serious intellectual attention to fall on traditional fictions only obliquely, through the mediation of other, contiguous sciences, where narratives in oral tradition might be instrumentally significant but yet not be the main objects of study. In Saint Paul's time, those other, preferred sciences were religious, being the sciences of ecclesiastical organization and theology; today, they are both religious and secular, ranging from social anthropology through psychology, social history, literary criticism, linguistics, art history, comparative religious studies, sociology, and a host of other intellectual 'disciplines' to such remoter fields as archaeology and even applied computer technology. In every such science there also continue to be champions of orthodoxy who, if they do not go with Saint Paul so far as actually to forbid the apostasy of any serious direct intellectual reflection on oral or 'folk' narrative traditions, do at least insist jealously on the exclusive claim of their own science's special methodology as the only path of salvation from perilous errors of the mind when dealing with the doctrinally polluting substance of oral traditions.

So until very recently in the history of Western learning there was no proper analytical science of oral narrative tradition in its own right. Indeed, the aspiration to such a science is still somewhat unorthodox and suspect even to the present day. In the beginning were the philologists, who like Jacob Grimm saw in modern folktales and ballads the wonderful survival of archaic language and, embedded in it, of esoteric words connoting old religious concepts that were thought to be characteristic of vanished or threatened ethnic identities first in Europe, and subsequently also in other parts of the world. What began as analysis of oral narrative traditions was thus gradually distracted into philological theorizing about the cultural history of nations that ultimately accomplished little general analysis of the narratives themselves.

Later in the nineteenth century came the effort, shared by many hands, to reconstruct the history of particular tales and their hypothetical diffusion from place to place. But the confident geographico-historicism of this movement, fathered as it was by the ebullient but often naive spirit of the Age of Discovery, assumed from the outset that it was merely a branch of existing literary science, and that oral literature was simply a system of fixed and numerically finite tale-types no different in principle from the historical succession of texts in any literary tradition. Because it knew nothing of oral narrative tradition as a fluctuating *process* of living human beings, the historico-geographic school saw no need for any methodology basically unlike that of ordinary literary historiography with its usual stemmata and searches for the probable authorship of anonymous compositions. Having made that assumption, that school had little choice but to accept by implication one or another literarily contrived theory about the genesis or 'authorship' of oral traditions that forever foreclosed the possibility of its tendering any useful explanation of the myriad fictitious and fabulous elements that so dominated such traditions everywhere. Condemned to sterility by the very closeness of its continuing affiliation with conventional literary science, the historico-geographic method was never anything more than a folklorist's form of *Textkritik*, and it never had anything to contribute toward the substantive understanding of the oral traditions it purported to 'analyze.'

The rise and decline of the historico-geographic method (sometimes called also the Finnish School) had, however, the virtue of attracting increased attention to the stuff of oral traditions among

Western intellectuals. And precisely because it was so destitute of comment on the value and sense of oral narrative traditions, the very ascendancy of the historico-geographic method created a great vacuum of interpretative criticism into which the representatives of many peripheral sciences have rushed in recent decades.

Many of these relative newcomers to the subject came from the so-called 'social sciences,' and they have brought with them a great diversity of outlook. Depending upon what their predilections were before they began to think about oral narratives, some have emphasized the information they find in oral tales about *personality,* while others find oral fictions more helpful in explaining the organization and activity of whole *social groups.* S. Freud, C. G. Jung, a host of their colleagues and followers including such well-known figures as Erich Fromm, Paul Radin, Joseph Campbell, Bruno Bettelheim, Thomas Szasz, and many others too numerous to name in a mere prolegomenon such as this preface, have all found occasion in their psychological and psychoanalytic pursuits to give some attention to oral narrative traditions and to such other phenomena as dreaming, wishing, and reminiscence, in which they have detected processes in some way comparable for their purposes to the processes in oral traditional fiction. Others such as J. Piaget have seen patterns of personal maturation and learning especially prominent in oral tales. Some sociologists have preferred, however, entirely to bypass the more usual distinctions between oral traditional fictions and other verbal forms, lumping all together under a general rubric of 'expressive culture,' by which they often imply that oral fictions are not actually 'things in themselves,' but only representations in speech of other things elsewhere in the body of a culture, whether material or abstract.

Still others say that such fictions as those I treat in this book are not so much communicative of other realities as of communicational technique *per se,* i. e., that folktales, myths, legends, and their congeners are better seen as models of communication and the *exchange* of thought than as any specific thoughts or ideas themselves (the medium being the message, as they say in their 'semiotical' slogan). But some others contend with equal energy that traditional fictions represent actual thought-processes, not merely the means of communicating thoughts, and so are the very epitome of philosophy in pre- or non-literate, 'primal' societies. Among the things most often formulated in such philosophy, we are told by still other authorities, is a rudimentary understanding of natural forces like climate, violent weather, sea and desert, forest and fen, and so forth. Some later scholars would, however, rather stress the formulation in oral narrative traditions of political ideas, or of kinship systems, or of economic concepts. For some of this school, traditional tales not only *represent* such categories but are also themselves active social agents that by their very telling formulate, revise, ratify, and enforce behavioural norms in a manner virtually independent of peoples' conscious intent. But others, though subscribing readily to such a *functional* interpretation of oral narratives, think of tales as only the structures wherein reside certain potent symbols which act upon society instead of the complete tales. Numerous advocates of this opinion have been especially interested in fictitious traditions as they relate to rites and ritual life.

Some, however, regard tales as mainly quasi-legal institutions, whose utility is chiefly to provide *justification* for various social actions rather than behaviourally to *cause* those actions outright. But scholars more concerned with veritable historical fact have more commonly seen formulations of history—a kind of primal historiography—at work in the genesis and perpetuation of oral traditional narratives. Still others (most notably C. Lévi-Strauss and those of similar persuasion), although they too are functionalists, do not like to think of traditional fictions as serving any one function to the exclusion of others. This school, which one might call 'multifunctionalist' in contrast to the unifunctionalism more common among social scientists of an earlier period, is most satisfied when they can discern the greatest number of disparate 'systems' of social, personality, philosophical, and natural order all integratively conceptualized together in the same texts of oral tradition, for they consider this integrative function as the paramount virtue in fictitious narrative tradition.

The passage of time and changes of intellectual fashion have somewhat eclipsed some of the latter-day theories and theorists of 'folk-narrative' just mentioned; but others remain to the present moment among the most respected and most imitated models and masters of their respective sciences. No doubt this is as it should be. It is not my purpose in this book to question or to intervene in any way in any of the various sciences of personality and society that have found sustenance in the study of oral traditions in this century. I have indeed a considerable personal debt to numerous modern social scientists whose works I have read and found helpful in my own studies. Among the living I should name especially C. Lévi-Strauss, Edmund Leach, Mary Douglas, Victor Turner, and Clifford Geertz, none of whom would necessarily take any pleasure in knowing of my indebtedness, but who also need no praise of mine to attest the suggestive force of their achievements.

But while I respect, and in some cases very much admire the work upon traditional tales and cognate matter performed by social scientists of several persuasions, their results and the aims of their sciences are not my concern in this book. There are only a few, incidental aspects of their work that bear immediately upon my subject as I conceive it, and those are as follows:

1. Social scientists as a class have very rarely evinced a truly primary desire to understand oral narrative traditions. The scholar like E. Leach or R. Firth who is already deeply imbued with thinking about moral and ethical categories in the abstract, about 'right' and 'justification' as variably interpretable categories of human thought and conduct, needs texts upon which to test and demonstrate his hypotheses. Oral fictions, whether tales, legends, epics, or myths, are often all the texts a small or primal social group can afford its students, and lo, the learned Western mind finds in them all it needs to prove its case. From just such a text emerges the demonstration and proof of the anthropologist's thesis about local notions of 'right' and 'justification,' or what-have-you. For Clyde Kluckhohn, the oral narrative tradition ratified an interpretation of ritual, while for Jan Vansina it yields with moderate coaxing a modicum of history. For Claude Lévi-Strauss, it shows the exquisite coordination of native ideas about kinship, economy, social order, and the gods, an hypothesis already incipient in Lévi-Strauss's mind before he encountered the texts of American Indian myths. Franz Boas got similar help from Tsimshian mythology, for him a happily concentrated compendium of all the randomly encountered, impossibly dispersed cultural significata he might otherwise have spent a frustrated lifetime trying without complete success to witness firsthand in the remote Pacific Northwest. Bruno Bettelheim, steeped beforehand in experience with diverse personalities and personality-traits, finds convenient explanations of those matters neatly encapsulated in folktale. And so forth. The scholarly or contemplative mind, already well prepared by general experience with some category in Western thought, turns to peasant or primitive or non-literate or small-group oral traditions and regularly finds there the very

details that its Western mode of thinking needed to give it a prize on the workings of the local culture. Clifford Geertz has recently praised this very process as 'the hermeneutic circle' upon which modern ethnology must depend for its understanding of diverse alien peoples: his 'hermeneutic circle' being a constant readiness of mind in a good ethnographer to shuttle mentally to and fro between the evident details of an alien culture and a theoretical matrix steadily evolving in the ethnographer's mind to help him classify and comprehend what he sees.

But is oral narrative fiction ever really so simply and unqualifiedly representative of the people who tell it that it can be relied upon no less than the people themselves to give true testimony of what they are and how they actually think? To what extent does the mere fact that a tale is found however frequently among a given people mean that it necessarily has in itself any power at all to explain anything about that people?

2. The very frequency and evident ease wherewith social scientists have found what they sought in oral narrative traditions suggests how right some of them have been when they comment that such traditions 'mirror' the societies where they are found. Is it not perhaps in the very nature of those traditions to mirror *anything* held up to them in *any* society, and to yield to the inquisitive outsider a schematic replica of any cultural sub-system he may care to take notice of, be it ritual, kinship organization, economic life, law and jurisprudence, cosmology, psychology, political order, religious thought, or whatever, at any time in the history of the given people? Does this universal reflective power of oral narrative tradition in fact require for its efficacy any substantive modification at all from one people to another?

3. Nevertheless a great many (though by no means all) social scientists insist upon confining the interpretation of oral narrative traditions to the immediate ethnic context where the traditions are found. For them, a tale of palpably Oedipal type from the Tangu of New Guinea does not, for example, imply that the Tangu people perceive anything in their world *or in their narratives* in a manner analogous to European perceptions. What is important, and to many social scientists the *only* important thing about the Oedipal typology of a tale indigenous to New Guinea is the distinctively different use to which they expect the New Guineans to put that tale as contrasted

to the import of the Oedipus story anywhere else.

It is, however, perhaps much as though one were to observe
that adult males in Cairo and in New York City typically consume
much caffein in the coffee they drink during the course of an ordinary
day; but then to insist that because the coffee is differently brewed
in those two cities, and because the drinkers react differently to the
stimulus of it, the fact of caffein in both their diets has *no* importance,
or none worth investigating. I am inclined to another opinion: though
it may have only *correlative* importance, it still has at least that importance, as one may readily appreciate by contrasting the behaviour of
coffee-drinkers in New York and Cairo with the behaviour of those
in New York or in Moscow whose preferred daily drink is not typically coffee but alcoholic. And the question becomes more compelling
the greater and the more subtle the nutritive value of the thing in
question is understood to be. So a myth of the Oedipal type in Europe
and as found indigenously in New Guinea may differently nourish or
inform the minds of its hearers in each place and yet be usefully compared as against the gamut of utility or the content of ideas that the
versions, let us say, of the Cinderella story native to those same two
places might have. The failure of the historico-geographic school and
of other, lesser comparative schools since it to do what they were
never designed to do—to contribute a comparative *interpretation* of
oral narrative traditions—is not sufficient grounds for totally dismiss-
ing and ignoring the great, obvious principles of likeness among the
world's innumerable local manifestations of oral traditional fiction.
There is, furthermore, no necessary contradiction between a comparative and an ethnically delimited approach to the criticism of oral narrative traditions. So long as they do not become confused one with the
other, each approach may in an open mind greatly enhance the potential of the other.

4. Finally, I am not alone in my disappointment with the general
level of analytical acuity achieved in the treatment of traditional
stories and story-telling by various other sciences since the decline of
the Finnish School. But since narrative *per se* has not often been the
real subject of those other sciences, which have for the most part only
used narrative as a vehicle for explication of something else, be it
social, psychological, linguistic, philosophical, or whatever, it is not
surprising that, intent as they were upon those other ends, the alternative sciences whose representatives displaced the historical geograph-

ers in this century have not produced much very general explanation nor even much widely accepted description of the actual phenomena displayed in traditions of oral narrative the world over.

THE TWO TREES: AN EXAMPLE OF ORAL NARRATIVE TRADITION'S UNIVERSAL ADAPTABILITY

When finally in the nineteenth century the Western intellectual habit of shunning 'godless myths and old wives tales' abatted enough to permit the emergence of a new science of oral narrative study out of the philosophical restlessness of Napoleon's Europe, the founders of that new science nevertheless still tended nervously to avoid the bogey of doctrinal perils in their new subject. It grew up accordingly as a science much more of forms than of ideas: forms of words and of linguistic development as with Jacob Grimm; forms of tale as with Antti Aarne; forms of motifs as with Stith Thompson or Vladimir Propp. While whole generations of those men's followers have continued to find refuge in their mechanical taxonomies and arid formalism, a new wave of less ideologically united but more ideologically inclined representatives of non-literary sciences has swept all before it in the criticism of oral traditional fiction. So we come to the present balance of dominations and powers in this subject, which leaves the desert of taxonomy and classification firmly in the hands of the tale-type indexers, formalists, and computer-assisted cataloguers, while a paladin of some other, alien discipline presides under the banner of his especial science at every fertile oasis of interpretative study. And for the most part the desert and the sown do not meet, for by their own choice they speak different and mutually uncongenial technical languages.

Manifestly I do not like this state of affairs, and am not willing to abide in it. So this is not a book about tale-types (though it is about types of tales), nor yet about the principles of social organization among particular peoples, nor does it concern the dynamics of anyone's psyche; nor is it about language, or religion, or social values, or law, or history, or any other of the myriad sciences that has each in turn sometime laid claim to oral traditional fiction as its own proper domain. *I freely admit the propriety of every such claim, but the exclusivity of none.* That I do at times myself touch upon some general traits of social order, psychic balance, language, religion, history, art, and literature I also do not deny, for on the basis of the evidence I know the chief use or function of fabulous narrative traditions everywhere is to *make men adaptable in their minds,* to enlarge the scope of their mental lives beyond the confines of their actual experience socially, psychically, and in every other way. I am so far persuaded of this that I have come to think of fabulous story-telling, and even of the stories so told in tradition, as proper aspects of human biology, although it is not my aim in this book to make a complete defense of that idea.

I do not, however, mean by this view to promote any grindingly functional way of thinking, for unlike Joseph divining at Pharaoh's command, I do not suppose that every traditional act of imagination among my own or any other people necessarily speaks symbolically to a particular contemporary social or psychic moment. That such juxtapositions of reality with popular fictions do occur is patent, and the study of them is no doubt useful for the declared purposes of those whose intellectual province those realities are. I maintain only that, given the inherent nature of traditional oral imaginative narration—the nature of the fictions in folklore everywhere—*such correspondences are always bound to obtain in every society* regardless of its place in history, how it is organized, or how divergent from others it and its members may be, and that furthermore *such divergence among peoples neither entails nor requires any basic divergence in the history, imagery, or construction of their traditional narratives.* Precisely in the protean ability of one finite complex of oral traditional fictions to inform and conform with every mode of action or being men have adopted lies its utility as an adaptive mechanism in human evolution.

This is a considerable claim, and it implies some departure from the tenets of both the old historico-geographic mode of thinking about 'tale-types,' and also from the uncompromising concentration upon ethnic and national idiosyncracy found in much modern anthropology of 'small groups.' It does not deny the reality of either tale-types or of ethnic idiosyncracy, but it does suppose the inadequacy of both those concepts as limits upon our understanding of oral narrative tradition.

This is accordingly a book written for others, who, like myself, are not entirely satisfied with the understanding of oral traditions that existing methods for the analysis of 'folk stories' already offer. I do

not think anyone should be content with the existing methods, but at
the same time I do not urge the overthrow of any received methodology. I say only that the science of oral traditions needs improvement,
and that to improve it one must have stories and their ideas—the tales
in and from oral traditions—more firmly at the center of attention than
the procedural presuppositions or prejudices of any other science. This
is, however, a great issue pregnant with occasion for polemic into
which I do not want to enter directly. For I find that, as in other
fields of intellectual endeavor, so too in the study of oral narrative
traditions: great issues usually devolve upon fine points of detail. If
these are carefully observed and understood, the larger considerations
of outlook and opinion tend to resolve themselves. For that reason I
have incorporated much actual story-material into this book, analyzing
it with considerable particularity, while at the same time restricting
the choice of tales to one class or 'strain' of narrative in what I regard
as the universal genus of oral traditional story. There is no attempt
here to portray the entire genus; rather I offer for the reader's appraisal a method and its premises which might, if one had time and will,
be extended in a number of directions.

My only desire in publishing these pages is therefore to set before
others who may share my interest in improving the fundamental knowledge of oral narrative traditions certain facts which may not be universally known or appreciated, together with an example of method
for finding out such facts, which my readers may freely evaluate for
themselves, improve upon, borrow, or discard, however they prefer.
And just as I make no claim of patent, so also I do not assert that
anything I have done in this study is definitive. On the contrary, this
is an altogether exploratory work, whose value to others, whatever
else it may incidentally be, must be mainly suggestive.

Few people generally, and not many professional scholars, are
well read in oral fable. I have tried in this book to indicate what some
consequences of being well read in oral fable might be. One essential
consequence is, I think, the disposition to recognize in fable the arrange-
ments of narrative material which I have chosen to call 'patterns.' There
are, however, numerous patterns present in even a short and simple
oral fable (though I argue that it requires knowing many tales to recognize the patterns in even one tale). For the sake of clarity about my
analytical method, therefore, I have preferred to do careful study of
just a few patterns rather than treating a large number superficially.

Indeed, the first chapters of this book deal almost exclusively with just one pattern, a pattern I call 'the Two Trees.' I know from my experience of discussing this pattern before a number of audiences before I wrote this book that different individuals differ in their rate of absorption and their tolerance for the sort of detailed exposition I have devoted to the 'Two Trees.' Some want and relish an uncompromisingly complete demonstration and proof of the universality of such mythic elements in oral tradition as the Two Trees, while others, as though already convinced by previous experience or the disposition of their own minds that such processes do exist and function in the ways I have described, want more to see how those processes articulate with others in the whole composition of different tales. For that reason much of the argumentation in this book has been relegated to its long Appendix, which is not essential to the thesis of the book, but rather to the proof of that thesis for those who want proof beyond what is provided in the main chapters.

I have throughout this work kept to a procedure of reasoning *propter hoc.* I have done this because I am conscious of a great incubus of *a priori* reasoning that has weighed upon the minds of scholars of oral traditional narrative from time immemorial. There is hardly a time-honored opinion in this field that does not have a main buttress in such recurrent and empty phrases as 'it must be,' or 'it stands to reason that,' or 'how else to explain,' or 'the only conceivable explanation must be. . . .' But what is merely plausible where oral traditions of narrative are concerned is usually mistaken, since their essence is the truth of wonderfully implausible things. And even when such presumptive reasoning does not falsify, it has the even more insidiously damaging power to cause mental stagnation, which is by all odds the most grievous problem we have to contend with in this subject. I have tried therefore never to offer any opinion as to method or theory without showing my reasons for it in the narratives themselves and their circumstances. This has meant giving up a large part of my book to occupancy by all manner of story-tellers and their stories. Professional folklorists and some literary scholars may find some of the narratives familiar, but they should not mind seeing again what they may not perfectly remember in every particular, since it is very much to the particulars that my considerations are addressed. I for one relish the stories in all their details, as I think most people do, most of all if they are not specialists in this branch of learning. I have preferred to make a methodical and thorough exposition rather than a speedy one only because I think the subject needs it, and has had already too much mischief wrought upon it by conventional, conjectural, and merely assertive judgements.

There is one form of presumptive reasoning I particularly deplore and have tried specially to shun as both intellectually stagnant and demeaning to my subject. That is the literary connoisseur's or aesthetician's affected pronouncement *ex cathedra* regarding the 'merit' of individual tales or renditions of tales. In particular, American scholarship on the subject of oral narrative has been infected with this pernicious tendency ever since Francis J. Child's landmark work on oral tradition in the form of British ballads. As a compiler and codifier of that balladry Child was a model, but it remains a marvel how little he understood the substance of what he laboured on so long and devotedly as accumulator and editor of texts. Lacking interpretative comprehension of the tradition, he introduced into learned ballad criticism the emotive and slight manner of the journalistic critic, which, conjoined in him with an unparalleled textual erudition, took on a spurious aura of authority that in his time effectively covered his real ignorance of the *causes* and *reasons* for ballad tradition. His method was to express his feelings about the ballads and their narratives epithetically, being in the process as attentive as a prudent stockbroker not to "rate too high" or "undervalue" any tale. So to him this ballad was "charming," while that one was "touching," "moving," "convincing," "one of the most beautiful," "honest," or "silly and insipid." The knowing crypticism of Child's critical comment set a style for later generations of academics, and whether in direct or indirect imitation of him, it has become conventional in American scholars of oral traditions to cultivate together with their textual knowledge a similar connoisseurship whereby they might make known their feelings as well as their information about the elements in tradition.

With the passage of time, a secondary rationalization of this emotive manner has arisen in the belief that such connoisseurship might contribute something positive to literary education, and ultimately to literary creativity in English. If, for example, William Faulkner, in part by borrowing and transforming matter from the German tradition represented in the Grimms' folktales, could so enrich the literary culture of his day as he did, then by refinement and extension of Child's manner as critic, scholars might not only *know* but also beneficially *influence* the course of literary history during and after their own time without ever having to risk themselves, their own energies, or their reputations (but only those of their idealistic or idolizing students) in the chancy artists' world of belletristic authorship.

Beyond noting the insipid results which such crypto-activism has tended to produce in practice, I am unconcerned with this more recent excrescence of academic literary thinking. I do, however, believe that it is fraudulent in a scholar to set himself up as arbiter of taste in any matter whose original causes and reasons he does not even try to understand. In the matter of oral narrative traditions, one may and must (as F.J. Child did) recognize tradition knowledgeably and competently performed on the part of its native bearers, discriminating between that and the faulty performances of ignorant informants; but we know too little about the causes and reasons of anything fundamental in oral traditions to legitimate arbitrary endorsements or exclusions of any parts of it from a canon of art. And before we become very much exercised about Faulkner's use of the Grimms' folktales, or Charles Dickens' or Shakespeare's use of other bits of oral tradition, not to speak of any use of that or similar matter by other writers still unheralded or unborn, we need a far better primary understanding than any yet formulated concerning the European traditions that gave rise to the Grimms' collection and earlier records of those traditions in the first place. But as regards the elements of tradition themselves, for reasons I have tried to make plain in this book, there can be no dispute about the merit or worth of those elements, which simply *are*— the unalterable data of tradition. Our task is not to choose, appreciate, approve, or disapprove, but rather in the simplest, most straightforward scientific sense, to understand.

Chapter One

HIDE AND SEEK

Le bon Dieu est dans le détail.

- Flaubert

Oral narrative a mnemonic art, but chiefly of things unreal.   *p. 35*

The miracle of the bees.   *p. 42*

Clusters, not single motifs, as the basis of narrative
    parallelism and comparison.   *p. 45*

The 'text' of oral narrative is the whole tradition, not
    single tales.   *p. 51*

L ike the manufacture of tools and weapons, like speech, or the
artificial production of dyes and pigments, story-telling is a
peculiarly human activity. It is in fact a unique property of *Homo
sapiens'* societies. Other animals than man communicate within their
own species by a variety of visual, audible, and chemical means that
help them to sustain life and maintain their communal identities. It
may sometimes be hair-splitting to differentiate between those
species' communications and our own uses of speech. But alone
among animals, only man converses with his fellows in a narrative
manner. Dolphins or other very intelligent beasts may someday be
taught to speak in a mode men will understand, or some of us
might learn their "languages," but it is wildly improbable that any
of them will ever tell any of us even a rudimentary story.

In moments of typically human fantasy, some natural scientists
who study the universe around our small planet enjoy telling the
story of how other "intelligent beings" similar to man may inhabit
a kind of astral Arcadia in other solar systems far from our world,
hidden from us beyond the reach of any present faculty except
imagination. Yet even if by diligent exercise of our mechanical
genius we earthlings do eventually contrive to discover and talk
with those invisible trans-galactic Arcadians, thus realizing one of
the most compelling fantasies of our so-called "science fiction,"
our sense of being truly like or unlike those "aliens" will depend
in large measure upon whether they can appreciate our traditional
narratives and we theirs. For unless they too are story-telling creatures
they will not be acceptably "like us" no matter how ably they otherwise speak, calculate, manufacture, or color themselves and their
artifacts with the paints and dye-stuffs of their worlds.

The amount of story-telling that happens in a single day on our
planet must be enormous. No one has ever tried to measure it, but
any experienced collector of oral tales knows that counting them is
like taking a census in China. The counting no sooner begins than
the reproductive process invalidates the count. All the engraved stones,
clay tablets, papyri, manuscripts, and printed pages devoted to records
of old stories in all the world's museums, archives, and libraries

probably amount to only a fraction of the stories told orally during
a few months' time in the modern world. Since the tales that have
been preserved in writing are so numerous, are by nature relics of
the past, and are often manifestly products of older traditions that
were never recorded at all, the social custom of telling stories by
word of mouth must long have been as highly developed and as pro-
lific as it is today. Indeed, no period of history is innocent of it,
and until comparatively very recent times most of the world's history
was itself composed of more or less standard oral narrative matter.

The original and still fundamental way of telling a story is by
speaking, although story-telling and speech are not the same thing.
Children ordinarily attain a fair proficiency in language during the
first years of life, but the evidence of modern story-collecting indicates that even a minimal competence in oral narration is seldom
achieved before adolescence. Furthermore, not all adults learn to
narrate well enough to satisfy the traditional expectations of their
peers, and I know of no culture where more than a small minority
of the whole adult population are recognized as expert story-tellers
by the rest of their society. Yet despite these limitations, spoken
narrative is an ancient and exuberant institution among men everywhere.

Erwin Panofsky expressed a common opinion about the purpose of story-telling in his small parable of a dog:

A dog announces the approach of a stranger by a bark quite
different from that by which he makes known his wish to go
out. But he will not use this particular bark to convey the idea
that a stranger *has* called during the absence of his master.[1]

Were Panofsky's dog able to bark at a stranger in the past tense, it
would indeed have mastered a first principle of narrative skill. The
basic utility of narration is memorial; it enables men to share memories of things which they may have never personally experienced.
For that reason oral stories are usually told about memorable events,
things somehow noteworthy or apart from routine occurrence. Even
the most ordinary oral tales obey this principle, like the following
Jewish (Hasidic) story from New York:

I heard a story about Z., the shohet. In that town there was
someone called Avrom the lumber dealer because he sold trees.
He had a sister-in-law who couldn't remarry because she wasn't
sure her husband was dead. Whenever he went to the Rebbe to

ask him what to do about it, the Rebbe used to tell him you
have to look through the newspapers and things like that. They
kept on going to the Rebbe, but nothing that they did and the
Rebbe did helped. They didn't find anything in the newspapers.

Then the Rebbe said, "You have to go to a certain shohet.
He could help you."

So they went to a big shohet who was also a relative of that
woman, and the shohet asked, "What could I do?" And they
started to think. They showed him pictures of the man. Now
this shohet used to go to a certain town to sell meat and buy
salt. He said that in that town someone looks like the picture
of the man. "Next time I'm in that town, since it's a matter
of life and death, I'll investigate."

The next time he went to that town he found that man and
it was her husband. And he gave her a divorce so that she was
able to get married again.[2]

This story is a good example of plain oral narrative. It tells of
something abnormal—a flaw in the fabric of society—and of a procedure for mending it. One has no way of knowing certainly whether the events narrated ever actually happened, but they are entirely
plausible in themselves. Like many plain narratives, this example is
equipped with names and social titles, which are not nearly so gratuitous as they might seem; how symbolically appropriate that a
shohet (ritual butcher) is the agent who duly disjoints the members
of the defunct marriage, finally severing the useless legal tie between
the uncertainly dead husband and the abandoned wife. The story
also contains a quantity of reported speech, which is one of the
commonest devices of oral narrative everywhere. Of course, one
might doubt whether the rebbe (unordained, Hasidic rabbi) in the
real event did actually say: "You have to go to a certain shohet.
He could help you." It is much more likely that the rebbe really
said: "You have to go to Z., the shohet. He could help you." And
as for the shohet, were his exact words just those quoted in the
story? "Next time I'm in that town, since it's a matter of life and
death, I'll investigate." Even the story-teller would probably admit
that he does not know what the butcher said *verbatim*, while in-
sisting that his story is nevertheless a correct account of the essential facts concerning the woman's search for her truant husband. In
other words, the story-teller has devised an imaginary conversation

to express not the absolute reality of the past events he narrates, but only the essential reality as he conceives it. To this extent at least, almost every oral narrative contains an element of fiction, something conceptual that is either somewhat more or somewhat less than a perfect report of simple, unembroidered fact. Story-telling is seldom, if ever, only a direct encoding of past happenings, like the hypothetical bark of Panofsky's dog to announce a visitor who has long since departed.

But if oral stories are not altogether factual, neither are they often wholly fictitious. The admixture of fiction can be considerable without doing any violence to fact; at times it is indistinguishable from fact. Even simple tales, like the story of the abandoned wife, the rebbe, and the butcher, contain some elements so typical of ordinary experience in the places where the tales are told that it is a hard and profitless task to determine whether they narrate facts about actual historical persons or just things that might abstractly happen in the lives of people like the characters in the narrative. Consider for example the story "What a Little Thing Did" which Clement Doke recorded in the early years of this century among the Aŵalamba, a Central African people who lived in present-day Zambia and Zaire:

> And one daughter and a son were born. And a man, her cousin, married the girl; and on the morrow he went hunting. His first father-in-law died, and his mother-in-law remained. One day a certain man came and said, "I (want) to marry your mother-in-law, my son-in-law." And that son-in-law of his said, "Marry, am I to deny my mother-in-law?" And sure enough he came and married his mother-in-law.
>
> One day he said to his son-in-law, "Come, son-in-law, let us go into the bush, that we may eat some honey." Ah, and the son-in-law went with him into the bush.[3]

Thus far, this too is a plain narrative, telling of entirely plausible persons and events. But it is highly selective in its depiction of those persons and events. Just as the Jewish tale of the abandoned wife identified its characters chiefly by reference to their social rôles as rebbe, ritual butcher, husband and wife—all categories of the real society where that story was recorded—so too the Lamba tale describes its cast of Aŵalamba[4] by their respective places in Lamba society, not by individual attributes or unique acts that

would identify particular historical persons. It is the qualities which
a character represents (and which he may consequently also share
with others) more than who he personally was (as distinct from anyone before or after him) that matters in oral narrative tradition.
The Lamba story begins by telling what might have happened to
four particular Lamba people once upon a real historical time, or
possibly to any past member of Lamba society who belonged to
one of the six categories of sex and kin that are mentioned in the
story. Thus, just as reported speech in oral narrative expresses an
essential rather than an absolute reality, so too oral narrative characters are not absolutely real, total historical persons, not even in
plain narrative with its ostensible quality of reportage. Not even
plain oral narrative reports total reality, but only meaningful parts
of it, or a presently significant reality.

The next events of the Lamba tale "What a Little Thing Did"
carry its hearers into an entirely different dimension of story, however, a dimension quite apart from plain oral narrative.

Then as they went along, the father-in-law said, "Son-in-law
here are bees!" When the son-in-law had gone, he found the
bees in a grass-stalk; and the son-in-law thought, "What sort of
a father-in-law is this, who calls me to bees in a grass-stalk?"
And he cut the honey from the grass-stalk there. Then his
father-in-law said, "Eat the honey that you have cut out." The
son-in-law refused, saying, "I have not yet eaten honey from a
grass-stalk." And his father-in-law ate alone.

Up to this moment, "What a Little Thing Did" has been a plain
narrative about supposedly real or at least typical Lamba people and
their lives in past time. But with the appearance of the bees in the
grass, the story-teller has departed from mere memory of either actual *or* typical past happenings. Clement Doke observed in a foot-
note to the story that the grass-stalk is "an impossible place in which
to find a nest of bees." The note was intended to avert misunder-
standing by city-bred readers in Europe and America who might know
very little about the hiving habits of wild bees or think anything
possible on a continent so full of marvelous plants and animals as
Africa. When oral stories are translated and published for urban people
to read in print they usually need many such explanations to make
them intelligible to an audience for which they were never intended.
But Mr. Doke's note also serves as a reminder that the detail of bees

in a grass-stalk is just as fabulous and as deviant from an Umulamba's[5] real experience as it is to us who are outside Lamba culture. While bees nesting in a stalk of grass may be permissible fiction in a Lamba story, they are not a plausible image of the real Lamba world; they are something no Umulamba has ever actually witnessed. The son-in-law of the story discloses an authentic Lamba attitude when he marvels rhetorically in a fictitious speech: "What sort of father-in-law is this, who calls me to bees in a grass-stalk?" [6]

A typical stand of grass on the Central African plateau (Zambia, 1969)

To be sure, there is nothing inherently unreal about the nest of bees in the Lamba story, nor about the stalk of grass, so long as they are kept separate from each other. For a Lamba man or woman, stalks of grass growing wild in the bush had some utility as thatch-ing,* but were otherwise utterly mundane and endlessly plentiful. Nor was there anything unusual about hunting wild honey; that too was a regular part of Lamba life. The only thing that makes these two details implausible in the story of "What a Little Thing Did" is that the story-teller has put them together as though they were one, which is impossible. Separately, they could be details in plain narrative, but conflated, they constitute decidedly another kind of story: fable. Whereas plain narrative recounts genuine facts, or at

---

*People live in grass houses, not bees.

least facts typical of reality, fable depicts those same facts together
with others that are fused or disjointed in ways which exist only in
imagination. Conflation (or sunderance) of real facts into fantastic
combinations is fundamental in fable-making. It is the same principle
that informs a pictorial artist's representation of monsters or other
imaginary creatures, as when he puts together the wings and legs of
a bird of prey and a woman's head to make a picture of a harpy,
or a human torso and an animal head to form a devil. In the same
sense, because they are a mixture of things which are never mixed
in reality, the bees in a stalk of grass are monstrous in the Lamba
story.

Once such fantasy has entered a story, its effects are not confined to the details which generate it by their fictitious combinations. The younger man in the Lamba tale is less concerned about
the miraculous or magical bees in a grass-stalk than about his father-
in-law, whom he holds responsible for their violation of plausible
hiving habits. Impossible things can be made real (or *vice-versa*)
only by unreal or preternatural means. The son-in-law's question
about his elder companion was rhetorical to the Aŵalamba who
heard the tale; they automatically recognized the father-in-law as
an unreal or preternatural person who could not be only what he
seemed to be when the story began, just a typical Lamba father-in-
law who once married a widow and liked to go hunting wild honey
with an agreeable younger relative. Simply because they were Aŵalamba, the natives who heard the performance of "What a Little
Thing Did" recorded by Clement Doke had inevitably heard many
tales like it before. To them, the father-in-law was obviously a
magician, or perhaps not a man at all but rather an ogre, devil,
witch, or other monster in human guise, himself an implausible
combination of separately plausible qualities. Nor does the infection of implausibility stop with the father-in-law. Obedient to his
elder's command, the son-in-law performs the unreal task of cutting
the impossible honey from its place in the grass and thereby himself
becomes an implausible character. Thus the fabulosity generated in a
single implausible juxtaposition of facts spreads by association to
neighboring details in an oral story until it embraces the whole matrix
of the narrative where it occurs and makes the whole narrative a fable.

THE MIRACLE OF THE BEES

Nothing in the tale "What a Little Thing Did" either before or after the discovery of the bees explains why the story-teller inserted such a fantasy into a narrative that was otherwise entirely reasonable up to that point. If there were nothing besides this story from which to derive an understanding, learning the source and the meaning of the fantasy could be very troublesome. Consider the plight of Biblical scholars confronted with a similar story in the Old Testament Book of Judges. There the story of Samson begins, like the Lamba story and like much of the world's oral narrative besides, with ostensibly plain narrative about sex and kinship (Judges 13:24-25).[7]

The woman gave birth to a son and called him Samson. The child grew, and Yahweh blessed him; and the spirit of Yahweh began to move him in the Camp of Dan, between Zorah and Eshtaol.

14:1 Samson went down to Timnah, and there he noticed one of the daughters of the Philistines. 2 He came up again and told his father and mother this. 'At Timnah' he said 'I noticed one of the daughters of the Philistines. Get her for me, then, to be my wife.' 3 His father and mother said to him, 'Is there no woman among those of your own clan or among your whole nation, for you to seek a wife among these uncircumcised Philistines?' But Samson answered his father, 'Get this one for me; get her, because I like her.' 4 His father and mother did not know that all this came from Yahweh, who was seeking an occasion for quarrelling with the Philistines; since at this time the Philistines had Israel in their power.

Samson's father has counselled endogamy, but Samson is firm in his desire to marry a foreigner. The marriage is destined to be childless and full of woe for both the bridegroom and his foreign relatives; indeed, the whole legend of Samson is about the terrible consequences of his exogamy and his liaisons with alien women.

But the plain narrative about Samson's ill-starred wedding plans has scarcely begun when, like the Lamba story "What a Little Thing Did," it too is interrupted by a digression into fable. The fabulous incident of lion-slaying at the vineyards of Timnah has no apparently logical connection with the previous account of Samson's resolve to marry abroad:

> 5 Samson went down to Timnah, and as he reached the vine-
> yards of Timnah he saw a young lion coming roaring towards
> him. The,spirit of Yahweh seized on him, and though he had
> no weapon in his hand he tore the lion in pieces as a man tears
> a kid; but he did not tell his father or mother what he had done.
> He went down and talked to the woman, and he liked her. Not
> long after this, Samson came back to marry her. He went out
> of his way to look at the carcase of the lion, and there was a
> swarm of bees in the lion's body, and honey. 9 He took up
> some honey in his hand and ate it as he went along. On return-
> ing to his father and mother, he gave some to them, which they
> ate too, but he did not tell them he had taken it from the lion's
> carcase.

Honey bees do not nest in carcasses of lions or other carrion in
the Near East any more than they inhabit stalks of grass in Central
Africa. Yet an impossible hive of wild bees intrudes in the ancient
story of Samson just as it did in the modern Lamba tale, and at a
similar place in the plot. In both stories a man proposes an exogamous marriage to another man who has jurisdiction over it but who is
not eager to permit it; then the bridegroom discovers honeybees
where they cannot be. The exact relevance of the bees to the marriage is initially as obscure in the legend of Samson as in the Lamba
tale, but they occur insistently early in both narratives.

Samson marries after he and his parents eat the wild honey. At
his wedding-feast he uses a riddle based on the fictitious bees in a
contest of riddling with his bride's countrymen. Since the famous
Riddle of Samson is something impossible that exists only in the
story of Samson, it is a riddle which no one could guess:

> 14:10 Then he went down to the woman, and they made a
> feast for Samson for seven days there, for such is the custom
> of young men. But because they were frightened of him, they
> chose thirty companions to stay with him.
> Then Samson said to them, 'Let me ask you a riddle. If you
> find the answer within the seven days of the feast, I will give
> you thirty pieces of fine linen and thirty festal robes. But if
> you cannot find the answer, then you in your turn must give
> me thirty pieces of fine linen and thirty festal robes.' 'Ask your
> riddle,' they replied 'we are listening.' 14 So he said to them:

'Out of the eater came what is eaten,
and out of the strong came what is sweet.'

But three days went by and they could not solve the riddle.
Finally the Philistines induce Samson's new wife to learn the secret
of her husband's riddle and betray it to them. She does this in an
adumbration or multiform of the Delilah story:

14:16 Then Samson's wife fell on his neck in tears and said,
'You only hate me, you do not love me. You have asked my
fellow countrymen a riddle and not even told me the answer.'
He said to her, 'I have not even told my father and mother,
why should I tell you?' She wept on his neck for the seven days
their feast lasted. She was so persistent that on the seventh day
he told her the answer, and she in turn told her fellow countrymen what the answer to the riddle was.

18 So on the seventh day, before Samson entered the bridal
room, the men of the town said to him:

'What is sweeter than honey,
and what is stronger than a lion?'

He retorted:

'If you had not ploughed with my heifer,
you would never have guessed my riddle.'

Samson is enraged by his wife's treachery, and after paying the wager
he has lost in riddling, he returns home alone to his own father. Meanwhile his father-in-law further disrupts the society of Samson's affinal
kin, giving Samson's unconsummated bride to another man. Samson is
again furious, and he cleverly incriminates his father-in-law so that the
Philistines intervene in their private conflict and publicly settle it in
favor of Samson, who is the younger of the two disputants:

15:4 So Samson went off and caught three hundred foxes,
then took torches and turning the foxes tail to tail put a torch
between each pair of tails. He lit the torches and set the foxes
free in the Philistines' cornfields. In this way he burned both
sheaves and standing corn, and the vines and olive trees as well.

6 The Philistines asked, 'Who has done this?' and received the
answer, 'Samson, who married the Timnite's daughter; his father-
in-law took the wife back again and gave her to his companion
instead.' Then the Philistines went up and burned the woman
and her family to death.

Samson's use of the lion and the impossible bees in his riddle does in one sense establish a connection between them and his marriage. Samson the exogamous bridegroom uses the bees to subordinate his new affinal relatives (as does the Lamba father-in-law), but they exploit their consanguineous kinswoman to turn the bridegroom's trick with the bees to their own advantage. Still, the question remains, why are specifically the lion and bees used when any unfair riddle (one whose answer is something that does not exist) might have sufficed to win Samson's wager with his bride's kinsmen? Or to put that question differently, why are the subjects of his riddle such as to taint Samson himself with fabulosity, and why did the Hebrews tolerate such a blatant aberration from plausible fact in a legend about Samson, a national dignitary? Thus the fabulous bees are a similar problem in both the ancient legend of Samson and in a modern African tale.

CLUSTERS, NOT SINGLE MOTIFS, AS THE BASIS OF NARRATIVE PARALLELISM AND COMPARISON

But as often happens when oral narratives have something in common, that one point of likeness is not the only similarity which the two stories share. Despite its preoccupation with extraordinary and marvelous things, oral fable (as distinct from plain narrative) has long been so much the same everywhere that small items of likeness between any two tales rarely stand alone, no matter how great the passage of time or the geographical distance that separate the moments when the tales were recorded. So in the present examples the small detail of the bees is part of an entire network of other similarities that are all the more striking because the two stories were collected nearly three millenia and some three thousand miles apart in distinctly different cultures that have no known historical links with each other.

"What a Little Thing Did" and the legend of Samson both narrate a contest between affinally related males of different generations. The immediate purpose of the contest is to acquire basic valuables, food or clothing. An exogamous marriage precipitates the contest in both cases, and in both cases one of the disputants uses a disloyal bride as a weapon against his opponent, who finds an impossible hive of bees and eats their honey.

When the Lamba father-in-law has finished eating the honey discovered in the grass-stalk, the two men continue their hunt. The elder
man finds another hive, but this time in a Wanga tree, ". . . a tree of
such hard wood, that natives seldom attempt to cut out a nest of
bees located in it."[8] The son-in-law tries to equal his elder's prowess
by cutting the honey from its difficult location. Not only is the wood
hard, but the hive is high in the tree and he risks falling. Although
the work is heroically arduous, still it is not strictly impossible, and
therefore not equivalent to the older man's downright magical act.
When the son-in-law has lowered the honey to the ground, the older
man again offers him some of it, but he again refuses, just as he
earlier refused to eat the honey from the grass-stalk. When the father-
in-law also will eat none of it, they carry it to their village.

The next day the two go hunting a second time; the father-in-
law again finds bees in both a grass-stalk and a Wanga tree. The son-
in-law behaves as on the previous day, but feels increasingly threatened by his elder's trickery (the grass-stalk) and dangerous demands
(to cut honey-comb from hard wood at a great height). On this day,
neither man eats any of the honey and their village gets all of it.

On the third day, the father-in-law once more finds honey in
both grass-stalk and Wanga tree. But now his younger companion
begins to work magic of his own. Aŵalamba used sections of tree-
bark as containers for portage of foodstuffs, children, and other
small objects, and made strings and cords from bark fibres. The son-
in-law decides on the third day of hunting with his tricky elder not
to use an ordinary bark-plate gotten from a tree-trunk in the bush.
Instead, he breaks off a section of bark from his own leg, puts the
honey-comb from the crown of the Wanga tree in it, and lowers it
to his father-in-law at the foot of the tree by a length of bark-string
which he also obtains from his own body. The two men then return
to their village with their contest in the magical procurement of
wild honey at a draw.

The next events in the tale intensify the rivalry between the
men. On this, the fourth day of their contest, they leave hunting
honey to seek bigger game. They meet a herd of bush-buffalo, animals that were in reality quite dangerous to the native hunter. The
father-in-law quickly kills five-at-a-blow:

And he took one arrow, and set it in the bow-string, and shot the arrow, and it went into an animal, and went through this one, and went through that one and it died, and it went through that one and it died, and it went through that one and it died; and the last one also it entered, and he who shot the arrow also entered the animals.

The son-in-law goes in bewilderment from one dead buffalo to another, calling his elder until at last he emerges from the fifth carcass. While the young man contemplates his elder's latest trick, the villagers carry off the rich provision of meat.

Thus a prodigious slaying of dangerous wild animals alternates with the discovery of impossible honey in both "What a Little Thing Did" and the legend of Samson:

	What a Little Thing Did	*The Legend of Samson*
First Journeys	Discovery of Honey	Slaying of Lion
Second Journeys	Slaying of Bush Buffalo	Discovery of Honey

The man who habitually finds honey in the Lamba story emerges from the carcass of a dangerous beast, while the honey comes directly from the carcass in the Biblical legend.

On a fifth day the two rivals again hunt game. They find a herd of Eland, a species of large antelope, and now it is the younger man's turn to show his skill. He shoots an arrow together with himself through each of four animals. But instead of lodging in a fifth beast as his father-in-law had done before him, he and his arrow fly on beyond the last of the antelope:

...and when it came to the last one, the arrow went right through, and entered a wild orange. The wild orange fell into the water, and a crocodile swallowed the orange. And in its turn a hippopotamus swallowed the crocodile. The father-in-law went to the animals, and said, "Son-in-law come out!" He did not come out. And he reached another, and said, "Son-in-law come out!" He did not come out. And yet another, but he did not come out. And the last one, but he did not come out. Then he said, "But where has my son-in-law gone? I have finished asking all the animals!" And the father-in-law went off alone to the village.

On the next day (the sixth) the father-in-law digs a pitfall. The hippopotamus with the crocodile and wild orange inside falls into the pit, dies, and the father-in-law has it cut up for meat:

> And they pierced that hippopotamus, and took out a croco-
> dile from the stomach of the hippopotamus. Then he said,
> "But where is my son-in-law?" He said, "Now men, pierce this
> crocodile." And they pierced the crocodile, and took out a wild
> orange. Then he said, "My son-in-law, come out!" Then it was
> that he came out of the wild orange with his bow in his hand.
> . . . and the people carried that meat.

Like the previous series of hunts for honey, the hunts for big game also end in a stalemate between the hunters. The young man is no equal to his elder in locating food, although he keeps pace with him in the actual acquisition of it. Yet the son-in-law has to take in-creasingly greater risks in order to match his opponent's displays of magical power. First he handled the ominous honey from the grass-stalks, then risked falling from the Wanga trees, and on one occasion used pieces of his own body to supply the utensils for moving the honey. Finally he chances being lost permanently in the wild, for whereas his father-in-law's buffalo and his own antelope were certain to be cut up for meat and carried to their village by their fellow villagers, the wild orange, crocodile, and hippopotamus were a place of concealment under no human control. The father-in-law could expect that he would be found and summoned out of his slain buf-falo, but the son-in-law chose a far more hazardous hiding-place in this strange game of hide-and-seek.

On the seventh and last day of their competition in hunting, the two men again go in search of honey. With this reversion in the object of the hunt, the father-in-law also now reverts to a plain character and remains so to the end of the story despite his earlier fabulous deeds. But the son-in-law undertakes still greater feats and personal risk, as though in inverse proportion to his elder's waning fabulosity: *

> And he went out with his son-in-law to cut out honey; and
> again located bees in a very tall Wanga tree. And he said, "Son-

---
* This common process of oral traditional narrative, whereby the fantastic element in a tale is progressively amplified, I shall hereafter refer to as *expanding fabulosity.*

in-law cut out these bees in the Wanga tree." And the son-in-law
came, and climbed that Wanga tree, and the son-in-law cut out
the honey. And he said, "Father-in-law, take this honey that I
have cut out!" Ah, and he received the honey; and then the
son-in-law fell hurtling down, and broke and smashed to pieces,
and not even a little bit of him was seen; and he entirely
crumbled up, and turned into dust. His father-in-law became
afraid, and said, "Today my son-in-law is dead, he has broken
to pieces." And off he went to the village, and reached the
village and said, "My son-in-law is dead, I don't see him."

With the men's return to hunting honey, the Lamba tale dupli-
cates the sequence as well as the kind of events in the legend of
Samson:

What a Little Thing Did	*The Legend of Samson*
Finding Honey (six times)	....
Slaying Dangerous Beast	Slaying Dangerous Beast
Finding Honey (once)	Finding Honey (once)

Tellers of oral fable commonly emphasize important parts of their
tales by repetition. Partly for that reason the same tale can have
long forms like the Lamba telling of "What a Little Thing Did" and
short forms like the legend of Samson. But variations in length because of emphatic repetition do not change the relation of a tale's
components to each other. So in the present tale, the wild honey
remains the focus of the men's contest in deception and concealment
no matter how often it is repeated. Samson challenges his wife's male
relatives by concealment of the impossible honey in a riddle, and they
triumph over him by finding it out. The Lamba father-in-law first
challenges his wife's male relative by concealing similar honey in a
grass-stalk, whence the son-in-law extracts it. At the same time when
Samson's affinal kin put an end to his concealment of the honey,
they also estrange his wife from him; the estrangement is part of
their victory in the matter of the hidden honey. The motif of wild
honey is repeated seven times in the Lamba tale (twice on three
days, once on a seventh day) but its last appearance is still the moment of the honey-trickster's final defeat and estrangement from his
wife, just as in the legend of Samson. The son-in-law's calamitous
fall from the last Wanga tree is only a ruse to bring public censure

and humiliation on his bothersome father-in-law:

> There where he remained, he revived, and joined himself together piece by piece, and changed into a woman. In the morning his father-in-law came saying, "Just let me go to where my son-in-law died." When he had gone some distance, he met that woman. He said, "Woman, where have you come from?" She said, "I have come from here in this country." Then he said, "I am going to divorce my old wife, and I shall marry this beautiful one that I have seen." All the time it was his son-in-law who had turned into a woman.

The father-in-law hastily sets up housekeeping with the girl, then after a single night as his bride the son-in-law resumes his former masculine shape and condemns his elder's depravity. Outraged by this supreme deception, the father-in-law begins a litigation, but the villagers' court finds in favor of the youth. Like Samson, the Lamba son-in-law is also finally satisfied with the damage he has brought on his elder social rival by public incrimination.

The tie of consanguinity between Samson's foreign bride and his male foes is the real cause of his undoing. The same must be said of the Lamba honey-trickster; his son-in-law exploits a woman of the most intimate consanguinity with himself, one whom he has created out of himself by transformation of his own person. It is of course an entirely fabulous and impossible transformation, but it does express the idea of consanguinity between the man and his female accomplice more forcefully than any real consanguinous kinship could do.

The contest between the honey-trickster and his bride's kinsmen is materially profitable for the foreign people among whom he has married. They go better clothed for their trouble in the Biblical version, while the Lamba villagers gain prodigious amounts of food. But whereas the results of the affinal rivalry in both tales are discovery and provision of material benefits to the bride's relatives, its means are just the opposite: deception and concealment between the rivals. The honey-trickster begins by hiding wild bees (in a riddle or in the conundrum of the grass-stalk) and for three days his rivals are confounded. For three days the Lamba men hunt honey and their contest remains undecided, while in the Book of Judges 14:14, "So he said unto them, 'Out of the eater came forth meat, and out of the strong came forth sweetness.' And they could not in three days

expound the riddle." But at the end of the third day the Lamba
son-in-law counters the trickster's artifice with a deception of his
own. The exogamous bridegroom's first trick involves only things
external to himself—the bees and honey—but the son-in-law invests
pieces of his physical self in his wile with the bark-plate, which
he strips from the side of his own leg. During the subsequent hunts
for big game (on the fourth, fifth, and sixth days) the contest in deception deepens as the two rivals play hide-and-seek in various animal and even vegetable guises (i.e., the wild orange). Finally on the
seventh day the son-in-law defeats the honey-trickster bridegroom by
the grandest deception of all, the concealment of himself and his in-
imical intent from the bridegroom in a *human* guise, in the very person of a substitute bride. The bridegroom fails to recognize his foe
concealed in the bride until the foe has gained enough private information about his secret life to ruin him publicly. Then the trickster cries foul, but it is too late, for the game is already lost. So too
in the Old Testament. Samson's affinal relatives make no progress
for three days in answering his deceptive riddle. Then on the seventh
day they suborn his bride. When Samson fails to recognize their design in his wife's nagging, they learn his secret and use it to humil-
iate him in public. Like the Lamba son-in-law, they too work a
greater deception than the honey-trickster's by setting themselves
and their interests in the place of the honey-trickster's bride. Samson
protests, but must pay his wager nonetheless. Even the numerical
cadence of the rivalry is the same in the two tales: three days of in-
decisive contest, then four more making use of other stratagems,
with the decisive intervention of the suborned bride on the seventh
day.

THE 'TEXT' OF ORAL NARRATIVE
IS THE WHOLE TRADITION,
NOT SINGLE TALES

Thus the narrative surrounding them in the Samson legend and
in "What a Little Thing Did" makes the bees of the two stories
very alike, despite the difference of their location in a lion's carcass
or a grass-stalk. Yet the sameness of the two stories does not explain
the fabulous conflation of the bees with the lion or the grass any
more than did either story separately. Anyone with a lively imagination could propose sundry reasons for the bees' being in a dead body
or a stem of grass—that suggestiveness is one of fable's prime virtues—

but a right understanding of it would surely depend upon knowing the Aŵalamba's and ancient Hebrews' reasons for the conflation. After nearly three thousand years it is too late to ask the ancient Israelites their opinion of Samson's bees, nor is direct inquiry any longer possible among the Aŵalamba whose story this was a half-century ago. But there is one vital asset in the Lamba case that is lacking in the Biblical one, and that is an ample supply of other contemporary Lamba tales for comparison with "What a Little Thing Did." When Clement Doke recorded the story, it was only one of many which he heard narrated in the same style and under the same customary circumstances. In his own words:[9]

> In order to hear these folk-tales effectively, one must hear them in their native setting. The native is happiest and most communicative in the evening after the substantial meal of the day when the thought of hot sun, a long, heavy march, and a hungry stomach has been banished under the beneficent influence of a crackling log fire and a great heap of stiff 'inshima' porridge in the hastily constructed zareba. Overhead is an inky-black sky dotted with brilliant stars, a slight breeze is moving the tops of the trees, and all is silent save the regular gurgling noise of the calabash pipes, as the men sit or lie around the numerous camp fires within the stockade. Then the narrator will refill his pipe, and start his story: *Mwe ŵame!* ("Mates!"), and at once they are all attention. After each sentence he pauses automatically for the last few words to be repeated or filled in by his audience, and as the story mounts to its climax, so does the excitement of the speaker rise with gesture and pitch of voice. A good story-teller will tell over again a story, well-known to all, in such a way that they will leave their pipes and crowd nearer to him around his fire, so as not to miss a single detail.

Plain narrative, like the Jewish story about the deserted wife, rebbe, and butcher, uses both fact and plausible fiction to recount something real, or presumably real. A plain story may of course be told many times by many persons and retold by the same person; it is as permanent as memory of the real things it somewhat fictitiously recounts. But the Lamba story of "What a Little Thing Did" is fable, not plain narrative. To extend Erwin Panofsky's parable, it is not one man's barking to tell another his conception of what actually happened at a real past time. It begins as a plain narrative might, but is soon interspersed with components that are fantasy, not experience. In contrast to plain narrative, the Lamba story's permanence—the number of times it may happen to be retold in the passage of years, decades, or centuries—does not depend on how long memory of real things endures. Instead, fabulous narrative enjoys its own special sanction in the custom of story-telling, which assures it an opportunity of being retold indefinitely on a regular, recurrent social occasion belonging specially to it when an impressive array of emotional, ritual, poetic, and musical habits convene to sustain it. Most plain stories survive no more than a single telling, because most actual events that men narrate to one another are not long remembered. But if plain narratives tend to be short-lived, fables tend to be immemorial, breeding not on history but on remembrance of other fabulous tales that have preceded them at previous story-tellings in a regression stretching back beyond remembered time. Only if Panofsky's dog had been told a fabulous story by his visitor, and could then retell it to his master at a reunion many years later, only then would the dog truly approach the condition of human narrative culture. It is the complex ability to create and maintain a tradition of fable and not mere recollection of things past that makes man the story-telling animal.

So Clement Doke described story-telling in Ilamba[10] as a Lamba custom, and said that it was customary to repeat old stories: "A good story-teller will tell over again a story, well-known to all ... " Because fabulous stories were customarily repeated, the Lamba man or woman listening to "What a Little Thing Did" when Doke recorded it must have heard it and other tales like it before. That experience was an inevitable part of being an Umulamba. The tale contains utterly fictitious and impossible details like the bees in a stalk of grass, but because those implausible things had precedents in many stories he had previously heard, an Umulamba could accept them as valuable parts of his culture no matter how unreal they were. The sanction of fable is a tradition of telling stories, not reality or anyone's actual experience. Those other tales he has heard collectively inform an Umulamba as to how he should understand "What a Little Thing Did." Without that same knowledge of other Lamba tales, we who are not Awalamba can hardly expect to understand aright either this or any other single Lamba story. Not the bees, nor the father-in-law and his way with grass-stalks, nor the son-in-law's strange powers of self-concealment, nor any other marvelous feature of "What a Little Thing Did" will submit to proper understanding until it is seen in its proper place among the various other customary fantasies in Lamba oral fable.

Chapter Two

TREES AND TRICKSTERS

Adam our fader was in blis,
And for an appil of lytil prys
He loste the blysse of Paradys
Pro sua superbia.

-Early carol

Guides, murderers, and tacticians: an atom of tradition.   *p. 57*

The atom in Eden.   *p. 69*

The Fall of Man: its meanings generic and parochial.   *p. 75*

A procedural envoi.   *p. 79*

The Lamba son-in-law asks himself: "What sort of a father-in-law is this, who calls me to bees in a grass-stalk?" Yet there is no hint of anything in the least fabulous about the Lamba father-in-law up to the moment when he finds the honey in the grass. Then, suddenly, he becomes a weird character and remains so until he is defeated at his own game of concealments by a younger rival with even greater preternatural talents than his. The peculiar location of the bees and their honey is the nub of the fable, and nothing in the story is fabulous until the bees are brought into it. But from the moment when they first appear their peculiarity is somehow a property of the father-in-law. It is as though he were one character before their appearance and another after it.

When Clement Doke wrote down "What a Little Thing Did," Awalamba did in fact hunt wild honey in the bush surrounding their villages. That was so typical of their life and so ancient a practice that a remarkable symbiosis had arisen between them and a certain species of bird they called iŋguni, which translated means 'honey-guide.' Mr. Doke described this creature and its part in the Lamba tradition of fabulous narrative:

> This little bird is held in such regard by the natives for its usefulness, that it has in Wulamba four or five distinctive names. In the stories, however, in addition to leading people to the bee-hive in rock or tree, it almost invariably leads them into danger. The bird is about the size of a sparrow, grey-and-white, and is most insistent in its shrill chattering, until followed by the man whose attention it seeks to attract. From bush to bush it flies, leading him on and on till at length it reaches the nest of bees. As a reward it hopes to pick up the young bees scattered about when the honeycomb is taken out. The persistent following of this bird is often a source of annoyance to the hunter, as it thus warns the game that a man is about, and efforts to drive it away often prove unavailing.[11]

The honey-guide appears in several tales in Mr. Doke's own collection. One of these, "The Story of Shichinongomunuma and Chilubwelubwe," is an account of five brothers' successive adventures with an ogre called Chilubwelubwe, whose name according to Doke means approximately 'The One Hopelessly Lost.'[12]

Beginning with the eldest, each of five brothers defies their father's prohibition against hunting small game toward the west and follows a honey-guide to a bee-tree in that direction. There, at the foot of the tree, the brothers one after another meet the hopelessly lost ogre. He gives each of them food, and when each has fallen asleep after the meal, it eats both him and his hunting-dogs. Only the last and youngest son saves himself from being eaten by remaining awake all night. At dawn, the ogre politely congratulates him on his prudent behaviour and gives him as the hospitality-gift which custom requires a bell containing "two little creatures." They are to defend the youngest brother against another monster which he must encounter as he returns homeward, Shichinongomunuma, 'The Ogre with the Big Pot at the Back.'

Leaving Chilubwelubwe alive (but cheated of his dinner and the bell), the surviving fifth brother goes to meet Shichinongomunuma, who attacks him twice. In the first attack the pair of uncanny helpers from the bell exhaust the ogre so that it faints, and as it falls the pot at its back is shattered. But he recovers, fits himself together, and attacks again, "the pot boiling behind him." This time the nameless creatures from inside the bell annihilate Shichinongomunuma. The youth proceeds until he arrives at Shichinongomunuma's village, where only a "vast crowd" of women live, the dead monster's wives. Here he remains as chief in place of the slain ogre, not returning home.

Much of this story echoes "What a Little Thing Did" and the legend of Samson. Those tales both began with disapproval or reluctance toward exogamous marriage; teleologically, this one does too. A father prohibits his sons' movements westward, yet by going westward his only surviving son becomes husband to a host of women in the dead Shichinongomunuma's village. Thus the journey westward is the first step toward exogamous marriage in the logic of this tale.

The journey itself is also an important similarity between this

tale and the other two. Once the exogamous bridegroom has decided
not to be deterred from marriage by the disapproval or reluctance of
a person in authority, his first act in all three cases is to travel. Samson goes to Timnah, the father-in-law takes his young relative hunting, and the five sons set out westward. Each of the three journeys
takes its traveller to the vicinity of a food-yielding tree: Samson
pauses at the vineyards of Timnah, the father- and son-in-law end
their series of hunts beneath a Wanga tree full of honey, and the
five brothers stop beneath another bee-tree where Chilubwelubwe
lives. Samson travels alone in the Biblical story (the text is short and
literary), but all the Lamba hunters travel in pairs of man and guide.

The honey-guide in "What a Little Thing Did" is of course the
exogamous bridegroom himself, the father-in-law who habitually finds
honey (seven times, four times in trees). As honey-guide, the father-
in-law's character corresponds initially to the *inguni* in the story of
Shichinongomunuma and Chilubwelubwe, for the *inguni*'s rôle there
is only its natural one of leading the five brothers to the bee-tree,
where each then meets Chilubwelubwe, a man-killing creature with
preternatural attributes (living alone in the wild and possessing the
strange bell with uncanny little animals inside). The *inguni* in this
story is therefore strictly a thing of Lamba reality, like the father-
in-law before he discovered the first hive in a grass-stalk. Even Samson behaved plausibly enough before his arrival at the vineyards of
Timnah, the Spirit of the Lord notwithstanding (Judges 13:25). But
in all three stories the bees mark a boundary between plain narrative
and fable, and the same boundary separates the beneficent, natural
character of honey-guide from another, malevolent kind of character
who inhabits the ground beneath the bee-tree. No matter whether it
is father-in-law or *inguni*-bird, the honey-guide gives way at the bee-
tree to a preternatural and mortally dangerous opponent of the person who has followed the guide to the bees' câche of food in the
wilderness. Samson meets his young lion, the five brothers meet Chilubwelubwe, and the father-in-law who was so friendly and helpful
at the beginning of "What a Little Thing Did" undergoes a sudden
change of character when he finds his first hive of bees, thereafter
threatening his son-in-law alternately with death from magical food
(the honey from the grass-stalk) and death by falling (from the high
Wanga trees). Thus a stable, uniform pattern of associative logic
persists in all three stories, regardless of whether one or a variety of

characters are used to supply the several pieces of the pattern:

Honey-Guide		Man-Slayer
(aid to life)		(peril to life)
$^{\circ}$	BEES	$^{\circ}$
(Samson)		*Lion*
Father-in-law		*Father-in-law*
Inguni		*Chilubwelubwe*

The wild bees in these stories are not only a boundary; they are also a point of equation between two larger halves of the under-lying logic. In all three stories the exogamous bridegroom jeopardizes important existing social ties (father and son, mother-in-law and son-in-law, husband and wives) in order to form new ties with aliens. To escape this dilemma, the bridegroom goes a journey into the wilder-ness to the site of a food-bearing (bee-) tree. He thereby moves out of his social dilemma into an even more serious economic and physi-cal dilemma of choice between the search for profit and avoidance of death, between preserving life and destroying it, between eating and being eaten. The sweet but stinging bees in the wild are a fitting symbol to accompany the bridegroom's bewilderment among the larger hopes and hazards of the fable.

As I have already said, the fable resolves the exogamous bride-groom's difficulties through a series of contests between himself and his affinal male kin. In the present three stories, the contests are ar-ranged in sequences of seven and subdivided into the unequal halves of seven: three and four. In the same way that the beneficent and malevolent characters before and after the bees' hive are represented by nominally different persons from one of these stories to another, so also the seven-fold contest has nominally different forms in each tale. Yet as a part of the fable's logical pattern, the numerical aspect of the contest is almost cabbalistically regular. The contest between Samson and his Philistine wedding-companions continues without change during the first three of seven days. Then the Philistines change their tactics. Instead of merely trying to guess the answer to his riddle as in conventional riddling, Samson's rivals turn to social skulduggery in order to discover the answer by means that have no place in an ordinary riddling-contest. The father- and son-in-law of "What a Little

Thing Did" compete with each other for three days in obtaining honey from the wilderness. When that thrice-repeated form of contest is inconclusive, they change their tactics and during the remaining four days of the seven they play at discovering one another in various wild animal and human hiding-places or disguises, a kind of trickery that has nothing to do with the ordinary conventions of hunting wild food. Four sons go to meet the Hopelessly Lost ogre in the story of Chilubwelubwe and Shichinongomunuma. Since they do not know who or what he is, Chilubwelubwe is able to deceive and eat all four. But his father arms the fifth and last son with foreknowledge of this killer:

> The next morning the father said to the son who remained with him, "You children of mine are foolish, because I forbade you to go westward: over to the west are Chilubwelubwe and Shichinongomunuma, the very ones who have made an end of human beings!" The son made reply, "Father why didn't you warn us of this while we were all here? Why have you hidden it from us? You merely spoke!" Then that youngest son arose and went right out westward.

After his brothers' four disastrous encounters with the ogre at the bee-tree, the fifth brother adopts a new tactic. Instead of falling asleep during Chilubwelubwe's entertainment of him, he remains awake and thereby vanquishes his cannibal host. But his ordeal in the western bush is not yet over; two further encounters with the even more dangerous Shichinongomunuma still await him to complete the full cycle of seven. The tactic that won his contest with Chilubwelubwe also wins him Chilubwelubwe's marvelous bell as a hospitality-gift, and the fifth brother uses it against The-Ogre-with-the-Big-Pot-at-the-Back in the same spirit of tactical innovation that prevailed against The-One-Hopelessly-Lost. For the fifth brother applies a principle against both the ogres of this story which his elder brethren had not observed and that was not part of the ordinary business of hunting small game: he understood that the successful hunter in the western bush had not only to overcome the game's avoidance of him, but also to avoid being himself caught and eaten like game by other hunters. By that policy the fifth brother completes the cycle of seven contests, reversing his elder brothers' four previous failures by his own three successes, once against Chilubwelubwe and twice against Shichinongomunuma.

"What a Little Thing Did" (3/4)	Shichinongomunuma and Chilubwelubwe (4/3)	Legend of Samson (3/4)
C O N V E N T I O N A L T A C T I C S		
1. Grass-stalk & Wanga Tree	1. First Brother & Chilubwelubwe	
2. Grass-stalk & Wanga Tree	2. Second Brother & Chilubwelubwe	Three days of guessing answer to Samson's Riddle
3. Grass-stalk & Wanga Tree	3. Third Brother & Chilubwelubwe	
	4. Fourth Brother & Chilubwelubwe	
T A C T I C A L I N N O V A T I O N		
4. Hunting Buffalo & Emergence of the Hunter	5. Fifth Brother & Chilubwelubwe	
5. Hunting Eland & Concealment of the Hunter	6. Fifth Brother & Shichinongomunuma	Four days of social quest for the answer to Samson's Riddle
6. Trapping Hippopotamus & Emergence of the Hunter	7. Fifth Brother & Shichinongomunuma	
7. Falling from Wanga Tree & Concealment of the Hunter		

The *conventional phase* of the seven-fold contest is dominated by preternatural deceptions and secrets:

Honey in the grass	Chilubwelubwe's masquerade as kind host	Samson's secret source of honey

The *innovative phase* of the seven-fold contest is dominated by disclosure of preternaturals' secrets:

Father-in-law's lechery	Chilubwelubwe's cannibalism & Shichinongomunuma's village	Answer to Samson's Riddle

In each of these stories the honey-trickster forfeits some property as the price of defeat in the contests. Chilubwelubwe gives up his bell, Samson pays his Philistine wedding-companions their thirty sheets and garments, and the Lamba father-in-law returns his widow-bride to her own people, divorcing her in favor of the illusory girl in the bush. Sometimes the honey-trickster in Lamba tradition forfeits his very life, as in another of Doke's tales, the story of "Mr. Little-Hare and What Ate Wulambe." 13

A man-eating lion catches its victims at the foot of a honey-tree. As in the story of Shichinongomunuma and Chilubwelubwe, four men go on four successive days to follow an inguni-bird. It leads them to the tree, and as they are about to lay fires for smoking the bees, the lion eats them; so instead of eating, they are eaten. The fourth victim is a certain Mr. Wulambe. His mother and marriageable sister survive him, and the sister offers herself in marriage to whomever will destroy "that which ate Wulambe." Little-Hare, an arch-trickster in Lamba fable, undertakes this labor and goes as the fifth person to follow the inguni, for as usual in these tales, the honey-trickster will be overcome only by invention and trickery craftier than his own. His four precursors had all immediately laid fires to smoke the bees when they reached the bee-tree, but Little-Hare adopts another tactic, ignoring the bees and waiting instead for the lion to appear. When it does, he varies the motif of smoking and asks the lion for some tobacco so that they two may have a social smoke together. After thus figuratively smoking the lion instead of the bees, Little-Hare proposes to show Lion a clever trick. He creeps into a sack and invites the lion to lift it. Lion accepts the challenge, but Little-Hare secretly slips his claws under a root, and the lion cannot move the sack for all his might. Hare then asks Mr. Lion to enter the sack and to call his wife and all his numerous children into it with him. When they are inside, rather than lift the bag Hare ties it shut and clubs the whole family of lions to death. Later Little-Hare opens the bag to display the corpse of What Ate Wulambe to Wulambe's sister. Seeing the dead lion, she rewards Little-Hare with marriage as she had promised to do.

This lion entertaining a visitor beneath a bee-tree in the wilderness is a fair equivalent of Chilubwelubwe. It is also like Samson in using the wild bee-hive to decoy its intended victims, and again like Samson in paying a forfeit for its defeat at the hands of a superior trickster who employs unconventional or surreptitious tactics against it. But this leonine Lamba honey-trickster also resembles Samson's young lion at the vineyards of Timnah, and not only because it too is a lion. Like Samson's lion it lies in wait for a would-be bridegroom in the vicinity of food-bearing wood, and there by a wonderful reversal of fortune it dies violently at the hands of the man whom it had intended to kill. Samson slays his lion by physical might and Little-Hare by prodigious cunning, but the result is the same: each subsequently marries by showing the dead lion to his prospective bride. Samson discloses the lion to his bride as the secret of his unanswerable riddle, while Little-Hare opens the sack full of dead lions to reveal What Ate Wulambe. Thus the lion in the Lamba story incorporates features of both Samson and the honey-yielding lion at Timnah, as if Samson and his lion were somehow only varieties of the same character.

These tales of honey-tricksters in Lamba tradition share yet another conspicuous resemblance to the legend of Samson. In all of them, food-trees are the location of crucial disappearances and concealments. Samson conceals everything that happened between himself and the lion at the vineyards of Timnah; keeping that secret was what he needed most to do. The son-in-law in "What a Little Thing Did" first disappears into the fruit of a wild orange tree, then when he is found out of that concealment he plummets out of the last Wanga tree to conceal himself absolutely from his dangerous father-in-law. Four brothers disappear forever in the story of Shichinongo-munuma and Chilubwelubwe, eaten by the dissembling honey-trickster Chilubwelubwe under his anonymous bee-tree. Finally, Little-Hare solves the murder-mystery of What Ate Wulambe and brings the criminal to justice by closing Mr. Lion in the sack under that honey-trickster's treeful of wild bees.

A tradition of oral fable is many tales together, but many nominally distinct tales are in truth only varieties or multiforms of each other. Because of that fact, careful comparison of the tales within a tradition is a main avenue to interpreting them. Moreover, this comparison of stories may and commonly does yield a considerable understanding of fabulous elements not only in that tradition but in other even very distant traditions as well. For example, the man-killing beasts and ogres that lurk about food-trees in Lamba stories not only threaten the lives of their visitors, but also entertain them in a polite and sometimes even gracious manner. By analogy, that fact provides a simple explanation for the honey in Samson's lion. It is, among other things, a vividly memorable and admirably concise way of expressing the man-slayer's hospitality, for as honey-trickster the lion must be both kind and malevolent toward his guest. This motif of provision, entertainment, or hospitality between the killer underneath the food-tree and his visitor resonates from one Lamba tale to another like a continuous echo of the Samson story.

Legend of Samson	Lion's provision of honey
Lamba Tales	
"What a Little Thing Did":	Father-in-law's provision of honey
Shichinongomunuma and Chilubwelubwe:	Chilubwelubwe's provision of food
"What Ate Wulambe:	Lion's provision of tobacco

Comparison of variants and multiforms may thus promote understanding of many individual bits of information in oral narrative which are impenetrably cryptic when isolated from their various equivalents in the tradition at large. *In traditions of oral fable, meaning resides in variety or multiformity of expression; above all else, motifs mean what they have in common with each other.* The same principle holds true furthermore for whole sets of motifs; the fundamental meaning of a cluster of motifs in any one tale lies in its identity of design with equivalent clusters in other tales that circulate with it in tradition.

Moreover, the equivalence of design that emerges from comparison of tales is a much more basic consideration for interpretative criticism than is the fortuity of a tale's immediate provenance from this or that linguistically or temporally defined tradition, for oral fable is and has long been much the same everywhere. So the design of the Samson legend is the same as the design of many tales in early twentieth-century Lamba fable, and the legend of Samson varies from the Lamba tales in the same manner as Lamba tales vary among themselves.

But variation and multiformity are not always a matter of one-for-one equivalence with a single different item representing the same basic motif in each tale of the same kind. It would be excessively simple-minded not to recognize that (a) sometimes one item represents a series of different motifs, and (b) sometimes more than one item represents just one underlying motif in a single text of oral fable. Even variation and multiformity are multiform and have diverse modes of variation.

Unitary, (b) variations are of course very common. The ubiquitous food-tree is an anonymous bee-tree in one tale, a vineyard in another, a Wanga tree in a third tale, and so forth. Sometimes duplications occur in one and the same tale. The Lamba son-in-law falls first from a wild orange tree to conceal himself, and later in the same story again from a Wanga tree for the same purpose.

I have already commented on an example of the other, (a) variety of variation, the transformation of the father-in-law's character in the story "What a Little Thing Did." There the father-in-law passes from the rôle of exogamous bridegroom through the rôle of natural honey-guide and thence on into that of preternatural honey-trickster, while elsewhere in Lamba fable the rôles of guide and trickster are assigned to separate characters. That was an instance of one nominal character playing two rôles, but there are equally numerous instances everywhere in oral fable of nominally different characters succeeding one another in the same rôle. Shichinongomunuma succeeds Chilubwelubwe as the exogamous bridegroom's preternatural opponent; in other Lamba stories a single person maintains that part throughout. So too Samson and his lion share the rôle of honey-trickster. First the lion threatens Samson's life, then posthumously fulfils the second requirement of the honey-trickster's part, that it be host to its guest and give him nourishment. Thereafter Samson assumes the lion's rôle as honey-trickster by means of the riddle, which being Samson's secret effectively transfers to him the lion's self-contradictory duality as simultaneous consumer and provider of sustenance. True to the defunct lion's nature, Samson too will either harm or benefit the guests at his wedding, the choice turning upon their success or failure against him in a contest of trickery centered on the equivocal lion; for to overcome Samson his foes have only to overcome the lion in his riddle.

Thus the names of characters may change, merge, and be divided from tale to tale as in a kaleidoscope, but as in a kaleidoscope the basic geometry or pattern of their relationships and deeds persists unchanged. The patterns or designs of fable, not the names attached to it, are the essence of fabulous tradition.

	Exogamous Bridegroom	Honey-Guide	Honey-Trickster	Arch-Trickster
Lamba Tales				
"What a Little Thing Did"	father-in-law	father-in-law	father-in-law	son-in-law
Shichinongomunuma and Chilubwelubwe	fifth son	*iŋguni*	Chilubwelubwe	fifth son
What Ate Wulambe	Little-Hare	*iŋguni*	Mr. Lion	Little-Hare
Legend of Samson	Samson	————	lion/Samson	30 Philistine companions

Changing the names of motifs and duplicating them in the same story are two of the most usual mechanisms of variation in oral fable. But there are others. The entire cluster of motifs that constitutes tales about honey-tricksters is no less variable as a whole than are the individual motifs in it. One common variation that effects a whole array of motifs is change in their sequence along the axis of the time it takes to tell a story. Thus one story-teller narrates the act of exogamy early ("What a Little Thing Did") while it is deferred to the very end of another tale (Shichinongomunuma and Chilubwelubwe). For this reason designs in oral fable give an impression of clustering rather than sequential regularity, despite the linear and non-recursive nature of oral narration. Motifs in fable do not need a fixed sequence to hold them together, because they have about them always the strong adhesive of customary association in the mind of every traditional story-teller, no matter which particular sequence one or another individual story-teller might happen to prefer. It is as if the motifs stand in a circle or orb which the narrator may rationally enter at any point and traverse at will, as did Clement Doke's Lamba narrators when they entered the sphere of fable about honey-tricksters and their trees.

THE ATOM IN EDEN

Another important kind of variation in clusters of motifs is omission. The honey-guide who leads the bridegroom to his encounter with preternatural danger and opportunity is on occasion expendable; the story is no less traditional and no less the same story without it. Indeed, like the clusters of particles in an atom, motival clusters in oral fable often seem to have nuclei, and these stark cores of fable make good narrative too. The three elements of food-tree, its preternatural denizen, and his hospitality to a human visitor were so significant a cluster of motifs in Lamba tradition that they could almost constitute a tale by themselves, as Clement Doke's "Story of the Man and the Ogre" shows. [14]

A certain man remained alone in a deserted village; so he went out to collect food. When he was out like this he came upon a fruit tree. It was then that it (an ogre) found him standing thus by the tree. On seeing him, it said, "What are you after?" He said, "Fruit!" Then it said, "Pick up these fruits!" and he picked the fruit up. Then he said, "These fruits I have begged, Sir, but what about those above? How do you climb?" It answered, "How about doing this!" and it lifted him and threw him up. So he went right up and picked the fruit. Then he asked, "And how now am I to get down?" It said, "How about doing this?" It drew down its arms, and lo! he is down.

So he tied up his bundle and went off to where he slept. Then again another day he came back and found the fruit. He shook (the tree) and the fruit fell. Thereupon he went in search of the owner of the fruit, who helped him to pick fruit; then helped him down again, and he went back home. But alas, one day he came back and found that the fruit didn't fall. So, when he saw that the owner hadn't come, he climbed up himself. Then the (owner) came and said, "And who has told you to climb up to the fruit?" And then, "Now you don't come down, you will go right away up with the fruit for ever!" Thereupon he didn't come back, not he; he was taken right away with the fruit. There was the end of him; he didn't come back, not he!

Here again the tale turns on the dual character of the preter-human person beneath the tree as alternately kind host and destroyer of men. The duplicity of the ogre's character is put to his guest in

the form of an enigma or paradox about food. First the ogre is
lavishly indulgent, and even condones the visitor's helping himself to
the fallen fruit without its owner's permission. Then, revoking all but
a little of his former liberality, he reacts ferociously to the unfortunate
man's last indiscretion and banishes him permanently together with
the food-tree. It is the end of the man, yet he takes with him in his
final disappearance the thing he needed most, the tree, meagre and
hard of access though its fruit had become.

In fact, the same paradox or enigmatic contradiction about
getting and eating food attends all these stories in one form or another, although one needs a good many variants to see exactly what
the paradox is in the tradition as a whole. But the more variants one
hears of a motif in oral fable, the clearer its meaning becomes as the
variants take their places one by one in a continuous spectrum of
nominal changes. Sometimes getting food seems easy in Lamba tales,
but before the hunter can eat it someone or something tries to eat
the hunter, and then the path of wisdom is to renounce eating ("What
Ate Wulambe"). Hunters become the hunted again in the story of
Shichinongomunuma and Chilubwelubwe, and even the trap of hospitality which Chilubwelubwe lays to snare his human prey is held taut
on the horns of a persistent little dilemma of whether to eat or not
to eat.

> *(The first brother meets the ogre)*...suddenly he came to a tree
> of bee-hives. The bees were everywhere. Then Chilubwelubwe
> greeted him, "Peace, friend!" And he said, "Peace to you!"
> Then he showed him to a house, which he entered. He cooked
> him some porridge with fly-relish; but he ate the porridge only.
> *(The second brother too)*...he heard the humming of bees, and
> then he reached the tree. When he looked round he saw his
> brother's weapons; then he knew that it was here that his broth-
> er was killed. Then Chilubwelubwe broke in saying, "Peace,
> friend!" And he said, "Peace, Sir!" Then he showed him to a
> house, which he entered and cooked him some porridge with
> flies for relish.
> *(And the third brother)*...off he went with the honey-guide; and
> drew near to the tree of bees. A humming, and he reaches it.
> When he looked round he saw his brothers' weapons, and he
> knew that this was where his brothers died. Then Mr. Chilubwe-
> lubwe greeted him, and he responded, "Peace to you!" He was

shown to a house, and porridge was cooked for him, and flies.
The flies he threw away, the porridge he ate.
*(The fourth brother understands the situation better, but not
well enough)...*he came to a tree of bees, they were everywhere.
He came and stood still. When he looked round, he saw the
weapons and axes of his brothers, and he knew that this (the
ogre had meanwhile appeared) was what ate people. Then he
was shown to a house, porridge was cooked, and flies.
*(Finally the fifth brother, who will undo the ogre)...*then he
reached the place where the bees were everywhere. When he
looked round he saw his brothers' axes. Mr. Chilubwelubwe
greeted him, "Peace, friend," and he returned, "Peace my
friend." He shewed him to a house, and cooked him porridge;
but he gave it to his dogs.

Chilubwelubwe's cuisine for visitors is basically ordinary; porridge
was the commonest staple of diet in Ilamba. But the relish of flies
is doubly strange. Not only are the flies inappropriate for Lamba
eating, they are also a kind of food that would be surpassingly hard
to procure in quantity enough for a relish if one did think of eating
them.[15] So Chilubwelubwe serves his guests a dish of food partly
easy to eat and partly hard to eat, but the wise man eats none of it
whether easy or hard, because in these tales the aftermath of eating
is the destruction (=disappearance) of the eater. Similarly, two men
go hunting expressly to find and eat wild honey in the story "What
a Little Thing Did," but again the prudent and ultimately victorious
one resolutely refuses ever to eat any of it. Moreover, like Chilubwelubwe, the father-in-law of that story tempts his intended victim with
some food that is easy to obtain and some that is hard, for if the
beehive in the Wanga tree was so difficult to open as to be virtually
impossible, then the stalk of grass was a câche of wild food effort-
lessly easy to exploit. Thus, by tracing the motif of dilemma concerning the ease or difficulty of obtaining food through the spectrum
of its variations from tale to tale throughout the tradition, one comes
to a plausible explanation and classification for the implausible detail
of the honey in a stalk of grass:

	Easy Food	Hard Food
The Man and the Ogre	Porridge	Fly-relish
"What a Little Thing Did"	Honey from grass-stalk	Honey from Wanga tree

The variations and multiforms of motifs in oral fable are often as various as these and more, yet not beyond understanding if the *tradition* (and not just a particular text) is what one tries to understand. But the problem arises of knowing the boundaries of tradition, if in fact it has any, because the organizing force of a few basic motifs underlying myriad variants in any one linguistically or historically defined tradition is rarely confined to that tradition alone. So Samson experienced the same paradox about food and eating as did his Lamba counterparts, and encapsulated it neatly in the enigma of his riddle.

Easy Food	**Hard Food**
Lion feeding on Samson	Samson eating from the lion

The lion that ordinarily might have killed and eaten of Samson feeds him instead, and by the enigma of feeding him accomplishes his permanent estrangement from the Philistines. So also the ogre in the tale of The Man and the Ogre paradoxically feeds, but in feeding also destroys, the mortal who frequents his orchard. In his enigmatic attitude about food and in the paradox that attitude creates for his human client, the preterhuman fruit-grower in the Lamba "Story of the Man and the Ogre" is reminiscent not only of Samson's lion at the vineyards of Timnah but also of the old orchardist who is comparably helpful and harmful by turns in the Pentateuchal story of Eden and the Fall of Man, Genesis 2 and 3.

> 2:8 Yahweh God planted a garden in Eden which is in the east, and there he put the man he had fashioned. 9 Yahweh God caused to spring up from the soil every kind of tree, enticing to look at and good to eat, with the tree of life and the tree of the knowledge of good and evil in the middle of the garden. 10 A river flowed from Eden to water the garden, and from there it divided to make four streams. *(Here intervenes the description of the four rivers, vv. 11-14)* 15 Yahweh God took the man and settled him in the garden of Eden to cultivate and take care of it. 16 Then Yahweh God gave the man this admonition, 'You may eat indeed of all the trees in the garden. Nevertheless of the tree of the knowledge of good and evil you are not to eat, for on the day you eat of it you shall most surely die.'

The Lamba ogre imposed a limit on when a man may harvest his fruit-tree, while the Lord God restricts which trees man may use. But the preternatural's human dependent cannot abide the restraint in either case. Both Adam and the Lamba man reach beyond the "domestic" food appropriated to their use to take forbidden or "wild" fruit from their preternatural host's tree. Like the taking of alien women, the taking of wild food costs the taker dearly in these stories. Genesis 3 enumerates the cost to Adam and all his descendants, culminating in the expulsion from Eden and the sentence of death:

> 3:22 Then Yahweh God said, 'See, the man has become like one of us, with his knowledge of good and evil. He must not be allowed to stretch his hand out next and pick from the tree of life also, and eat some and live for ever.' 23 So Yahweh God expelled him from the garden of Eden, to till the soil from which he had been taken. 24 He banished the man, and in front of the garden of Eden he posted the cherubs, and the flame of a flashing sword, to guard the way to the tree of life.

The expulsion from the garden could hardly have surprised Aŵalamba had someone in Clement Doke's era told them the Biblical story of Eden, because all their experience of fable in their own tradition taught them to expect a disappearance or a concealment, or both, in tales about food-trees. Like the Lamba ogre expelling his human guest from his garden, the Lord God makes Adam and his wife vanish forever out of Eden, but not before they have themselves learnt to practice concealments under the tree:

> 3:6 The woman saw that the tree was good to eat and pleasing to the eye, and that it was desirable for the knowledge that it could give. So she took some of its fruit and ate it. 7 Then the eyes of both of them were opened and they realized that they were naked. So they sewed fig-leaves together to make themselves loin-cloths.
>
> 8 The man and his wife heard the sound of Yahweh God walking in the garden in the cool of the day, and they hid from Yahweh God among the trees of the garden. 9 But Yahweh God called to the man. 'Where are you?' he asked.

After the game of hide and seek, the Lord God grants the man meaner food but better concealments than he had enjoyed in the Lord's garden:

> 3:17 To the man he said, 'Because you listened to the voice

of your wife and ate from the tree of which I had forbidden
you to eat,
> 'Accursed be the soil because of you.
> With suffering shall you get your food from it
> every day of your life.
> 18 It shall yield you brambles and thistles,
> and you shall eat wild plants.
> 19 With sweat on your brow
> shall you eat your bread,
> until you return to the soil,
> as you were taken from it.
> For dust you are
> and to dust you shall return.'

21 Yahweh God made clothes out of skins for the man and his
wife, and they put them on.

Like the Lamba ogre, the Lord God sends man away condemned
to the irrevocable disappearance of death, but with a source of nourishment (however meagre) to sustain him in exile. The Biblical story
of the Fall of Man thus has just the elements which its analogues in
Lamba tradition would lead one to expect.

The data from any tradition of fable in the ancient world is scant
compared with the abundance of information available from modern
traditions. For this reason, analogical studies of ancient and modern
traditions generally proceed best when they begin in modern materials
and then reach back in time to consider relics from the past. Where-
ever vigorous traditions of oral fable have been found in the modern
world, the stories in tradition present a continuous spectrum of multiforms like the Lamba tales about food-trees. When such a tradition
is well collected or otherwise well attested, the records of it preserve
the effect of that narrative spectrum, and the mind moves easily
through the spectrum appreciating each new tale as a further development or restatement of things already known but never before so
well understood. What is usually wanting in records of ancient traditions (like the Bible) is just this sense of a spectrum with its gradual
and connected modulation from one tale to the next, for ancient
records rarely contain enough fable to fill up the gaps between the
few broken pieces they do preserve. Yet the spectrum of a modern
tradition may to a great extent compensate the lack of one in the
scantier records of ancient fable, and thus supply the missing typo-

logical links between unsuspected multiforms of the same tale in an
ancient literary compilation. By itself the legend of Samson does not
readily suggest its own likeness to the story of Eden and the Fall of
Man, but as analogues of Lamba fable the two biblical stories are indeed alike.

The Lamba
Continuum: **"What a Little**
    Thing Did" ~ **Shichinongo-**
        munuma and
        Chilubwelubwe ~ **What Ate Wulambe** ~ **The Man &**
                         the Ogre

Biblical
Relics: **The Legend of Samson**   ~   †   ~   †   ~   **The Fall of Man**

Motifs: 1. Vineyards of Timnah   1. Garden of Eden

    2. Honey   2. Fruit of Knowledge

    3. Lion first feeds Samson,   3. Lord first feeds Adam,
      then by a paradox about   then by a paradox
      food destroys his bliss and   about food destroys
      expels him from Philistia   his bliss and expels
                           him from Eden

    4. The paradox: 4. The paradox:
      "Out of the eater   Not to eat the fruit
      came forth meat;   is wisdom; to eat
      out of the strong   the fruit is to be
      came forth sweet-   wise
      ness

    5. 30 wedding companions   5. The subtle serpent
      suborn Samson's bride   suborns Adam's bride

THE FALL OF MAN: ITS MEANINGS
GENERIC AND PAROCHIAL

Surely no tale in oral tradition has been more important than the
short, simple story of the Fall of Man. Still, as a piece of fable it does
not materially differ from a hundred multiforms which I might adduce
here from a variety of oral traditions, though none of those tales have
anything like the history of significance attached to the Biblical story.
Not even the legend of Samson has retained a comparable significance,
if ever in ancient times it had such. So far as the basic components

and the design of the Samson legend and the Fall of Man are concerned, they are the same tale, but it is only parody to say

In Samson's fall
We sinn'd all.

One can only conclude that the greater importance of the Fall of Man
is in the burden of theological and moral ideas which it has come to
bear by interpretation during the long philosophical development of
the peoples who have known the tale as a literary relic. The only real
difference between the two Biblical forms of the story, and the thing
that makes one of them a vehicle for a more portentous cargo of
extra-narrative ideas than the other, is the difference in names assigned
to the tales' motifs. Not that the name Samson was trivial; he was an
important figure in Hebrew legendary history, his lion was at least a
serviceable symbol of Philistine manhood, and the real historical rivalry between the Hebrews and Philistines was a substance well suited
to be cast in the mold of oral fable about honey-tricksters. The vineyards of Timnah must also have had local significance when the story
was first told with these names, although that significance is not obvious any more now. But the lion, Samson, and the vineyards of Timnah were nevertheless only names for stock motifs in oral fable, and
when those motifs were fitted with other names, the same mold of
fable could shape other moral and philosophical substance too. By
naming the motif of preternatural host Yahweh, his human guest
Adam, the ancestor of all mankind, and the food-tree the Tree of
Wisdom, the same oral tale was equipped to carry one of the most
impressive loads of interpretation any tale has ever borne. That burden
of interpretation has in the course of time even become something of
a tradition in its own right in the West, although it is by no means
either so ancient or so universal a tradition as is the fable upon which
it rests.

But while it is clearly wrong to regard the whole hermeneutical
superstructure about original sin and related matters as somehow
inherent in the tale of Eden, it would be just as wrong to deny that
anything besides the names that are attached to the story's motifs
enable it to support ideas about sin and divine retribution. Like all
its many oral variants, the Fall of Man has a logical pattern that is
especially suited to reasoning about the relationship between men
and any kind of supernal beings. It is the story of a man whom an
expropriative impulse drives away from ordinary human dwelling-

places and to a rendezvous *sub rosa* with a preterhumanly powerful
being whose enigmatic and paradoxical behaviour the man must then
endure in the satisfaction of his own most compelling needs: to eat,
to beget and protect progeny, and to survive the malice of others.
Because of that fixed design, oral tales of this kind are well adapted
to be told about the beginning of adult manhood and its responsibilities; and such in fact is their use, as several of the multiforms
already cited show, for even Adam was a man at the beginning of
responsible manhood.

From the foregoing comparative evidence and other evidence
like it in the experience of many folklorists, it seems to me that the
underlying, essential motifs of oral fable *with their durable generic
meanings* must be distinguished from the various local names and
interpretations which men in particular cultures associate from time
to time with their own local inheritance of fable. Such names as
Samson, Mr. Lion, Eden, and Wanga undoubtedly helped to fill the
ancient Hebrew and modern Lamba variants of the honey-trickster's
tale with an ethnically distinctive and parochially valuable content of
moral ideas for the Israelite or Umulamba who heard the variants as
parts of oral fable in his own language. And yet, for all its momentary
descriptive or explanatory relevance to the personal and corporate
lives of Hebrew and Lamba listeners, the vernacular meaning which
they might find in the tale was after all only their interpretation of
it and not nearly so lasting or permanently valuable as the tale itself.

Like the Israelite or Umulamba, the historian or ethnographer
of Hebrew or Lamba culture always meets oral fable clothed in local
names and intimately associated (as it must be in those localities) with
characteristically Hebrew or Lamba ideas and values. It is easy to forget in these circumstances, or not to know (as the Israelite and Umulamba did not know) that oral fable is a universal cultural property—
universal not only because every people tell fabulous stories, but also
because they share in the telling a common fund of generic motifs
and story-patterns. Furthermore, generic motifs and their patterns
have generic meanings. Dressed in Hebrew costume as the story of
Adam's fall, the tale of the food-tree and its preterhuman keeper conveys an elaborate vernacular meaning that could not be guessed from
either the generic story or its Hebrew multiform alone. One must
know more than the story to comprehend all it meant in ancient
Israel or all it has come to mean in later cultures that were influ-

enced by the Scriptures. Nevertheless, even after three thousand years, the generic tale underlying the Pentateuchal account of Adam's disobedience still limits the Hebrew story's hermeneutical cargo. It is a tale generically able to bear and integrate all manner of ideas about marriage, property-rights, divinity, and even economy, but by itself it is ill-suited to support ideas about cosmology or government. For those matters, there are other tales in oral fable with different motifs and different designs. The scholar concerned with the meaning of particular tales in a particular culture spares himself much confusion and many mistakes when he recognizes generic motifs and their concomitant patterns in the local, vernacular tradition of fable which he studies.

But regardless of whether one is interested more in the universal or in the parochial aspects of oral fable (or to put it differently, more in its nature or in its uses), one must unavoidably deal with fable in its parochial manifestations, because every text of oral fable comes from some particular story-teller in some particular language at some particular time and place. Generic motifs and the designs that hold them together exist only in their myriad parochial variants where fable is actually composed. These actual manifestations of motifs often seem barbarous, irrational or foolish at first encounter, but a little experience with them soon reveals their high order of abstraction, as for example in the Lamba son-in-law's plunge from the Wanga tree to conceal himself from an enemy too crafty at discovery, or the Timnite lion's yielding honey to fulfil his motival obligation as a preterhuman host. The parochial forms of fabulous motifs commonly have so little logical necessity by themselves that they are quite cryptic, and often no less cryptic to natives who have known a tradition of fable all their lives than to aliens who meet it for the first time in an oral performance or a record thereof from some out-of-the-way part of the world. The purpose in comparing variants of fable and extracting generic motifs from them is precisely to lighten the otherwise heavy work of deciphering variants, which, if taken one by one and without reference to each other, constitute a truly insurmountable labor of decipherment. But as in any process of discovery, a good deal of effort must go to finding out the generic motifs and refining their descriptions before they can be useful for typing and classifying a wide variety of tales. Thus criticism and the practice of classification should march together. When they do not, classification ιof folktale types and motifs becomes idle and useless cataloguing, while criticism looses touch with the reality of multiform tradition and starves on a steady diet of nothing but identical or nearly identical texts.

A PROCEDURAL ENVOI

This book is about essential or generic motifs and the webs of design that keep them together in traditions of oral fable. It is concerned essentially with what fabulous motifs and patterns are, not with their origins nor with their uses in any surroundings other than their own proper ambient of oral narrative. Whether the things described here are innate psychic categories or learned types of imagery is quite beside the present point, because whatever their origins might be, they are the objective fundamentals of oral fable and beg to be understood in their own right, apart from anyone's prepossessions about their ulterior utility. Much mischief has been wrought in the study of oral narrative by treating it as if it consisted of its applications in religion, witchcraft, history, social organization, the private phantasmas and reminiscences of disturbed individuals, or a dozen other occupations of the mind beside story-telling. Oral fable is so ingenious an instrument that it is capable of many uses, but like other instruments it is not the same thing as its applications. And if it is to be thought of as an instrument of culture or social behaviour, then its instrumentality is that of a highly adaptable vehicle giving conveyance and mobility to many ideas of many kinds and having a better record of service to the negotiation and exchange of ideas than to their selection or enforcement in particular systems of thought.

I conceive the eldest and most universal components of oral fable to be *story-patterns*. I owe the phrase 'story-pattern' and my understanding of it to Albert Lord. I define a story-pattern as a traditional cluster of generic motifs, and I distinguish among such clusters two kinds, *bounded* and *unbounded*. I call the bounded kind of motival clusters *themes*, and I regard them as the basic small pieces of which oral fables are made, while unbounded patterns constitute the larger, as it were architectural design in oral narrative tradition. I consider *generic motifs*, like the fibres of a timber or the atoms in a molecule, capable of analytical separation from patterns but incapable of entering into the composition of traditional stories except as

integrants of patterns, where they are held indissolubly in their orbits
of association with other motifs by the powerful cohesive force of
story-telling custom. *Nominal motifs* are the local varieties of generic
motifs found in the same story-patterns, equivalents of each other
like the Lamba ogre's fruit-tree and the Hebrew Yahweh's tree of the
knowledge of good and evil.

Finally, there are everywhere associated with oral fable certain
interpretative traditions of diverse age and universality which attach
to motifs and make them *symbols*. As symbols, many motifs found
in fable have considerable employment outside narrative, in religious
ritual for example, or in decorative art, where indeed part of a motif's
symbolic function may be as an economical or compact means of reference to the story-pattern where it also occurs. In this manner some
narrative motifs do achieve a more or less independent existence in
other cultural processes apart from fable and thereby form important
links between fable and other kinds of reasoning. Through the symbolic links with narrative tradition which these single, "liberated"
motifs provide, the virtues of narrative patterning can be exploited
for various philosophical and practical purposes without the demand-
ing necessity of actually narrating whole fables every time one wants
to transfer an idea traditionally maintained in fable to some depart-
ment of social or intellectual activity other than story-telling.

I therefore find unacceptable the older scholarly fashion of
treating as though they were the same thing *motifs* in oral fable and
symbols in other contexts such as ritual. I find this unacceptable even
when motifs and symbols reside together in exactly the same images,
as they often do. A symbol is by nature a perfectly adequate purvey-
or of meaning in its own right whenever it passes between persons who
are initiate into its symbolism. But a narrative motif by itself means
nothing and *cannot even be identified* apart from the other motifs
surrounding it in the story-patterns to which it belongs. Moreover,
when one is not privy to the symbolism of an image used symbolically , it means little or nothing, and no amount of effort will suffice
to extract its symbolism from it alone, because symbolism is meaning
associated with an image and not resident in the image itself. But in
their proper patterns, narrative motifs bear certain meanings inherent
in narrative regardless of whether anyone apprehends that meaning
or puts it to any extra-narrative use whatsoever. In order to use a
symbol effectively, one must (as in enactments of ritual) be taught

in detail what it symbolizes, but to convey the generic ideas in narrative motifs one learns to tell stories.

In summation, I consider that the meaning of a narrative image derives from its place among other narrative images, while symbolism derives from an image's conventional associations in other spheres outside narrative. Symbolic reasoning and fabulous tradition meet in nominal motifs, but while they are complementary processes, they are not the same, for each has its own rules of procedure and composition. The long history of oral narrative tradition abundantly demonstrates how closely wed the two cultural processes of symbolic thought and storytelling have been, but it also shows how independently of each other they have functioned. The ponderously weighty symbolism of this or that nominal motif seems today to dominate the minds of a whole people, but it is gone tomorrow, while their neighbors remain oblivious to it the whole time, seeing their most precious values reflected in some other nominal motif instead. Yet both peoples will tell the same tales with the same motifs, because in the long run their precious tradition of story-telling is more precious to them both than all the high values and all the ethnic peculiarities of themselves which they once associated with some of their tellings of fable. A modern description of oral fable must reveal why this is so.

	COMPONENTS OF FABLE	MEANINGS OF FABLE
Local Multiforms and Their Uses:	Nominal Motifs	Interpretative Tradition
The World Tradition:	Generic Motifs in Story-Patterns	Generic Meanings

Chapter Three

INTER DVOS ARBORES

There is an old tale goes that Herne the Hunter,
Sometime a keeper here in Windsor Forest,
Doth all the winter time, at still midnight,
Walk round about an oak, with great ragg'd horns;
And there he blasts the trees, and takes the cattle,
And makes milch kine yield blood, and shakes a chain
In a most hideous and dreadful manner.

-The Merry Wives of Windsor

Trees of oneness and trees of separation.   *p. 84*

The hewn wood of redemption: Squeezer, Beowulf,
    and Christ.   *p. 88*

The hewn wood of retribution: Helen of Troy, and
    other misappropriated rights in women.   *p. 98*

The hewn wood of exchange: the manifold marriage
    of Mandu and the mission of Moses.   *p. 122*

Given enough time, everything that man is or creates undergoes changes of form and composition. Palaeontologists deduce from the fossils of prehistoric primates that even the biologically inherited apparatus of the human body has changed over a long period of time. Nevertheless, the forms of the body have seemed to be the least mutable data of the human condition, and they supply the only presently accepted scientific criteria for determining which of the prehistoric primates were human.

But it must still be obvious even to prehistorians of human anatomy that the only sure proofs of humanity lie in the functions of the mind and not in the shapes of the body. This must be true whether or not we possess or know how to interpret evidence of prehistoric human mental activity. And just as the physical form of fossil men is judged human or hominid by comparing it with the form of living men, so too any evidence which we might have or acquire of prehistoric mental activities is subject to comparison with the intelligence of living men and of men who have left records of their intelligence in historic times. Following this procedure, one should have to say about his own evolutional ancestors just what was said here earlier about hypothetical "intelligent beings" on planets in other solar systems or in other galaxies. If they had a tradition of fable, then they were human, but otherwise not, no matter how much their fossilized physical remains might suggest the shapes and functions of modern men's bodies. Moreover, without fable, not even a rudimentary use of language were enough in itself to make humans out of prehistoric hominids. One can imagine, and even witness in the routine life of present-day peoples everywhere a considerable use of imperative and indicative language without any conception of fiction or past time. But the first true humans were the ones who first remembered fiction about the past and told each other those memories. Judging from the universality of such activity among living peoples, the development of a capacity for fable took place much before any men had learned to write. But how long a time separated the two innovations of fable and writing is hard to know, because fable began by virtue of a mental development whose physical consequences

in the anatomy and material remains of prehistoric men are still un-
discovered or uncertainly appreciated, if they exist at all.

Changes of shape and of substance are the rule throughout culture. In time, they effect the production of intangibles like language
and ritual no less than material requisites such as tools and containers. It is so in story-telling too. Oral traditions of fable are impossible without story-tellers' sometimes changing their tales, and the names
of fabulous motifs as well as their arrangement in patterns are different from place to place and from one people's tradition to another.
But while these variations are very numerous, they are also quite
superficial. An anatomical analogy is again useful: be it great or small,
whole or broken, a femur or a mandible by any other name is still
the same thing, no matter how well or badly it serves the organism
to which it belongs. For oral fable answers to innate functions of the
mind, just as accurate marksmanship answers to human optics or
grasping to the shape of the hand. And like those traits of inherited
physique and their functions, the legacy of memorable fiction in
traditions of story-telling seems to have kept its basic form unchanged
over very long intervals of time and in the most diverse environments
which men have found habitable.

It is therefore not an accident nor necessarily a fact of recent
provenance that the Philistine tale of Samson, the Hebrew account
of Eden, and Lamba fable have much in common. They are alike
because they consist of the same generic motifs. And curiously, the
nominal differences among them *emphasize by variation* those very
features in themselves wherein their likeness lies.

One such difference between the Lamba tale of "The Man and
the Ogre" and the Hebrew story of orchard-robbing in Genesis Two
is in their motifs of food-trees. For all his preternatural power to
help or harm his human client, the Lamba ogre is not so great an
orchardist as the maker of Eden, whose garden held "all trees pleas-
ant to look at and good for food; and in the middle of the garden
. . .the tree of life and the tree of the knowledge of good and evil."
In contrast, the Lamba ogre has only one tree, and it is the only
one in the whole tale about him.

But though the trees in Eden are of every kind, the story about
the ogre and his one tree is patterned in exactly the same fashion as
the Hebrew story of Yahweh and his entire orchard with its three
distinct categories of planting: trees for food; tree of knowledge; tree

of life. Perhaps only the association of Eden with the Hebrew cosmogony necessitated the mention of Yahweh's ordinary trees—those from
which Adam might take fruit whenever and however he pleased— but
they are notable not only because Yahweh created them. The traditional pattern of the story calls for an experienced fruit-picker to
play opposite the preterhuman owner of the fateful tree. Adam's
employment as Yahweh's orchard-keeper assured him the requisite
experience, even though he was himself a recent invention. On the
other hand, Adam's counterpart in the Lamba story needed no such
preparation for his encounter with the ogre, because every Lamba
man from time immemorial had in reality plenty of experience in
gathering food from fruit-trees in the wild.

The two remaining kinds of trees in the story of Eden are the
significant ones, because their fruit has moral as well physical nutritive value. The first of these, the tree of the knowledge of good and
evil, yields fruit with the extraordinary power to make the mind of
the eater understand moral distinctions. It is thus a tree of *separation,*
that causes its user to apprehend differences among things, actions,
and conditions of being, and, ultimately, to be himself separated
from Eden as a person whose heightened powers of discernment
make him a dangerous and bad thing in contrast to the undifferen-
tiated good of Eden. The other morally significant fruit-tree in Yahweh's garden has just the opposite virtue. Those who eat of it loose
their distinctive natures and become like Eden's creator. It is just this
abolition of difference which Yahweh fears and obviates by expelling
Adam and his mate from paradise, for he does not want them to become like himself and never experience the most awesome of all
separations, that of the living from the dead.

The single tree in the Lamba story represents both of the generic
motifs that are given different names as the tree of life and the tree
of knowledge in the tale of Eden. A change in the African tree's
fruiting signals the transition from the one generic motif to the other.
The sequence of the two motifs as they are presented in the Lamba
tale is just the opposite of that in Genesis, but since sequential order
is a variable that has no effect on basic patterning, the pattern of the
two stories remains the same. The Lamba ogre's tree at first yields
abundant fruit, and its owner (who enjoys plenty while men starve)
shares it with a man whom he treats as his peer, as one with himself
even to the extent of enabling the man to ascend and descend the
tree by the same bird-like maneuver he himself habitually employs.

It is for a moment as though Adam had achieved the likeness of Yahweh. Then the fruit-tree changes. It begins to yield its fruit grudgingly,
as if it were not the same tree. The man then forgets his dependence
and *oneness* with the ogre, undertaking instead to feed himself from
the tree *apart* from the agreement and help of the tree's owner. The
ogre reacts to the man's display of independence with an unexpectedly well-developed concern for the separateness of his own property-
rights, and he finally completes the round of separations by severing
the man from life on earth.

So the African tale contains the same two types of arboreal
image found in the story of Eden, even though the Lamba narrator
represented them with only one actual tree-motif, the ogre's single
fruit-tree. The images are typologically the same in both stories not
only because all are fruit-trees, but also because they carry the same
associations of meaning arranged alike:

		bearing:	Union of man with a preter-natural, and man's redemption.
"The Man and the Ogre"	*Ogre's fruit-tree,*		
		not bearing:	Separation of man from a preternatural, and the man's perdition.

		bearing:	Union of man with a preter-natural, and man's redemption.
Genesis Two	*Yahweh's fruit-tree*		
		not bearing:	Separation of man from a preternatural, and the man's perdition.

THE HEWN WOOD OF REDEMPTION:
SQUEEZER, BEOWULF, AND CHRIST

Lamba story-tellers also had in their tradition of fable other
motifs besides living, green trees to express these same ideas about
unity and *separation*. Sometimes they used those other motifs supple-
tively with trees to form the same pattern. Clement Doke recorded
the evidence of this in such tales as "The Story of the Sons of Squeezer and Mr. Water-Lizard," [16] where the pattern of the two trees is
represented by three nominal motifs, only one of them a living tree,
and the other two a pair of wooden flutes.

Mr. Squeezer had three children; and he carved two flutes. He said, "My children, don't blow the 'going-right-away,' blow the 'near-at-hand.' " When one of the children went, he blew, "Ne ne near near e near near e. . . !" But the honey-guide didn't come. Then he took the flute 'going-right-away,' and blew, "Away ay. . . !" Behold, a honey-guide flew down. (Away) flap flap flap, ...

Here the two flutes bear the burden of signifying union and separation, notions associated directly with the trees of other tales. The flute named "near-at-hand" is designed to assure the continued community of father and sons, while "going-right-away" separates them:

. . . (and) they (the bees) are sitting in a tree. When he had gone swish swish swish swish, he said, "Indeed, ah! ah!" (and) he found that the bough was growing stretched out over the middle of a pond. Then he arrived, and put down his weapons, and lit a fire; then he climbed. When he had chopped with the axe chop chop, lo, the head flew off whirr into the pond. Then he climbed down, and undressed, and dived in to look for the axe.

Appetite, the same consideration that drove Adam and his Lamba counterpart to violate the preternatural's tree, also drives the first son of this story to use the flute of separation, for while there is safety in the flute "near-at-hand," it gets its user nothing to eat nor any hope of discoverying food. A meeting with a preterhuman beneath the tree must inevitably follow, for the traditional story-pattern dictates it; the only uncertainty is which species of unreal creatures in Lamba fable will appear:

While he was searching in the water, he came upon a Water-Lizard lying. It said, "Who are you?" He said, "I am the son of Squeezer!" It said, "First squeeze me, let us feel!" He said, "I do not know how, he who knows how to squeeze is my father." Then it swallowed him.

The remaining two sons of Squeezer go the same way into the belly of Mr. Water-Lizard. Then their father goes in search of them:

Where the father was, he thought, "Now (my) children are finished, I myself remain." Then he hastened to blow the 'going-right-away.' It sounded, "Away ay. . . !" And the honey-guide came, and led the way to the tree. Then he hastened to climb, and chopped his axe into it, slip! and it fell in. Then he dived in to look (for it). And he came upon Mr. Water-Lizard. He said, "Who are you?" He said, "I am Squeezer." He said, "First squeeze me, let us feel!" And he caught (him) and squeezed. Lo, a child and an axe. And he squeezed (again). Lo, a child and an axe. And he squeezed (yet again). Lo, a child and an axe. And he cast (the Water-Lizard) on the land, and went to the village with his children.

Squeezer has a famous elder cousin in the eponymic hero of an eighth-century Anglo-Saxon epic, *Beowulf*. The meaning of the personal name "Beowulf" has been disputed, but in view of the story-pattern which *Beowulf* shares with African and ancient Near Eastern fable, it is certainly reasonable to see an apian reference in the first part of the name, and so to associate Beowulf with (wild) bees. In any case, the hero Beowulf also overcame water-monsters, named Grendel and Grendel's dam, by "knowing how to squeeze." Like Water-Lizard, Beowulf's pair of swallowing monsters also haunted a pool under a grove of unnamed trees (the only stand of trees mentioned in the story) where one particular tree leans suggestively over the water. Before Beowulf sees this place for the first time, his patron Hrothgar tells him certain rumours about Grendel, Grendel's mother, and their underwater home:

1345   Ic þæt londbūend,   lēode mīne,
        selerǣdende   secgan hȳrde,
        þæt hīe gesāwon   swylce twēgen
        micle mearcstapan   moras healdan,
        ellorgǣstas. Ðǣra ōðer wæs,
1350   þæs þe hīe gewislīcost   gewitan meahton,
        idese onlicnes;   ōðer earmsceapen
        on weres wæstmum   wræclāstas træd,
        næfne hē wæs māra   þonne ǣnig man ōðer;
        þone on gēardagum   Grendel nemdon
1355   foldbūende;   nō hīe fæder cunnon,
        hwæþer him ǣnig wæs   ǣr ācenned
        dyrnra gāsta.   Hīe dȳgel lond
        warigeað wulfhleoþu,   windige næssas,
        frēcne fengelād,   ðær fyrgenstrēam
1360   under næssa genipu   niþer gewīteð,
        flod under foldan.   Nis þæt feor heonon
        milgemearces,   þæt se mere standeð;
        ofer þæm hongiað   hrinde bearwas,
        wudu wyrtum fæst   wæter oferhelmað.[17]

1345   I have heard my people who live in that land
     and who have houses there say
     that they have seen two such
     huge wanderers keeping watch on the bogs,
     alien spirits roaming the wastelands.
1350   Insofar as they could exactly understand,
     one of the pair was like a woman. The other hapless
         creature
     endured in man's shape the loneliness of a hated
         outcast condemned to wander in desert places,
     though he was mightier than any other man.
     In former times, those who dwelt among men
1355   named him Grendel; but they do not know his father,
     or whether earlier he begat any other
     furtive and baneful spirits. The secret land
     which they inhabit is the refuge of wolves, the windy
         bluffs
     and the perilous fens, there where the mountain
         torrent
1360   plunges into the misty shadow of the cliffs,
     joining the waters beneath the earth.
     The place where that pool lies is not far hence,
         reckoning in miles;
     over it hang rimy groves,
     and a tree held fast by its roots reaches over the
         water.

The Old English story-teller described the same tree and pool
again when Beowulf later approaches the place and prepares to squeeze
the witch-like mother of Grendel in an underwater, hand-to-hand combat with her:

     hē fēara sum   beforan gengde
     wīsra monna   wong scēawian,
     oþ þæt hē fǣringa   fyrgenbēamas
1415   ofer hārne stān   hleonian funde,
     wynlēasne wudu;   wæter under stōd
     drēorig ond gedrēfed.[18]

     He went ahead with a few
     wise men to inspect the region,
     until suddenly he found the mountain-trees

1415   leaning over the gray rock,
        and the joyless tree among them; beneath lay the
            water,
        dreary and troubled.

Plunging into the pool, Beowulf finds the water-monster in the depths
and grapples it there just as the Lamba Squeezer did, because like the
Lamba Water-Lizard Grendel's dam and her brood are also proof
against cutting implements and conquerable only by squeezing:

1531   wearp ða wundenmǣl   wrǣttum gebunden
        yrre ōretta,   þæt hit on eorðan læg,
        stīð ond stȳlecg;   strenge getruwode,
        mundgripe mægenes. . . . . .
1535   . . .   .

        . . .   .
        Gefēng þā be eaxle   —nalas for fǣhðe mearn—
        Gūð-Gēata lēod   Grendles mōdor;
        brægd þā beadwe heard,   þā hē gebolgen wæs,
1540   feorhgenīðlan,   þæt hēo on flet gebēah.[19]

1531   The angry fighter threw down the etched sword,
        and it lay on the earth
        hard and steely. He trusted instead in his own strength
        and in the powerful grip of his hand . . .
1535   . . .   . . .

        . . .   . . .
        Then the War-Geats' man resolutely seized
        Grendel's mother by the shoulder,
        and raging now, he pressed
1540   his deadly enemy so hard that she fell to the ground.

When they have defeated it, both Beowulf and his Lamba counterpart dredge up the monstrous aquatic cannibal and take it ashore (or
its head, the part that eats men). Then the squeezers return to the
familiar paths of home in company with their own kind. Their con-
vivial return is counterpoint to the lonesomeness and strangeness of
their descent to meet the uncouth creature in the pool:

1632   Ferdon forð þonon   fēþelāstum
        ferhþum fægne,   foldweg mǣton,
        cūþe strǣte;   cyningbalde men
1635   from þǣm holmclife   hafelan bǣron

earfoðlīce;   heora ǽghwæþrum,
felamōdigra,   fēowar scoldon
on þǽm wælstenge   weorcum geferian
tō þǽm goldsele   Grendles hēafod,[20]

1632   They went thence by the beaten path
            glad at heart, marching along
            the familiar road. The king's valiant men
1635   carried the head from the bluff.
            It was heavy work
            for four stalwart men
            to bear Grendel's Head on a spear-shaft
            to the gold-hall. . . .

Beowulf has much in it besides the story of Mr. Squeezer. Yet one group of motifs distributed discontiguously in *Beowulf* represents the same narrative paradigm found consolidated as the major part of the Lamba tale: *A man of mighty grasp dives alone into a pool under a tree; either he or the tree is associated with wild bees. He finds a cannibal under the water, but acts of hewing or cutting are futile in combat with it and it is ultimately defeated only by pressure. The man with the strong hand squeezes, throws, and lands the monster, then returns home convivially with past companions.*

As part of this scheme, the *wudu wyrtum fæst* at verse 1364 in *Beowulf* is an Anglo-Saxon equivalent of the trees of separation seen here earlier in both Lamba and ancient Hebrew fable. Under that live tree Beowulf must struggle alone to win or lose everything. So we have before us now four tales, all sharing the pattern of the separation-story with its central motifs of tree and ogre. In all four tales the ogre under the tree destroys men whose only sin is in their desire to eat and drink; Grendel and Grendel's mother make the utopian eating-place Heorot as uninhabitable for men as Yahweh made Eden. One of the two Lamba tales ends tragically with destruction of the hungry man, as in Genesis. That happens again under different names in the "Story of the Sons of Squeezer and Mr. Water-Lizard," but there Mr. Squeezer intervenes after the disappearance of his hungry sons and turns tragedy into salvation by rescuing them from the ogre. Beowulf serves Hrothgar to the same end. The story of Squeezer's sons and *Beowulf* are different from the Fall of Man and the "Story of the Man and the Ogre" only because they have a sequel with a redeemer whose powerful grasp saves hungry men from the devouring ogre.

This saviour is in fact only a rank imitator of the ogre, who turns the ogre's characteristic acts of sunderance upon itself. When Grendel grips the men in Heorot, Beowulf grips Grendel. When Grendel's mother grips Beowulf in the pool, he grips her; and when subsequently she tries to stab him in the neck, he beheads her. When the water-lizard swallows his sons, Squeezer engulfs the water-lizard in the grip of his hand. When the lizard has taken his sons out of their proper terrestrial ambient and retained them underwater, Squeezer takes the lizard out of its proper aquatic ambient and lays it to rest permanently in the terrestrial world above. By reflecting the ogre's sundering effects upon itself, the rescuer civilizes its powers in his own person and places them at the service of humanity. His mastery of ogreish techniques not only neutralizes the ogre, it also reunites men with the customary activities and companions from which the ogre had earlier separated them. Squeezer and his sons return to their village in happy camaraderie, while revelry resumes in Heorot. It is a neat trick: from imitating an alien, anti-social power of disintegration a new integration results.

The tree of separation stands where it is expected in this story, towering over the ogre, but where is the tree of unity? As in the Lamba telling, so too in the Anglo-Saxon: once Squeezer and Beowulf have descended into the water, the tree overhanging the pool is not mentioned again. Plainly that tree signifies only separation, and the squeezer's victory over the man-eater in the pool is the end of separations.

♦ The Sons of Squeezer	♦ The Man and the Ogre
♦ *Beowulf*	♦ The Fall of Man
+ redeemer	+ tree of unity
− tree of unity	− redeemer

Instead of trees, the dominant motifs of object after the struggle underwater are the bodies of the dead monsters and the cutting instruments associated with them: the axes spewed up by the water-lizard when Squeezer grips it, and the marvelous sword which Beowulf finds in his water-ogre's hoard of looted weaponry.

1557   Geseah ðā on searwum   sigeēadig bil,
           ealdsweord eotenisc   ecgum þȳhtig,
           wigena weorðmynd;   þæt (wæs) wæpna cyst, −

1560   būton hit wæs māre   ðonne ǣnig mon ōðer
            tō beadulāce   ætberan meahte,
            gōd ond geatolīc,   gīganta geweorc.[21]

1557   He saw a lucky sword there among the weapons,
            an ancient one made by the voracious titans, with
               a hard edge,
            such as warriors prize. It was the best of swords,
1560   though too ponderous for any other man to carry
               into battle,
            a fine and splendrous weapon, the handiwork of
               giants.

The prominence of cutting-tools at the end of the combat suggests
where to look for the opposite of the tree that signifies separations.
I have already said that the flute "near-at-hand" which Squeezer carved
for his sons is the wood of unity in that tale. It is opposed to the
lizard's bee-tree in the same manner as the Tree of Life was opposed
to the Tree of Knowledge in Eden. The flute called "going-right-away"
is at first an intermediate, transitional term between the bee-tree and
the flute "near-at-hand." When Squeezer's sons play it, it is a device
for separating them from their father and from each other. But then
Squeezer plays it with just the opposite effect: in order to be reunited
with his sons. Both flutes are ultimately devices of unification in the
hands of their maker, Mr. Squeezer.

	Union	⇔	Separation
	↓		↓
− Rescuer	Tree of Life		Tree of Knowledge
+ Rescuer	"Near-at-Hand"	"Going-Right-Away"	Water-Lizard's Bee-Tree

The flutes are not trees, but they are wooden. More exactly,
they are wood hewn and fashioned to human uses. They in the realm
of objects are what the squeezer is among animate creatures, a kind
of monster who is in the service of men to inflict ogreish punishments
on ogres. He represents the domestication of ferocity. In a similar
manner, wood that is hewn and fashioned to human purposes in
these tales of ogres brings with it into the service of men those same
virtues which it possesses inaccessibly to men while it remains in a
natural or wild, unhewn state. No wonder that Squeezer and Beowulf

—both cutters, carvers, and hewers—have motifs of tools for cutting
and the products of their hewing clustered about them: Squeezer
with his pair of magic flutes and Beowulf with his two hewn things,
Grendel's fearsome head on the spear-shaft.

The scene with the ogre's terrible head (the dead engine of its
destructiveness) on the pole at verse 1636 *ff.* signals the triumph of
human authority in *Beowulf*. Yet that scene is only an exact domestic
replica of the earlier scene in the wilderness (verses 1357 *ff.*) where
the live ogre waiting dangerously under the *wynleasne wudu* represented the ultimate degree of human impotence. Even in death Beowulf's
ogre retains its association with the wood, except that now both are
in a hewn state. But although the pole with the dread head on it is
fashioned from wood and fitted with the product of Beowulf's hewing in the wilderness, it is still only a transitional motif, an equivalent of the Lamba flute "going-right-away" and not the primary wood-
en artifact that represents human unity in *Beowulf*. That motif, the
Anglo-Saxon equivalent of the Lamba flutes and the Hebrew Tree of
Life, is Heorot itself, Hrothgar's magnificent wooden banquet-hall,
assembly-place, and seat of government, the very home of men's
desire to eat, be merry, and enjoy companionship. The praise of
wooden Heorot in *Beowulf* is too frequent and too famous to need
repeating here. It is, moreover, to Heorot that Grendel's head is borne
on the spear-shaft. Thus, after serving as a bridge between the two
arboreal extremes—wild and domestic, hewn and unhewn—the intermediate wooden motif of the shaft is finally assimilated to Heorot,
the primary emblem of human unity, as in the Lamba treatment of
the second flute.

The Man and the Ogre, the Fall of Man, the Story of the Sons
of Squeezer, and the corresponding part of *Beowulf* all contain the
same cluster of motifs: the ogre, the two kinds of wood, and the
confrontation of ogre and solitary man in a place which the ogre
holds. The first two tales use these motifs to tell of a comity between man and preternatural that ends in man's perdition, while the
other two stories tell of just the opposite: an enmity that leads to
salvation. The difference is achieved by adding certain new motifs
to the cluster. The old wood of unity, invariably a live tree, is cut
and fashioned for human use, and its carver is a new champion against
the exigent old ogre who expelled men from paradise. The ogre correspondingly descends underwater beneath the tree instead of meet-

ing men where it did before, on a common level under the tree of separation.

By elaborating the cluster which they both share, the Story of the Sons of Squeezer and Mr. Water-Lizard complements the story of the Man and the Ogre. The one story is an unrelieved tragedy, but the other tells the formula for relieving that tragedy. This complementarity of stories in an oral tradition makes them quite different from much of literary narrative, even when individual literary and oral tales are substantively indistinguishable from each other. Unlike its parallel in Lamba fable, the Hebrew Fall of Man is isolated in a literary canon, cut off from the multiforms that would surround it in oral story-telling. That isolation makes Adam's tragedy in Genesis not only horrible, but also final and hopeless. It is equally horrible in Lamba fable, but there it remains hopeful because the same story exists in multiforms, like the Story of the Sons of Squeezer, that provide alternative *dénouements*. Or to put the matter in another way, the durable grandeur which a tale may gain by isolation in literature is often bought at the expense of complementarity, whereby in oral fable multiforms of the same story-pattern are playfully combined with other patterns to demonstrate or explore the patterns' logical possibilities.

Occasionally literary tradition also shows the effects of complementarity, especially when it is a long tradition that has drawn upon oral fable from time to time. It would seem from the two complementary Lamba tales that the right procedure for overcoming Yahweh's expulsion of man from the Garden would be to supply the story of Man's Fall with a sequel wherein a human saviour equipped both with hewn wood and with the preternatural enemy's own powers could defeat man's ancient foe. Without entering into the details of apocryphal literature, it is enough to note that the many stories of the Rood-Tree and the heroes associated with it in Hebrew legend from Seth to Christ complement the pentateuchal Fall of Man in a manner quite like the complementarity of our two Bantu stories. Esther Casier Quinn has given a useful account of those legends in her book, *The Quest of Seth for the Oil of Life*.[22] So too Christ and his redemptive tree of hewn wood on Calvary is the antidote in Christian legend to Yahweh and his green tree of perdition in Eden.

After finding the two trees, the one green and the other hewn, in ancient Hebrew, in Old English, and in recent Lamba fable, one is prepared at least to meet them again in the story-telling of other

peoples on the Central African plateau. During the same early years
of this century when Clement Doke was collecting Lamba fable, another people of Bantu speech who were known at that time as the
Bene-Mukuni occupied lands south of Ilamba and maintained a well-
developed tradition of *chante-fable*, which they called *ka-labi* (meaning: 'it opens a little one's eyes'). The collector of the Bene-Mukuni's
oral tradition was Julius Torrend, S.J., who published several Mukuni
stories about trees among his *Specimens of Bantu Folk-Lore from
Northern Rhodesia; Texts (Collected with the Help of the Phonograph)
and English Translations.* [23]

THE HEWN WOOD OF RETRIBUTION: HELEN OF TROY
AND OTHER MISAPPROPRIATED RIGHTS IN WOMEN

The Lamba, Hebrew, and Anglo-Saxon examples which I have
used thus far have shown the two trees standing nearly side-by-side,
or sometimes even merged in the same nominal motif (the Lamba
ogre's fruit-tree). That arrangement occurred in Mukuni fable too,
as in the tale "Mother, Come Back." [24]

    This is what a woman did.

    She was then living in the bush, never showing herself to any-
one. She had living with her just one daughter, who used to pass
the day in the fork of a tree, making baskets.

    One day there appeared a man just when the mother had gone
to kill game. He found the girl making baskets as usual: "Here
now!" he said, "there are people here in the bush! And that
girl, what a beauty! Yet they leave her alone. If the king were
to marry her, would not all the other queens leave the place?"

*The man reports his discovery to the king, who sends a troop of men
to fell the tree and bring him the girl:*

    So they put the axes to it. The girl at once started this song:

        "Mother, come back!

        "Mother, here is a man cutting our shade-tree.

        "Mother, come back!

        "Mother, here is a man cutting our shade-tree.

        "Cut! Here is the tree falling in which I eat.

        " Here it is falling."

The mother drops as if from the sky:

        "Many as you are, I shall stitch you with the big needle.

> "Stitch, Stitch!"

*The mother leaves only one alive to go and report the killing of the
whole troop to their king. Hearing that report, the king is undeterred
and sends a second company on the next day, who die in the same
manner, stitched to death by the mother's needle.*

Like Grendel's dam and the Lamba water-lizard, this ogress beneath the Mukuni tree of separation also collects the cutting tools
of her victims:

> Next morning early, the men ground their axes and went to
> the place.

> They too found the mother gone, while the porridge was
> ready there, and the meat was hanging on the tree. . .

> "Bring the axes." Forthwith they are at the shade-tree. But
> the song is already started:

> "Mother, come back," etc. (as above).

The mother drops down among them, singing in her turn:

> "Many as you are, etc. (as above).

> They are dead. The woman and her daughter pick up the axes. . .

But the king is not yet defeated:

> "Halloo!" said the king. "To-day let all those that are pregnant
> give birth to their children."

> So one woman after another straightway brings forth her child.
> Soon there is a whole row of them.

> There goes the whole band, making a confused noise.

> When the girl sees that, she says: "There is no joke about it
> now. There comes a red army with the umbilical cords hang-
> ing on."

This army of innocents cuts down the tree and carries the girl to
town. Being themselves instant products of separation from their
own mothers, they naturally have the power to separate the girl
from her mother. The mother in turn is helpless against the troop
of babes, for they are the most awful spectres in Bantu folklore. All
she can do is set an intolerable taboo on the employment of her
daughter once they have brought her to civilization:

> "Since you have carried away my child, I must tell you some-
> thing. She is not to pound in the mortar, nor to go to fetch
> water at night. If you send her to do one of these things, mind
> you! I shall know where to find you."

> There is the mother going back to her abode in the bush.

The following day the king said: "Let us go a hunting." And
to his mother he said: "My wife does not pound in the mortar.
All she can do is to stitch baskets."

While the husband was away there in the open flat, the other
wives as well as the mother-in-law said: "Why should she not
also pound in the mortar?"

*They force the girl to take up the pestle and pound grain. With each
stroke of the pestle she sinks farther into the ground (as if she were
the mortar) until she has completely vanished; but the pestle continues by itself to pound the earth at the spot where the girl has
disappeared. The women call upon crane, crow, quail, and doves
for help. Only the doves know the name of the girl's mother and
can summon her with their call: "Kuku! Ku!" Finally the mother
appears and extracts her daughter from the ground by means of
medicine and song.*

The shade-tree in the forest and the wooden pestle in the town
stand in the usual relationship of unhewn tree-of-separation and hewn
wood-of-unity. The girl's place in the crown of the living tree separates
her from the rest of mankind and from a Mukuni woman's usual
career. Her seclusion there engenders other separations too. The
entire adult male population of the town except the king is divided
from its families and lost under the tree. Then unborn babes are un-
timely separated from their mothers in order to approach the tree
and separate the girl from her mother. The ground beneath the tree
is as usual mortally dangerous to the men who visit it. Their attempt
to take property from it in a free or lawless manner is met with the
ogreish mother's equally lawless destructiveness. The tree is the scene
of absolute division and uncompromising hostility between sexes,
and both sexes are untrammeled by any unifying conventions of
civility.

The hewn wooden pestle is the opposite of the green shade-
tree in many ways. Bantu men customarily shun it and the work it
represents with the same resolution they display here in this story
by their determined advance toward the wild shade-tree. Like the
Hebrew Tree of Life or the Old English Heorot, the Mukuni pestle
is surrounded by strict rules of reciprocity, price, and requital. They
are the same rules or laws of behaviour which neither of the opposing
male and female forces in this Bantu story would acknowledge under
the shade-tree. When they want her help in pounding whole grain for
porridge (an important act of food-production) the women pay the

Ill. 1. Women pounding grain for porridge in equatorial Africa. Alternating blows with their wooden pestles in a wooden mortar, each claps her hands as her pestle rebounds of itself, then catches it in mid-air.[25]

price of the girl's gradual withdrawal. Even the rate of her withdrawal is exactly metered by the rhythm of her cooperation, the number of her strokes with the pestle as she cracks the grain in the mortar. Then, pounding on the place where the girl has withdrawn into the ground, the pestle unifies the townspeople and the girl's wild mother in a joint effort to restore and fix the girl in her new matrimonial setting. As it provides the rhythm for their songs when they call the birds and the focus for their reciprocal acts of demand, concession, and reconciliation, the pestle figuratively domesticates and blends the girl into the life of the town in a preternatural but perfectly logical extension of its actual function as an instrument for domesticating and blending whole grains in the preparation of meal for porridge. Mother, daughter, birds, townswomen, and the girl's husband are all thus united in a common cause by the visible and audible effects of the pestle, and by the reciprocity it evokes in the behaviour of everyone concerned, even the girl. She is initially as recalcitrant in the town as her mother was in the bush, but finally, as she emerges from the earth, she too submits to the new comity and mutual good will in the town.

Each text of oral fable is a forest of motifs growing on an old terrain of logic whose configuration was determined long before the present nominal motifs germinated and took root there. Which nominal motifs grow on that terrain depends upon the husbandry of the story-tellers in each particular local tradition, but the terrain itself decides what kinds of motifs—what generic motifs—they may plant upon it. Like good arborists everywhere, oral traditional story-tellers know what plantings or substitutions of motifs are possible, because they know what nominal motifs have thriven before on a given tract of story, and they make their own choices accordingly. Distributed in separate stories, their choices complement each other in such a way that a single narrative pattern may have much greater power to organize logically the diverse data of a people's real world (represented in nominal motifs) than any one text of story alone would suggest. So the wild girl's place in the tree in the Mukuni story "Mother, Come Back" implicitly equates her with wild food as an occasion for conflict between men and a preterhuman person, in this case the stitching ogress who holds the tree and the girl. Eve and the apple are the same character in this story. The crown of the wild shade-tree where the girl rests is the place where wild fruit or lawlessly appropriated honey triggers a similar course of events in so many other Central African tales. Indeed, the equation of food and fertile womanhood (or progeny) is not only characteristic of African story, it is also itself a fundamental pattern in oral fable generally. We shall see more of it anon.

The identification of the girl with food in the present Mukuni story is reiterated (emphasized by repetition) several times after her initial appearance in the place where other, complementary tales (tales with the same pattern) would lead a Mukuni or other Bantu listener to expect the discovery of food. Initially, a single individual finds the girl where food is expected, but when the company of king's men goes to take possession of her, they notice food instead of the girl:

> They too found the mother gone, while the porridge was
> ready there, and the meat was hanging on the tree. . .

Finally the townswomen tame the girl in their king's house as if she were grain, or an analogue of grain, a food-material raised like the girl outside the town, then imported and reduced to an urbanely useful form by pounding. As the girl herself moves from a wild state to a domestic one, the references to food keep pace with her, pro-gressing from the mother's game-hunting at the beginning, through the dressed meat and porridge at the tree when the last company of the king's men dies, to the thorough, simultaneous, domestic pro-cessing of the grain and the girl together at the end of the narrative. Thus *complementarity* and *emphatic repetition* are both employed to reinforce the identity of the girl as an analogue of food through-out the tale.

It is plain to see from this example that complementarity is simply emphatic repetition at work across the boundaries of individ-ual oral narrative performances or their texts. Complementarity is to a whole tradition, to the sum of narrative performances, what em-phatic repetition is within the confines of a single traditional perform-ance or its text. But the fact of complementarity, which is obvious, is not so important as its consequences, which are not always so ob-vious or so well-known. Complementarity means that a given pattern may govern the composition of many individual tales without neces-sarily being complete in any one of the tales. And even when a pattern is generically complete in one performance (as the pattern of the two trees is complete in "Mother, Come Back"), the scope of its generic meaning can still be grasped only by exploring the whole range of nominal variations on the pattern in other, complementary performances. But when a single pattern is distributed over more than one performance, then not even its generic outline can be seen in any one story alone, and there is no hope at all of understanding it properly unless it is heard together with its traditional complements in other tales.

Moreover, there is hardly any performance in an oral tradition of fable which is not defective in some of its patterns, for every tale is constructed of numerous patterns, and some are normally less perfectly reproduced than others. Were it not so, every tale would be a sufficient tradition of fable in itself, and while there are good performances and bad in any tradition, no one tale is ever quite that good. The hearing of numerous tales together as complements of each other is a luxury often beyond the modest resources of fable recorded from dead cultures, but it can be done to some extent with any moderately large, synchronously collected corpus of a living people's oral fable. Julius Torrend's Mukuni collection fits that description, and the two famous tales "How Can I Silence Katubi?" and "Let the Big Drum Roll" supply good examples of the two trees segregated into separate performances.

"How Can I Silence Katubi?"[26] begins like the Legend of Samson, with an ill-starred marriage and ineffectual opposition to it:

This is what some people did.

The son said: "Mother, go and find a wife for me, as I am now grown up."

The mother said: "My child is now grown up."

Other people said: "Dear me! He is not grown up yet."

The mother got up and went to look for the wife. . .

Time passed. The wife gave birth to a child, and later on to another. At last she said to her husband: "Let us get up and go and see my mother."

The husband said: "We will go."

They got up, both of them. It happened to be a time of famine. On the way they found wild figs. The woman then said: "Do climb up and give me some figs."

The husband went up the tree. He then began to shake the branches, and figs fell in abundance, the woman, meanwhile, and her children eating them.

Again he shook, and more figs fell, among them a particularly big one: "Wife," said the husband, "do not eat that one fig; if you do I will kill you."

"Hunger has no law," said the wife. "Besides, really! Would you kill me, your wife, for a fig? I am eating it; let us see whether you dare kill me."

The woman ate the fig. Seeing that, the husband came down and with an assegai pointed at her, said: "My fig, what has become of it?"

She said: "I have eaten it."

He there and then killed his wife, his younger child just staring at him.

The murderer and his two children continue their journey to visit the dead wife's parents. The youngest child chants riddles on the way:

> "Silence Katubi!
> "Silence Katubi!
> "My brother has become my mother!
> "My brother has become my mother!
> "Silence Katubi!"

> "What a lot of vultures!
> "What a lot of vultures!
> "Over the fig-trees at Moya's,
> "What a lot of vultures!"

The child continues to chant these verses when he reaches his mother's native village, and eventually his maternal kin understand them:

The grandmother said: "Stop, baby." She added: "We are just going to kill your father also."

People then set to dig inside of a hut, to dig a deep, narrow hole....

He was called. As he entered the hut, he said: "We may as well sit just there on the mat." And, as he said so, he tumbled into the hole. He died in boiling water (which was then poured over him).

Torrend's gloss on the name 'Katubi' is helpful:

Katubi, lit., "Make-the-thing-white," *i. e.,* "Expose-the-truth," is the name of the baby.

Torrend also noted that the fig tree of this tale was a recurrent (nominal) motif in Mukuni fable:

Moya is the name of a chief introduced here merely to localise the story. The fig-trees of Moya's kraal are famous in both the Mukuni and the Tonga folk-lore.

Moya's fig, a Mukuni equivalent of the Hebrew Vineyards of Timnah, is the familiar tree of separation, and of course the father is the ogre of the piece, who first liberally feeds and then kills his needy human dependent. Enigma ("my brother has become my mother") is the means of the bridegroom's undoing in this tale just as in the Legend of Samson and its Lamba congeners. Vengeance is wrought upon the ogre, but that only adds new bereavement and deepens the tragedy. One must seek elsewhere in Mukuni fable for the hewn wood and the restorative retribution that attends it, as in the story "Let the Big Drum Roll:"[27]

> This man was a young king. As he had gone with other people to trade, his companions noted that he was bringing back a large amount of goods. So, being mere blacks, they became quite jealous and said: "Let us kill him."

This lawless acquisition of goods in the bush has no tree about it; the goods are not food, female, nor wild, nor is the adversary preternatural in this part of the story. The whole cluster of tree, ogre, and supporting motifs is missing until the dead man reappears in a preterhuman form that is able to invoke artifacts of hewn wood for his revenge:

> He was then changed into a little bird, with pretty colours and cowries all over the body, which went and perched on the top of a tree in front of the criminals. He then sang:
>
> > "Let the big drum roll!" —Chorus: "Let the big drum roll!"
> > "It flaps the wings,
> > "The little bird that has come out from the deep river,
> > "From the great river of 'them.' Let the big drum roll!
>
> > "Let the big drum roll! Let the big drum roll!
> > "At the great river of beads and pearls
> > "I have found fowls which pound,
> > "Using mortars hewn from blood trees. Let the big drum roll!
>
> > "Let the big drum roll! Let the big drum roll!
> > "Using mortars hewn from the blood-trees,
> > "Their beaks are all white.
> > "Here, Nemba, where are you? Let the big drum

roll! . . ."

Nemba was the sister of the dead chief.

When those people heard that song, they caught the little bird and killed it by beating it.

The dead man cannot return to life as man. No victims in tales composed according to this pattern do. But the bird is indestructible. The dead man has in it an avenger who, like Beowulf, will destroy the violators of property-rights and assure the enjoyment of the property by its rightful owners, the victim's own kin and heirs. True to the international type to which he belongs, this Mukuni redeemer also accomplishes his mission of vengeance by turning the villain's destructive techniques against themselves. They first try to destroy the tattling bird by beating it, then by burning it, and finally by pulverizing its ashes:

> They had hardly resumed their march when they saw the little bird alive once more going ahead of them, and heard it sing:
>
> "Let the big drum roll," etc. (as above).
>
> Once more they caught it and killed it, then this time said: "Let us burn it to ashes."
>
> So they put it on the fire, reduced it to a cinder, then ground it to ashes.
>
> But it got up again, flew into the air, and went on singing as before:
>
> "Let the big drum roll!" etc. . . .

Yet, despite their ferocity, the culprits' beating and grinding is nothing to compare to the relentless roll of the wooden drum and the steady pounding of the 'mortars hewn from blood-trees' in the bird's song as it inexorably conjures the villains to death-by-burning at the end of the story:

> Now those people are coming to the kraal: "You have reappeared!" —"We have reappeared."
>
> "And the king, where have you left him?" They answer: "On the road."
>
> Then: "Really? On the road! Come and see a little bird which is on the roof of the royal house."
>
> They at once said: "Let us kill it."
>
> Meanwhile some people are digging a hole in the ground.
>
> Then Nemba says: "No, don't kill it. Let us hear the news first."
>
> Just then the little bird started its song again:

"Let the big drum roll!" etc.

"Go into the hut, that you may explain to us exactly what the little bird sings."

They went and sat down in the hut on the mat spread there, but then *powowowo,* they tumbled down into the hole. Boiling water was brought at once and poured on top of them. That is how they died.

So the bird incants exactly the same three acts of retribution against its persecutors—thumping, burning, and pulverization—which they had earlier inflicted physically upon the bird. But whereas the culprits use coarse, elementary methods—cudgeling, direct burning with fire, and crude grinding, the soul-bird incants more refined procedures of the same kind:

	Striking	Heating	Friation
Physical Acts of Living Men without Allies	cudgeling	burning with fire	grinding without special tools
Incantation of a Dead Man with Allies	drumming	scalding	mortaring

Thus, like all of his type, this Mukuni retributor also inflicts upon the original wrongdoers only those same injuries which they first inflicted on the innocent.

The culprits of this Mukuni story die like Beowulf's envious enemies, at the bottom of a hole under falling water. And like Beowulf returning from the *wynleasne wudu* to Heorot, the soul-bird in the equivalent Mukuni telling moves from the wild tree where it confronts its enemies at the beginning of the tale to the royal house where it completes its victory over them at the end. There is thus at least one vestige of the wild tree even in this Mukuni narrative, and close scrutiny might reveal still other bits of hewn wood connected with the murderers' lawlessness and the compensatory meting out of justice to them, for example in the sticks implied in the cudgeling of the bird and in the fire that burned it to a cinder. But these are only vestiges of other trees complementary to the wild green one that fleetingly presides as the vengeance-bird's perch over the acts of discord and separation at the beginning of the story. The real inanimate 'hero' of the piece is the wood of unity, the hewn wood of the drum and mortars in the bird's song. No less than five successive repetitions of the song in this *chante-fable* emphasize the central motifs of hewn wood and keep them at the center of attention as the tale progresses. The bird's oft-repeated song finally unites the spirit of the dead man with his kin in joint vengeance against the murderers.

The Mukuni narrator who told Julius Torrend "Let the Big Drum Roll" was a mature woman named Mumba. Torrend admired her knowledge of tradition and her narrating skill, and recorded numerous stories from her as well as consulting her about the details of other informants' stories. As good oral narrators usually do, Mumba knew several nominal varieties of each generic motif in her repertory. She could embody the hewn wood of unity in a drum and in 'mortars hewn from blood-trees' in a story about retribution for murder like "Let the Big Drum Roll," and then give it another, different form in a story of retribution for bride-denial and bride-theft such as her tale "What Do You Mean, Block of Wood?" [28]

How now? "You, my mates," said a girl, "let us go and have a look at the village yonder, where lives the man Kasere" (that is, 'the little dancer' —*Torrend's note*).

There is no delay. They already perceive the man there at a distance, and near him heaps of meat. "Yes, and no mistake," they say, "that is a husband worth having."

They come near: "You girls," says the man, "why don't you get married?"

"Well now," they answer, "is a woman going to ask a man to marry her?"

"All right," says the man, "just now we shall go and look for a wife."

And so he did. But as soon as he appeared in sight, the girls disappeared.

Their mother, too, would you believe it? said: "No, you may come back another day."

The refusal was evident.

The hewn wood of unity is a universal motif in African fable, as elsewhere in Old World story-telling, but only occasionally does one see the wood a-cutting as here in Mumba's tale of an African Pygmalion:

> Another day he came again in the same direction, but a tree of the kind What-is-it-good-for standing on the road caught his fancy. He set to work cutting it and stripping it for its branches, then began hewing it. He carved, carved, carved, and put it upright against a tree there in the forest. Then he went to buy a cowry, and came back to put it on the head of his block of wood. What do you think? He finds it turned all of a sudden into a maiden: "Enough! mother!" he said, "I have found the wife they refused to give me."

Ovid says that Pygmalion too made shells the first gift to his carved lady (*Metamorphoses* X, 259-260):

> . . . modo grata puellis munera fert illi conchas teretesque
> lapillos

> . . . and now he brought it gifts that please girls, shells and
> polished stones

The bride brought to life from a statue remains nameless in both Ovid's and Mumba's versions of the tale, although the name of her creator and lover, Pygmalion or Kasere, is carefully pronounced in both cases. But Pygmalion's carved bride was cut from ivory according to Ovid, not wooden like the Mukuni effigy. Still, there remains a close resemblance at least in the hue of the two different materials used for the carving in the ancient and modern forms of the story. If ivory was an ideal simile for feminine flesh in the classical world, then wood gotten from a tree of the kind "What-is-it-good-for" must be granted the same distinction in a Bantu setting. The name "What-is-it-good-for" results from a kind of metonymy or antonomasia that was common in Bantu fable. The tree it signifies is a euphorbia, or so-called 'milk-tree,' a species of the plant called spurge in English that is arboreal in Central Africa. Many Bantu peoples strongly associate this tree with womanhood because of the thick white, milk-like sap which the live wood exudes when cut. This natural property of the live wood marks it as feminine in their minds, while in a similar manner the blood-red sap of the so-called 'blood-tree' in Mumba's other tale "Let the Big Drum Roll" marks that wood as masculine. Thus Mumba knew two nominally different varieties of hewn vengeance-wood, one masculine for use in a tale of male conflict over property, and the other feminine for use in a tale of dispute about possession of women.

Ill. 2. A 'milk tree' growing in the compound of a Senior Chief in southern Zambia. Regarded as feminine by the inhabitants of the compound, the milk tree twines as a palpable dependent on its deciduous 'masculine' host.

Ill. 3. A fresh cut in the milk tree showing the milky white sap that gives the tree its common name. An ordinary Zambian coin lies beside the small, profusely oozing cut, for scale.

But that locally significant variation on the name of the hewn wood in no way changes its vengeful purpose in Mumba's stories. It will still be placed in the hands of an avenger who will use it to destroy those who have wronged him; an avenger who will imitate and inflict upon his enemies the same treatment they have inflicted on him or on his kith and kin. Nor does the local choice of blood-wood or spurge change the strong unifying effect which either wood in hewn form has upon the whole cast of characters in each tale. The bride made from the spurge-tree attracts the other persons of the story to her like a magnet:

Ill. 4. A fresh, bright scarlet cut on a 'blood tree' in Kangaba, Mali. Below and to the right of the larger, fresh cut is an older, smaller cut with a scab-like appearance in the process of healing.

On the following day he went to look for honey and brought some to his wife. When they had finished eating, they went to bed.

Next morning early, the man went out once more in search of honey. While he was away, people came and found the girl seated alone outside: "Give us fire and water," they said. She brought fire and handed it to them, she brought water and gave it to them. There they smoked and smoked again (admiring her silently), then went back to their kraal.

As they reached the place, they said: "Is she not a beauty, the girl we have seen over there?"

The following day the king, having heard that, said: "Go and bring her here to me."

Kasere is no sooner 'wed' than he goes to search the forest for wild honey. Once again we have to do with a honey-trickster. We might have expected as much from his marriage, which is exogamic to a preternatural degree. Predictably, Kasere will not be able to keep his bride, and characteristically, he is separated from her while he is away at some unnamed bee-tree in the wilderness.

Mumba was indeed the fine narrator Torrend supposed her to be. Once she had embodied the wood of unity in Kasere's bride, she lost no time implicating an opposite, wild tree of separation:

That day the man bethought himself of going once more in search of honey. The girl then said to him: "Some people were here yesterday, who asked for fire and water, and I gave both to them."

"To-day," said the man, "lock thyself in the hut." He went off.

When those people came they found her seated outside. They took her away.

For a moment Kasere has had the best of everything. He is a wealthy man by Mukuni standards, as the heaps of meat around him proved to the girls who visited him at the beginning. Then he gets a wife who seems better than other women, not only because she is more beautiful than others, but also because she comes to him free of all the social entanglements and duties which a real woman of his own people would inevitably bring upon him. She is moreover a remarkably potent wife. At one and the same time she is the most beautiful of women, i.e., an ideal means for a man to get progeny, and is also made from a kind of wood that symbolizes the nourishing power of motherhood to many Bantu peoples. She is thus a living embodiment of the equation which I have mentioned earlier as another stock pattern in fable:

$$\text{Food} \cong \text{Progeny}$$

Kasere too does what he can as a male to reinforce that equation. First he surrounds himself with remarkable heaps of food, then gets himself a more perfect wife than other men have. That done, he thinks again of food-getting (the wild honey) and returns from it to pursue his abducted wife. His whole activity is encompassed in two cycles of pairing food and nubile woman:

<table>
<tr><td>First
Cycle</td><td>1) Hunting and cutting meat
2) Hunting and cutting a wife</td></tr>
<tr><td>Second
Cycle</td><td>3) Pursuing bees to honey
4) Pursuing wife to king's kraal</td></tr>
</table>

There is no ground for hope that Kasere will regain the woman once the king has taken her away. Kasere the eater of wild honey may not keep his bride; the pattern of the honey-trickster tale forbids it. But Kasere the carver must do unto the wrongdoer as the wrongdoer has done unto him; the pattern of the vengeance-wood tale demands imitative retribution. The king has robbed him of a wife; now he must rob the king. He begins by again cutting wood:

The husband came home. . . . "Ugh! What!" he said, "they kept refusing me a wife, and now today they have taken this one! One whom I carved!"

He has soon made up his mind. Drums, that is the thing. He goes to cut them and adjust them. He loses no time: "Let us go," he says.

He goes beating the drums and singing on the way:
"My wife made by carving!"
Chorus: "What do you mean, block of wood?"
"Stop that."
Chorus: "What do you mean, block of wood?"
"My husband, who gave them meat!"
Chorus: "What do you mean, block of wood?"
"My wife, who gave them fire and water!"
Chorus: "What do you mean, block of wood?"

"They were denying me a wife in the land."
Chorus: "What do you mean, block of wood?"
"The block that I carved!"
Chorus: "What do you mean, block of wood?"

Singing his riddling song, Kasere the little dancer excites the whole
country on his way to the king's house:

He came to a village occupied by common people. At once
the principal woman of the place, good gracious, said: "Those
who can accompany dances, come and see a dancer."
Good heavens! They heard the song falling down: (as above).

Kasere begins to take tribute of those he meets:

"Come on," says the woman, "throw presents to the man."
They are showered upon him. They make him quite red.

He then asks: "Have you not seen people passing this way and
carrying away a woman?"
"They have passed," is the answer. "They have gone further."
"What is she like?" he asks.
"Beautiful," they say, "beautiful. She has a cowry on her
head."

He then goes further, singing on the way: "My wife made by
carving," etc. (as above).

He reaches another kraal. . . . "Come and see a man who beats
the drum. . . ."

Then: "Come on, you who accompany the dance, throw presents to the man."

At last he stops for a little rest.

Others help Kasere to find his abducted wife:

A little man then said to him: "Come near, I will tell you. . . .
That kraal over there, that is where your wife is, in the big hut.

There goes the man, beating the drums once more: (song as
above).

Good Heavens! He is in view of the place. . . . "Come and
see a man who is on the road beating a drum."

Now Kasere insinuates himself into the abductor's compound:

As he comes near, he goes toward the king's house, as if to
go and pay homage. Then he starts again: (song as above).

"Good gracious!" says the king himself, "come and throw
presents to the man."

But he does not stop to receive any. He just goes on round

the court-yard (beating the drum all the time).
He engages in a contest of will with his wife, calling to her in his song
to make her come forth from her place of concealment:
A servant then says (to the king): "Shall we bring thy wife? . . ."
He is already near the hut. Good Heavens! This is what he
hears from within: "This is his wife, who has been carried away."
The drums then roll with full sound:

> "My wife, a gift for them!
> "What do you mean, block of wood?
> "My wife made by carving!
> "What do you mean, block of wood?"

"Come," say the people to the woman, "you too come and
give presents to the man. All your mates have already thrown
some to him."

"All right," says the woman, "go and throw him presents your-
selves. I shall do nothing of the kind."

The drums are at last at the door:

> "My husband, the carver!
> "What do you mean, block of wood?
> "My wife, a gift for them!
> "What do you mean, block of wood?"

Great Lord! "Let us just peep," says the woman.
"Carry her out," say some people.
In fact, their hands are already on her.
Finally Kasere completes his elaborate dancing-manoeuvres and strips
the king of his prize:
Then they see the little man going on dancing like a fly around
the king himself, and singing:

> "The tree which I carved!
> "What do you mean, block of wood?
> "They refused me a wife in the land.
> "What do you mean, block of wood?"

"Let us look outside," she says at last. And she stands just at
the door.

Heaven help me! Drum and song now sound and resound.

> "My husband, to give me to them?
> "What do you mean, block of wood?"

She now just lets her head appear with the cowry on it. By

a rapid movement of the hand the husband takes this off. . . .
Great Heavens! She is already transformed into a simple block
of wood, no, she has become but a bush standing at the door. . . .
Then the little husband comes home humming his own tune,
while the king and those who had seized the woman remain
there with their shame.

I collected a variant of this tale from a middle-aged woman at
Senior Chief Mukuni's compound outside Livingstone, Zambia, in
August, 1969. My informant did not know of Torrend's printed tale,

My source of a
central African
Flood story.

nor could I discover any reason why she should or even might have
known of it. She nevertheless followed the same plot as in Mumba's
story, except that in her version a great flood issued from the bush
to which the wooden bride had reverted, and spreading over the earth,
drowned the king and all his company. The tale was told me in the
presence of three other experienced women narrators from the same
district, who said when I questioned them that the flood from the

bush was the only ending of the tale which any of them knew. It is
tempting to think that Mumba was careful about reciting flood-stories
into the phonograph of Julius Torrend, a Jesuit missionary. Perhaps
someday, when and if a proper survey of Central African Bantu oral
fable has been made, it may be possible to determine which ending
is the more common—the one assigning mere shame, or outright bodily
destruction to the rapacious king and his court. At present it is possible only to observe that there is a cataclysmic denouement of some
sort to this story in Central African Bantu tradition.

Regardless of the ending, Mumba gave Torrend a splendid example
of the story about two trees in this Mukuni tale. It is a decidedly short
tale even by Mukuni standards, which did not require much length. Yet
it contains fully developed examples of both the honey-trickster's and
the avenging carver's stories, neatly coalesced in a single narrative. Even
the seven stages of the honey-trickster's story (Samson's seven days of
riddling/seven days of hunting competition in "What a Little Thing Did")
are perfectly reproduced in Mumba's tale of seven journeys to secure
marital rights:

1. The girls' visit to appraise the bachelor Kasere
2. Kasere's visit to the girls and their mothers to seek a bride
3. Kasere's journey to the forest to carve and animate the
     spurge-wood bride
4. Kasere's journey to the bee-tree and home to bed with the
     spurge-wood bride
5. The first visit of the king's people to Kasere's home, ending
     in the command to abduct the bride
6. The abduction
7. Kasere's pursuit

The honey-trickster traffics in riddles and in paradox. So too
does Kasere, whose wooden wife paradoxically seems to be one thing
(a real woman of flesh and blood), while in truth she is something
else (a block of wood) quite incompatible with what she initially
appears to be. She is an enigmatic object used at the same place in
the story-pattern and for the same purpose as the verbal enigma of
the sweet lion in the Legend of Samson, or the enigma of the alluring
young woman's identity at the close of the Lamba story "What a
Little Thing Did." And just as those riddles were unfair, so too is
Kasere's riddle unfair, because it conceals a preternatural identity, the
identity of something that cannot be. Spurge may symbolize woman-

hood, but it cannot in reality *be* a woman. Finally the honey-trickster's riddling ends, as it must, with a loss that is embarrassing to him, but even more embarrassing for his foes. Mumba's telling of the conclusion is only a minor rearrangement of the data found in the Legend of Samson:

> **Samson's enemies get his riddle from him by means of his wife**
>
> . **Kasere's enemies take from him his wife, who is a riddle**

The alternative, cataclysmic ending to Mumba's tale, whereby the king and all his company are destroyed, calls to mind another tale of vengeance-wood that is somewhat longer and better known in the Western world than any of Mumba's tales will ever be: the so-called Troy Saga. Composite though it is, the ancient Greek legend about the Rape of Helen and her husband Menelaos' pursuit of her with the help of his brother Agamemnon's army is a replica of Mumba's tale about the rape of Kasere's wife. Like Kasere's spurge-wood bride, who begins and ends her marital career as standing green wood (but who in the meantime betrays no hint of her arboreal nature), fabulous Helen in ancient Greek tradition was also a daimon or goddess of living green trees. The two aetiological tales that survive from ancient Greece to explain Helen's deification as an object of tree-cults rationalize her arboreal connections specifically in conjunction with her marriage (to Menelaos at Sparta) and her demise (on the island of Rhodes, where she was venerated explicitly under the name Ἑλένη Δενδρῖτις —Helen of the Tree).* Modern authorities disagree as to when in Greek antiquity the actual cults of Helen the tree-goddess arose, but they are united in recognizing her as a wood-dæmon who, [†] like the African Kasere's wife, came into the world by non-uterine means, and who was during her life-time the wife of two men whose

---

* Helen's tree at Sparta, in Theocritus, *Idylls*, 18. 43 ff.; for Helena Dendritis at Rhodes, Pausanius, *Description*, 3. 19. 10.

† So Carl Boetticher, *Der Baumkultus der Hellenen*, pps. 119-120; R. Engelmann, 'Helena,' in: W.H. Roscher, *Ausführliches Lexikon der griechischen u. römischen Mythologie*, 1928-1978; Lewis Richard Farnell, *Greek Hero-Cults and Ideas of Immortality*, pps. 323-5 et passim; Martin P. Nilsson, *Geschichte der Griechischen Religion*, especially pages 211, 315 and 487 (vol. I); Herbert J. Rose, *Handbook of Greek Mythology*, and 'Helen,' in: M. Cary, A.D. Nock, et al., *The Oxford Classical Dictionary*.

rivalry over her caused a great communal uprising ending in the complete extinction of the initially more powerful faction. Furthermore, the pursuit and recapture of the abducted wife in both the old European and the modern African tales devolve upon wooden effigies and wood hewn expressly to accomplish vengeance. Despite nearly three millenia of difference in date, the Mukuni and ancient Greek versions of the story are so alike that a single summary serves them both:

Citizens of a distant, powerful kingdom visit the home of a wealthy but less powerful man. His wife, who is uniquely beautiful, entertains the guests while her husband is absent, then they abduct her to their city to be a wife of their royalty. When the rightful husband returns home and learns of the abduction, he equips himself and pursues his wife, alarming the whole country and acquiring help and tribute from others on the way. He (or a helper) makes an enigmatic wooden effigy which the abductor's compatriots take into their city as a thing of value. After extensive manoeuvres outside, the husband eventually insinuates himself into the city of his rival by means of hewn wood (wooden drums or a δουράτεος ἵππος —the Trojan Horse sculpted in wood). There in the abductor's city the wronged husband and his wife engage in a calling-contest, each trying to summon the other out of concealment. Finally the husband invokes the power hidden in the hewn wood to ruin the city.

The Troy-Saga is not just one tale, but many tales associated with each other by mutual association with the Siege of Troy, the oldest oral traditional tale that survives in European literature. The part of it that is like Mumba's tale of Kasere is only the beginning and the end, the framing story of the rape of a beautiful female wood-daemon and of retribution by her first husband through carved wood. Mumba narrated that story as a single piece, with no interval between the abduction and the retribution, but the ancient Troy-Saga accommodates the whole Homeric *Iliad* and more besides in an enormous narrative interval between Paris' taking of Helen and the Fall of Troy. This difference of treatment is instructive. It shows that although the pattern of story surrounding the two trees is quite definite in the number, character, and cohesion of its constituent motifs, yet it is also prodigiously elastic and tolerant of agglomeration with other patterns and their motifs.

So far in this book I have dealt mostly with short tales, or with discrete episodes in longer tales that manifest the story-pattern of the Two Trees. But the discovery of the Green and Hewn Wood pattern in the Troy-Saga reveals that the same story-pattern is also sometimes the undergirding which supports and unifies much longer and more complex narrative. This reality can be observed even in the case of the modern African narrator, Mumba herself, who could put the wild and hewn wood strictly side by side as when she told Julius Torrend the tale of Kasere, or separate them with wide intervals of other story-material, as she did in a much longer tale which she knew by the catch-word title "Kapepe."

THE HEWN WOOD OF EXCHANGE: THE MANIFOLD MARRIAGE OF MANDU AND THE MISSION OF MOSES

The Bantu word *Kapepe* is a proper noun meaning in English 'little feather,' and referring to a feather-badge worn as a divinational fetish by Kalombe, the hero of Mumba's other tale. The personal name Kalombe means 'Little Blood-Wood Tree.' Like Mumba's other hero Kasere, Kalombe too was a tormented bridegroom, and the tale about him is also a wedding-story.

Torrend wrote that "Kapepe" was "one of the most popular stories all over the Zambesi region" and that it was by nature "rather long." He heard the tale from several narrators besides Mumba, and he listed her among three Mukuni women (Munje, Mumba, and Rumba) who "know the story quite well." The main Mukuni text which Torrend chose to publish with his own English translation was "from the mouth of a man called Mwana Mbirika, who has given the whole story twice on the phonograph."[29] But he annotated Mwana Mbirika's text copiously with Mumba's comments where her telling of the story differed in substance from the man's, and he inserted in brackets bits of text from Mumba's version into Mwana Mbirika's text wherever Mumba told things not found at all in the man's version. In the end there was no great difference, and it is apparent from Mumba's recorded comments that she sanctioned Mwana Mbirika's performance, for her whole concern in commenting was not to change but only to clarify and embellish the story as he had told it. It was the same tale of precocious childhood and marriage for both of these Mukuni story-tellers, and it was full of trees.

The Bene-Mukuni had two kinds of *chante-fable,* as do many

Bantu and other equatorial African peoples. One is a kind of narrative told with intermittent singing of a single tune, like Mumba's tale
of Kasere or "Let the Big Drum Roll." The verses of the song in such
a tale are sometimes quite numerous, and like the tune itself may (or
may not) undergo considerable alteration from one reprise to another.
The reprises too may be few or many in number. Yet regardless of
how elaborate variation and repetition may make it, this simpler kind
of story-telling is characterized by the rule: one tune to a tale. The
other, more complex kind of *chante-fable* is stylistically only a concatenation of performances in the simpler manner, with the tale divided into episodes, each having its own tune linked in series with
the others. This kind of tale is also subject to reprise in its sung por-
tions, but here the narrator not only repeats or varies one tune at a
time, he may also take up again one or another of the tunes used before and repeat them in alternation with other, new tunes. With the
participation of a chorus or individual choral respondent that is usual
in this tradition, these multi-cantata performances take on the character of oratorios, and like oratorio in Western music, they are usually
quite long. One recently published example of this many-tuned African species of *chante-fable* from the Banyanga (eastern Zaire) took
twelve days to perform, though it certainly does not contain twelve
days' worth of narrative (since a good part of the performer's time
was taken up in use of the tunes for dancing).[30] The tale called "Kapepe" among Torrend's Bene-Mukuni (and still remembered by that
name among the Mukuni, Leya, Lenje, and Tonga peoples whom I
visited north of the Zambezi in 1969) was composed in this same
complex form of *chante-fable*.

Not surprisingly, the Mukuni hero named Kalombe or Mandu
in the tale "Kapepe" had a series of adventures that runs step-for-
step parallel to those of the Nyanga hero Mwindo in the twelve-day
performance from Zaire mentioned above. The likeness of Mwindo
and Mandu suggests that their story may be a kind that lends itself
readily to long narration, or perhaps even requires it. In any case,
"Kapepe" in Julius Torrend's experience was regularly a long tale
with a number of tunes. Its length was certainly not the result of
anyone's piecing together several randomly selected short tales with
single tunes to make from them one long story with many tunes.
The agreement of Torrend's other informants with Mwana Mbirika's
performance shows that "Kapepe" was a discrete tale in Mukuni

tradition with a traditional stability of content. The sinews of that content are the traditional patterns in it, like the pattern of story about two trees, and they bind together the various episodes of the tale with their different songs into a narrative unity that would remain indissoluble even if the narration were somehow interrupted and the narrator forced to tell the episodes separately on different occasions.

Torrend identified fourteen distinct songs in Mwana Mbirika's performance, and divided the published text into fourteen corresponding episodes. In summary, they are as follows:

First Song[31]

A dreadful rumour circulates among the women of a village whose chief has just gone away on a protracted hunting-expedition. According to the rumour, he desires any of his pregnant wives who may bear a child during his absence to rear the child carefully if it be a girl, but cast it out to die if it be a boy. One wife bears a son and carries it into the reeds near the river where she abandons it on a piece of bark floating on the water. A "little old woman," who lives like a wild creature alone in the bush, discovers the baby and undertakes to raise it, predicting that it will become a great man. Its natural mother takes food to the bush, where the old woman feeds the child, and it matures precociously.

Mumba said that the infant's name was originally Kalombe, " but the little old woman changed his name to Mandu," the name which Mwana Mbirika used throughout.

A female cousin of Mandu goes hunting for edible rodents with her girl-friends, and discovers Mandu living in a hole in the ground. They dig him up, and report their finding in the village. Mandu's mother bids them not to tell what they know to the chief when he returns. The girl-cousin's name is Ngoma, "Drums."

Torrend recorded the next episode from Mumba; his other informants did not know it. In it Mandu hews wood wherewith to unite his various kin and friends with each other and with himself:

Second Song

When the chief returns home, he finds a diseased baby girl born in his absence, but no male children. Mandu, still living in the bush, carves drums and startles the townspeople with his unexpected drum-

ming. *They ambush the mysterious drummer and deliver him to the chief, who recognizes and embraces him as his son. A fight ensues between the chief and the little old woman from the bush over possession of the boy, but the chief and townspeople appease her with gifts and with their display of devotion to the son whom she has reared. His natural mother then tells Mandu to go and marry the daughter of the Rain-Lord.*

Third Song

Travelling toward the Rain-Lord's city, Mandu sees a pretty little bird that permits him to touch it. He tries to capture it in order to take a feather from its plummage, and pursues it for two days until it comes to rest atop the half-ruined hut of a little old woman. She explains that the bird is her food-scout and cannot be captured. Mandu declares his intention to marry the Rain-Lord's daughter, mercifully extracts worms from a foul ulcer on the old woman's body, and receives in return a night's lodging and a small feather from the bird.

Fourth Song

Kapepe, the little feather from the beautiful bird that scouts for food, instructs Mandu how to pass the obstacles which he en-counters on the way to the Rain-Lord. The obstacles are excrements, a river, a herd of hostile elephant, a precipitous mountain, bush buf-falo, lion, and an entanglement of snakes.

After the blood-wood (Kalombe) and drums (Ngoma) in the first and second episodes, a third tree now appears in the tale:

Fifth Song

"On reaching the place, he goes and sits down under a tree with his arms folded over his knees. (This is the attitude taken by boys when they go courting."—Torrend).
The rest of the episode is about shelter. The people of the place offer Mandu lodging in one of four different huts. Each time he con-sults his feather fetish whether to accept, and on its advice he accepts the fourth, seemingly most ungracious offer: 1) the hut of his intend-ed mother-in-law, 2) the hut of a female slave, 3) the hut of the Rain-Lord's niece, and 4) an abandoned hut standing in ruins.

After shelter in the fifth song comes the subject of entertainment in the sixth:

Sixth Song

Mandu's hosts bring him sitting-mats, drink, and food, which he accepts or rejects at the bidding of his feather-fetish. He 1) rejects a mat belonging to his intended mother-in-law, but accepts one from his bride-to-be. He 2) rejects wine that is a commingling of his future parents-in-law in disguise; 3) he rejects two kinds of food which are his father-in-law and mother-in-law in disguise; and 4) he accepts the same two kinds of food when his bride-to-be brings them to him personally.

With shelter and food provided by the eight steps of the fifth and sixth episodes, it remains only for Mandu to gain the bride for whom he has come to the Rain-Lord's strange city. He has acquired what he needed in each of the two previous episodes by *progression* through a series of four decisions, each correct choice bringing him nearer to his goal. In a similar manner, he is also required to make four choices in order to get his bride.

The problems of identification and selection which Mandu and Kapepe had to solve were simpler in the fifth episode than in the sixth. In the fifth episode the questions demanded simple 'yes' or 'no' answers without nuance or equivocation; only three answers of 'no' and one 'yes' in that order were necessary. But there was enigma and duplicity in the preternatural combinations which the Rain-Lord's people presented to Mandu and his feather in the four progressive steps of the sixth song. There each of the four problems had two components (two mats; two intended in-laws in the wine; two intended in-laws disguised as two dishes of food; two dishes brought by the Rain-Lord's daughter) and the right choice involved distinctions of either/or as well as of 'yes' and 'no.' Considering this larger progression from four simple questions in the fifth episode to four manifold ones in the sixth, it would be surprising if the next four problems of identification about to be posed to Mandu concerning his bride were not even more difficult in some respect than those he had to solve to obtain food and shelter.

So in the seventh episode, the problem is to select the right woman as bride, and *none* of the alternatives is the right one, although the pressure upon Mandu to accept what is offered him mounts at each step.

Seventh Song

Four imposters are brought to Mandu to take as his bride, each more beautifully dressed and more desirable than the others. Each of the women in this progression represents a diminishing degree of in—cestuousness for the future husband of the Rain-Lord's daughter:

> *Mother-in-law*
> *Mother-in-law's younger sister*
> *Rain-Lord's niece*
> *Sister-in-law*

On the advice of his feather, Mandu correctly refuses all of them.

Measured in terms of the avoidance of incest, the progression in the seventh episode brings Mandu very near to claiming his intended bride. It stops just short of that goal. In that respect the seventh episode is unlike the two before it. Each episode since Mandu's arrival at the Rain-Lord's city has contained a progression of four steps:

> **Fifth Song:** four steps to inferior shelter
> **Sixth Song:** four steps to food of ordinary quality
> **Seventh Song:** four steps to a matchless bride

Clearly the number four in this tale signifies wholeness or completion. Yet the daughter of the Rain-Lord is such a peerless bride that something beyond common completion is required to win her. Marriage with her represents more than mere fulfillment; it is perfection, at least one step beyond any ordinary marital attainment. So another test of recognition with her as the winner's prize lies ahead in a subsequent episode (the ninth song).

But the significance of four as the measure of completion in this tale exceeds the individual progressions of four questions to be decided in each of the fifth, sixth, and seventh episodes. There is additionally an overriding scheme of four at work in the progression of episodes themselves. This larger progression concerns Mandu's accumulation of an adult man's assets:

> **Fifth Song:** housing
> **Sixth Song:** nutrition
> **Seventh Song:** affinal kin

Obviously the fourth member of this larger progression must concern getting the bride herself, i.e., the consummation of Mandu's marriage. But since the marriage was deferred beyond completion of the four tests of recognition in the subordinate progression in the seventh song, one may also readily expect to find it deferred beyond the eighth song in the larger progression of whole episodes. And in fact Mwana Mbirika did just that. He built his tale with four-stage progressions both great and small, the small ones nestled within the great ones as in a set of Chinese boxes:

Fifth Song	*Sixth Song*	*Seventh Song*	*Tenth Song*
◆	◆	◆	◆
Four Tests	Four Tests	Four Tests	Four Tests
to Obtain	to Obtain	to Obtain	to Obtain
SHELTER	FOOD	MARITAL KIN	THE RIGHT
			TO MOVE
			THE BRIDE

So at the eighth song Mwana Mbirika interrupted the immediate sequence of four episodes (with four tests of Mandu's manhood in each) in order to return to an even grander progression of four which he had begun much earlier, in the very first episode. Instead of consummating Mandu's marriage in the eighth song, Mwana Mbirika paused to consummate his hero's manhood in another aspect, by completing the four-stage progression of Mandu's experience with trees. Born into the world as Kalombe, the Little Blood-Wood Tree, Mandu had hewn the wood of unity in his boyhood (the drums carved and beaten to announce his approach to the settlement in the second song) and then sat under the Rain-Lord's shade-tree to signify his maturation to marriageable age. Now the narrator makes him leave his comfortable seat as a suitor beneath the third tree and accept the more hazardous rôle of provider as he climbs to the top of a fourth tree:

Eighth Song

The Rain-Lord commands his daughter's suitors, who are Mandu and two competitors, to fetch him bark from the top of a great Baobab tree if they wish to marry the girl. The fully grown Baobab (Adansonia digitata) being a perilous tree to climb, with an enormous trunk, smooth, slippery bark, soft wood that breaks easily, and no low branches, the first two suitors who attempt the climb fall to their deaths; but Mandu with the help of his feather nimbly ascends, gets the bark, and comes safely down again.

Ill. 5. General view of a typical Baobab tree (Adansonia digitata).

Ill. 6. Detail of a typical Baobab tree (Adansonia digitata).

The progression of four trees with the Baobab as its final member dwarfs and subsumes the lesser progression of four four-stage episodes in the subsidiary plot about Mandu's courtship. His successful progress through the various series of four tests in the Rain-Lord's town are momentous for his future, but the grander progression of trees represents the continuity of his entire career and marks the principal stages of it before as well as during his marriage-suit, indeed from his very birth to the day of his wedding. The series of trees in the substance of the story is subordinate only to the sequence of fourteen songs as an overall organizational scheme in this long tale.

M A N D U ' S   B O Y H O O D

First Song	*Second Song*	*Third Song*	*Fourth Song*
1st Tree (green): Kalombe	2nd Tree (hewn): drums	Journey to an old woman living alone	Journey to a young woman surrounded by society

M A N D U ' S   C O U R T S H I P

Fifth Song	*Sixth Song*	*Seventh Song*	*Eighth Song*	*Ninth Song*
3rd Tree (green): shade-tree at the Rain-Lord's city; 4 tests to obtain shelter	4 tests to obtain food	4 tests to obtain marital kin; 5th test adumbrated; First day of courtship ends	4th Tree (hewn): Baobab	Consummation of marriage by completing a 5th test; Second day of courtship ends

With the grand progression of four trees completed in the eighth episode, the story is ripe for the bride to go to her husband:

Ninth Song

*The Rain-Lord's people shave his daughter bald, cover her in
ashes, and give her only a fragment of animal skin to wear on her
wedding-night. They dress one of the bride's slave-women in finery
even more sumptuous than the women wore in the seventh episode,
and send the two of them to Mandu's ramshackle quarters. As the
two women approach his hut, the Rain-Lord's daughter lightens and
Mandu thunders. His feather tells him which is his bride, and he
passes the nuptial night with her.*

Mandu began life as Kalombe, the Little Blood-Wood Tree, in
a state of separation from the rest of mankind so absolute that no
real infant could have survived it. He survived because he possessed
the remarkable power of attraction of his namesake—the same unifying power that the blood-wood had in Mumba's other tale "Let the
Big Drum Roll." Kalombe's attraction for his mother is perhaps only
natural; in any case she continues to take food to the wild for him
even after she has relinquished all other control over his fate. Beyond
her, his power of attraction beguiles first the little old wild woman
and then his young cousin Ngoma ('Drums'), who both join with his
natural mother to raise Kalombe outside the village. Thus three generations of women dwelling both within and without the confines of
the town stand united at the end of the first episode in the common
cause of protecting and rearing Kalombe. In the second episode,
Kalombe renamed Mandu manifests in himself the very essence of
hewing when, all untaught, he carves the drums wherewith he soon
attracts and unites the entire personnel of the story, male and female,
young and old, around himself. But this perfect unity precipitates the
first gesture of separation seen in the tale since Kalombe began to
exert his unifying power at the time of his abandonment. This first
breach of the newly achieved social solidarity in Mandu's village occurs when his mother tells him that he should woo the daughter of
the Rain-Lord, which means that he, the new-found focus of perfect
unanimity in the village, must leave it and go to live at least for a
time among strangers with whom not comity but conflict will be the
dominant mode of life. From this time forth separations and rifts of
all kinds multiply in the career of Kalombe/Mandu, and other trees
both living and cut are introduced to mark each major new phase of

the separative and reunifying processes.

In short tales, the difference between the two extremes of unity and separation is measured by a journey between just two trees, with perhaps at most only a single intermediate stage like the wooden flute "Going-right-away" in the Lamba tale about the Sons of Squeezer. Or sometimes, in very short tales like the Mukuni "How Shall I Silence Katubi?" only one of the two trees is carefully articulated, while its opposite appears elsewhere in some other, suppletive tales. It is interesting to note that the Mukuni narrator of "How Shall I Silence Katubi?" was an adolescent named Mwana Rumina who was only fifteen years of age. His relative inexperience as a traditional narrator may be a reason why only one of the expected two trees appeared in that story. Yet even experienced and altogether knowledgeable story-tellers like Mumba sometimes gave one of the trees much more prominence than the other and used no intermediate motifs between them at all, as in "Let the Big Drum Roll." But when it came to telling a long story in complex style like the tale of Kapepe, Mumba agreed with her fellow Mukuni story-tellers that the two trees must proliferate into many trees and be arranged in progressions to show more gradually the same movement between separation and unification that would occur abruptly between only two trees in a short tale. So we have not just two trees in the nine episodes of Mandu's youth and courtship, but four.

Those four trees are in turn arranged in pairs of two, one pair belonging to the tale of Mandu's boyhood, and the other pair to his wooing of the Rain-Lord's daughter. The two halves of each pair are of course green wood and hewn; but the two pairs themselves replicate the same contrast on a grander scale. Thus, the woods of Mandu's boyhood are green (Kalombe, the Little Blood Wood Tree) and hewn (the drums), but both taken together emit primarily the notion of hewing and cut wood, for while Kalombe is named (and resides in the wilderness like) the living tree, it is nevertheless he who spontaneously carves and beats the wooden drums that are the cut and purely civilized implements of social consolidation. By contrast, the pair of green and cut trees in the period of Mandu's courtship are, despite the usual internal difference between them, nevertheless predominantly an unhewn set of arboreal images, for only the bark is taken from the Baobab—a hewing that is literally only skin deep—, while the Rain-Lord's shade-tree is (as an inviolable green sanctuary against the scorching equatorial sun) utterly remote from even the faintest suggestion of hewing. Thus, even in larger progressions of nominal tree-motifs that multiply the basic dualism of the cut and uncut trees and impart graduated nuances of local meaning to them, the fundamental opposition of green and hewn wood persists with its stable polarity of generic meaning.

The third, greenest, and most unhewable of the four trees is the one beneath which Mandu introduces himself to the people whose princess he has come to woo and marry. He indicates to them by the courting attitude which he assumes under that tree and by the words which he speaks there that he has come to *separate* the Rain-Lord's daughter from that place and from her kin in that place, and to take her away as his bride (fifth episode). Then in the crown of the Baobab tree he finally wins the right to possess the girl, which is reciprocally the duty of the Rain-Lord to separate his daughter from her people and give her to the foreigner Mandu. When finally at the consummation of their marriage they are left alone together in the tumbledown hut, both Mandu and the girl alike have been substantially alienated from their respective kin.

Still, the process of separation is not complete in the ninth episode. Though separated from their respective kin, Mandu and the girl are at last maritally united, they are still in her native town, and Mandu might think of returning to his own village with his bride since that was the normal course of events in Mukuni marriages. Those facts constitute at least three more circumstances wherein further separations might occur:

       1) Mandu from his bride's town,

       2) the bride from her own native town,

       3) Mandu from his bride.

If indeed these three separations were to occur, then a fourth possibility would also arise:

       4) the bride separated from her husband's village.

With so many potential occasions for the play of unity and division still remaining in the tale, it would be strange if there were not also more trees forthcoming to preside over the successive stages of that play. The tenth episode accordingly supplies two more trees, the fifth and sixth in the overall arboreal progression of the whole narrative.

Tenth Song

The events of this episode occupy the third, fourth, fifth, and sixth days of Mandu's sojourn in the city of the Rain-Lord. The Rain-Lord ordains five lethally dangerous labours for his new son-in-law. On the first day he commands Mandu to 1) hoe and trample mortar in a pit; on the second day, to 2) cut down all the branches from the crown of a live thorn-tree, and 3) fetch dry branches for fire-wood from an old woodpile infested with termites; on the third day, to 4) help the Rain-Lord forge lightning-bolts; on the fourth day, to 5) repair a damaged roof with patching-material of bark. The Rain-Lord conjures the object of each labour to separate Mandu from his city: 1) the mortar-pit to engulf him; 2) the thorn-tree to carry him up into the sky; 3) the woodpile to incinerate him; 4) the hammer to pull him away by its centrifugal force; 5) the roof to fly away and transport him. Mandu asks the Rain-Lord to hold his feather-badge while he does the prescribed work so that the valuable fetish will not be soiled or damaged. He conjures the feather to inflict a corresponding injury on the Rain-Lord for each of the Rain-Lord's attempts to hurt him. At the end of the labours the Rain-Lord yields and Mandu remains in the city.

The four days of exercise which the Rain-Lord requires of Mandu are the Lenje version of another international narrative pattern. Lords of the sky in fable commonly resist young men who come claiming rights of kinship by threatening them with four kinds of peril. The generic motifs of the pattern are:

      1) danger of being swallowed
      2) danger of falling
      3) danger of being crushed
      4) danger of being burnt (or cooked)

There will be more examples of this pattern further on in these pages. Of course Mwana Mbirika knew the pattern only in its familiar Lenje dress:

      1) Mandu threatened by ingurgitation in the gastrogeneous contents of the mortar pit;

      2) Mandu in danger of falling from Baobab, thorn-tree, and rooftop;

     3) Mandu imperiled by the Rain-Lord's hammer;
     4) Mandu burning in the woodpile.

The Mukuni narrator linked this pattern with the pattern of the two trees by making Mandu climb the trees and undergo the prescribed risk of falling from them. The pattern of the sky-lord's four tests thus dictated that the trees in this part of the story should be alike in being heights from which to fall. Simultaneously, the pattern of the Two Trees' story dictated that each of the trees should have an ominous preternatural beneath it (the Rain-Lord) contending with his human guest about enjoyment of food or nubile women (the food/progeny pattern).

    The pattern of the Two Trees' story also requires, however, that the trees presiding over Mandu's marriage be diametrical opposites in other ways. Accordingly, Mandu climbs the enormous, glaubrous, and soft-wooded Baobab during the day preceding his wedding-night, but on the following day he climbs the thorn-tree, a tree of naturally modest size, yet so spiny and of such hard wood that no man would ever conceivably climb or cut it for any purpose except to fell it at ground level and be rid of it. And unlike the live Baobab whose bark-fibre was useful, a living thorn-tree yielded nothing but deep and painful lacerations, while a dead one was good only for firewood. Consequently, another difference between the Baobab and the thorn-tree is the utility of the one when alive and standing versus the utility of the other when felled and dead.

    Mandu approaches both of these sequentially proximate but typologically very different trees in exactly the same manner, climbing them to take wooden material from their crowns as the Rain-Lord commanded. Yet the results of that identically repeated action are as different as the trees themselves; they, and not Mandu, determine the profit or loss of his labour. Indeed, the trees not only decide what becomes of Mandu's effort, they also decide what becomes of Mandu himself, moulding him in their own image even while he works. Like the fibre from the living Baobab, Mandu is useful as social binding-material before his wedding when he serves to connect his own people with those of the Rain-Lord. But after his marriage he is like the thorn-tree. He cuts the thorn-tree's wood in such a way (in the crown of the tree) that it must inevitably injure him as much as he injures it. For each

cut he inflicts upon the tree, it will reciprocally inflict laceration upon him, and the blood must run from his cuts as freely as does the
sap from the tree's wounds. When finally Mandu and the tree have
cut each other down according to this absolute law of mutual retribution, neither of them is good for any better purpose in the Rain-
Lord's eyes than to be burnt as firewood. Mandu accordingly goes on
the same day directly from the impossible job of cutting the thorn-
tree to the woodpile for a test of his inflammability. There the Rain-
Lord tries to infest him with termites as though he were the same as
any other stick or splinter of felled wood left to decay in Central
Africa, where the ubiquitous 'white ant' visibly attacks even living
trees when they have been injured. The conclusion is inescapable:
Mandu's experience is identical with that of the two trees that frame
his wedding-night. Before his wedding, he is figurative binding material, intangibly and in a social sense like the bark which he brings
down from the Baobab for physical bindings; but after his wedding
he is only an economic substance to be consumed in the service of
his new kin like thorn-wood in their fires. He and his trees are simply
human and arboreal forms of the same principles, with the sole difference that Mandu, the animate representative of those principles,
is with the passage of time capable of metamorphosis from one aspect of the principles to another, whereas the inanimate trees are not.
Being inanimate, they can only succeed each other in a dynasty of
separate existences (i.e., a progression of multiforms), woodenly following one after the other in a series of graduated but mutually exclusive contrasts and contradictions. The Baobab cannot be like the
thorn-tree, nor can their different utilities ever be reconciled in their
own persons. Mandu experiences the same contrasts and contradictions
as do they, but differently. For him they are only stages in the un-
broken cycle of his whole life, and he has an ability to escape contradiction which no tree has: the power to change. Therein lies the
essential difference 'twixt the man and his trees, and the maintenance
of that distinction is every wit as important in the story "Kapepe"
as is the obvious analogy of Mandu with the trees. He and the trees
are exactly identical, but only for a moment and in certain momentar-
ily primary respects.

　　As Kalombe, Mandu was in his infancy identified with the blood-
wood tree, but in time his name was changed. Ceasing to *be* wood,
he became a hewer of wood and made the socially unifying drums

when he was a boy. In a parallel manner, he is briefly identical with
the thorn-tree on the second day of his marital career, but on the
fourth day he comes into a new character as repairman of his father-
in-law's wooden roof. That wood is like the wood of Heorot in the
Old English epic of *Beowulf*, already completely hewn and domesticated before Mandu's coming. Like Beowulf, Mandu is charged with
the responsibility only for that hewn wood's preservation. Thus, after
his marriage, he no longer hews *new* things from wood as he did when
he made the drums in his youth; yet he is still a woodworker, and the
progression in his maturity parallels that found in his childhood: from
identity with wood to former of things wooden. So the progression
of trees and other motifs of place make Mandu's marriage a major
demarcation in his life, second only to his birth:

Mandu's Minority

Place of Beginning	Identity	Product
Shallows of the River	Kalombe	Drums

Mandu's Majority

Place of Beginning	Identity	Product
Mortar-Pit	Thorn-Tree	Roofing

The Rain-Lord commanded Mandu to climb the Baobab as a
way of preventing the marriage with his daughter. By his unexpected
success in the Baobab, Mandu won the right to possess the girl in her
native village. Having thus failed to prevent Mandu's divisive entry into his city and into the circle of his kin, the Rain-Lord next attempted
in the tenth song to purge the intrusive son-in-law from his community.
Purgation of an entrenched opponent being harder than mere opposition to a newcomer, the Rain-Lord correspondingly used more violent
means in the second instance than in the first: two trees instead of
one, and magical attempts to make the trees act against Mandu instead of leaving the outcome of the perilous climbing to natural chance

as in the case of the Baobab. But Mandu meets the Rain-Lord's concerted effort to force his departure in the tenth episode with an even stronger determination to remain, and he succeeds. He unites himself definitively with his new affinal kin and asserts his right to remain in their village by enduring the trials of service to them and their chief on the thorn-tree and roof-top. Like the second episode before it, the tenth episode also ends in perfect unification of all the tale's *personae.*

If Mandu's reward for climbing the Baobab was possession of the girl (partially alienating her from her kin), then his reward for climbing the thorn- and roof-tree is the right to carry her away from her native village to his (in a physical sense at least alienating her completely from her kin). The perfect unity that crystalized around Kalombe and his drums in the second song ended paradoxically in Mandu's separation from his people. In the same manner, the perfect unity achieved in the Rain-Lord's city in the tenth song ends with Mandu's paradoxical decision to leave that city in the eleventh song. Mandu's and the Rain-Lord's postures toward each other in the tenth episode (Mandu wanting to remain and the Rain-Lord wanting to expel him) are reversed in the eleventh, where Mandu struggles to depart while the Rain-Lord exerts all the obstructive force which he can deploy as lord of waters to stop Mandu's homeward progress:

Eleventh Song

Mandu and his bride leave the Rain-Lord's city on the seventh day after his arrival there as suitor. Her people give the bride provisions, slaves, and cattle, and Mandu gives her his feather-fetish and wild-cat skin (a badge of royalty) to carry on the journey. She lags behind as they walk, and Mandu summons her to follow more promptly. She replies in song, calling Mandu by a new name: Ximutemambaro, 'Child of Woodcutter.' The bride looks back toward her father's city twice during the journey, and laments that the Rain-Lord has forsaken her. Her father causes a torrential rainfall each time, which paralyzes the bride's procession. But Mandu conjures the sun to shine, and the procession resumes its march.

Mandu outdistances his wife's company and sits down to await them under a big shade-tree beside a stream on the outskirts of his native forest.

The patterns found in long tales are not different from those in short ones. They are only more extended and more frequently repeated in the telling, while the essential ideas which they convey are more completely and more intricately developed. The same generic motifs cluster around the recurrent pairs of contrasting trees in "Kapepe" as in any single-tuned Lenje (or other Central African Bantu) story about the Two Trees. "Kapepe" has its exogamic bridegroom Mandu, its ogre under the tree (repeated in the eighth and tenth episodes), its riddles of identity before marriage (sixth episode), its seven days of contest for possession of a woman, its host and guest who, meeting under green wood, find their expectations of each other inverted by untoward fortune, and its hewer of wood with his characteristic policy of an eye for an eye, who inflicts upon a preterhuman figure the same injuries which that disguised ogre attempts to inflict on him. If certain motifs of this familiar cluster are still missing, one may reasonably anticipate that in a tale as long as "Kapepe" they too will eventually appear. Experience teaches a hearer of Central African tradition to expect, for example, that sooner or later one of the trees in "Kapepe" will yield wild food which some trickster will try to use hurtfully. And the exogamic bridegroom will somehow lose his bride. . .

Twelfth Song

The bride overtakes Mandu at the shade-tree where he awaits her, and bids him go on with her entourage through the forest to his own village while she pauses to bathe in the stream. A honey-guide calls to Mandu in the forest, and he follows it to a bee-tree. Taking some of the honey from it, he returns with the honey to his wife's entourage, but an imposter has meanwhile taken the wildcat skin from his real wife and assumed her place in the procession. He gives some of the honey to this substitute bride, and they march on together toward his village.

The true bride pursues them from the west, singing as she goes. Mandu and his mother recognize the substitute at the threshold of his house because she does not have his feather-fetish. Mandu rushes back along the path by which he has just come and meets his real wife.

Thirteenth Song

Mandu's people welcome his bride to his village with great feasting. She will not eat, but consents at the end to taste a little beer.

Fourteenth Song

The Rain-Lord's daughter cannot endure life in Mandu's village because its people are immoral. After ten days she flies home to her father's city with Mandu in pursuit. He cannot overtake her until she has reached the city, where they then reside together permanently.

The shade-tree in the eleventh episode is an obvious twin of the one at the beginning of the fifth song. Both are liminal motifs, the first standing on the threshold of Mandu's married life in his wife's village, and the second verging on married life in his own village. Mandu goes from sitting under those trees to climbing first the Baobab and then the bee-tree, where in each instance he obtains economically useful material.

So in "Kapepe" there are not just two trees as in short tales of the same pattern, but eight trees arranged in two parallel progressions with four nominal arboreal motifs apiece. The pattern is still generically two-fold, but nominally eight-fold in this particular tale. The same contrast between unification and separation obtains between the two progressions as between two single trees in short tales, and internally each of the two progressions moves from domestic to wild imagery, from hewn to unhewn wood (or vice versa) as is usual in tales with only two nominal motifs of trees. The numerical elaboration of the two generic motifs into eight nominal ones simply permits a fuller, more leisurely application of the Two Trees' pattern to a greater variety of situations. Tales like Mumba's "Let the Big Drum Roll" and "What Do You Mean, Block of Wood?" apply the Two Trees' pattern to single courses of action or single phases of experience like marriage or crime and punishment; but the elaborate form of the pattern in "Kapepe" provides the plot for an entire male career from birth to middle-age. The first of the two progressions of trees in "Kapepe" provides the framework for a course of primarily social events, while the second organizes a narrative about economic activities; correspondingly, the first progression coincides with Mandu's bachelorhood, and the second with his being a husband.

UNITY   **SEPARATION**

ACTS OF UNIFICATION AND SOCIAL PURPOSE

Mandu as a juvenile and ceremonial hewer

	Kalombe	Ngoma (Drums)	Rain-Lord's Shade-Tree	Baobab
	Hero becoming completely domestic	Domestic, hewn	Wild, unhewn	Becoming partly domestic
	Unity aborning	Unity perfected, Mandu departs	Liminal	
	Little Blood-Wood (Kalombe) becomes Child of Woodcutter (Mandu) [i.e., green, then dry]	Dry wood	Green wood	Partly green, partly dry
		Cutting is for ceremonial manufacture	Man underneath awaits wife	Cutting is mostly ceremonial, partly practical
	FOOD BROUGHT TO MANDU		*Man and wife soon to be joined*	

ACTS OF DIVISION AND ECONOMIC PURPOSE

Mandu as an adult and practical hewer

	Thorn-Tree	Roof	Mandu's Shade-Tree	Bee-Tree
	Hero becoming completely domestic	Domestic, hewn	Wild, unhewn	Becoming partly domestic
	Unity aborning	Unity perfected, Mandu departs	Liminal	
	Green, then dry	Dry wood	Green wood	Partly green, partly dry
	Cutting is mostly practical, partly ceremonial	Binding is for practical repair	Man underneath awaits wife	Cutting is entirely practical
			Man and wife soon to be separated	MANDU BRINGS FOOD

1st Tree: Green wood as hewer's alter-ego	2nd Tree: wholly dry and domesticated by hewer	3rd Tree: wholly green and untouched by hewer	4th Tree: Dry/green, cut/uncut, domestic/wild

Torrend observed rather shyly that "Kapepe" was like the Biblical legend of Moses. He gave only a thumbnail sketch of the likeness, but few know it, and it is worth knowing.

In this tale, as in others, the narrators take, of course, all the liberties of fiction, but, even so, there are in it too many details reminding one of the authentic story of Moses to allow us to reject as entirely absurd the notion that some parts of it sound like an echo, however faint, of Mosaic traditions.

We have, in suggestive combination, a chief ordering the murder of newborn boys, a boy taken to the river and deposited there in some sort of cradle, a woman taking care of him, and the very mother of the boy knowing all about it, while a near relation, called Drum or Drums, is also in the secret. There is also a wonderful feather with some of the magic power of Moses' wand. Then the filth which blocks the way of our hero makes one think of the plagues of Egypt. The river Putu, which he has to cross, is said to be somewhere in the direction of Egypt. Here, as in Exodus, we have a high mountain and a plague of snakes. By our hero, as by Moses, the Lord is found on a high mountain. In both narratives lightning and thunder play an important part. In both narratives the hero, to secure the treasure upon which he has set his heart, has to go twice to the mountain of God.

And after all, what did the author of the original tale mean by speaking of "a daughter" or "the daughter" of God "coming with water from the clouds?" It is quite possible that he may have meant "the law of God" given to the hero amidst thunder and lightning. A number of passages of the tale are evidently meant to teach certain Mukuni laws supposed to come from God. And one of its notable features is that the sight of wrongdoings is enough to make the daughter of God run away.

What is beyond doubt is that the present narrators have not sought their inspiration in the Bible. They are perfectly illiterate, and the principal narrator, Mwana Mbirika, has probably never entered a church.

Just as this is going to press I note in *Anthropos* (1909, p. 946), the following observation of Father Trilles: "In our Northern Fam tribes, far from all European infiltration, in villages which had never seen a white face, I found a legend in which the the principal actor, *Bingo,* saviour of his people whom he

frees from the persecutions of an enemy nation and whom he
leads through a thousand dangers to the land they are going to
occupy, reminds one strongly of the Moses of the Bible. . . ."[32]
It is now fifty years since Julius Torrend published those words, and
we are still no nearer to an exact understanding of the relationship
between Central African and ancient Near Eastern fable than he was.
Not even a basic description of Central African tradition toward which
Torrend contributed has yet been compiled, and unless it is done soon,
it may never be possible to do at all. But even the scant data which he
made available shows the kinship between Moses' burning bush and
fabulous staff on the one hand (Exodus 3 and 4) and the two trees
in African fable on the other.

Walking alone in an uninhabited place ("the far side of the wilderness"), Moses finds a bush so resolutely green that not even the
flame of the angel of Yahweh will burn it (Exodus 3:1-3). There the
mortal visitor Moses meets a supernal host, Yahweh, who without
bidding or any offer of recompense promises to feed not only Moses
but also his whole people with milk and honey (3:8). As the lonely
interview between man and preterhuman progresses however, it appears
that the preternatural being is mortally dangerous as well as gratuitously bountiful. Moses hears Yahweh proffer an unheard-of deliverance
and riches, but is also hideously infected with leprosy by the same
donor, who does this awful thing to him even as he makes the spectacular promise of plentiful good things (4:6). Here in the wilds of
Mount Horeb where Moses is not only remote from his own people
but also separated from all other human company of any kind, he
hears Yahweh describe how the Hebrews are likewise to go forth
into the wilderness after separation from their host Pharaoh, whose
one-time kindness has in the course of history been unaccountably
turned about, and so become a deadly oppression. But the Hebrews
who have thus witnessed the reversal of their expected good fortune
in Egypt are soon, says Yahweh, to observe the ogreish Pharaoh's
reversal of fortune; for whereas Pharaoh has made the Hebrews his
victims, Pharaoh is paradoxically soon to be the victim of the Hebrews. Moses in the rôle of trickster is to be the agent of this turnabout, but not before he too experiences an unanticipated reversal
of his own personal fortune. For, having endued him with amazing
magical power (Exodus 4), Yahweh then paradoxically pursues Moses
and in Exodus 4:24 attempts to assassinate him. As the husband of

Zipporah, a Midianite woman, Moses is of course an exogamic bride-groom whose marriage among aliens now brings trouble upon both himself and his foreign affinal kin, as Zipporah is quick to say (4:25) and to repeat (4:26).

So the notions of separation, gratuity, and an unpredictable dead-ly danger cluster about Moses' burning bush (that will not be burnt) just as they do about the green wood of the heroes elsewhere in the Old Testament or in modern African fable. Meanwhile the ideas of unification, recompense, reciprocity, and the meting out of punish-ments to ogres as ogres mete out injuries to men cluster about the hewn wood of Moses' staff. It is this piece of wood cut and fashion-ed to human purpose which Yahweh in the bush on Mount Horeb specifically designates as the ceremonial implement for uniting He-brew allegiances on the one hand and for the practical exaction of penalties against the Egyptians on the other hand. Both functions are merely extensions in logic of the same staff's ordinary uses in Moses' shepherding of his animal flocks. Thus, unity (not only of the Hebrews as one people, but also of the Hebrews and Yahweh in a common cause), a justice that exactly retaliates hurt for hurt, and a divinely guaranteed prediction of escape from mortal danger all at-tend Moses' wooden staff just as they attend Beowulf's lance-shaft and Heorot, Mandu's hewn trees, or the flutes of Mr. Squeezer. Thus experience with a living tradition of oral fable shows once again that no tradition is intelligible in isolation from the continuum of story-telling in other languages all around it, whether past or present. As Lamba fable revealed a pattern shared between the Biblical Legend of Samson and the Fall of Man earlier in this discussion, so now the tales told by a Lenje woman named Mumba and her fellows reveal the formal kinship between the Legend of Samson and the tale of Moses, for it too is a multiform of the Two Trees' story. Like Sam-son denied his alien bride, so Moses also struggled to acquire alien property which in the end he could not himself enjoy. If, as some think, the Legend of Samson was originally a Philistine story which the Hebrews borrowed from northerly neighbors, then the immediate cognates of the Mosaic legends point southward into Africa.

Indeed ancient Hebrew legends surviving in the Old Testament abound with multiforms of the Two Trees' pattern. Abraham under the Oak of Mamre in Genesis 18 is another founder of Hebrew nationhood who, like Adam before and Moses and Samson after him, met fatefully with a preterhuman agent and the preternatural, paradoxical effects of that agent under greenwood. There Abraham supposed himself to be Yahweh's benefactor, but in the end it was Yahweh who benefitted Abraham with the remarkable gift of Isaac. Not, however, before the supernal being had alloyed his unbidden generosity with the fearful danger of an equally gratuitous reprisal for Sarah's indiscrete laughter. But what Yahweh gave him gratis under the green tree in Genesis 18 Abraham is obliged to repay completely in Genesis 22, and for that purpose of requital he hews wood (22:33). So capriciously exigent a demand from the erstwhile benefactor at the green wood is of course only to be expected in the regular pattern of the Two Trees' story. Yet in the end the incident of the sacrifice of Isaac is governed by the hewn wood which Abraham has cut and Isaac carried upon his back to the place of sacrifice. Accordingly, the whole episode concludes purely as a test of the true mutuality of Abraham's and Yahweh's devotion to each other, and the hewn wood triumphs in the sworn and proven unity of Yahweh and Abraham's descendents forever.

Like "Kapepe," the legends of Abraham and of Moses are long tales full of progression, a device of oral narrative patterning whereby great tales are made from basically simple and easily remembered designs. But they remain stories of a trickster's encounter with a preternatural who offers his human client food/progeny in the presence of a green tree, and of the preternatural's alternate helping and hurting, mitigated by a champion who hews wood (as Moses did when he caused the hewing of Acacia for the ark and the tabernacle) to unite his people and to limit the preternatural's depredations against them. The ancient Hebrews well knew (without necessarily understanding) that fabulous champions and saviours are hewers of wood, and they constructed the written chronicles of their legendary beginnings as a nation accordingly, on the unshakeable bedrock of a fundamental pattern in oral fable.

Chapter Four

THE RITUAL FALLACY

Many years ago the people in a neighborhood near Pittsboro had assembled at the church for service. Before the service began, a man out in the grove encountered a large snake. He looked for something with which to defend himself. The snake ran toward him, and the man to protect himself dodged behind a tree. The snake at once threw himself against the tree fastening himself to the tree by the horn on the end of his tail. There he hissed at the man, who struck at him with a pole until the snake was killed. The man left him there in the tree and went into the church. When the service was over, he found that the leaves on the tree had withered and later the tree died.

- told by Clara Hearne of Chatham county,
North Carolina, in 1922

Victor Turner's tree of puberty.   p. 149

James Frazer's tree of priesthood.   p. 155

Arthur Evans' tree of aniconic divinity.   p. 164

The prehistory of the Two Trees.   p. 239

Vladimir Propp's tree upon the grave.   p. 244

It has often been observed that certain motifs found in fable occur also in cult and ritual. So Helen of Troy, of whom no cults are mentioned anywhere in Homer, had cults later both at Sparta and on Rhodes. This happens to be true also of the two trees in Central Africa. The coincidence of the same motifs in narrative and religion naturally raises the twin questions of how story-telling and rites come to share particular imagery, and whether ritual may conceivably have caused narration at some time, or vice versa.

I have already argued in the preceding pages that sunderance and conflation of real perceptions into fabulous images according to traditional patterns, and the reiteration of those images in traditional clusters, are innate and necessary functions of the human mind. I also contend that the patterns expressed as motival clusters in oral fable are so widely shared among various peoples and races, and their antiquity is so great where historical evidence of them subsists, that one may reasonably speak of a single tradition of oral fable with many local variations and styles throughout the world. Similar arguments can be made about the origins or universality of ritual practices, and have been made to various degrees by various scholars. But regardless of whether one is interested in the broader genetic or typological relationship between stories and rites (or more sonorously, myth and ritual), or only in ascertaining the meaning of particular motifs that occur in both narrative and cult, the case of the two trees in Central Africa cannot fail to be informative.

In mid-twentieth century, a British anthropologist named Victor Turner found the two trees enshrined as *mudyi* tree *(Diplorrhyncus Mossambicensis)* and *mukula* tree (blood-wood) in rituals of another Bantu people, the Ndembu, who lived in the extreme northwest of the present state of Zambia. Like the Lenje euphorbia and *mulombe*,[33] the Ndembu *mudyi* had a milky white sap and the *mukula*'s sap was blood-red. Turner was interested in what these trees meant to the Ndembu as ritual objects, and in the manipulations of them prescribed by Ndembu ritual custom. He called the two trees 'symbols,' and described their symbolism in an article dated 1957 and entitled "Symbols in Ndembu Ritual." [34] He said in that article that the *mudyi* tree was the 'dominant' or principal symbol in a day-long rite for pubescent girls called *Nkang'a.*

Participants in that rite met around a young *mudyi* tree and placed under it a pubescent girl whose breasts were just beginning to develop. Turner found that the celebrants understood the young girl and the young tree as similes of each other, since each could or would soon be able to yield 'milk.' But he found too that the tree had abstract meaning, or 'symbolized' certain abstractions, which the girl did not. Participants in the celebration of an *Nkang'a* ceremony understood the *mudyi* as symbolizing their harmony and cohesion while they celebrated the rite, but the tree also stood for certain shared principles of outlook and behaviour that tended to unite them at all times, both during and apart from such ritual moments as *Nkang'a.* Among those principles were matriliny, tribal custom, the continuity of Ndembu society, the personal dependence of individuals on their fellows, nourishment and learning, female sexuality and fertility. In keeping with the simile of the girl and the tree and with the abstract idea of nourishment which the *mudyi* symbolized, ritual eating, or a kind of communal supper in the presence of the tree, was part of the celebration. Thus the *mudyi* had the same association with feeding and eating in Ndembu ritual as did the wild food tree that was known under so many different names in Central African fable.

The *mudyi* tree resembled the green tree of fable in other ways, too. Turner found that although his Ndembu consistently appreciated it as a symbol of unity and unifying processes in their culture, their manipulations and behaviour during the rites under the tree in some ways belied their conscious understanding of its meaning. By their ritual acts, women symbolically opposed themselves to men; representatives of other villages opposed themselves to the natives of long extraction from the village where the rite was being performed; mothers were opposed to daughters; the anonymity of female childhood was opposed to the personal identity, worth, and responsibility of adult womanhood; a girl's matrilineal kin were opposed to affinal kin at her future marital virilocality; matricentric society was opposed to wider society; and the other tribeswomen were opposed to the pubescent girl's mother. This striking contradiction between the participants' conscious thoughts of unity on the one hand and their ritual acts of differentiation on the other hand was something of a conundrum to Turner.

He encountered the same paradox again in the rites performed around the *mukula* tree. He says that the *mukula* was used in several ceremonies: in *Nkula,* a menstrual rite; in rites of the hunters' cult; in rites of purification for homicides; and in propitiation of ancestral spirits. Thus, despite the greater diversity of its cultic contexts, the *mukula* was a plain opposite of the *mudyi.* While the uncut *mudyi* determined the site of *Nkang'a* by the accident of the place where it happened naturally to grow, the wood of the *mukula* was ritually hewn and deliberately transported to its ceremonial sites, just as experience with its narrative counterpart suggest it should be. It symbolized parturition, violence, killing, skill in hunting game, murder, victimization by witches. The polarization of ideas around the *mukula* was just as paradoxical as in the case of the *mudyi,* for while the *mukula* symbolized all manner of disruptions and meant, in Turner's words, "to breach, both in the social and natural orders," it also implied such ideas as the unity of hunters in the hunters' cult, and the unity of living men with their dead ancestors.

In their rites under the *mudyi* tree, the Ndembu thought of unity, but enacted a great variety of divisions and distinctions among themselves. Inversely, they contemplated a great variety of disruptions and contrasts in their rites connected with the *mukula,* but ritually enacted order and unification. Turner reasoned ingeniously in highly technical language to explain this double paradox, using such special and rather obscure terms as 'field setting,' 'structural perspective,' 'reference and condensation,' 'predominance of orectic quality,' etc. But neither philosophical abstrusity nor the jargon of social science disclosed what is amply apparent from reading Central African fable. The processes of separation and division in the story of the Two Trees regularly generate unity, while unification generates parting and rifts. Any multiform of the Two Trees' story displays that scheme in one guise or another. The wild, green trees in "Kapepe," for example, preside over separation of old acquaintances and the bringing together of new ones, while the dry, hewn trees occur in scenes where old friends are brought together and new ones parted:

H E W N

Drums	Rain-Lord's Roof
Mandu's male and female consanguinous kin are united in acceptance of Mandu, and Mandu departs	Mandu's male and female affinal kin are united in acceptance of Mandu, and Mandu departs

U N H E W N

Rain-Lord's Shade-Tree	Mandu's Shade-Tree
Mandu is separated from consanguinous kin and allied with a stranger	Mandu is separated from established affinal kin and allied with a stranger

It was customary among social anthropologists of Turner's era to seek present values and present motives in the cultural systems of the peoples they studied. But the polarization of ideas about junction and disjunction around the *mudyi* tree did not spring from Ndembu motives, and neither did the association of that tree with feeding. Both of those implications together with the tree itself as their vehicle were part of a pattern in oral fable which the Ndembu inherited as other Central African peoples had, and then put to their own uses, filling up the prefabricated philosophical system given them in tradition with their own present values. Turner argued brilliantly that the idea of nurturing, the idea of killing, and the other values polarized around the two trees were crucial to Ndembu individually and collectively at the moment when he observed them. But his synchronic treatment of Ndembu ritual hid from him the fact that his Ndembu had nothing to do with inventing the two trees as *foci* of symbolism, or the fields of ideational polarization surrounding the trees. Ndembu were users of that system, and attached their own nominal values to the system, but they were not its makers. And even as users of the system they were not notably efficient, if one may judge their efficiency from Turner's own description. Only a small part of the Two Trees' story entered into any particular Ndembu rites, despite the richness of the Ndembu symbolic use of that small part, and the sum of the motifs common to both the rites and the story-pattern was a good deal less than the sum of the motifs in any multiform of the story alone.

Collectively, the various Ndembu rites around *mudyi* and *mukula* did use somewhat more of the Two-Trees' story-pattern than just the trees with their surrounding fields of conjunctive and disjunctive association. The pubescent girl upon whom the Nkang'a rites focused was placed at the foot of the *mudyi* during the rites, and prohibited from making the slightest physical movement during the whole day of the celebration. Thus, like the ground beneath the wild tree of fable, the novice-girl's place under the *mudyi* was charged with jeopardy. Turner said that the Ndembu called it " 'the place of death' or 'the place of suffering.' " Moreover, the *mudyi* was literally a place of feeding where the tree's "owner," the novice-girl's mother, hospitably entertained those who visited the tree. It was the mother's ritual duty to prepare "a huge meal of cassava and beans. . .for the women visitors." The mother was of course a natural person, not the preternatural host under the wild food tree of fable, but there was an interesting question about the ownership of the food. Turner wrote:

> Before eating, the women return to the milk-tree from their eating-place a few yards away and circle the tree in procession. The mother brings up the rear holding up a large spoon full of cassava and beans. Suddenly she shouts: "Who wants the cassava of chipwampwilu?" All the women rush to be first to seize the spoon and eat from it. 'Chipwampwilu' appears to be an archaic word and no one knows its meaning.[35]

We may never know for certainty whether Chipwampwilu was an Ndembu equivalent of such Lamba preternaturals as Chilubwelubwe or Shichinongomunuma, although it seems very probable from comparison of the story-pattern and the Ndembu rite of Nkang'a that he was. Turner apparently did not record any Ndembu fable; at least if he did, he gives no report of it. Yet I do not doubt, nor do I think it reasonable to doubt, that even a modest effort to collect fable from the Ndembu who practiced Turner's rites would produce a number of multiforms of the Two Trees' story. Countless past studies of the diffusion of tale-types in both the Old and New World make it unthinkable that any story so widely attested as is the story of the Two Trees among other peoples on all sides of the Ndembu would not also be well represented in their oral fable. Until a proper survey of Ndembu fable is made, this opinion cannot, of course, be anything more than mere supposition, no matter how plausible it may be. But all conjecture aside, the fact remains that the mystery of Chipwampwilu's identity and the enigma about his ownership of the food that is dispensed at the wild tree occur at exactly that point in the Nkang'a rite where the preternatural host would appear in fable.

Yet despite all the correspondence of individual motifs between Ndembu cultic imagery and the ubiquitous Bantu story of the two trees, there are still many more regular elements in the narrative than have counterparts in Turner's description of Ndembu rites. It is as if the Ndembu saw the pattern of the story through a partly closed Venetian lattice when they celebrated their various rites involving arboreal symbols. If one thinks of Ndembu symbolic concerns as their window on the story-pattern, the window through which they could consciously contemplate and interpret the pattern in terms that were germane to their own life as a group, then the metaphor of a partly opened blind is accurate enough. Part of the story—some of its motifs—were brightly visible in the light of Ndembu symbolism, while other motifs, although present in fable, remained opaque to both the interpretative acts in Ndembu rites and the interpretative thinking of adept Ndembu individuals when reasoning about their rites. So, for example, in celebrating Nkang'a, the Ndembu ritually used and attached symbolic value to the wild food tree, to the polarization of differences that produced unity at the tree, to the dangerous ground under the tree, and to the hospitality of the tree's "owner" toward visitors. But other, no less integral components of the narrative pattern went unnoticed in either the words or deeds of the ritual, if we may judge by Turner's report: the pitting of human against preternatural power; human imitation of ogreish techniques; the contests in trickery; forfeiture of property; the food-trickster himself; the motif of disappearance or concealment at the tree; the quest for food or wife (=source of progeny) that leads to the tree outside the circle of consanguinous kin; and so forth.

True, Turner's account of the Ndembu rites that used arboreal imagery is sketchy. There may have been more of the narrative motifs in the rites than he reported. But regardless of whether his report is complete or not, the dependence of the Ndembu ritual imagery on a prior narrative pattern is obvious. An Ndembu ritual like Nkang'a or Nkula is only a kind of vignette abstracted from the narrative and charged with local, Ndembu meanings. Yet, to judge once more from Turner's own report, the ritual vignette is so incomplete a reflection of the narrative that one could not possibly reconstruct the narrative

from it. I say that the narrative pattern is prior to the Ndembu rites
not only because the narrative is the entity of which the rites are only
dismembered pieces, but also because one cannot even begin to trace
such a ritual vignette of narrative motifs as Nkang'a or Nkula over the
spans of time and territory occupied by the story of the Two Trees.

Some will think that because Turner's purpose was only to find
out the nature of Ndembu values and Ndembu philosophy, he did not
need to know whether their expression of values and philosophy in
their ritual life had any connection with narrative. So long as he could
extract meaning from Ndembu symbols, why should he care whence
their symbols came? But just how much of the meaning which he extracted was in fact of Ndembu patent, and how much was not "their"
meaning at all, but rather the meaning of a story which they happened
to possess by dint of nothing more than the conservatism of individual
Ndembu who had kept up a tradition of oral fable quite independently
of Ndembu ritual life? For Turner found what anthropologists of his
time had so often found, and he was able to explain no better than
they, why his "primitive philosophers" were conscious of only a part,
and a lesser part at that, of the meaning which he could discern in
their customary acts and imagery. Turner's own account shows that
the Ndembu ritually cast the flux of their experience in the mold of
certain narrative motifs (although Turner did not know them as components of narrative). But those motifs and the story to which they
belonged were more than merely formal constituents of narrative. One
of the trees generically *meant* separation, its opposite generically
meant unification, and the two of them together constituted a general
proposition of logic complete with corollary: *ex uno multa,* and *e
pluribus unum.* The story and its constituent motifs are themselves
an elaborate, prefabricated system of general meanings ready-to-hand
for the "primitive philosopher," who need only hit upon interesting
analogies between fable and experience to be a thumping success.
Philosophy of this kind needs little or no abstract reasoning to create
prodigies of symbolism.

JAMES FRAZER'S TREE OF PRIESTHOOD

The case of the two trees as Ndembu symbols is no isolated example of motival linkage between narrative and cult. In view of that
fact, it is hard to understand how Turner and others like him have

thought they could succeed in their analyses of cult and ritual without making an equally careful study of the story-telling among their subject peoples. No doubt part of the explanation lies in their reaction to an earlier school of ritual studies which went so far in comparing myth and ritual that it recognized hardly any distinction at all between them. The doyen of that school was an eminent precursor of Victor Turner in British anthropology, James George Frazer, who also preceded Turner in writing on the subject of trees and their meanings in cult. Frazer incorporated much of what he had to say about tree motifs in his monumental (and lately much maligned) compilation of cultural oddities entitled *The Golden Bough*. His scholarship was very different from Turner's, and many of Turner's contemporaries have attacked Frazer's work for all manner of good reasons. But J.G. Frazer is still a more prominent authority on trees in cult than any of his detractors, or any later writer at all for that matter.

Frazer wrote most of *The Golden Bough* between 1890 and 1915; in its final form it occupied thirteen large volumes. He called this colossus of Victorian learning "a general work on primitive superstition and religion," but it was first and last a study of trees and the other motifs clustered around them in story and in cult. The very title of the work bespeaks Frazer's concern with tree motifs; the title is a Virgilian gloss on an arboreal detail of ritual from the ancient Latin cult of Diana at Aricia in the Alban hills.* Frazer began the study which grew into *The Golden Bough* with discussion of a forbidden tree in Diana's sanctuary at Nemi, and ended twelve volumes and twenty-five years later with the sacred oaks of sky-gods in Indo-European mythology. In the vast intervening space, Frazer made passing reference to myriad other trees—too many, indeed, and with too fleeting scrutiny of them for his study to be of much value today except as a lumber-yard of references. But he was a more poetical than analytical writer, and one cannot fault his poetic appreciation of the dangerous wild tree as a nexus of motifs that is crucial alike to narrative and to cult. Imitating classical authorities (Ovid, Strabo, and Servius), Frazer commenced *The Golden Bough* with his own literary sketch of a bloody ritual scene under a dangerous tree that belonged to the Latin goddess of the wild, Diana:

In the sacred grove (of Diana Nemorensis) there grew a certain

_____

* The birthplace of Caesar Augustus.

tree round which at any time of the day, and probably far into
the night, a grim figure might be seen to prowl. In his hand he
carried a drawn sword, and he kept peering warily about him as
if at every instant he expected to be set upon by an enemy. He
was a priest and a murderer; and the man for whom he looked
was sooner or later to murder him and hold the priesthood in
his stead. Such was the rule of the sanctuary. A candidate for
the priesthood could only succeed to office by slaying the priest,
and having slain him, he retained office till he was himself slain
by a stronger or a craftier.[36]

...Within the sanctuary at Nemi grew a certain tree of which
no branch might be broken. Only a runaway slave was allowed
to break off, if he could, one of its boughs. Success in the attempt entitled him to fight the priest in single combat, and if
he slew him he reigned in his stead with the title King of the
Wood *(Rex Nemorensis).*[37]

The Darwinian overtones ring loud and clear in this lurid description of a gladiatorial moment in the supposed Arician cult of Diana.
But popular understanding of the then-fashionable doctrine of the
survival of the fittest encouraged worse intellectual abuses than this
in Victorian England. A more important weakness of Frazer's portrayal is the strong possibility that even in his classical sources the account
of the ritual combat at Nemi was only a piece of local legend and not
the description of a real ritual contest actually reenacted from time
to time in the Arician grove. It was quite common for Greeks and
Romans alike to attach just such bits of fable to sacred localities like
the Arician grove, and not even Frazer supposed that any of his three
classical authors except possibly Strabo had in fact ever seen the *Rex
Nemorensis,* not to speak of the bizarre duel to the death with a runaway slave, which of course no ancient writer had seen, not even Strabo. Nor will anyone who has had much practical experience as an ar-
borist of taking healthy branches from live trees think that that is a
very probable act with which to begin a mortal combat with a vigilant
foe, unless the challenger meant simultaneously to fell both Diana's
hierophant and the branch from her tree with one stroke of a prun-
ing-bill. The very parallel between tearing the branch from the goddess's tree and tearing the life out of her priest makes the whole scene
more plausible as fable than as rite. Frazer himself wrote that "the

strange rule of this priesthood has no parallel in classical antiquity, and cannot be explained from it." Indeed it cannot, because it was probably not the rule of any real priesthood whatsoever, but only another instance of fable masquerading as reality.

Frazer characteristically took no notice of that difficulty, although he proceeded immediately after recreating the scene of ritual murder at Nemi to quote a number of other ancient legends about Nemi which he treated strictly as tales. The fact is that he was not clear on the difference between fable and cult when he began to write *The Golden Bough,* and he never firmly grasped the difference at any time during the three decades of his continued work on the subsequent volumes of it. He preferred to avoid the issue, because he had no interest in narrative apart from those tales which he could somehow connect with cult, and he declared early in his writing what he thought of such tales. He had only the strictest Pauline contempt for them:

> It needs no elaborate demonstration to convince us that the stories told to account for Diana's worship at Nemi are unhistorical. Clearly they belong to that large class of myths which are made up to explain the origin of a religious ritual and have no other foundation than the resemblance, real or imaginary, which may be traced between it and some foreign ritual.[38]

Frazer neglected to say who he thought might have "made up" such myths, or whence their imagery might have come, although he tried to make it appear by such grand and resolute words as "origin" and "foundation" that he had some opinion on that subject which he would reveal in due time. But after all a "resemblance" is not the same thing as a source, and "foundation" is not origin. In fact he had no understanding and proposed no theory of fable; the only opinion of fable which he ever revealed was disdain. To the extent that his sentiment allowed him to notice narrative, he noticed it only in its bearing on cult. And that had unfortunate consequences for his understanding of cult.

The difficulty was not really of Frazer's own making. He no less than countless other Western men of learning was a victim of the Pauline doctrine. The historic power of the Pauline doctrine concerning fable can hardly be overestimated. Possibly no doctrine in Christianity has deprived peoples in the West and in the Western sphere of cultural influence of more of their inherited culture, and to less purpose, than has this destructive bit of Christian moralism. The source of the trouble is a passage in the New Testament, in Paul's First Epistle to Timothy. Paul's evident concern in that Epistle was to keep Christian cult and the sectarian organization which supports it free from influences that might change them. Among those possible influences he particularly feared fable. The anathematic setting for his condemnation of fable is at least as damning as what he actually wrote against story or myth itself. Clearly it was the intellectual stimulation of fable and its power to alter ideas that Paul feared most (Timothy I, 3-11):

> When I was starting for Macedonia, I urged you to stay on at Ephesus. You were to command certain persons to give up teaching erroneous doctrines and *studying those interminable myths and genealogies, which issue in mere speculation* and cannot make known God's plan for us, which works through faith.[39]
>
> The aim and object of this command is the love which springs from a clean heart, and from a good conscience, and from faith that is genuine. Through falling short of these, some people have gone astray into a wilderness of words. They set out to be teachers of the moral law, without understanding either the words they use or the subjects about which they are so dogmatic.
>
> We all know that the law is an excellent thing, provided we treat it as law, recognizing that it is not aimed at good citizens, but at the lawless and unruly, the impious and sinful, the irreligious and worldly; at parricides and matricides, murderers and fornicators, perverts, kidnappers, liars, perjurers—in fact all whose behaviour flouts the wholesome teaching which conforms with the gospel entrusted to me, the gospel which tells of the glory of God in his eternal felicity.[40]

Set in a context of such terrific rhetoric of denunciation, the brief mention of myth or fable takes on by association a religious horror out of all proportion to the brevity of the reference. Moreover, Paul is still at it three chapters later, where he makes the unquenchable human interest in fable not only irreligious but also degrading to manhood, in an old-womanly metaphor that is itself borrowed straight from fable (Timothy IV, 7):[41]

> But refuse profane and old wives' fables, and exercise thyself rather unto godliness.

Even in the twentieth century there were still authorities and fellows of great English-speaking universities to whom the Pauline doctrine about fable or myth was an unquestioned, if not often conscious, tenet of morality and of permissibility in intellectual pursuits. It matters not at all what St. Paul really meant by his strictures on fable; the point is that throughout Christian history he was believed to have condemned just such fiction as is the subject of this book. No wonder then that in the Cambridge University of W. Robertson Smith's day with its decided theological prepossessions, the study of religion even in the form of pagan cults might be permissible, while only contempt could be accorded to any uncanonical narrative matter, no matter how nonsensical the study of the cults might be without a parallel but separate attention to and understanding of fable. No wonder either that Smith's disciple, James Frazer, who was a poetic but not a notably analytic mind, should neither know nor want to know anything he could avoid knowing about "old wives' fables." And even the most analytically minded anti-Frazerian successors of Frazer in British anthropology have not done much to disabuse their science of the Pauline doctrine's lingering effect.

Victor Turner's information about tree-cult among the Ndembu showed how the two trees of narrative were separated and distributed apart from each other in different Ndembu rituals. The *mudyi* "presided" at Nkang'a, and the *mukula* at Nkula; but neither the *mukula* nor any (hewn) equivalent of it figured in Nkang'a, and neither the milk-tree nor any other wild food-tree had any place in Nkula. That same separation of the two fabulous trees into different ritual contexts was common also in the classical world. Now Frazer saw all cults everywhere as the primitive, evolutionary antecedents of ancient Greek and Roman cults; again he was indebted to Darwin for the idea of evolution, which he no doubt used too loosely and too much in his cultural studies. Yet partly on account of his evolutionary bias, he fully recognized the importance of trees as cultic motifs in the classical world, even though he thought they were archaic and somewhat barbarous elements in the advanced civilization of the Greeks and Romans, and he was perfectly willing to extend the same recognition to other trees in both cult and narrative elsewhere. But he gave cult an absolute priority over narrative, and viewed all cult from the peculiar vantage of a classicist, which does not in any case give a very full or unobstructed prospect of either cult or fable.

Had Frazer given to narrative anything like the amount of attention which he lavished on cult and religion, he might sometime have realized that there were two irreconcilably different types of trees in classical cults as elsewhere. But he did not. Instead he tried to reduce all tree-cults (and the tales which he found associated with them) to a single type. Because the two trees were often segregated from each other in ancient cults just as they were in Turner's modern Ndembu rituals, the same confusion has somewhat afflicted other classicists too, but none has ever tried so hard as Frazer did to reduce the irreducible differences between the two types of trees. Other writers' lesser insistence on the homogeneity of tree motifs has therefore saved them from the kind of muddle which Frazer made in the second volume of *The Golden Bough,* where he wrote in Chapters IX and X about "The Worship of Trees" and "Relics of Tree-Worship in Modern Europe." [42]

As Frazer himself acknowledged, much of his information about tree-cults came from the work of a German scholar, Wilhelm Mannhardt's *Der Baumkultus der Germanen und ihrer Nachbarstämme; mythologische Untersuchungen* (Berlin, 1875). But Frazer, not Mannhardt, became the world's leading authority on the subject. Despite numerous inconsistencies, his opinion of trees in cult and story has been more widely received and more influential than any other scholar's in the past hundred years. That fact is due not only to the failure of later scholars to develop better alternatives to Frazer's views, but also to Frazer's revealing treatment of the trees as parts of a larger array of motifs that belong together by virtue of an ancient and universal tradition. He confused the two trees, but he was aware of their persistent concatenation with certain other motifs in a traditional motival cluster. He maintained, moreover, that the cluster is no mere aimless group of images; it is in effect a system of ideas. No matter how much one disagrees with his formulation of that ideological system, his general thesis that it is a system still deserves attention.

Even though he confused narrative with cult, and looked upon both from the strange vantage of a classicist seeking an evolutionary explanation for an ancient Latin rite which probably did not exist, Frazer was able by the very magnitude of his enquiry to approximate many features of the narrative pattern. Ancient legend did not tell whether Diana's tree in the Arician glade bore fruit, but Frazer knew of ancient engraved gems which he thought portrayed Diana herself as a bearer of fruiting branches. He knew that preternatural persons frequent green trees and may harm ordinary men who meet them there; he called them tree-spirits, supposing (after Mannhardt) that in belief they dwell in the green wood itself. He cited examples of the trees' ritual association with marriage, and examples of hewn wood used to defeat the malevolence of preternaturals. He knew of many instances in ritual when men behaved as guests in the presence of trees, and when they donated or forfeited property or life to the spiritual owners of trees. Most of all, he perceived that the combat between Diana's incumbent and aspirant priest-kings in the imagined rite at Nemi was a contest in which a man who had hitherto enjoyed the favor of a preterhuman person might unexpectedly lose that favor, and in losing it, die. If only Frazer had respected narrative more than he did, he might also have discovered how like Eden the vale of Nemi was, and how much the *Rex Nemorensis* resembled Adam, or Moses, or Samson, or Mandu, and all the other innumerable equivalents of this cosmotactic* character-type in oral fable.

While Frazer appreciated that all these motifs belonged together, the many examples of them from the researches of other men which he recited to support his own theory were mostly ritual, and none of those examples exemplified more than one or two of the motifs.

---

* Further in this book (in the chapter "Up, Down, All Around, and Who Made the World") I describe a kind of character in fable who is systematically instrumental in the creation of the world, or the maker of some outstanding feature of the universe. Because he is thus an agent of cosmogony, I call that character-type a "cosmogonic hero," or simply a *cosmogone*. I consider, however, that there is an important distinction to be recognized between the cosmogonic hero and his adventures on the one hand, and another kind of character who does not make or create anything in the fabulous cosmos, but who rather reorganizes, delimits, amplifies, or otherwise *arranges* things that are depicted as already existing in the universe, or who discovers the necessity of their arrangement in ways more useful or more suitable to himself and subsequent generations. Sometimes called a *changer* or *transformer*, this type of character is still not unambiguously distinguished from the cosmogone by those names, and so I prefer to call him a *cosmotact*, forming this new term on the analogy of *cosmogone* by a neologistic combination of my own invention from the two Greek words κόσμος, 'world, universe,' and τάσσω, 'marshal, appoint, place in order, assign, ordain, settle,' hence: cosmotact (n.), cosmotactic (adj.), 'who or which orders or arranges the world.'

He was unwilling ever to think that the alleged ritual of priesthood at Nemi was unique—the whole argument of *The Golden Bough* was to the contrary—yet he never found evidence of any real parallel to the rites of Nemi as a whole, only individual bits and pieces which severally paralleled the particular elements of Diana's cult. In the end, he pieced together a reasonable facsimile of the narrative pattern, but it took him thirty years to do it, and even then he had still not found any specific, concrete case of the whole pattern in any one ritual anywhere except the alleged ritual at Aricia. Unwittingly, he gave the clearest and most exhaustive proof of how little the narrative patterning is ever employed in any ritual.

James Frazer's ignorance of the ways of narrative and his mistakes in distinguishing narrative from cult set a bad precedent for later British anthropology. None have been so keenly aware of Frazer's mistakes as later British anthropologists, who, like Victor Turner, have adopted methods calculated to help them avoid errors of the kind Frazer made. Frazer took the whole of primitive cultural manifestations everywhere for his province, and relied for his information entirely on other scholars, be they ancient or modern; he was a stay-at-home with no inclination to field-work. In contrast, Turner relied in the only manner acceptable to his generation upon no one but the Ndembu themselves for his data, and confined his study of tree-cult to them alone. Frazer was concerned with the historical development of what he thought was a very archaic pattern in cult; Turner's later enquiry was strictly synchronous. One practical benefit of that procedure to Turner was that he could not confuse the two trees as Frazer had; indeed, he could not even think of confusing them because the Ndembu themselves made such a sharp distinction between them. By the same policy, Turner also avoided confusion of cult and story; the Ndembu did not narrate while they celebrated their rites connected with trees, nor did they go out of their way to point out the links between their rites and their tradition of fable. By obedience to that Ndembu separation of narrative and ritual performances, Turner avoided all notice of their story-telling while he was studying their rites, and thus avoided any such confusion of ritual and fable as Frazer experienced. But as it happened, that way too led to imperfect results, because Turner's Ndembu tree-cults were no more capable of explanation without knowledge of fable than were Frazer's hypothetical rites of Diana at Nemi. Whereas Frazer had, however inadequately, taken at least some notice of fable, Turner took none. Later British anthropology has surmounted numerous bad procedural precedents set by James George Frazer, but his crippling ignorance of the nature of narrative still endures among his successors.

ARTHUR EVANS' TREE OF ANICONIC DIVINITY

Frazer was not the only prominent British scholar of his day who studied the two trees. Another equally distinguished classicist and author on this subject was Arthur John Evans (1851-1941). Famous for his archaeological work on the Cretan Bronze Age and for his discovery of Knossos, an ardent traveller, and a life-long collector of ancient sealstones, Arthur Evans was an almost exact coeval of the more sedentary Frazer (1854-1941). Evans published his important work on trees in 1901, a decade after the first edition of *The Golden Bough* had appeared. A more modest work than Frazer's, Evans' treatment of the trees took the form of a long article entitled "Mycenaean Tree and Pillar Cult and Its Mediterranean Relations."[43]

Trees were conspicuous elements in the pictorial art of the eastern Mediterranean in the Bronze Age. Despite a pause in artistic production possibly coupled with some change in the ethnic composition of the region during the early Iron Age, arboreal motifs were once again as prominent in the art of the classical Greek world as they had been earlier. This continuity, and certain architectural associations of the trees in Bronze-Age portrayals, made Evans think that a cult of trees had been a major part of religion in Bronze-Age Crete, and he used the images on the ancient gems and gold finger-rings which he knew so well as the main data for an attempt to reconstruct that cult. Thus, like James Frazer before him and Victor Turner later, Arthur Evans also first approached the trees as elements in cult.

It must be said in fairness to Evans that he enjoyed much less choice about whether to study the trees in cult or in narrative than did Frazer or Turner. Frazer did not know the difference, while Turner, who surely knew the difference, elected to ignore narrative. But Arthur Evans' information from the Aegean Bronze Age was incomparably more rarified than either Frazer's or Turner's information about Latin or Ndembu tree-cults. No tales survive in writing from either Mycenaeans or Minoans; all that is now or was in Evans' time known about their story-telling comes indirectly from reflections in later written sources, or from just such incised, modelled, or painted artistic representations of narrative motifs as Evans studied for evidence of a tree-cult in prehistoric Crete. So Evans had no such immediate analogues in story to fall back upon as did Frazer and Turner. His scantier evidence of an Aegean tree-cult in the Bronze Age did not even permit Evans to surmise what rites might have been customary in that cult; there were no verbal records of Bronze-Age ritual to help him interpret what he saw depicted in Mycenaean and Minoan pictorial art. It was as if some later archaeologist of a dead Christian culture were to unearth icons and crucifix in the ruins of churches, and then try without Bible, prayerbook, or liturgy to reconstruct the beliefs and practices of Christians. Without direct records of either story *or* ritual from the Aegean Bronze Age, it would have been achievement enough for Evans just to prove the probable existence of a particular cult by demonstrating the regularity and frequency of certain pictorial motifs on objects of Bronze-Age manufacture. But in the event he was able to do more than that.

Whether they were intaglios on sealstones and gold signets, or figures modelled on plaques or in statuary, or paintings on walls and pottery, the prehistoric images which Evans set out to explain were much poorer in detail and much more cryptic than Frazer's legends about the vale of Nemi. But Arthur Evans had a more discriminating mind than Frazer's, and although he entertained no doctrinaire prejudice against comparing his information from Mycenaean Greece and Minoan Crete with like data from other cultures in later times, he was more circumstantial than Frazer in his treatment of facts wherever they came from. For that reason he recognized distinctions within his very restricted body of data that had escaped Frazer in the great sea of information which he had tried to compass. By careful discrimination of types in Bronze-Age portrayals of trees, Arthur Evans showed that the same system of two trees that is so familiar in oral narrative was embedded also in Mycenaean and Minoan cult.

Evans' first reason for assigning the trees in Mycenaean and Minoan decorative art to cult was architectural. He thought the remains of a curious oblong building among the Bronze-Age ruins at Goulas on Crete had once been a kind of roofless temple or shrine of the same type as he had found portrayed elsewhere on the fragment of a soapstone vase which he had dug up near Knossos (Figure 7), or again on such signets of stone or gold as those reproduced here in Figures 8 and 9.

Fig. 7. Fragment of steatite pyxis from *Gypsades*, Knossos. (After Evans).

Fig. 9. Steatite lentoid signet bezel from Ligortino, Crete.
(After Evans).

Since it served no evident practical purpose, Evans supposed that this
type of unroofed enclosure around a tree was cultic. He called it an
'hypaethral sanctuary,' and reasoned that if the enclosure was cultic,
then the living tree enclosed within it was sacred. He observed that
where the workmanship in these depictions permitted identification
of the enclosed trees' species, as it did on his steatite fragment from
Gypsades (Fig. 7), they were often figs. One might object that such
an enclosure around a fruiting tree need serve no other purpose than
the practical one of keeping hungry goats away from the tree, like
the ruder fence in the African scene in Figure 10.

Fig.10a. A young fruit tree fenced against the casual nibbling of passing
goats.

Fig. 10b. A fence that failed marks the place where the sapling died.

There were both domestic and wild goats aplenty on Crete in the Bronze Age, and they were undoubtedly just as destructive of young trees then as they are today. But an enclosure to protect a new tree from goats need not be so elaborate a piece of masonry as that shown in the Mycenaean and Minoan portrayals. And other features of those scenes bespoke cult too. The devout attitude of the anthropomorphic figures who face the trees as on the sealstone from Ligortino (Fig. 9), or the ritualistic postures of other figures such as those on the gold signet from Mycenae (Fig. 8) seem to denote some manner of cult.

Evans knew of several species of trees besides the fig which were sometimes 'sacred' in the Aegean Bronze Age: palm, plane-tree, cypress, and grape-vine. Later, in classical Greece, the oak and the black poplar also figured in cult, while in Italy the cornel and beech were used ritually, together with the oak and fig. Among the Semitic neighbours of the Mycenaean world, there were in addition the Hebrew mulberry and acacia, and later the Arabic gharcad. So Evans was well informed about the standing, green trees of ancient Mediterranean cults.

James Frazer had depended considerably on a German, Wilhelm
Mannhardt, for his notions about tree-cult, and Evans similarly owed
much of his thinking about 'sacred' trees to the work of another German, Carl W. Boetticher's *Der Baumkultus der Hellenen* (Berlin, 1856).
Both Boetticher and Mannhardt stressed the green trees in cult, and
regarded them as the embodiment of deities. According to this notion,
which was perfectly in keeping with the poetical conventions of German Romanticism, the green trees of ancient cult *were* gods and spirits and not just botanical associates or properties of preternaturals like
the trees in fable which I have discussed in the earlier chapters of this
book. Evans called this cultic merger of the tree and its frequenting
spirit 'aniconism,' and the green trees of cult he called 'aniconic images' of the gods. But there were difficulties with the German scholars' doctrine of aniconism, because the pictorial artistry of the Aegean
Bronze Age emphasized the standing, green trees much less than did
nineteenth-century Germans, and gave much greater prominence instead to pillars and rods of hewn wood. As Arthur Evans expressed it:

> . . .a special feature of the Mycenaean cult scenes with which we
> have to deal is the constant combination of the sacred tree with
> pillar and dolmen.[44]

He followed Boetticher unswervingly in the latter's explanation of
the pillar's origin. It was hewn wood:

> . . .the living tree. . .can be converted into a column or a tree-
> pillar, retaining the sanctity of the original.[44]

But when it came to giving a reason why the sacred tree should be
cut down and rendered into a pillar, Evans chose his words so as to
leave the relationship between the wood and the preternatural less
exactly defined than Boetticher had done:

> It would appear that the indwelling might of a tutelary God was
> secured by using in the principal supports of important buildings
> the wood of sacred trees.[45]

Evans thus accepted Boetticher's explanation that the sacred trees
were hewn in order to endue architecture with the same influences
that emanated from them in cult before they were cut down. Evans
did not try to specify what exactly those influences or meanings of
the trees might have been, but he did think that in time the desire to
make buildings more permanent had led to the substitution of stone
columns for wooden ones. The stone columns had, however, retained
the foliation and other decorative marks of their wooden antecedents:

The Mycenaean column in its developed architectural form, as can be seen from its entablature, essentially belongs to wood-work structure. The fundamental idea of its sanctity as a 'pillar of the house' may at times. . .have been derived from the original sanctity of the tree trunk whence it was hewn, and a form, in this way possessing religious associations, have been taken over into stone-work.[46]

Boetticher thought that the ancient Mediterranean tree-cult had evolved from an early 'animistic' stage of reverence for green trees themselves as deities to a more refined spiritualism that would have distinguished between the pure spirit of godhead and sacred trees as its material symbols. Correspondingly, the ancients should have hewn sacred wood more and revered green trees less with the passage of time. Evans was loath to contradict Boetticher on that point of theology, but his archaeological evidence from the Bronze Age did not conform to Boetticher's scheme. The hewn pillars of wood did not succeed green trees in Mycenaean and Minoan art. On the contrary, the green wood and the hewn were perfectly simultaneous. The hewn pillar was, for example, just as regular a feature of Evans' 'hypaethral sanctuaries' as was the fruit-tree; no such sanctuary was complete without both the green tree growing within and the hewn pillar standing either within, or within view outside. The pillar usually stood free at the entrance to the green tree's enclosure, or visible at a moderate distance through the doorway. The gold ring from Mycenae (reproduced in Fig. 8) was a case in point, as was another gold signet which Evans himself unearthed at Knossos:

Fig. 11. Gold signet ring from Knossos.

Later discoveries and publications of other signets have tended to confirm Evans' judgement in 1901:

Fig. 12. Gold signet ring from Crete.

Fig. 13. Gold signet ring from Asia Minor.

Fig. 14. Gold signet ring from the island of Mochlos.

Sometimes the pillar supported a corner of the green tree's enclosure:

Fig. 15. Gold signet ring from Mycenae.

Fig. 16. Gold signet ring from Mycenae. (After Evans).

Fig. 17. Impression of gold signet ring.

The green tree was not always enshrined in an hypaethral enclosure. Sometimes the hewn pillar stood instead in a shrine of its own, which probably had a roof, and in that case female figures might be shown carrying foliage from the opposite side of the picture where some leafing plant stood unenclosed in opposition to the enshrined dry pillar. The ritual action in portrayals of this type was thus played out between the two extremes of greenery on the one hand and dead pillar on the other, in a manner highly reminiscent of fable:

Fig. 18. Gold signet ring from Mycenae.

Fig. 19. Gold signet ring.
(Courtesy of the Antikenmuseum, West Berlin.)

There were also some cultic representations of the two trees which showed them singly; sometimes the green tree without the pillar:

Fig. 20. Gold signet ring from the Vapheio tomb, Mycenae.

Fig. 21. Gold signet ring from Mycenae.

In other instances the pillar stood alone without the green wood:

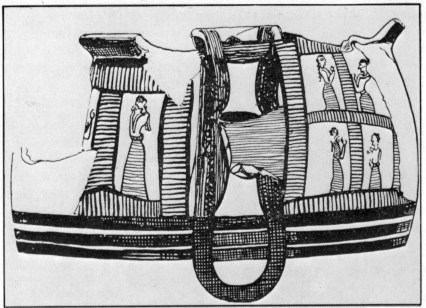

Fig. 22. Shard of a vase from Old Salamis, Cyprus. (After Evans).

But no matter whether they were shown singly or together, the green tree and the pillar were simultaneous phenomena in Mycenaean and Minoan art. Boetticher made the same mistake in his theory of theological development in ancient tree-cult that Schliemann had made in supposing that the course of events in Homer's *Iliad* was historical, when in fact it only followed a fabulous pattern in oral narrative tradition. Similarly, Boetticher mistook the developmental idea expressed in the imagery of the cult (movement from green wood to hewn pillar) for the historical development of theology through successive generations of the cult's practitioners. In the Aegean Bronze Age as in modern Africa, the two trees undoubtedly provided the two extremes between which the adherents of tree-cult could ritually enact those periodic changes in themselves and in their surroundings that were essential to the continuity of their lives. But today, one can only speculate, as Arthur Evans, Martin Nilsson, Axel Persson and others have done, what the ideological substance of Mycenaean and Minoan cults really was. One cannot go to the Bronze-Age peoples of the Mediterranean as Victor Turner went to the Ndembu to observe and interpret their rituals. And even if that were possible, there is no reason to think that tree cult in the Bronze Age would have been any more self-explanatory than was tree-cult among the Ndembu. As it is, all that survives of Minoan and Mycenaean cult is certain of its three-dimensional emblems and several dozens of ritual scenes on seals and in painting. If Turner's Ndembu rites were only vignettes of a more complex pattern of motifs in fable, then the surviving scenes of Minoan and Mycenaean rites are only vignettes of vignettes. They do not even begin to describe ritual in the Bronze Age, not to mention any patterns of oral fable that might have informed such ritual.

Nevertheless, certain elements that belong to the fabulous pattern of the Two Trees other than the trees themselves can be discerned in Minoan and Mycenaean iconography. The green tree, for example, was consistently associated with food, not only vegetable but also animal. Sometimes it was a fruit tree, as in the 'hypaethral sanctuaries' on the margins of the Bronze-Age seals already displayed in these pages. But the green tree sometimes stood also at the center of engravings, usually without fruit, and when it did, it often had herbivorous, edible animals flanking it on either side:

Fig. 23. Lentoid gem with intaglio from Goulas, Crete. (After Evans)

Fig. 24. Impression of crystal signet ring from Mycenae.

Fig. 25. Impression of lentoid gem with intaglio from Mycenae.

This same arrangement of figures, two four-legged animals and a tree, was otherwise used with the hewn pillar instead of the green tree at the center. In that case the flanking animals or preternatural theriomorphs were carnivores and potential manslayers, but they were posed tamely beside the pillar as though they were thoroughly domesticated. The contrast between the domesticity of the hewn pillar with its ferocious attendants and the wild scene with its green tree and timid herbivores is nowhere clearer than in the famous lion-gate of Mycenae:

Fig. 26. The gate of Mycenae.

Fig. 27. The pillar-and-lion relief over the Mycenaean gate.

It is paradoxical that the pillar hewn for an architectural purpose, to support the habitations of men, should be attended by creatures either real or fabulous that are such potential dangers to men as lions, sphinxes, and griffins. Enigmatic too that such horrendous beasts should appear so docile as they do in these Bronze-Age portrayals. Without more information about Minoan and Mycenaean ritual than has been discovered to date, it is certainly not possible to know whether the paradox of the benevolent ogre figured in Bronze-Age ritual, but the paradoxical scene depicted in Figures 26-29 is entirely consistent with the character of man-killers and ogres in the narrative pattern of the Two Trees. Beside the vineyards of Timnah Samson's lion threatened him at one moment, and benevolently fed him the next; Moses' supernal being in the burning bush promised him and his people food and protection against Pharaoh (Exodus 3:7-8), but soon after tried paradoxically to kill him (Exodus 4:24); the Mukuni Rain-Lord sheltered and fed Mandu, and then threatened him with mortal dangers. The same enigmatic duality of character informs the real and imaginary predators who appear so docile and inoffensive in the iconography of the Aegean Bronze Age, but who are by nature the most terrifying and most dangerous to men of all creatures.

Fig. 28. Lentoid gem with intaglio from Zero, Crete. (After Evans).

Fig. 29. Gold signet ring from Mycenae.

(Courtesy of the National Museum, Athens.)

Significantly, the potential man-killers were sometimes shown tethered to the pillar:

Fig. 30. Impression of lentoid gem with intaglio from Mycenae.

Fig. 31. Gold signet ring from Mycenae.

Such pictures raise the question: what human or preterhuman person had subdued and tied these fierce creatures? Evans observed:

> It is possible, for instance in the case of the Lions' Gate scheme, to give a series of examples in which a divinity is introduced between the lion supporters in place of the column.[47]

He illustrated that point with another sealstone (Fig. 32):

Fig. 32. Lentoid gem with intaglio from Kydonia, Crete.

(After Evans.)

It was probably Boetticher who was responsible for Evans' speculation that this male anthropomorph who replaced the column was a deity. But there was not in Evans' time nor is there now any factual evidence *pro* or *con* concerning the divinity of this figure. It is nevertheless noteworthy that the male figure, be he deity or not, replaced *only* the hewn column between carnivores, and never the corresponding green tree flanked by herbivores. As in modern oral fable, this Bronze-Age subduer of potential manslayers and ogres was also identified with the hewn pillar, not the green wood.

Rods of dry wood as well as hewn columns were attributes of male figures, as on Evans' gold signet from Knossos (Fig. 11) or on the ring of electrum from Mycenae in Figure 33.

Fig. 33. Electron signet ring from Mycenae.

Whether, as in fable, the subduer of manslaying ogres and lions was also the hewer of the columns and rods cannot be surely decided from the extant iconography. But there are suggestions of that correlation. Following earlier writers (Brunn, Perrot, and Chipiez), Evans conceded

that the docile lions and pillar over the gate at Mycenae might have
had military and political meaning:

> The lions have. . .been recognized. . .as symbolic figures of the
> military might of those who held the walls of the citadel, and
> as a challenge to their foes. The column itself and the architrave
> and beam-ends that it supports have been taken, with the altars
> below, to stand for the Palace of the Mycenaean Kings.[48]

The male anthropomorph who took the place of the pillar in Figure
32 might also reasonably be thought to symbolize political power as
did the pillar, since he and the pillar alike subdue and control the two
fierce mascots of the city-state (compare Figures 31 and 32). Thus
both the pillar and its male anthropomorphic double may have been
military and political symbols. If so, they were not the only such symbols. The famous Cretan double ax shown above in the ritual scene
on a gold signet ring from Mycenae (Fig. 21) was also a prominent
emblem by itself at seats of political authority in Bronze-Age Crete.
It was associated especially with the so-called 'Cretan Zeus,' who was
worshipped *inter alia* at cave sanctuaries high on Mounts Ida and Dikte,
locations particularly in keeping with his character as a 'high' or sky-
god. He was apparently the supreme male person in Cretan cosmology
of that time, and the frequent occurrence of his double ax emblem
at centers of government suggests that he was supreme too in the political hierarchy of men and gods. As the ultimate protector of political
order in Minoan Crete, this Zeus of the double ax may well have been
the same type of politically significant hewer as was Moses, maker of
the Ark, Tabernacle, and Altar of acacia-wood in Hebrew legend (Exodus 25-27), or Beowulf, the protector of Heorot in the Old English
epic. The possible simultaneity of the double ax and hewn column as
symbols of political authority lends special interest to the offertorial
scene on a painted sarcophagus from Hagia Triada in the Messara,
where several double axes surmount round wooden pillars (Fig. 34).

If, like the pillar on the Lions' Gate of Mycenae, the pillars on
this sarcophagus were also transmutable into male figures according
to the laws of substitution in Minoan iconography, then we would
have before us the missing hewer of oral narrative tradition, whose
axes, pillars, and rods are otherwise so common in Mycenaean and
Minoan art. At least one of his multiforms would certainly be Cretan
Zeus, god of the fig and plane-tree in Minoan times, and later in classical Greece, god of the oak, the best of all architectural woods.

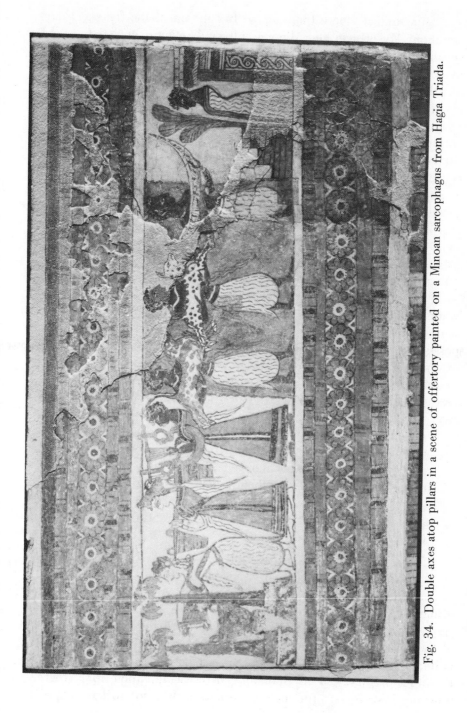

Fig. 34. Double axes atop pillars in a scene of offertory painted on a Minoan sarcophagus from Hagia Triada.

In a subject where there are so few incontestable facts as there are about Mycenaean and Minoan cults and religion, speculation and guessing must come into heavy play, and the best scholarship is that most nearly abreast of current thinking about the cults and religion of other peoples whose cultures are better documented. Because there is extraordinary scope for surmise, disagreement about the reconstruction of this or that feature of Aegean religion in the Bronze Age may continue indefinitely even when all parties are equally well informed. But it is also generally true that the narrative correspondents of Mycenaean and Minoan cultic motifs have not been adequately known or appreciated among the various authorities on this subject. Arthur Evans, for example, did not see the lion-tamer in the male anthropomorph that replaced the hewn pillar between two lions (Fig. 32). To him it was only an aniconic pillar-deity that had somehow become iconic (he did not say how) and assumed the pillar's function as a tethering-post for the lions. Here again the unfortunate idea of aniconism which he owed to earlier German scholarship played him false, for while he believed that the pillar and the male anthropomorph were the same motif, i.e. *identical* with each other, he could not explore the possibility that the male figure and the column were only *concomitants* of one another as they are in oral fable. Without a proper knowledge of narrative, he fled from that idea even when it presented itself to him quite forcefully in his own *métier*, the iconography of the Bronze Age:

> These religious schemes in which the divinity simply replaces the pillar must be distinguished from some other designs, also exemplified by Mycenaean signets, bearing a certain superficial resemblance to them, in which a male hero is seen in the act of grappling with a pair of lions. These have another origin and should more probably be regarded as adaptations of the familiar Chaldaean type of Gilgames.[49]

The operative words in this statement are: "...also exemplified by Mycenaean signets."[50] What Evans meant to say by these words, or had to admit, was that the figures of lion-tamers and other subduers of dangerous predatory beasts in both Minoan and Mycenaean iconography were in no formal or stylistic way distinguishable from the rest of the imagery in that art. Only he thought that the pillars and the lion-tamers had different origins; the one 'native' to the Aegean, and the other originally Mesopotamian. There was not then nor is there now any basis in fact for such a distinction, but not to have made it would have meant abandoning the idea of the pillar's aniconic divinity, and accepting that the pillar was only a concomitant of the male deity or hero, not identical with him. In the event Boetticher's authority was too great for Evans to resist, for knowing nothing systematic about narrative, Evans had nowhere else to turn than to such speculations about cult as Boetticher's for an explanation of the obviously close relationship between the pillar and the lion-tamer. It is of course an old if unworthy procedural rule of humanistic scholarship that when one does not understand the pertinency of something in culture, one should call it foreign, dismiss, and forget it. Not even Arthur Evans was above occasional compliance with that rule.

Far from demarcating a boundary between the iconography of the Aegean and Babylonian worlds Evans' comment about the pillar and the lion-tamer only serves to draw Babylonian cultic iconography and the story of Gilgamesh into the general fund of evidence about the existence and ritual use of the Two Trees' story in antiquity. The Akkadian epic hero Gilgamesh was indeed a subduer of lions, among other ogres. Evans' own glyptic example of the divine male tethering post from Khania on the northwest coast of Crete (Fig. 32) shows the two lions in the same rampant, scratching attitude as Gilgamesh's lion displays on the famous relief from the palace of Sargon II, now in the Louvre in Paris (Fig. 35).

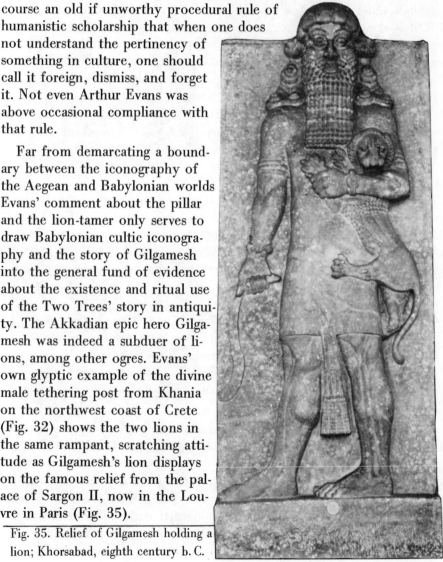

Fig. 35. Relief of Gilgamesh holding a lion; Khorsabad, eighth century b. C.

Assyrian and Neo-Babylonian glyptic art of about the same time (late eighth century b. C.) employed a parallel scheme of figures that explains the instrument in the hero's lowered hand: it is a cutting tool (Fig. 36).

Fig. 36. Carnelian cylinder seal.

The lion alternates with a griffin in this same pictorial scheme (Fig. 37).

Fig. 37. Cylinder seal of white calcedony.

True to the character of his counterpart in narrative tradition, the hero of this scene is both a cutter and a subduer of ogres. These two aspects of the hero were rendered in separate, complementary pictures in Aegean art of the Bronze Age, but they appear together simultaneously on single seals in Mesopotamia, as in Figure 37. There were technical reasons why in Mesopotamia more of the story of the Two Trees entered into individual productions of visual art than was usual in the Aegean. From its earliest relics in the fourth millenium onward, Mesopotamian glyptic was more elaborate and generally richer in detail than its counterpart in the Aegean region. One important reason for the difference was the often large and always cylindrical shape of Mesopotamian seals; they provided a larger surface for engraving than the more elegant gold ovals and flat or lentoid stones that were worn as finger-rings, items of jewelry, in the Aegean. Yet the pattern of story underlying the cults that are reflected in both the Mesopotamian and Aegean artistic traditions was the same. It called for hewn pillars or stocks as concomitants of the hewer and ogre-tamer, and in the eighth century b. C. the glyptic artists of both northern and southern Mesopotamia, Assyria and Babylon, perpetuated that tradition. Two of the requisite stocks duly appear between the hewer and his ogre on the cylinder of white calcedony in Figure 37. There the stocks are hewn into shapes taken to be symbolic of two Assyrian 'high' or sky-gods, the supreme male deity Marduk on the right, and his son Nabu on the left.[51] The association of these hewn stocks with father and son 'high' divinities is powerfully suggestive of Zeus and Apollo in the Aegean region during the same era.

The subduer of ogres in Aegean glyptic was usually portrayed not with one, but with two creatures flanking him (or his pillar) on either side. This was the usual treatment of him in eighth-century Mesopotamia too (Figs. 38-40). Variations with one or three ogres were merely for the sake of variety. Two recent writers, Edith Porada and Briggs Buchanan, comment on the prominence of this scheme during and after the hegemony of Sargon II (721-705 b. C.):

> ...the favorite scheme of Assyrian seal cutters from the time of Sargon onward [was] a hero with two monsters or animals.[52]
>
> The most frequent scheme...is that of a symmetrical group with a central hero grasping two rampant animals or monsters.[53]

Mesopotamian glyptic art from the end of the eighth century b. C. or later is much too late to be of any direct interest in connection

Fig. 38. Cylinder seal of green and white siliceous stone.

with Mycenaean or Minoan art in the Aegean, which belongs mostly
to the millenium before 1100. But Sargon II and his artists were
archaizers, and their iconography resumed a much older Mesopotamian
tradition:

> This scheme (a symmetrical group with a central hero grasping
> two rampant animals or monsters) differs from that in most of
> the contest scenes on cylinders dating from the fifteenth century
> to the time of Sargon. In such earlier representations the hero is
> usually depicted charging his antagonist with a weapon. However,
> those of the present group revert to the scheme of the Akkad
> period, in which the heroes vanquish the beasts with their bare
> hands. This return to ancient tradition may be accidental, or it
> may reflect a conscious attempt on the part of the artists, at
> the prompting of Sargon, to revive the style associated with his
> great namesake, Sargon of Akkad.[54]

Just as modern variants are indispensable for the study of oral fable,
chronologically late pictorial art may be of great value for establish-
ing the types in an iconographic tradition. Thus the type of the scene
shown on the Neo-Assyrian seal in Figure 38 rises to a high antiquity
in Mesopotamian glyptic art, and its elements taken severally are all
as old as the earliest relics of that art. Two ogres flank their subduer,
with a post or stock in the background beside the hero as on the seal
in Figure 37. The post is cruciform with a short cross-piece and a spher-
ical finial. A tall green plant stands at the outer edge of the scheme in
tidy opposition to the cruciform dry post beside the hero at the center
of the scene.

Another multiform of the ogre besides the lion and griffin was
the ostrich, whose powerful legs and clawed feet can disembowel a
man at a single stroke. This particular ogre's tamer is associated with
the aerial world of the sky by the wings which he wears, or by celes-
tial bodies above the scene of his grappling with feathered adversaries
(Figs. 39 and 40).

Fig. 39. Cylinder seal of yellowish chert.

Fig. 40. Cylinder seal of brown and grey jasper breccia.

Marduk's armorial device, an upright stock or spade-haft, alternated with the ogre-tamer in Mesopotamia in the same manner as hewn post and hero alternated with one another between two flanking ogres in Aegean glyptic (compare Figs. 31, 32, 38, and 40).

Fig. 41. Cylinder seal of greenish calcedony.

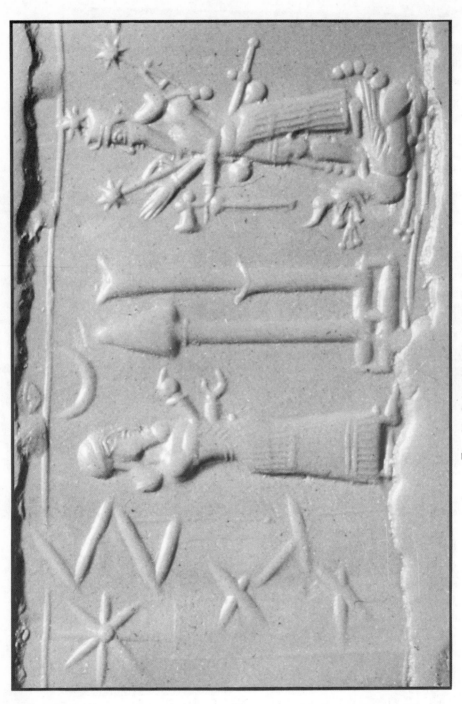

Fig. 42. Cylinder seal of bluish calcedony.

A worshipper (on the left) indicates the divinity of the ax-bearing hewer on the sealing in Figure 42, which is perhaps a century older than those in the preceding Figures,[55] while the hewer shows his mastery over a griffin by standing on its back.

Another seal, also thought to be of the ninth century,[56] portrays the ogre-tamer in the same relationship to the worshipper and post as was the ax-bearer atop the griffin in Figure 42, except that now he grapples his griffin rather than standing on it (Fig. 43).

Fig. 43. Cylinder seal of black serpentine.

The same scheme of griffin-grappler with a cutting instrument in the left hand was incised hundreds of years earlier on the next seal, a Middle Assyrian piece attributed to the thirteenth century,[57] a time corresponding to the close of the Minoan period on Crete. Here too a green tree stands at the outer edge of the scheme, as on the eighth-century seal of green and white siliceous stone above (Fig. 38), in opposition to the long dry rod employed as the haft of the hewer's ax. This seal is a good example of what Porada and Buchanan

meant when they wrote that

>...Assyrian realism and use of landscape parallel similar tenden-
>cies in the contemporary art of Egypt and of the Aegean regions.[58]

But there is substantive as well as stylistic likeness in this case, where
two herbivores frequent the green tree just as in the iconography of
Aegean glyptic; here they are an ibex and a monkey (Fig. 44).

Fig. 44. Damaged cylinder seal of pink chert.

A green tree with exceptionally graceful foliage but without the
herbivores attends another monster-tamer in the same position on the
following seal, which is also Middle Assyrian (Fig. 45).

Fig. 45. Hero with griffins. (Courtesy of the Museum of Fine Arts)

I cannot agree with Henri Frankfort that the tree on this seal is a "bedecked maypole." He did not derive his opinion of it from his own great erudition in Assyriology, but from Sidney Smith, who got it *verbatim* from James G. Frazer, whose confusion of the two trees I have rejected earlier in this chapter. The essential difficulty with Frazer's understanding of arboreal motifs was his untenable idea that ancient and primitive cults and their supporting myths made no distinction between the symbolic properties of stripped, dry trees on the one hand and foliated, green ones on the other. In order to apply Frazer's notion to the archaeological evidence of Assyrian religion, Frankfort cited certain findings of others that in fact argue strongly against any such confusion of green wood and dry stocks in Mesopotamia, especially when those findings are compared with the glyptic iconography. Quoting Sidney Smith further, Frankfort affirmed that a

"...bare pole...was the object of ritual practices...just as was the case [of the *ashera*] in Syria and Palestine."

The tree is, in all probability, a cedar tree: and in front of the temples at Khorsabad cedar trees bound with copper bands, decorated with religious scenes, stood on either side of the entrance.[59]

A tree bound about with metal bands and "decorated with religious scenes" is of necessity a dead tree, a dry stock girdled against splitting, with its cultic associations carved into its very wood. Standing at the entrance to temples, this dry tree is an obvious relative of the many ringed and tasselled stocks and gateposts elsewhere in Mesopotamian glyptic art (e. g., Figs. 51 and 54 below). Frankfort objected that "...the very artificial structure on such seal designs as [in Fig. 45]...are unintelligible as the rendering of natural trees...."[60] The same thing would have to be said about the modern piece of folk art on the Moravian mural in Figure 46a, or the designs painted on the exterior walls of the famous mosque at Travnik in Yugoslavia (Figs. 46b-e).

Fig. 46a. Women's mural painting from Moravia, Czechoslovakia.

Fig. 46b. The painted mosque in Travnik, Yugoslavia.

Fig. 46c. Facade of the painted mosque.

Fig. 46d. Arboreal decorations on the painted mosque.

Fig. 46e. A stylized fruiting tree on the painted mosque.

But the Moravian and Yugoslav Moslem figures are certainly green plants, not maypoles, and so by the same token is the tree in Figure 45. Frankfort's own earlier explanation of the ornate tree in Fig. 45, that in it "purely decorative values are paramount"[61] was quite sufficient without his becoming involved in Frazer's careless arboreal typology, which never in the thirty years of Frazer's work on this subject could tell the difference between a hewn and a green tree.

In connection with this same seal (Fig. 45) Porada and Buchanan wrote: "The style of Middle Assyrian seals is curiously reminiscent of the Akkad style of a thousand years earlier."[62] Some of the subject matter was reminiscent too, to say the least; ogre-grappling, for example, with an erect dry rod or stock beside the grapplers (Figs. 47-49) was prescribed by a tradition even older than Akkad. The dry wood is a radiant spade-haft on the Early Akkad seal in Fig. 47, whose manufacture probably about 2300 b. C.[63] corresponds in time to the Early Helladic period on mainland Greece, Early Minoan III on Crete, and Early Cycladic on the other islands of the Aegean.

Fig. 47. Cylinder of greenish black and olive buff serpentine.

Other seals of the same time show other multiforms of the dry stock. It is a reversed gatepost in Fig. 48.

Fig. 48. Concave shell cylinder.

An upright post stands in the background on a seal from the time of Sargon I (Fig. 49).

Fig. 49. Cylinder seal from Tell Asmar (Courtesy of the Oriental Institute, University of Chicago).

The fierce adult bull and male bison join the lion as varieties of ogre on the two foregoing Akkadian pieces. An explicitly fabulous kind of ferocious bull opposes the hewer in the rather unusual scene on the Akkadian seal in Fig. 50 too. The scheme is different, with additional anthropomorphic and theriomorphic figures in it expressing a larger than usual complement of narrative motifs, but the hewer as usual still faces his ogre with his upright post beside him.

Fig. 50. (Courtesy of the Trustees of the British Museum).

Rarely can contemporary narrative be used to such an extent in the interpretation of ancient glyptic iconography as is possible in this instance. Henri Frankfort seized this exceptional opportunity, and analyzed the scene on the seal in Fig. 50 as follows:

> Drought is symbolized by a bull; here we must quote the Gilgamesh Epic, which obviously refers to the Bull of Heaven as a symbol of the aridity of the Mesopotamian climate. It is thus described when Ishtar asks her father Anu to give her the bull that she may destroy Gilgamesh who has scorned her:
>> Father, Oh make me a Heavenly Bull which shall Gilgamesh vanquish
>> Filling his body with flame.
>
> But Anu warns her of the dangerous character of the creature:
>> If I the Heavenly Bull shall create for which thou dost ask me
>> (Then) seven years of (lean) husks must needs follow after his onslaught.
>
> And a Sumerian fragment makes it even clearer that Ishtar plans to punish Gilgamesh by striking his city with famine:
>> It was reported to the Lord Gilgamesh:
>> Inanna has brought forth the Bull of Heaven!
>> She made him pasture in Erech
>> And drink at the waxing river:
>> A double-hour the waxing river flowed, then only his thirst was slaked;
>> Where he pastured the earth is bare.
>
> The heroic king of Erech succeeds in killing the bull:
>> Gilgamesh, like an able slaughterer, strikes with his sword the Bull of Heaven forcefully and precisely between shoulders and neck.
>
> It is this action which we see illustrated. . . . The kneeling god there is hardly the Gilgamesh of the Epic, for the scene appears on our seal, not as part of the personal conflict between Ishtar and the King of Erech, but in the more general cosmic form which may have supplied the epic poets with the theme. But it is clear that the killing of the bull on the seal signifies the breaking of the drought. The Thunder-god with mace and leather-tongued whip is seen approaching from the left on his dragon of lightning, and abundant rain descends, called up by the goddess who appears with outstretched arms in the sky.[64]

So the action portrayed on the seal in Fig. 50 is a fragment of narrative. But it is surely not narrative for its own sake, and not a whole narrative. The various figures all marching from left to right across the scene constitute a kind of processional that terminates with the subduing of the bull under the upright column or post on the extreme right. This *taurobolion* is the focus of the scene, and it has a decidedly ritual character for two reasons. If Gilgamesh the epic slayer of the Bull of Heaven is the type of the ogre-tamer on this seal, then one must not forget what Gilgamesh did with the Bull when he had slain it. Tablet VI in the Assyrian version of the Akkadian Epic of Gilgamesh tells the story:

> Between neck and horns (he thrust) his sword. (150)
> When they had slain the Bull, they tore out his heart,
> Placing it before Shamash.
> They drew back and did homage before Shamash.
> The two brothers sat down.

> Then Ishtar mounted the wall of ramparted Uruk,
> Sprang on the battlements, uttering a curse:
> "Woe unto Gilgamesh because he insulted me
>   By slaying the Bull of Heaven!"
> When Enkidu heard this speech of Ishtar,
> He threw the right thigh of the Bull of Heaven,
>   Tossing it in her face:
> "Could I but get thee, like unto him. (160)
> I would do unto thee.
> His entrails I would hang at thy side!"
> (Thereupon) Ishtar assembled the votaries,
> The (pleasure-) lasses and the (temple-) harlots.
> Over the right thigh of the Bull of Heaven she set up a wail.
> But Gilgamesh called the craftsmen, the armorers,
> All (of them).
> The artisans admire the thickness of his horns:
> Each is cast from thirty minas of lapis;
> The coating of each is two fingers (thick); (170)
> Six measures of oil, the capacity of the two,
> He offered as ointment to his god, Lugalbanda.
> He brought (them) and hung them in his princely bed-chamber.[65]

Gilgamesh and his bosom companion Enkidu (compare the pair

of ogre-subduers in Fig. 49, above) use the ritually significant parts of
the slain bull—heart, horns, and thigh—to do genuine homage to two
male deities, and to parody proper homage to the powerful goddess
Ishtar. Of these three deities, Ishtar is far the most important at this
point in the Epic of Gilgamesh. She it is who brought the fabulous
beast into being as a chastisement to Gilgamesh, and to her Enkidu
gives in anger (but gives nonetheless) the choicest joint of its flesh,
the right thigh. Similar rites of dedication must be expected as the
normal sequel to the *taurobolion* on the Akkadian seal in Fig. 50.
The incipiently votive character of the scene on this seal gives meaning to the pillar behind the bull-slayer. It must be one of those banded and carved cedar-wood poles which Frankfort and others knew
stood before the entrances to Assyrian temples.[60] Undoubtedly it
stands on the seal before the temple or shrine where the rites of offertory must be performed when the bull is dead.

Even the clearest of ritual scenes in ancient pictorial art are almost impenetrably cryptic without the kind of help from narrative
tradition toward their interpretation which the Epic of Gilgamesh
provides in the case of this Akkadian seal. But once the light of narrative has fallen upon such a scene, the schematic continuity in an
iconographic tradition may make it possible to understand similar
scenes where no contemporary narrative is available to give such help.
A case in point is the following seal from the Uruk period in the fourth
millenium b. C., which is prehistoric in that there are no written documents (and hence no recorded tales) from that time.

Fig. 51. Cylinder seal showing a scene of offertory.
(By courtesy of the Staatliche Kunstsammlung, Dresden).

This scene is explicitly offertorial. As on the preceding Akkadian seal, the procession of men and beasts moves from left to right toward a sanctuary marked by the pair of ringed and tasselled gateposts. These tasselled posts have been identified with the Sumerian goddess Inanna,[66] who was to Akkadian Ishtar much what Greek Aphrodite was to Latin Venus. A scene of dedication to Inanna in the glyptic art of Sumerian Uruk may thus be compared with the offertory to Ishtar implied on the Akkadian seal in Fig. 50. The most important difference between the two scenes is that in the Sumerian instance (Fig. 51) the fruits of the earth quickened by rainfall and the meat gotten by slaughter are shown already prepared and laid out as if in preparation for dining, whereas the Akkadian seal depicts the same things at an earlier moment of their development: the coming of rain to stimulate the growth of vegetable food, and the slaughter of the meat-yielding animal (Fig. 50). If the connection between drought and the slaughter portrayed on the Akkadian seal seems obscure, it has only to be remembered that slaughtering is the natural and usual recourse of cattle-keepers in time of drought, when they must reduce their herds and flocks to conserve water and pasturage. The scene of offertory incised on the seal from the Uruk period is of much too early a date to be compared directly with any extant Aegean iconography, but it is strongly suggestive of the offertory on the sarcophagus from Hagia Triada shown in Fig. 34, where food-animals and vegetable food and drink are similarly borne toward free-standing dry pillars.

Two ringed and banded dry pillars stand before the entrance to a shrine as an offertorial procession approaches it again on the seal in Figure 52, which is also from the Uruk period:

Fig. 52. A cylinder seal in the National Museum of Iraq.
(By courtesy of the Director General of Antiquities, Baghdad).

The essential contrast between green wood and the dry pillars of the sanctuary is brilliantly expressed on the next seal, again from the Uruk period, where two gentle herbivores flank the green wood as in later Assyrian and Aegean iconography (compare Figures 23, 44, and 53).

Fig. 53. (By courtesy of the State Museum, East Berlin).

Henri Frankfort explained this scene as feeding of the temple herd. If his explanation is correct, then the green wood and the dry column in this very early Sumerian scene may have had opposite and complementary symbolic properties not unlike those of the *mudyi* and *mukula* trees among Victor Turner's modern Ndembu of Central Africa. Be he man or god, the anthropomorph is the trickster and the ogre under the green wood in the scene on this seal. He feeds his animal clients at the green wood one moment, but the next moment may be expected to slaughter them himself or to sanction their slaughter by others under the sign of the temple pillars for his own sustenance and that of the gods. Ndembu similarly celebrated the distribution of plant food at the *mudyi* tree and their hunters' killing of animals for meat at the hewable *mukula* tree. What more abstruse metaphorical symbolism may have attached to these two Sumerian trees, green and dry, must remain for scholars of Sumerian archaeology to decipher if they can. But it is amply apparent that the same arboreal dyad with its usual concomitant motifs as found in cults of the modern world was also operative in the earliest cults of Mesopotamia more than five millennia ago. Arthur Evans said, "the coincidences of tradition are beyond the scope of accident," and indeed they are. But the coincidences of this particular motival tradition cannot be accounted for in the history of religion and cult. They are only within the scope of oral fable.

In respect to cattle, the type of Sumerian temple that is represented by the gateposts on the seals in Figs. 51-53 had to be as paradoxical as the behaviour of its anthropomorphic attendant who is pictured feeding the cattle green branches in Fig. 53. The temple was a place of protection and nourishment for its herds, yet it was also their *abattoir*. As the sign of such temples, the dry pillar could not escape having the same dual, self-contradictory, simultaneously benevolent and baneful signification. If the temple was indeed Inanna-Ishtar's, then her strange behaviour in the Akkadian Epic of Gilgamesh, where at one moment she offers her love and favours to Gilgamesh and at the next moment prosecutes a vicious vendetta against him, is entirely consistent with the character of her temple in relation to its animal clients, who are similarly first protected and nurtured, then slain. A small cylinder from the Jamdat Nasr period[67] neatly encapsulates the paradox (Fig. 54). Outside the temple, the cattle were to be fed, but to be eaten inside.

Fig. 54. (By courtesy of the Trustees of the British Museum).

In sharp contrast to the Sumerian temple herds, wild herbivores frequented green trees in the absence of any hewn rods or posts on other seals, like the one in Fig. 55, which has also been assigned to the Jamdat Nasr period.[67]

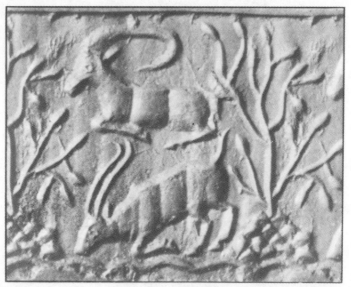

Fig. 55. Cylinder seal showing a scene of green tree and herbivores. (Courtesy of the Directorate General of Antiquities, Baghdad).

But the temple cattle were a domestic herd or flock, and therefore their feeding takes place in the simultaneous presence of both the green and the hewn wood. Were they wild, they too might feed at a green tree without the presence of the dry pillar, because the green tree of oral fable is regularly associated with unreciprocal, lawless, or merely emotionally motivated giving or taking of goods and benefits. In contrast to it, the dry wood customarily signifies reciprocity and consequence, or the rule of law in all matters of property and exchange. The temple herd is kept and cared for, but in time it must recompense its keepers and their gods with its own flesh; meanwhile the feral herbivore takes from the green tree at its own pleasure and owes nothing in return. If innumerable human and animal heroes in every age have found themselves caught in the web of this same paradox of domesticity as they move between the green and dry trees of oral fable, then it must be because the Sumerian temple herd's dilemma of having to give back to its keepers as much as it receives is inherent in the very nature of culture, whether animal or human. No doubt the story of the Two Trees has persisted in oral narrative tradition because it is about an equally persistent and essential feature of culture: the need for reciprocity and recompense. That would explain the longevity and universal appeal of the story-pattern, but it still leaves unanswered the question of why the pattern should persistently and universally consist of its particular motifs: the two trees, the schizotropic ogre, the concealment or disappearance of persons, etc. One can find sufficient reasons for a tale's existence, some of local and some of more general validity, but still not merely on that account know anything certain about the tale's origins.

All that is certain is that the temporally tenacious motifs of a story-pattern have their equally tenacious generic meanings. The dry wood of the Two Trees' pattern signifies the law of reciprocity in men's dealings whether among themselves or with other beings in either the animal or the supernal order. It is therefore only logical that the hewn wood should persistently be associated with an enforcer of reciprocity, the familiar hewer, subduer of monsters, and master of preternatural techniques, who protects men and their goods against the depredations of alien powers by using the techniques of such aliens against themselves. That champion or saviour was also portrayed in the glyptic art of the Uruk period, and beside him, the upright hewn post as expected. With minor facial differences, he was the same type of carnivore-fighter who grappled and vanquished outlaw creatures, either killing or making mascots of them, in later Akkadian and Assyrian iconography. The seal in Fig. 56 shows him in the usual act of carrying two subdued lions, one on either side (cf. Fig. 35), while above his head two other lions tamely form a pyramid in the manner of the Lions' Gate of Mycenae (cf. Figs. 26-27), but without the central pillar seen on that monument, which is displaced here by the ogre-tamer himself. The hewn tree takes instead the form of a tall post at the open gateway to the large enclosure where the lion-tamer stands barring the way in an apotropaic posture. Another daemonic or masked figure with a ram's head and a human torso grasps the post as if in supplication. This and the other ram-headed figure within the fence to the right of the lion-tamer give the enclosure the character of a hallowed sheep-cot like the one on the cylinder from the Jamdat Nasr period in Fig. 54. The present seal, assigned to the Uruk period in the fourth millennium b. C., is accordingly a complete prototype of the

Fig. 56. A cylinder seal of the Uruk period.

Fig. 57. Impression of the seal in Fig. 56, showing a sheep-cot and its cyclopean keeper.

iconography of contests and sacred pillars that continued in Mesopotamian glyptic art for nearly three thousand years. That long visual
record of the hewer/ogre-tamer and his hewn wood is valuable evidence for the existence of the Two Trees' story-pattern in oral tradition at an earlier date and in greater multiformity than is attested by
any surviving verbal monument from any people anywhere in the world.

The fundamental motivation for the innumerable contests with
ferocious animals seen in the Mesopotamian glyptic tradition is the
same as that in oral fable and in the many literary offshoots of fable
like those in the Old Testament. Like the combatants in modern African tales, like Beowulf, Samson, Moses, or even Adam, the monster-
tamers in Mesopotamian glyptic art are also the keepers of eating-
places and food-supplies, and champions of the hungry. Their dry
pillars and rods, so often portrayed in holy places, have the same
value as symbols of reciprocity as they have in oral fable. They are
a liminal motif in Mesopotamian art as they were in the ancient Aegean, marking doorways and gateways where property-rights and the
enforcement of rules of exchange commence. The carnivores and monsters whom the hewer overcomes at the sign of the upright post or
rod are just those invaders of property and takers who give nothing
in exchange for what they consume, and who can serve no useful
purpose except eventually to join the hewer in guarding the precincts
of property against others of their own kind from beyond the pale.
In keeping with his mascots, the monster-tamer is himself frequently
monstrous in some fashion, although indispensable to men. Like the
policeman with his night-stick or fire-arm in the modern urban world,
he is a dangerous figure employed by civilization to ward off other,
less tractable dangers.

For all their obvious interest in contests and stocks of dry wood,
the seal-cutters of Mesopotamia did not neglect the green tree. Sometimes they included it on the same seals in various modes of opposition to upright hewn wood, but it figured too on other seals by itself
as fruit tree, shade tree, or browsing place for herbivores (as in Fig.
55 above). Often it was a palm. A seal thought to have been cut during the dynasty of Akkad (Fig. 58) shows a group of women taking
fruit from one of four different trees arranged in a progression of size
(or perspective):

Fig. 58. (Courtesy of the Koninklijk Kabinet, 's-Gravenhage).

Three seals that are said to be of Middle Assyrian style again associate the green tree with herbivores as prescribed by the old tradition; one of these seals also shows a progression of different kinds of green trees (Figs. 59-61).

Fig. 59. (Courtesy of the Bibliothèque Nationale, Paris).

Fig. 60. Cylinder seal of milky white chalcedony.

Fig. 61. (Courtesy of the Musée d'art et d'histoire, Genève).

This tradition continued in Assyrian times (thirteenth-tenth centuries b. C.) as seen in Fig. 62, and still later in the ninth century b. C. (Figs. 63-64).

Fig. 62. (Courtesy of the State Museum, East Berlin).

Fig. 63. Cylinder seal of black serpentine.

Fig. 64. Cylinder seal of black serpentine.

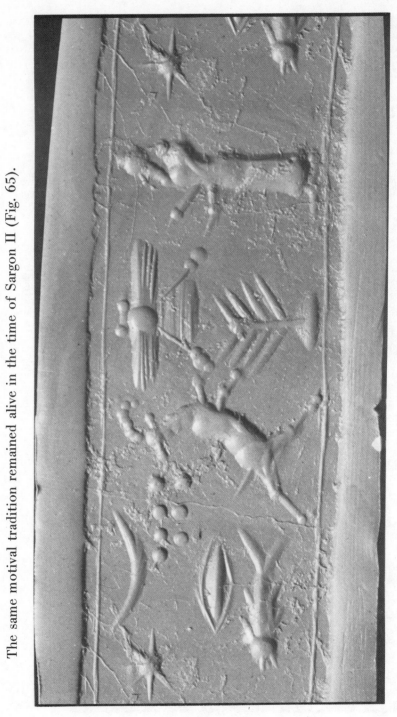

The same motival tradition remained alive in the time of Sargon II (Fig. 65).

Fig. 65. Cylinder seal of orange chert.

Henri Frankfort, a distinguished authority on Mesopotamian cylinder seals, wrote: ". . .it is with ritual, not with myth, that the seal-cutters of the Uruk period seem to be concerned."[68] Much the same can be said about Mesopotamian glyptic art in its later periods as well. There were in certain periods recognizable schools of glyptic artistry, and no doubt individual artists in other periods too stressed the decorative qualities in the seal-cutting tradition, giving more attention to the preservation or development of particular artistic styles than to the completely faithful reproduction of traditional scenes in all their details. But even then the substance of the iconographic tradition remained cultic and ritual. It is impossible to construct a whole integrated tale of any kind from the bits and pieces of imagery in even the best preserved periods of Mesopotamian glyptic. Moreover, not even the simplest tales that are actually preserved in writing from ancient Mesopotamia are represented in glyptic art by more than a paltry few scenes which may (or may not) portray isolated narrative incidents. As in the modern case of Ndembu ritual and Central African story-telling, only a small part of Mesopotamian story entered into Mesopotamian ritual and cultic iconography, and the sum of the motifs common to both narrative and cultic depiction was much less than the sum of the motifs in any attested story of that time.

Nor is any of that at all surprising. On the contrary, it arises from the very nature of pictorial art. Pictures by themselves were never able to tell a story until the advent of cinema. They could allude to and evoke remembrance of narrative in persons who already knew the tales to which pictures referred, but they were never more than a stimulating supplement to verbal story-telling, and not even pictorial art's more recent elaborations such as cinema have ever approached the efficiency of speech as a means of narration. It is perfectly natural therefore that Mesopotamian glyptic imagery was cultic and ritual, not mythic. Like the cults to which it was a religious or decorative adjunct, Mesopotamian glyptic iconography was an abstraction from narrative of certain elements that were at some time or other symbolically significant in Mesopotamia. It follows that much may be gained for the study of Mesopotamian cult and glyptic from a prior knowledge of narrative. But the inverse is not true; not even a long and richly attested iconographic tradition like this one will, unaided, tell its modern viewers much about the tradition of narrative that was contemporary with it.

Luckily, some tales have come down in writing that betoken an abiding Mesopotamian tradition of story-telling about a hewing, cosmo-tactic hero and ogre-taming enforcer of reciprocity. He was Gilgamesh, the legendary builder of Uruk, a fabulous person about whom various tales were told in Sumerian and Akkadian; no doubt there were more such tales than survive in writing. The best-preserved story concerning him is the so-called Epic of Gilgamesh, in Akkadian, wherein he subdued not one but three different monsters in a series of adventures that took him from a hewn post in his own city of Uruk (Erech) through a great forest of green cedars (in Lebanon?) to another, tamer woods at the very edge of the world where he manufactured a hundred and twenty long punting-poles (three hundred in the Old Babylonian Version) to help him navigate the perilous Waters of Death.

Gilgamesh was unlike numerous other stock characters of ancient Mesopotamian narrative in that he had nothing to do with the creation of the world, and did not himself come into being until after the Great Flood, which gave the world its present shape according to ancient Near Eastern opinion. But he travelled widely through the world not very long after the Flood, discovering as he went how the world is organized and governed by mutual accommodation or compromise be-tween the will of the gods and the will of men. As the legendary founder of Uruk, Gilgamesh must be understood as a figment of the fabulous age at the very beginning of civilization. From the ancient Mesopotamian point of view, the time of Uruk's founding was a cosmo-tactic era when men generally were only just learning the finer points of how they ought to live, and the things which Gilgamesh learned in his adventures and travels were worthy to be preserved for the instruc-tion of all men thereafter:

> He who saw everything [to the end]s of the land,
> [Who all thing]s experienced, [conside]red all!
> . . .
> . . .
> The [hi]dden he saw, [laid bare] the undisclosed.
> He brought report of before the Flood,
> Achieved a long journey, tiring and resting.
> All his toil he engraved on a stone stela.
> —I, i, 1-2, 5-8.[69]

Indeed Gilgamesh saw and endured more than any ordinary man could experience and yet live. But that was because he was not strictly a

man. Only a part of him was human, while most of him was preternatural:
> Two-thirds of him is god, [one-third of him is human].
> > —I, ii, 1.[70]

Thus, like countless others of his cosmotactic type in oral fable everywhere, Gilgamesh too was sufficiently alloyed with monstrosity to be
a capable subduer of monsters. He was champion and defender of
Uruk, but at first he played that part monstrously, adulterating his
protective function with exploitative behaviour of his own that did
not recompense the citizens of Uruk for his extravagant use of them.
One difficulty was Gilgamesh's taking of women who did not belong
to him:

> The nobles of Uruk are worried in [their chamb]ers:
> "Gilgamesh leaves not the son to [his] father;
> [Day] and [night] is unbridled his arro[gance].
> [Is this Gilga]mesh, [the shepherd of ramparted] Uruk?
> Is this [our] shepherd, [bold, stately, wise]?
> [Gilgamesh] leaves not [the maid to her mother],
> The warrior's daughter, [the noble's spouse]!"
> The [gods hearkened] to their plaint,
> > —I, ii, 11-18.[71]

Reacting to the citizens' protest against the ogreish element in
Gilgamesh, the same goddess who created him makes another monstrous mixture of disparate natures to be a foil to him. This new
preternatural person is Enkidu, a compound of human and herbivorous animal characteristics fit to match and offset the blend of human
and predacious qualities in Gilgamesh:

> With the gazelles he feeds on grass,
> With the wild beasts he jostles at the watering-place,
> With the teeming creatures his heart delights in water.
> > —I, ii, 39-41.[72]

But though he is a different mixture (animal and human as distinct
from the blend of human and divine in Gilgamesh), Enkidu is just as
disturbing a person as is Gilgamesh. He denies hunters their game in
the same way Gilgamesh had denied familial rights to the citizens of
Uruk:

> The hunter opened [his mouth] to speak,
> > Saying to [his father]:
> "My father, there is [a] fellow who [has come from the hills],
> He is the might[iest in the land]; strength he has.

[Like the essence] of Anu, so mighty [his strength]!
[Ever] he ranges over the hills,
[Ever] with the beasts [he feeds on grass].
[Ever sets he] his feet at the watering-place.
[I am so frightened that] I dare not approach him!
[He filled in] the pits that I had dug,
[He tore up] my *traps* which I had [set],
The beasts and creatures of the steppe
    [He has made slip through my hands].
[He does not allow] me to engage in fieldcraft!"
                    —I, iii, 1-12.[73]

The remedy for Enkidu's interference with orderly hunting on the steppe is the same as the remedy for Gilgamesh's interference with orderly family life in Uruk. The two monsters, Gilgamesh and Enkidu, meet, grapple, and subdue one another in a perfectly reciprocal manner beside a doorpost of hewn wood in Uruk:

They met in the Market-of-the-Land.
Enkidu barred the gate
With his foot,
Not allowing Gilgamesh to enter.
They grappled each other,
Holding fast like bulls.
They shattered the doorpost,
As the wall shook.
        —II (Old Babylonian Version), vi, 11-18.[74]

Before Enkidu's arrival at Uruk from the wild steppe where he was born, Gilgamesh dreams of his coming. In the dream Enkidu is an axe destined to be Gilgamesh's inseparable tool and companion:

[Again Gilgamesh says] to his mother:
"[My mother, I] saw another dream:
[In ramparted Uruk] lay an axe;
    There was a gathering round it.
[Uruk-land] was standing about it,
[The land was gathered] round it,
[The populace jostled] towards it.
[I] placed it at thy feet.
[I loved it] and was drawn to it as though to a woman,
[Thou didst] make it vie with me."
                    —I, vi, 7-15.[75]

Thus Gilgamesh the tamer of monsters is also a hewer: he begins his career as ogre-fighter in this epic by associating himself with an axe. And appropriately, his first joint adventure with Enkidu after they have fought and tamed each other is an expedition to cut down trees for timber. Together they go to an enormous cedar forest on a mountain far from Uruk where, before felling the trees, they must first fight and defeat the forest's guardian daemon, Humbaba (Babylonian Huwawa). Before leaving Uruk on this hazardous mission, Gilgamesh and Enkidu had equipped themselves with axes:

> Mighty adzes they cast;
> Axes of three talents each they cast.
> —III (Old Babylonian Version), iv., 30-31.[76]

When Gilgamesh and Enkidu struggled with one another, their contest ended in a draw, and Gilgamesh accepted Enkidu as his companion and equal. But the ferocity and preterhuman qualities of Gilgamesh's next ogreish opponent, Humbaba, are more ample than were Enkidu's. This second step in the progression of Gilgamesh's contests with ogres is more dangerous, occurring as it does in the forest of live cedars, and cannot end in mutual accord as did the wrestling-match with Enkidu beside a single hewn post within the civilized precincts of the city.

Gilgamesh stopped Enkidu's violation of hunters' rights to game on the open steppe, and reciprocally Enkidu stopped Gilgamesh's violation of citizens' rights in Uruk. But although it was thus subdued, these two tamed ogres' transgressive nature still drove them to trespass in Humbaba's forest, which was a sacred precinct of the goddess Ishtar. After their long journey, the two friends reach the Cedar Forest where Humbaba is a kind of resident care-taker. The description of the Forest as they approach it in the Assyrian Version of the epic is short and fragmentary, but still better than James Frazer's rendering of the comparable scene in the Vale of Nemi:

> They stood still and gazed at the forest,
> They looked at the height of the cedars,
> They looked at the entrance to the forest.
> Where Humbaba was wont to walk was a path;
> Straight were the tracks and good was the going.
> They beheld the cedar mountain, abode of the gods,
>   Throne-seat of Irnini.
> From the face of the mountain

The cedar[77] raises aloft its luxuriance.
Good is its shape, full of delight.
                                —V, i, 1-8.[78]

Humbaba challenges them when they enter the forest and begin to
cut the great cedar:

[Gilgamesh] seized [the axe in (his) hand]
[. . .and] felled [the cedar].
[But when Huwawa] heard the *noise,*
[He] became angry: "Who has [come],
. . .
And has felled the cedar?"
                                —V (Hittite Recension), 8-12.[79]

Humbaba is a terrible yet purely defensive monster, who valor-
ously guards the Cedar Forest but is otherwise unaggressive. Gilgamesh
and Enkidu subdue him with the help of Gilgamesh's patron god Shamash. As god of the sun, Shamash was a 'high' god like Greek Zeus,
and could effect changes in the weather as could Zeus. Shamash im-
mobilizes Humbaba by causing winds to blow against him. Thoroughly
defeated, Humbaba entreats Gilgamesh to spare his life and to accept
him as a loyal servant. But Enkidu, who seems to be less generously
disposed than Gilgamesh, objects, and Humbaba is not permitted to
join the less monstrous Enkidu as an additional guardian of Uruk or
companion to Uruk's Lord Gilgamesh. Gilgamesh is reluctant to see
him killed, but in the end Humbaba is hewn down like one of his
own cedars and beheaded:

Thereupon Huwawa replied to Gilgamesh:
"Let me go, Gilgamesh; thou [wilt be] my [master],
And I shall be thy servant. And of [the trees]
Which I have grown, I shall [. . .]
. . .
. . . ."
But Enkidu [said] to [Gilgamesh]:
"To the word which Huwawa [has spoken]
H[ark] not [. . .]
Let not Huwawa [. . .]."
                                —V (Hittite Recension), 21-30.
[. . .] the head of Humba[ba *they* cut down. . .].
                                —Assyrian fragment, line 47.[80]

This scene of decapitation was familiar to at least one Assyrian seal-
cutter (Fig. 66).

Fig. 66. Cylinder seal of black serpentine.

Ishtar admired Gilgamesh's manliness after his exploit in the
Cedar Forest, though it was her forest and her guardian monster
which he and Enkidu had violated. She invited Gilgamesh to be her
lover, but he spurned her, and she sent the third monster of the story
against him. It was the Bull of Heaven, a mixture of animal and mineral substances, and temperamentally the opposite of the purely defensive ogre Humbaba. The Bull of Heaven is pure trespasser and ag-
gressor. Again Gilgamesh and Enkidu subdue the ogre, but this time
they kill it as quickly as they can, without the least hesitation or debate, because it is utterly useless as a protective agent to either men
or gods.

Each of the monsters in this epic is different, and each is disposed
of differently. The differences are arranged in two parallel progressions:

Kind	Disposition
Gilgamesh: God/Human	Lord of Erech and guardian of its human flock, destined to die in the distant future.
Enkidu: Human/Animal	Companion of Erech's lord and guardian of its animal flocks, destined to die in the near future.
Humbaba: Animal/Aerial Substance (see Old Baby-lonian Version III, iii, 18-20, and v, 16-17; Assyrian Version II, v, 3).	Inimical guardian of a distant, wild precinct, denied servitude under the Lord of Erech, dies presently at the hands of hesitant slayers.
Bull of Heaven: Animal/ Terrestrial Substance (Lapis)	Inimical invader of Erech's domes-tic vicinity, guardian of nothing, dies presently at the hands of urgently prompt slayers.

The impudent killing of Ishtar's two ogres Humbaba and the
Bull of Heaven, and Gilgamesh's insulting refusal to recompense Ishtar
for that loss by becoming her lover, lead directly to the death of Enkidu. Ishtar's father, Anu, exacts payment of Gilgamesh for killing
her creatures by decreeing that he must similarly give up his favorite
creature, Enkidu, to death:

And Anu said to Enlil:
"Because the Bull of Heaven they have slain, and Huwawa
They have slain, therefore" —said Anu— "the one of them
Who stripped the mountains of the cedar must die!"
But Enlil said: "Enkidu must die;

> Gilgamesh, however, shall not die!"
> > —VII (Hittite recension), 5-10.[81]

Gilgamesh recognizes in Enkidu's consequent death the basic problem of mortality, his own as well as that of others whom he loves as he loved Enkidu. The pain of bereavement and the fear that he must eventually suffer the same fate drive Gilgamesh to distraction and vagrancy:

> For Enkidu, his friend, Gilgamesh
> Weeps bitterly, as he ranges over the steppe:
> "When I die, shall I not be like Enkidu?
> Woe has entered my belly.
> Fearing death, I roam over the steppe."
> > —IX, i, 1-5.[82]

After aimless wandering and other degenerate behaviour, Shamash and the gradual condensation of renewed purpose in his own mind bring Gilgamesh to the outer limits of the world. First he comes to a mountain that is the junction of the world's vertical and horizontal axes:

> The name of the mountain is Mashu.
> When he arrived at the mountain range of Mashu,
> Which daily keeps watch over sunrise and sunset—
> Whose peaks reach to the vault of heaven
> (And) whose breasts reach to the nether world below—
> > —IX, ii, 1-5.[83]

He passes through this mountain along the path which the sun takes (his patron deity was the sun-god, Shamash). Many leagues of the way are in total darkness, but then he emerges into a brightly lit, fabulous grove of precious stones which grow and bear fruit like plants (a conflation of vegetable and mineral). Beyond this place he finally arrives on the seashore at the edge of the world, where he meets the ferry-boatman named Urshanabi in the Assyrian Version (Sursunabu in Babylonian), who is the sole means of communication with Gilgamesh's immortal ancestor, Ut(a)napishtim. Utnapishtim, like Hebrew Noah in Biblical legend, was the only survivor of the Great Flood in Mesopotamian legend. By special dispensation of the gods, Utanapishtim alone of all men enjoys immortality, but as a condition of that gift he resides with his wife beyond the Waters of Death in a place of utter seclusion from all other men. Instructed by the boatman Urshanabi, Gilgamesh takes up his ax once again, cuts, and finishes punting-poles wherewith to cross the Waters of Death to Utnapishtim. There, in conversation with his ancient ancestor, Gilgamesh is at last reconciled with the bitter fact of his own mortality which the great gods had forced him to recognize in consequence of his various acts of dishonour to Ishtar beginning in the Cedar Forest.

From the doorpost beside which the two heroes fought in Uruk through the Cedar Forest to the forest hewn for punting-poles, the progression of trees in the Epic of Gilgamesh is threefold. The sole import of the doorpost at the Market-of-the-Land in Uruk is that of hewn wood. As they approach it, Gilgamesh and Enkidu are opposed both in their natures and in their intentions. The élite urbanite Gilgamesh, a mélange of man and divinity dedicated to the defense of Uruk, confronts the rude ruralite Enkidu, a blend of man and animal bent upon a barbarous invasion of the city. But like Victor Turner's Ndembu at the *mukula* tree, the two Akkadian heroes find the means to reconcile their differences and be united beside the hewn doorpost. The remaining two steps in Gilgamesh's progression of trees are both whole forests, each partially green and partly hewn. The Cedar Forest however derives its significance from its green state, while the nameless woods where Gilgamesh cuts the punting-poles for the last stage of his quest have again the primary sense of hewn timber. Contumacious and preterhumanly assisted in the first forest, Gilgamesh is a pitiable figure purged of arrogance in the second, where he has no powers left to him except those same skills and resolution in himself which any ordinary man can summon to help him surmount trouble. Ishtar and Shamash both seem virtually to conspire in Gilgamesh's success in the Cedar Forest, the one permitting and the other aiding in his cutting down Humbaba and the trees. That verdant forest also unites Gilgamesh and Enkidu in their first joint enterprise. Finally even Humbaba begs to join in common cause with Gilgamesh. But the appearance of united purpose among gods, men, and brutes in the episode of the evergreen Cedar Forest is deceptive. Humbaba is not allowed to serve Lord Gilgamesh as he offered to do, nor will Gilgamesh serve Ishtar. Thenceforth the rift between men and gods that began with Gilgamesh's hewing of the cedar grows steadily wider until, through his hewing and use of the punting-poles, he finally reaches wits' end in the land of Utanapishtim and is reconciled to the laws of recompense and reciprocity laid down by the gods.

Gilgamesh enters the wood to cut poles at a time when all the characters in the tale seem to be irremediably at odds. Everyone whom he meets during his great wandering after the death of Enkidu (itself a form of social division) is amazed at his unkempt appearance and his eccentric purpose in being where he is, so far removed from his home in Uruk. Ultimately Utnapishtim too disapproves Gilgamesh's coming to him as not worth the labour or the risk. Even Gilgamesh's patron god Shamash has counselled him to change his ways, and having counselled, left Gilgamesh to his doom. But out of this divided and discordant situation Gilgamesh achieves through the agency of the punting-poles a reunion with his own kind and a new, stable harmony in his relations with both men and gods. Crossing the Waters of Death by means of those poles to visit Utnapishtim, he consults the eldest of all men, the one man in the world whose being unites in itself the whole accumulation of human wisdom extending even to the era before the Great Flood. From this oracle, who unifies and reconciles in himself all of human history, Gilgamesh learns to unite and to be reconciled to the diversity of influences that shape his own experience.

So the green cedars of Humbaba's forest seemed to promise unity and cohesion for Gilgamesh's world, but in the end they produced instead discord and divisions. Inversely, the sadder, tamer, and less glorious wood where he went at Urshanabi's behest to make punting poles seemed to betoken Gilgamesh's irrational resolve to separate himself altogether and perhaps forever from the society of other men by the crazy voyage to Utnapishtim. But out of that wood and the voyage which it enabled him to make came not only Gilgamesh's reconciliation with his own mortal nature, but also the knowledge that for any man nothing else is possible. Gilgamesh carries that invaluable knowledge home to record on a stone stela for the people of Uruk and their descendants ever after, thus uniting all generations of men through all time from Utnapishtim downward in the certain knowledge of the limits of human capability. This accomplished, Gilgamesh returns to his proper place in Uruk a thoroughly subdued, tamed man, able contentedly to resume both service to the gods and life among his own kind, accepting at last the law of reciprocity, the give and take essential to civilization.

Gilgamesh is, moreover, uniquely equipped by his personal adventure in search of the immortality which he could not achieve to rule

—or to maintain unity among—other, less experienced men: the citizen-ry of Uruk. So this ancient tale of two woods has also its political implications. Gilgamesh has learned not only what he must know to be content with his own circumstances, but also what he must know to govern, which is to say, to help other men toward contentment with their circumstances. The lesson of his experience beyond the Waters of Death—the lesson of the punting-poles—pertains therefore to the political life of the state as well as to the regimen of personal ambition in private life. Man is mortal; nothing which he possesses is absolutely his inalienable property, because he is insecure even in his own life, the necessary premise of all other property-rights. Where in nature security of possession is so tenuous, there must compensator-ily be in civilization fair rules of exchange justly enforced to protect every kind of property, even life itself. Lord Gilgamesh as ruler of Uruk accordingly had the bounden duty to obey and to enforce fair rules of exchange and reciprocity in all matters under his jurisdiction. *Memento mori* was thus the crux not only of Gilgamesh's personal rehabilitation and reunification with the people of Uruk after the death of Enkidu, but also of his rehabilitation as governor of his people. The same slogan, *memento, homo, quia pulvis es et in pul-verem reverteris*, would equally well fit any of Gilgamesh's myriad cosmotactic counterparts in oral fable from Hebrew Adam to Lenje Mandu, for to a man all these foresters and ogre-tamers learn the law of exchange, price, and payment through an actual or certainly im-pending experience of death.

The written preservation and archaeological recovery of the Epic of Gilgamesh were extraordinary pieces of good luck. That tale proves what Mesopotamian glyptic by itself could never prove, rich though it is: that the pattern of the Two Trees' story was the same in Meso-potamia three or four millennia ago as it is in modern oral fable. And as though that good luck were not enough, there is extant also a multiform of the story, a Sumerian tale wherein a stream of water separated the green tree growing in the wild from its hewable domes-tic opposite. Again the preternaturally alloyed man Gilgamesh met ogres at the tree when the time came to hew its wood, and subdued them, in this way embroiling himself once more in questions of prop-erty and possession: *Shortly after the creation of the universe, a tree growing on the bank of the Euphrates was uprooted by the south wind. Inanna (Ishtar) took the floating trunk and planted it in her garden in Uruk. She intended to use it, in due time, as timber for her bed and chair. When several hostile beings interfered with Inanna's plan, Gilgamesh came to her rescue. In gratitude, Inanna made from the base of the tree a* pukku, *probably a magic Drum, and from the crown a* mikkū, *apparently a Drumstick of magic potency similar to the Drum, and gave them both to Gilgamesh. One day both these precious objects fell into the nether world. Gilgamesh sought to retrieve them but could not. Lamenting his loss, he cried "O my* pukku, *O my* mikkū. *"*[84]

THE PREHISTORY OF THE TWO TREES

When Arthur Evans wrote seventy years ago about glyptic art and other forms of ritual iconography of the Aegean region in the Bronze Age, he wove an intricate web of speculation concerning the connections between that tradition and other neighboring traditions in Mesopotamia, Asia Minor, Canaan, and Egypt. He tried to trace the influence of those traditions upon the conventional portrayal of 'sacred' trees and posts in the Aegean region. Whether he was right or wrong about the sources of influence on Aegean iconography, he did a lasting and little-known service in demonstrating that the dyadic system of tree-motifs as found in modern oral fable was known throughout the eastern Mediterranean and the Near East from the earliest historic and even prehistoric times.

Another, more recent investigator of prehistoric arboreal lore has in a similar manner unintentionally proven the existence of a similar dyadic system in early Indo-European understanding of trees. Studying the cognate names for various species of trees in Indo-European languages, the historical linguist Paul Friedrich matched those names with botanical and palaeobotanical facts about the plants which they designate in a monograph entitled *Proto-Indo-European Trees.*[85] The bare onomastic and natural facts, together with some information about the utility of diverse trees in ancient material culture, are all the data which Friedrich chose to use in his investigation. He therefore worked with an even more attenuated body of knowledge than did Arthur Evans or Victor Turner, who could at least adduce information about ritual to help them explain the prominence of the two trees in Bronze-Age Aegean or modern Ndembu culture. Since little has yet been firmly established about the content of either Proto-Indo-European ritual or story-telling, Friedrich cannot be blamed for caution in surmising much about those aspects of early Indo-European culture. But partly because he did limit his inquiry to linguistic, natural, and economic facts, he unknowingly detected certain probable reasons in the realms of nature and economy for the persistent discrimination between standing green wood and hewn wood in the pattern of oral fable and in contingent rituals.

Friedrich found that prehistoric Indo-Europeans shared knowledge and use of eighteen broad types of trees. Of these, ten provided food for men, for meat-yielding domestic animals, and for game. The ten types of food-tree were apple, cherry, beech, oak, hazel, hornbeam, elm, ash, linden, and aspen/poplar. The wood of nine kinds of tree was used in construction and to make various instruments: oak, ash, yew, elm, juniper/cedar, willow, conifers, aspen, and linden. The kind of tree with the highest utility-quotient, most useful of all both as a source of food for men and animals and as a source of timber for furniture, wooden weaponry, and terrestrial and naval architecture, was the oak, which goes far to explain its supremacy in Indo-European religion as the tree of 'high' gods, the supreme male deities of the various Indo-European peoples: Greek Zeus, Latin Jupiter, Germanic Thor, Balto-Slavic Perkunas/Perun, etc. The oak's supremacy as a useful tree was quite logically translatable into association with the supreme divine persons in cult and religion. To this extent the cognate lexica of Indo-European languages give evidence that prehistoric Indo-European peoples regularly identified certain trees with certain very potent preternatural persons. At least that much of the motival cluster around trees in oral narrative was surely known at an early date in Indo-European prehistory. It is very probable, moreover, that the green food-tree and the hewn wood were systematically opposed to each other too, although no narrative texts have come down in writing from that time to prove or disprove any such assumption. But the basis in nature for that distinction was certainly as firm for Indo-Europeans as it could have been in Mesopotamia or in the Aegean region. All ten of the major types of food-trees known among prehistoric Indo-Europeans were deciduous. Like the preternatural hosts at food-trees in fable, the real food-trees of the Indo-Europeans would therefore ordinarily have fed their Indo-European clients in late summer and autumn with an abundance of fruits and nuts such that men might well have considered themselves blest like dwellers in paradise at that time of year. But deciduous food-trees would have behaved much like the ogres of oral fable: out of season or in a bad year, such trees withheld their potential largesse in a manner that could only be interpreted as malevolent meanness or outright enmity were the trees persons capable of such feelings and motives. This is not to suggest that any sane Indo-European ever actually thought trees were persons. But oral fable throughout the modern world supplies such trees with ogreish attendants who might well have borne the blame for such inhospitable stinting in prehistoric Indo-European fable too.

Thus real Indo-European peoples in prehistory may indeed have lived in real circumstances where the cyclical ebb and flow of arboreal generosity in and out of fruiting-season was comparable to the mercurial relationship between men and ogres who meet at wild food-trees in oral fable. In such circumstances, the threat of famine out of season would have required just such vigorous defensive measures as the hewers and ogre-tamers of fable are wont to take. The same trees that sustained human and animal life by their bearing of fruit in season threatened inanition and death by refusing to yield out of season. That threat had to be overcome, and paradoxically, the same trees that posed the threat could be used to overcome it despite their seasonal refusal to bear fruit. Prehistoric men's first tools and weapons were neither stone nor metal, but wooden, and throughout the world the majority of ordinary hand-tools and weapons continue to be hafted with wood down to the present day. From prehistoric digging-stick to modern ship's timber, men's first line of economic defense against the inconstancy of natural increase has been wooden. While they are dependent for sustenance upon green trees growing in the wild, men are no better than animals, subject to and victims of every caprice of the invisible forces that govern natural increase. But when deep in prehistory men (whether human or hominid) first hewed wood to cultural purpose, they quite literally took their destiny into their own hands, and began the long process of reversing the relationship between themselves and the fickle, figurative ogres of undomesticated nature who sometimes let them eat, and other times ate them. Armed thenceforth with hewn wood in many multiforms, men would rule nature, by turns nourishing and victimizing it at their pleasure, as earlier it had alternately nourished and victimized them. This turnabout must have brought with it, however, new and unexpected difficulties, for with their new-found rule over nature men also inherited from nature the subtle and complex problem of apportioning property-rights and defining possession—the same problem which the hewers and ogre-tamers of fable still struggle with daily and hourly in oral story-telling all around the world. If the pattern of the Two Trees' story in oral fable does not indeed date from the very beginning of these developments in men's material and political culture, then at least it is a highly exact logical encapsulation of those developments that continues even now to communicate both the tangible facts and the philosophical essence of men's escape from feral bestiality into a human condition far better than any modern, literary piece of scientific palaeontological or palaeoanthropological exposition could possibly do.

The arboreal beginnings of the Hominidae are well known; the green, food-yielding tree in the wild was truly the mainstay of life for man's earliest evolutionary ancestors. As a whole, mankind has been more intensely intimate with trees longer than with any other kind of plant or animal, with the possible exception of certain insect parasites such as lice and fleas. Yet the history of the Hominidae's intimacy with trees has been one of slow but steady divorce. The very first step which the first hominids took toward becoming men was to free themselves from total dependence on an ambience of green trees. The most immediate benefits of that liberation accrued, moreover, in regard to eating. In the words of a notable prehistorian, Grahame Clark:

> It would seem that, whereas the great apes were adapted to life in the forest and so specialized in a brachiating mode of locomotion (that is, one in which they still made considerable use of their arms) the hominids developed in more open country and early adopted an erect, bipedal carriage.
>
> From an evolutionary point of view the most significant step in the emergence of the hominids seems to have been the assumption of an erect posture. It was this which released the hands from locomotion, making them available for tool-making and the securing and preparation of food. . . .[86]

Like the ogre-tamers and hewers in oral fable, even so-called Australopithecine men must have been to some degree caught up in the problem of choosing when to identify themselves and the satisfaction of their wants with green trees, and when to exploit the products of broken wood and the various activities away from wild trees which tools and weapons fashioned from dry wood made possible. As hominid skill in using dry wood increased to include making shelters and refuges, storage, heating, cookery, and transportation, so must the subtleties of dependence and independence in early men's economic relations with natural trees also have increased.

The two trees in their opposite characters have thus been prominent economic facts of hominid and human experience from the very onset of hominid evolution. They have furthermore endured as such down to the recent past or present of very many peoples in both the Old and New World. The relatively recent Indo-Europeans were surely less dependent on trees for sustenance and equipment than were Australopithecines or other very early hominids, but they too evidently lived in a material culture where the balance between a commensal relationship with green trees and exploitation of dry ones still mattered, if only in the apportionment of their time to food-gathering and herd-tending on the one hand, or to manufacturing or building from wood on the other. The history of men's intimacy with trees has been one of progressive divorce, but it has been a very prolonged divorce, and its end is nowhere in view.

Unfortunately it is not possible at present to determine from natural history when the two trees together with the other typical elements of the Two Trees' story-pattern were first condensed into oral narrative. That was an event in cultural, not natural history. But the story of the Two Trees has persisted with equal tenacity in cultures geographically far separated from one another where the kinds and degrees of economic use of trees are radically different. It therefore appears that the separation of the races of men on different continents is younger than the story of the Two Trees, and consequently younger also than oral fable. I do not know of any reason why *prima facie* the Two Trees' story should not be considered of the same age as oral fable itself, which is by definition exactly as old as humanity. But while it is inherently reasonable to argue that humanity and oral fable are conterminous, neither the study of prehistory nor the study of oral narrative has yet advanced far enough to permit dating the inception of any particular pattern in oral fable. Much in nature and in archaeologically attested prehistoric human behaviour suggests the motifs and patterns of fable, but we do not yet know when those suggestions first stimulated men to fabulous narration. The global range of some motifs and patterns like the story of the

Two Trees signifies that oral fable was already a strong habit in the Palaeolithic Age, but a more exact dating of fable's origin and a chronology of motival and pattern inventions must await further advances in both the prehistorical and oral literary fields.

One does not know, for example, where or when between Australopithecine and Proto-Indo–European times the hewing of wood as a narrative motif took on social significance. But certainly it has that generic significance in the pattern of the Two Trees' story in sharp contrast to the anti-social, segregational significance of the green tree. I have already remarked the social reunions accomplished through hewn wood in African fable and in *Beowulf.* The Ark, Tabernacle, and Altar which biblical Moses caused to be wrought from Acacia wood at the Lord's direction (Exodus 25-27) had a comparable effect in uniting Israel under the leadership of Moses and Aaron, and through them, under the guidance of the Lord himself in the great contract of Hebrew religion. The ritual reflexes of the hewn tree follow suit: the Mesopotamian temple with the pillar or post before it was preeminently a place of reunion where gods, men, and even domestic animals periodically met together; the pillar of the Lion's Gate at Mycenae demarcated the physical premises of human comity; Ndembu hunters joined together in cult at the sign of the *mukula* tree; and so forth.

VLADIMIR PROPP'S TREE UPON THE GRAVE

Although Arthur Evans knew the two trees principally in multi-forms from the Aegean Bronze Age, he had one first-hand ritual experience of his own with one of them, the green tree of segregation and severance. He like many other learned men of the nineteenth century believed that ancient rites had survived over prodigious lengths of time in the customs of uneducated rural populations in Europe. According to this 'doctrine of survivals' it was reasonable to suppose, and Evans did suppose, that modern peoples within the geographic sphere of ancient Aegean culture would have inherited and continued to practice rites like those portrayed in Aegean art of the Bronze Age. Being an enthusiastic traveller and life-long amateur of the modern Balkans, Evans missed no opportunity to observe and even participate in contemporary rituals in districts contiguous to his archaeological

research. At Tečino selo in Yugoslav Macedonia he helped to celebrate
a modern Moslem ritual at a gravesite:

> . . .A personal experience may thus supply a more living picture
> of the actualities of this primitive ritual than can be gained from
> the discreet references of our biblical sources or the silent evi-
> dence of engraved signets and ruined shrines.
>
> For the better understanding of the ritual employed, I went
> through the whole ceremony myself. . . .
>
> The worshipper who would conform to the full ritual, now
> fills a keg of water from a spring that rises near the shrine. . .
> and makes his way through a thorny grove up a neighbouring
> knoll, on which is a wooden enclosure surrounding a Moham-
> medan Saint's Grave or Tekke. Over the headstone of this grows
> a thorn-tree hung with rags of divers colours, attached to it. . .
> by sick persons who had made a pilgrimage to the tomb. . . .
>
> In the centre of the grave was a hole, into which the water
> from the holy spring was poured, and mixed with the holy
> earth. Of this the votary drinks three times, and he must thrice
> anoint his forehead with it. . . .[87]

Evans thought that he had witnessed in this modern ritual scene the
same scene intended by ancient Aegean artists in their depiction of
rites beside green trees.

Evans' analogy was generically right, but nominally wrong: none
of the Bronze-Age portrayals show a green tree bedecked with rags
or on a grave. Nor was there any other certainly verifiable motif
beside the green tree itself and the paling around it to warrant the
supposition of any direct line of ritual continuity linking the tree at
a modern Moslem saint's grave with the green trees in ancient Aegean
iconography. The 'doctrine of survivals' as applied to ritual or religion
was no more demonstrable in this instance than in the many other
equally uncertain cases cited by so many other scholars in the nineteenth century.

Had Arthur Evans known more about oral fable in the regions
where he carried on his archaeological research, or anywhere else in
Europe or the Near East for that matter, he would surely not have
been so quick to think that a tree growing at a modern grave necessarily owed its identity as an object of ritual to such a remote historical origin. But Evans knew next to nothing about fable, and he shared
to a high degree the peculiar single-minded devotion to historical

explanations that so typified serious nineteenth-century English intellectuals and so often concealed from them the sources and utility of
necessary fictions such as those in oral fable and cult. Partly because
of the effect of the Pauline Doctrine, and, because it is not a body of
historically exact facts, as a corollary of that Doctrine oral fable in
all its forms was for the most part debarred from the canon of dig-
nified knowledge in the England of Evans' time, and so it largely
remains down to the present. A man like Arthur Evans would have
been ashamed to display very much acquaintance with the substance
of oral narrative tradition even had he been able to so so, which he
was not.

The opinion that oral fable is not worthy of serious research because it is 'untruthful' would not matter were it confined to Britain.
But through the writings of such influential men as James Frazer,
British contempt for fictions as subjects of learning (except in law)
has spread everywhere, even into scholarly circles otherwise averse
to British influence. A case in point is the work of the eminent Soviet
folklorist and scholar of folk-tale and epic, Vladimir Jakovlevič Propp.

Propp knew all those things about green trees on gravesites in
modern European fable which Arthur Evans should have known. He
published what he knew about that subject in 1934 in one of his
three best-known writings on folk-tale, an article entitled "Volšebnoe
derevo na mogile" (The Magical Tree on the Grave).[88] He knew that
the sepulchral kind of green tree was a stock motif in the Cinderella
story, one of Europe's most common tales: *An orphaned maiden (or
youth) is mistreated by step-relatives. A tree grows from the grave
of her (his) parent(s) or an animal mascot. The tree provides means
of distinguishing the orphan from its step-relatives, and helps the
abused step-child to marry into another family.*[89]

Another multiform of the sepulchral green tree was less common
in European oral tradition, but still a frequent motif. It occurred in a
type of story about murder and revenge very similar to Mumba's tale
"Let the Big Drum Roll" from the Lenje in Central Africa: *a youth
is murdered and the corpse or dismembered parts of the corpse are
buried by the murderer(s). Out of a tree growing at the place of burial a tattling bird flies up or a flute is hewn, which sings a song of
vengeful accusation until the murderer is slain and the guiltless members of the murdered youth's family are reunited.*[90] Had Arthur Evans

known these details of modern European fable so familiar to present-
day scholars of folk-tale, he might have recognized in the sepulchral
green thorn-tree at Tečino selo the same tree that succoured and
avenged the weak and outcast in oral tales being told all over Europe
and the Near East even as he performed the rites of an obscure Moslem cult in a by-way of Yugoslav Macedonia. No doubt it brought a
tingle to Evans' spine to think that a 'primitive ritual' among the
colourful modern people of the Balkan hinterland at the turn of the
twentieth century had descended from an Aegean ritual prototype
of three millennia ago. That same excitement is still a major source
of inspiration to many an Old World archaeologist and ethnographer.
But in truth Evans' Macedonian thorn-tree with its sepulchral and
succouring concomitants in rites to be performed by the poor, the
sick, and the injured had infinitely more corroboration in contemporary Mediterranean fable about poor, anonymous orphans and murder-
victims than in the scant reliques of state religion surviving on the
monumental architecture, elegant ceramics, and costly jewelry of
wealthy men and women who lived in the great commercial centers
and occupied the opulent tombs of rich and mighty Aegean states
in the Bronze Age.

But if Evans was nominally wrong in his identification of the
green tree in a Macedonian cult, he was nevertheless right in supposing that that tree was generically akin to the green tree in "the silent
evidence of engraved signets and ruined shrines" from the ancient
Aegean. Like it, the tree on the grave in modern oral fable is a separa-
tor, and stands in a place where giving and taking need not be reciprocal. Marking the grave of the dead, the green tree is set apart from the
habitations of the living, and so denotes the segregation of the dead
from the living. It is, moreover, the particular resort of outcasts; the
relatives and friends of orphans and murder-victims shun it, nor will
the green tree respond to them if they do happen to approach it. Its
help lies only to the injured or disabled individual whose human society will not or cannot help him. Only when this tree is hewn and the
hewn portion is carried away, as in the fashioning of a flute (or a
Cross) from its wood, will it act upon a group of persons. In that
case it first separates the wicked from the righteous (or the damned
from the redeemed), and then reunites the righteous with their own
kind, as may be expected of any hewn wood.

Evans' ritual thorn-tree had the same segregational significance,
even down to such minute votive detail as the bits of rag torn away

from whole cloth and stuck individually on the spines of the tree.
This tree too marked the separation of the dead from the living,
standing apart from the dwellings of the living and segregated from
the usual walks of men by a thorny copse. As Arthur Evans himself
witnessed, the injured and disabled resorted to it individually for help
which their living kin and friends could not or would not give them.
Evans' experience of the Macedonian ritual did not include any witness of the tree being hewn, and he did not on this occasion observe
any other true equivalent of the hewn wood in fable. Perhaps there
was some such hewn concomitant of his green thorn-tree which he
did not see ritually manipulated; or perhaps not. But had there been,
knowledge of modern oral fable such as Propp's would not have bene-
fited him as Propp's knowledge of green trees might have, because
Propp knew less about the pairing of green and hewn wood in story-
patterning than did Evans. In fact, he knew nothing of it at all, and
the reason for his ignorance was mainly the effect upon him of scholars like Arthur Evans and James Frazer, who sedulously pursued the
most obscure details of heathen ritual to the farthest corners of the
earth while ignoring the most obvious facts of oral narrative tradition
that pressed upon them begging for recognition at every step they
took along their chosen way to the distant circus-entertainments of
pagan and pre-Christian religion.

Vladimir Propp's earliest important monograph on folk-tale was
Morfologija skazki (The Morphology of Folk-Tale), published in Leningrad in 1928. It was a reaction against the prevalent emphasis on nominal motifs in earlier European scholarship on folk-tale. Propp argued
that previous attempts to classify and interpret the tales in modern
European oral tradition according to their typical or characteristic
nominal motifs were misguided. He did, however, accept the old notion that the units of oral tradition were whole tales exactly as told
to the various collectors whose records of oral story Propp had to
rely upon (since he was not himself a collector). As other students of
folk-tale both before and after him usually have done, Propp too
noticed that the plots of many nominally different tales are much
alike. He tried in *Morfologija skazki* to describe that likeness in one
hundred Russian märchen from the secondary collection of an earlier
Russian folklorist and conflator, Aleksandr Nikolaevič Afanas'ev (1826-
1871). It was not an entirely happy choice of material, since both
the texts and the tales in Afanas'ev's publication were 'idealized,' i.e.,
considerably altered both verbally and substantively from the reality

of oral narrative tradition in Russia. But like the Grimms' earlier collection in Germany, Afanas'ev's in Russia (a conscious emulation of its German precursor) was a familiar part of civil culture in the twentieth century, and Propp could be confident that those who read his Russian monograph would be able to find in print and read the material on which it was based.

Propp sought to resolve all one hundred of his chosen Russian märchen into a single plot. He went about this by first asserting that the *personae fabulae* in numerous tales can be reduced to a few character-types. Then he reduced the events in tales to thirty-one functions of character-types, and finally he said that the various beasts, plants, and inanimate objects of story should be reduced to a few categories of instruments and means whereby folk-tale characters discharge their prescribed functions.

The results of this reductive analysis were banal. Shorn of its residual Russian peculiarities, the common plot which Propp was able to extract from his sample of Afanas'ev's Russian tales amounted in sum to the statement: All heroes in folk-tale have trouble; someone helps them; they exert themselves to vanquish other characters and/or to surmount various obstacles which represent their troubles; thus they gain happiness and achieve tranquillity. Such an undiscriminating truism flatly contradicted the ingenious conceptual variegation of real folk-tales. It explained none of the things in tales that needed explanation, things which other scholars of folk-tale before Propp had been trying for generations to explain about oral story-telling: why men tell tales, why their tales are fabulous, and why they are multiform. Indeed, Propp had only deepened those long-standing mysteries by his anticlimactic results. For when he had done his work, he had left himself no way to account for the variety of multiforms in which characters, functions, and objects actually occurred in tales—the variety that gave rise to a hundred Russian tales all radically different in detail and yet similar in plot. He had knowingly and intentionally eliminated from consideration all motival multiforms, the only possible avenue to an explanation of motival multiformity. In doing that, he had incidentally also eradicated every trace of fabulosity—the preternaturally sundered and rejoined pieces of reality—from his material. The effect was to make the fabulosity of oral fable appear even more irrational and senseless after than it had seemed before Propp's formalist exercise. And that result was truly a disaster for folk-tale scholarship, because fabulosity—the lack of correspondence between tangible reality and the stories in oral tradition—was the very thing that militated most against admission of oral narrative into the charmed circle of 'legitimate' and 'worthwhile' subjects of learning in the historiographically oriented scholarship of western Europe and its cultural satellites.

Robbed in this manner of its two most distinctive traits—its multiformity and its fabulosity—oral fable in Vladimir Propp's hands in 1928 ceased to be oral fable and became something else instead. The terms of his plot-analysis betray the identity of that something else. Propp saw nothing in folk-tale that others before him had not previously seen in cult. The terms of his narrative analysis did not derive from narrative itself (as it pretended to do), but rather from religious studies and religious terminology of the same kind as James Frazer and Arthur Evans and other men like them had developed for use in their several 'respectable' branches of learning: anthropology, archaeology, history, literature, psychology, sociology, etc. Scholars of all these academic subjects had at least found ways of coming to grips intellectually with religious phenomena if not oral fable, and clearly Propp's ambition was somehow to assimilate the unacceptable 'nonsense' of traditional oral story-telling into acceptable, polite learning by assimilating it to religion. Accordingly Propp cast his parsing of narrative morphology in ritual categories and ritual terms. The specifically Christian reason for Saint Paul's elevation of ritual and abomination of fable had perished from Russian academic life with the passing of the Romanoffs and the Orthodox Russian Empire, but the old Pauline contempt for story as such lived on in Propp's mind as vigorously as ever it had in any Church Father.

So Propp's folktale heroes in *Morfologija skazki* moved in a world of taboos, victims, magic spells and entrancements, occult instructions, ritual paraphernalia, ritual contests, ritual markings, persecutions, rites of recognition, epiphanies, transfigurations, and all the other physical and conceptual trappings of religious ritual. For Vladimir Propp, folktale was not more nor less than it had been for James Frazer: the scenario for performance of rites. Yet Propp did not attempt in *Morfologija skazki* (nor in any of his later writings) to explain how it happened that no rite had ever been observed anywhere in the world which contained more than a scant few of the many motifs in any of his hundred Russian folktales. He made folktale a scenario for ritual, but curiously he never discovered any rite that followed more than an occasional random passage in the scenario. Worse, he seems never to have so much as noticed, not to say reflected upon, that discrepancy.

Nominal motifs had been the focus of attention among the European scholars who gave their attention to folk-tale before Propp. But Propp discarded motifs as the fundamental units of oral narrative tradition and, fleeing from one extreme to another, put whole stories in their place. Although traditional performers of oral narrative mistakenly think that they have a certain repertory of different tales, actually they all tell the same story all the time according to Propp's findings in 1928. What is always the same without change cannot, of course, hold any clues about its own history, and since Propp's analysis yielded no evidence that the basic plot of folktale had ever changed, nothing useful could be expected to come from historical study of folk-tale. Historical studies of ritual might help to illumine the origins of folk-tale, but folk-tale as Propp defined it could have no history of its own. It was truly an aberration and a *cul-de-sac* in man's intellectual evolution, just as James Frazer had said it was; oral stories were nought but primitive chop-logic and the philosophical gibberish of mentally incompetent savages. From an initial position of challenge to the narrow rationalists and historicists of European scholarship, Propp had in a few bold moves placed himself in an opposite attitude of abject capitulation to the worst enemies of oral narrative studies.

If folk-tale was what Propp said it was, then no one need ever bother about acquainting himself with much of it. All stories were essentially the same anyway, and nothing could be gained by cluttering the mind with an excessive number of variants and multiforms. Propp recognized that admonition in the results of his own work, and obeyed it. He was never widely read in oral tradition. What he knew and wrote about in later years as in 1928 was confined principally to the established literary canon of Russian folk-tale and epic, together with some other material that came under his hand to edit, and some well-known western European collections of tales such as that of the brothers Grimm. But comparative study of folk-tale would have been anomalous in a man of Propp's views.

Rites were another matter. While Propp stayed within close boundaries in his acquaintance with story, he energetically followed James

Frazer's advice that man's history as a ritual animal had, unlike his
history as a knower and teller of fable, led civilized mankind out of
the moral and political morass of savagery to the orderly bliss of good
government and ethical religion. The opinion was quintessentially
British, but it found a vigorous exponent in Soviet Leningrad. In
keeping with it, even a Soviet folklorist should know all he could
learn about ritual and cult, even the rites and cults of peoples unrelated to Russia or to Europe. So Propp's next important work after
Morfologija skazki was the article "Volšebnoe derevo na mogile,"[88]
where he broke with the precedent of his own earlier formalistic work
and adopted instead the historicizing and religiously oriented precedent
of James Frazer's work in *The Golden Bough*. In this way he returned
to the nominal motifs which he had so decisively discarded from his
previous analysis of folk-tale, and began to review them one by one
as historical, ritual antecedents of tales. His motto now was Frazer's
old dictum about

> . . .that large class of myths which are made up to explain the
> origin of a religious ritual and have no other foundation than
> the resemblance, real or imaginary, which may be traced between
> it and some foreign ritual.

The years that followed publication of "Volšebnoe derevo na mogile"
in 1934 were the most difficult period of Russian history in three
centuries, and one can only guess at the pressures that bore upon
Propp as upon other Russian urbanites and intellectuals during those
years. But he did not waver in his Frazerian mission to find the ritual
causes of folktale motifs no matter how intense official disfavor toward
any kind of serious religious studies might be, and in 1946 he published another, longer monograph entitled *Istoričeskie korni volšebnoj
skazki* (The Historical Roots of Märchen).[91] It was an enlargement of
the research on ritual and cultic counterparts of folk-tale which he
had begun with the article in 1934, informed by the same axiom that
ritual practices were somehow the antecedents of tales (he did not say
how).

Propp's next original book was on another form of oral narrative
tradition, Russian oral epos. His treatment of it was even more prosa-
ically rationalistic than his writings on folk-tale had been. Oral epic
poetry to him was folk-history, and a scholar's service was to refine
true historical knowledge from the unreasonable mixture of truth and
fantasy in it. Again Frazer and Propp were of one mind: historical
truth was precious stuff, but fantasy was only worthless dross. Thus

the book *Russkij geroičeskij èpos* (Russian Heroic Epos)[92] was an exercise in refining historical verity from the impure ore of the kind of Russian oral fable that was composed in verse. Finally Propp left the field of narrative studies altogether and gave his undivided attention to investigations of ritual, cult, and customs entirely apart from fable. The book that resulted, *Russkie agrarnye prazdniki* (Russian Agrarian Festivals), was surely the best of Propp's several monographs. It was a logical conclusion to the intellectual development that had begun in him more than thirty years before. It was also a crowning achievement in research on ritual in modern Europe, for not many men in this century have understood the continuum of European cultic and ritual traditions as well as did Vladimir Propp. He also offered the most interesting new thoughts about folktale that have appeared in this century. But Propp no less than other men was a product of his own era, and in Propp's era men of learning gave precedence to religion and ritual, eschewing the substantive perplexities of oral narrative with an almost frightened avoidance. Cult and ritual were more tangible, and did not so much demand the gift of tongues. Ritual was sometimes nonsensical—it exploited narrative imagery and narrative tropes of action—but the adepts of heathen cult who performed strange rituals could invariably give a foreign observer some sensible explanation of his rites if he wanted to do so, and a thoughtful observer could discern other unarticulated causes as well, as did Victor Turner in Africa.

In contrast, traditions of oral narration are not so easily accountable. The native's reason for knowing and telling a tale is scarcely ever so immediately utilitarian as his reason for a rite. And the substantive complexity of even simple tales is exponentially greater and more elusive than anything men do physically, whether it be for material gain or in performance of rite. So despite his erudition in cultic and ritual matters, Vladimir Propp could not have given Arthur Evans any help in understanding the necessary relationship between the green and hewn trees. Nor does he give us any. In his preoccupation with ritual, he had not studied oral fable deeply enough for that. Both of those generic motifs existed plentifully in the ancient and modern cults and rites which Arthur Evans and Vladimir Propp both knew. But the tie that bound the two trees together and kept them together during at least four millennia in Europe and the Near East was not religious or ritual. It was narrative, or more exactly, it was the two trees' traditional association with one another in a pattern of oral fable—a cluster of generic motifs indissolubly adhering to each other by virtue of countless oral story-tellers' timeless and immutable narrative habit. Propp knew tales, he knew nominal motifs, and he knew of variations in both of those categories, but he did not understand the patterns of oral fable. Less than whole performances, and larger than single motifs, they are the real entities of narrative tradition, because they are what a traditional oral story-teller must know to make any tale, long or short, simple or complex, in prose or in verse. Cults and rituals that occasionally draw from the fund of motifs in oral fable for renewal may themselves be widespread and very old; but still they cannot be traced so widely or in such diverse multiformity as the tales that periodically serve them as motival reservoirs. In relation to narrative, cultic and ritual imagery is moreover systematically incomplete, and it regularly lacks the continuity of narrative multiforms over vast geographic ranges unobstructed by the ethnic, linguistic, or other boundaries of cultural differentiation that have played havoc with the younger diffusions of particular cults and religions. Scholars of ancient and primitive religion cannot therefore afford to ignore oral fable any more than can scholars of literary narrative, for whereas narrative motifs and religious symbols are, as they have long been known to be, intimately affiliated, their common matrix is story, like the story of the Two Trees.

Chapter Five

UP, DOWN, ALL AROUND, AND WHO MADE THE WORLD

And here were gardens bright with sinuous rills,
Where blossomed many an incense-bearing tree;
And here were forests ancient as the hills,
Enfolding sunny spots of greenery.

-Kubla Khan

About other patterns. p. 257

1. Vertical Journeys. p. 259

2. The Four Zones. p. 261

3. The Three Women. p. 265

4. The Restorative Journey. p. 270

5. The Cosmogonic Triad. p. 277

It follows from the foregoing considerations that the historical reason why a tale like the story of the Two Trees is told in Africa (or elsewhere) must be sought in narrative itself, not in the material life, religion, or social experience of those who tell it. Oral fable gets its fundamental character from its own past, not from the chance persons or peoples whom collectors have randomly caught telling fable. From an historical point of view, who tells a tale or how he tells it palls into insignificance before the tale itself.

The most important evidence for an antiquity of the Two Trees' story greater than that witnessed in ancient writings and iconography is inferential. The universality of the Two Trees in the story-telling of widely separated peoples whose mutual influence upon one another, or whose common subjection to an imperial influence emanating from one of their number, cannot account for that universality argues not only that the story is very old, but also that its age is universal. The diffusion of man, not the diffusion of the narrative within any already existing population of man, must be looked to as the real origin of the story.

The popular supposition that at some time a single "great mind" must have invented every common trope of imagination or fantasy in oral traditional narrative is not so much disproven as rendered superfluous by the evidence of the Two Trees' story and other patterns of fable like it. As are most popular suppositions on this subject, the "great-mind theory" is founded much more upon the ostensible reasonableness of the theory itself than upon the facts of fable. For if we admit that some prehistoric great-minded individual invented this story (rather than 'merely' reconstituting a tale already known to him from preceding tradition, in the manner of modern oral traditional narrators), we must also admit that the central concerns of the story, and hence its probable date of invention, lie more within an actuality crucial to the dryopithecine antecedents of mankind than to the diverse human cultures where the tale has so persisted into modern times. The ingrainment of the Two Trees in the narrative culture of the modern Eskimo at one extreme and of the Iraqi Arabs on the treeless plains of Mesopotamia at the other extreme is in any case

less obviously vital to them than it would have been to the sylvan
hominoids who in so many other ways "invented" and genetically
willed to us their innovations of form and behaviour. And if we thus
come to admit that the "great mind" behind the story of the Two
Trees was as possibly that of a thoughtful tree-ape as it was human,
why should we not also admit that some inscrutably deep, subcon-
scious dryopithecine psychic legacy in untold generations of human
story-tellers has caused perpetual re-invention of the tale in every age
and every branch of humanity for tens and hundreds of thousands of
years? But again, such an hypothesis is more superfluous than demonstrably wrong. A tale such as the Two Trees' that is always and everywhere present in oral narrative culture needs no invention; and given
what generally is known in natural science about the rise and diffusion
of the human species (apart from the disputations of palaeology in detail), what is both unique (as is fabulous storytelling) and truly ubiquitous in man (as is the tale of the Two Trees) is *ipso facto* a feature
assignable to the origin of our species.

In the previous chapters of this book I have described the pattern
of the Two Trees' story by reference to examples of it in certain traditions of the Old World, specifically African, European, and Middle
Eastern. I claim, however, a much wider sphere of prevalence for this
and other story-patterns like it—that they are in fact world-wide phenomena found in the oral narrative traditions of every people whose
traditions of that kind have been made accessible to learning. To prove
the truth of this averment completely would require an encyclopaedic
treatise beyond the patience or the actual needs of any reader. Those
who find the idea and the method I offer in this book useful will be
able to proceed for themselves from the more limited demonstration
I provide to a broader application of their own in other narrative of
particular interest to them. I rather hope therefore to suggest the
worth of the method than to exhaust its applicability through my
own exposition, which in any case I do not think I could do.

For some readers, however, prior ideas about distinctions of genre,
about stages of civilization or cultural 'progress,' and about the ethnic
genius of individual peoples may effect understanding of story-patterns
and how they 'work' in a broader spectrum of cultural diversity than
my few preceding African, European, and Middle Eastern examples
display. For those readers and others who may be interested, I have
incorporated further discussion of the Two Trees and further examples

of them from other parts of the world in the Appendix of this book. There I have examined at greater length the diversity within which a single pattern may be expressed and still be itself.

But there are many patterns in oral fable. The exact enumeration and description of all of them is a task for the future. For the most part, the material in this book illustrates only one general kind of pattern, which I call unbounded or *disjunctive*. Disjunctive patterns are coherent constellations of generic motifs like the Two Trees and their satellites, but they are permeable by the motival elements of other patterns which are found interspersed with them in given performances of fable. Bounded or *conjunctive* patterns on the other hand are motival clusters that traditionally resist penetration by elements of other conjunctive patterns and so present clear-cut textual boundaries in the linear progress of particular performances. Disjunctive patterns require to be analyzed like the constituents of a compound chemical; conjunctive patterns are arrayed sequentially like the beads on the strand of a necklace. Bounded patterns are in the technical sense the *themes* of oral fable, but skill in the analysis of disjunctive patterns remains an essential preliminary to thematic studies.

In order accurately to observe the characteristic intermeshing of disjunctive patterns, it is necessary to have at hand the descriptions of several others besides the Two Trees. This chapter concerns five patterns that are often interwoven with the hewn and green wood. A general proof of the universality of the five patterns described here will not be provided as was done for the trees in the preceding chapters and in Appendix I. Such a tale-by-tale verification of these five patterns' range and age would fill several volumes, and is unnecessary in any case. Once the existence of patterns is recognized, verification of their presence in particular tales from various ethnic traditions becomes an automatic consequence of reading the tales sensitively.

1. VERTICAL JOURNEYS

Journeys and quests have long been recognized as essential components of oral fable in all its genres. But this pattern discriminates between ordinary travel and the kind that may have fabulous results. The contrast is often very explicit, as in the following tale recorded in August, 1964, from the Turkish *conteur* Sukru Dariji in Kavshit village, Sungurlu, in the Turkish province of Chorum:[160] *A potentate is disabled by blindness and tells his three grown sons that the only remedy for his impaired vision would be a handful of earth from a place where his horse's hooves have never trodden. The eldest son undertakes the quest, travels for three months in a straight line, collects a handful of dirt, and returns the same way. It is dirt often trodden by his father's horse. The second son journeys six months outward bound, and comes to a high wooded mountain. Climbing to the peak, he collects a handful of dirt, descends, and returns home. Again the dirt is useless.*

The third son finds a dragon under whose head there is dirt uniquely never trodden upon by his father's horse. He obtains the dirt and three peerless brides for himself and his brothers. But on his way home his brothers waylay him and cast him into the netherworld, into which he descends on the back of a black ram. By means of a great bird he is able to fly home, where he avenges himself and claims his rewards.

The third son's vertical journeys down into the underworld on the back of a ram and up into the air on the back of an eagle-like bird of prey expose him to hazards and bring him rewards which his more horizontally pedestrian competitors cannot experience.

The pattern of the vertical journeys is maintained in myriad nominal motifs. The same Turkish *conteur*, Sukru Dariji, who told the story about the blind ruler's three sons also told a tale about Shemsi Banı, Emporer of the Pidgeons:[161] *An old woman begging for food observes a caravan of pack-animals burdened with comestibles and follows it. The caravan enters the sea and goes to a mansion on the bottom. The crone hides in the underwater palace and observes a host of pidgeons gather there one by one. Each of the pidgeons is transformed into a young man, and these dine together opulently. Their emperor is eventually domesticated, abandoning his aquatic and aerial haunts to live as a ruler in stable residence among men.*

The capacity for vertical journeys distinguishes this pidgeon-king from other men as the best husband for the mortal heroine of the story and makes him the best heir to her father's imperial properties; for more than any other of her suitors he is an habitual traveler in both the underworld of the sea-bottom and in the aerial zone of bird-life.

The superior competitor for fabulous rewards and benefits may be ingeniously endowed with vertical capacities of various descriptions; one way or another traditional oral fabulists keep the pattern intact. Another Turkish narrator, Mehmet Anli of Samsun, conferred the pattern of vertical journeys on his hero without obliging him to digress from the direct pursuit of bliss, by associating him with two travelling-companions whose sole function was to represent the prior achievement of prodigious journeys up and down:[162] *A young prince falls in love with a vision seen in a dream, The Most Beautiful Girl in the World. He is warned that many have searched for her in vain for many years, including his own father. He sets forth on the quest anyway, and is joined on the way by two other young travelers, the Prince of Stars and the Prince of the Seas. He possesses the girl where all others have failed.*

The well-known story of the Frog Prince, Number One in the famous early collection of German fable by the brothers Grimm, provides another example of the pattern of vertical journeys.[163] *A princess goes one day to amuse herself in a cool grove of trees. Her plaything, a golden ball, falls into a deep well under an old linden tree in the grove. A man bewitched in the likeness of a frog descends into the depths of the well to retrieve the toy, then pursues the girl up the stairs of her father's palace and into the royal dining room. After it has dined, it gains entrance to the girl's bedchamber. When in anger she lifts the frog and sends it flying through the air, it becomes a handsome youth and possesses her.* Thus even so unlikely a hero as a frog needs the pattern of the vertical journeys, down to the depths of the well and flying through the air high in my lady's chamber, to achieve its fabulous destiny.

2. THE FOUR ZONES

Conventional wisdom has it that the cosmos of oral traditional fiction is divided into two parts, 'this' and 'the other' world. But in fact the districts traversed in the fabulous journeys of traditional storytelling everywhere fall into a distinct quadripartite pattern. As with any disjunctive pattern, the order of the four parts is completely variable, and they may or may not be distinguished by separate nominal motifs in particular texts.

Again the Grimms' German Frog Prince is typical. Princess and bestioform prince meet in "Ein grosser dunkler Wald. . .unter einer alten Linde." Everywhere in traditional German fable such a location is foreboding (this being the verdant member of the Two Trees' pattern), and the potential duplicity of the linden's zone is soon realized. Here both of the interlocutors give up old companionships and assume new ones. The frog renounces his froggy surroundings and begs for acceptance into human society. And whether she knows it or not, the princess's impulsive donation of her company to the frog when he has offered to retrieve her lost toy is a lifelong commitment to a new companion, the princely husband that is destined to be liberated from the frog's form. The great dark wood is accordingly a kind of limbo that forebodes danger, but where old associations give way to new ones. As such it represents one of the four zones of fabulous geography in the German tale of Der Froschkönig.

The next zone in the linear sequence of the German narration in Grimm No. 1 is the bottom of the frog's well. It is an untenable location for all the *personae* of the story. The princess cannot contentedly leave her lost ball there—it is 'lost' solely because it is in the well. Nor can the Frog Prince remain there happily. It is a place from which the only value that can be securely extracted is escape. As such it represents the second "otherworldly" zone in the Four Zone pattern.

The third zone is the palace to which the princess and the frog alike retire from the "great dark forest." It is a place where all good things are found (especially *food* and the hope of *progeny* implicit in the cohabitation of prince and princess), but where a monster must be met and overcome (= the frog transformed).

Last comes the domestic zone of the tale, the place where ordinary relationships (and plain narrative) prevail. 'Der treue Heinrich' conveys the transformed, newly-wed prince and his princess away to this zone in a carriage, to the patrimonial home of the prince.

Another German tale chosen at random displays other multiforms of the Four Zones. Number 16 in the Grimm collection, Die Drei Schlangenblätter (The Snake's Three Leaves) tells of a man whose career begins in the plain, true-to-life setting of home, his native place: *A poor man can no longer provide for his only son. The youth tells his disabled elder that he will go on a journey to seek the means of overcoming the parental disability and so provide for himself. He goes accordingly to a "powerful kingdom" that is at war, defeats its enemies, and is rewarded with the premiership and marriage to the king's daughter. But the daughter dies after she becomes his wife, and he is obliged by the terms of their peculiar marriage contract to be confined with her corpse in the burial crypt. Here in a place that forebodes his own death the man obtains from a snake three leaves of an herb wherewith he resurrects his dead wife. He and she are then released from the burial chamber, but a "great change" has come over her and she is no longer the good and loyal companion she formerly was. During a sea voyage she takes the ship's captain for her lover, and the two of them throw the husband into the sea while he is in a deep trance. He drowns, but a faithful servant sets out in a small boat, finds the dead man, and revives him with the snake's three leaves. Master and servant then row safely to shore.*[164]

The sequential order of the Four Zones is of course different in this tale from the order in which other storytellers express them in other tales. Obviously too the nominal motifs are different. Instead of the limbo of a forest grove, Grimm No. 16 gives us a burial vault where danger forebodes and companionships are altered. Home is a poor old man's estate, not the princely palace native to the Frog Prince before his bestial transformation. The place whence no value is retrievable except escape is again watery, but this time a salt sea rather than the frog's well-bottom. Finally, the "mighty kingdom" where the youth struggles fiercely to overcome powerful public enemies is also the place which bestows on him every imaginable comfort and happiness. The pattern of the Four Zones is thus again complete:

1. Home, a scene of plain domesticity.
2. Limbo, a foreboding place where old companionships and associations are discarded and new ones assumed.
3. The 'good' otherworld, where violent enemies must be overcome in hard struggle, and where all good things are forthcoming.
4. The 'bad' otherworld, where nothing matters but escape.

Literally any ethnic tradition from any historic era affords abundant examples of the Four Zones pattern. Many of the narratives cited elsewhere in this book demonstrate the pattern. Thus, the hero of the Middle English Breton lay of King Orfeo (see Appendix, pps. 402-406).

has his home in Thrace, but the orchard where his wife sleeps under
an *impe tre* is a limbo where she exchanges erstwhile human companions for the companionship of the fairies. Her disconsolate husband
goes to live for a decade in the wilderness, whence he desires to retrieve nothing but his and his wife's eventual deliverance. Finally he
comes to the fairy king's castle, a place abounding with all manner
of richness and indulgences not to be found in other zones. Here Orfeo confronts and subdues his monstrous adversary, gaining thereby
both wife and a return to power and riches. In the ancient Near Eastern Epic of Gilgamesh, Uruk is plain home to Gilgamesh, while the
wilderness where the temple harlot makes Enkidu exchange his erstwhile companionship with animals for the new companionship of herself and Gilgamesh is the limbo of the Four Zones' pattern. Humbaba's Forest is a blessed tract where the violent struggle with a monster ends victoriously and Gilgamesh is preternaturally enriched. Finally, from the time of Enkidu's funeral to his own return to Uruk from
the land of Utanapishtim, Gilgamesh's Wanderings take him through
the complex zone from which nothing is ultimately retrievable except
his escape homeward.

The Apinayé tale of Tečware (see Appendix, pps. 429-430) again
discloses the Four Zones. First comes the limbo where the piquy tree
stands, and where the old companionship of brothers-in-law gives way
to the terrified near-victim's flight to his fellow villagers. The village
where the deaths occur and ritual means are found to oppose the murderer is of course the domestic precinct of the tale, or home. The open
woods, where the villagers pursue Tečware into the wilderness of his
perdition, offer no benefit to anyone except mutual escape; but the
roadside where in the end Tečware is violently overcome is also the
place where the mangaba tree sprang up over his grave. From the latex
of this tree young men first made the rubber balls used in the enrich-
ing peny-kra game, says the Apinayé storyteller.

The pattern of the Four Zones has been widely used in Western
literature. It is basic, for instance, in the popular modern short story
by Charles Dickens, "A Christmas Carol." There Home is Ebenezer
Scrooge's own house. The Spirit of Christmas Past shows Scrooge a
foreboding limbo where he exchanges old acquaintances for new. Then
the Spirit of Christmas Present leads the hero to a bounteous scene,
but one where the monstrous crippling of an innocent child must be
overcome by energetic measures against the culprit, who for a moment

is both the ogre and the ogre-slayer of the piece. Finally the perdition of Christmas Yet to Come is revealed, a scene from which no good can be extracted except escape.

Less widely familiar but more beloved of modern *literati*, the conventional Christian literary cosmology which Dante Alighieri employed in the *Divina Comedia* is also a latter-day derivative of the ancient fourfold pattern of geography in oral fable. From that literary poet's first evocation of place with the words 'nel mezzo del cammin di nostra vita, mi ritrovai per una selva oscura,' his literary epic exploits the Four Zones throughout Inferno, Purgatorio, and Paradiso.

3. THE THREE WOMEN

Another tale in the Grimm collection affords an example of this pattern. Die drei Federn (The Three Feathers), Grimm No. 63, is about a contest among three sons for succession to their father's throne:[165] *A king's two elder sons are intelligent, but the third and youngest is a taciturn simpleton. When old age disables the king, he commissions his three sons to seek fine carpets; whoever returns with the finest will inherit the kingdom. The two eldest travel together. Thinking their younger brother too stupid to compete with them, they find a shepherd's wife and strip her ragged clothes from her, returning to offer these to their father as carpets. The dunce obtains a superior fabric from a toad. A second competition is set—to obtain a fine ring; the elder sons bring carriage nails pulled from a piece of junk, the youngest a good article from the toad. The third and final competition is to obtain the fairest woman. The elder sons obtain a pair of coarse peasant women; the simpleton returns with one of the toad's daughters transformed into a peerless damsel. He inherits.*

All of the women in this little *histoire buffe* belong to one or another of three types. The hapless shepherd's wife is of no ultimate use to anyone. Indeed, she were better left completely alone, for the clothes robbed from her are the cause of her assailants' failure in the first of the three contests. The two peasant women whom the elder brothers later recruit are more promising. In the event, they lack the delicate beauty of the toad's daughter, but as their two sponsors in the contest are quick to say in their defense, they appear to be decidedly stronger. On that ground they are for a time serious aspirants to the peerage. They are, so to speak, temporarily or transiently interesting women, and belong therefore to the second type in the pattern of the Three Women. The third type, of course, is represented by the toad's beautiful daughter, a woman of unique attainments and devotion who contributes priceless benefits to the estate of her male consort.

The Turkish tale about the blind emperor told by Sukru Dariji (already quoted above in discussion of the Vertical Journeys) also displays the paradigm of the Three Women.[160] *The youngest of three sons searches for an elixir to restore his father's eyesight. He asks a night's lodging in the house of an old woman who lives alone with one beautiful daughter. He betroths the daughter on behalf of his eldest brother and continues the journey. On the next evening the same events happen again at another house; the girl is betrothed this time to the traveller's next eldest brother. On the following day the young man is directed to a third woman whose help he needs to obtain the elixir for his father. After several more days of travel he finds this woman alone in the act of prayer.*

Each of the first two nubile women whom the hero meets on this journey is paired with an old mother, and each lives in a house. In contrast, the third woman is quite alone and inhabits the open air. And whereas the first two damsels are like the two peasant women in the German story,[165] good matches for some *other* men (the young hero's elder brothers), the strange woman praying alone in the midst of a grassy plain is a superior being whom none but the most blessed of men can claim. It takes longer to reach her (several days' journey instead of just one day) but she is correspondingly worth the greater effort. She is fabulously powerful: *The young traveller approaches the woman and calls a greeting to her while she is yet praying. She does not reply. He calls again, and is struck blind. When she finishes her prayer, she invites him to speak, but he is too amazed by the sudden loss of his sight to remember his business with her. She admonishes him against the impiety of interrupting prayer, for she is an utterly fabulous and unreal person, a female Moslem priest, and accordingly has the sobriquet of 'Khoja (priest) girl.' Next she passes her thumbs over the young man's eyes, and his sight is restored. He says that he needs her help to obtain the elixir for his father's eyes, but she assures him that she can restore vision to the father too without any recourse to* materia medica.

Besides having instant power to restore and take away eyesight, and in addition to being a learned prelate of religion, the Khoja girl is also an accurate prophetess. Above all, she is a completely autonomous woman in traditional Turkish society (which in reality did not tolerate such autonomy in women any more than it tolerated women in the office of khoja). She is the peerless woman destined to be the lucky hero's lifelong consort. He travels homeward with her and with the two transiently interesting women whom he has selected for his brothers until the brothers waylay him and cast him into the netherworld, taking all three women for themselves. There in the zone whence only escape is possible he meets yet another (third) pair of women, the one ancient and the other nubile. *The youth comes to a small house where an old crone lives by herself. He asks her for water to drink, and she serves him her fresh urine. She apologizes, saying that a dragon permits water to be drawn from the well in that land only when it is given a girl to eat. The emperor's daughter is about to be sacrificed to it that very day. The youth kills the dragon and saves the girl. While they are alone together, the girl marks the young man's back with the print of her hands dipped in the dragon's blood. When the girl returns to her father's house, he determines to give her in marriage to her saviour, and all the young men in the kingdom are summoned to pass in review so that the girl can identify her husband-to-be. All young men answer the summons, but the man sought is unknown to the census of that kingdom. Ultimately he is found hiding in the old crone's little house because he fears for his life should he disappoint the girl and her father—he is adamantly determined not to marry her.*

Like the shepherd's wife in the foregoing German tale about the simpleton and his helpful frog,[165] this netherworldly emperor's daughter is ultimately of no use to anyone. In the end she does not even contribute to her saviour's own salvation, nor to the one thing which he accomplishes while he is in her zone that is of value to himself— his escape. That is done instead by an enormous female bird of prey whose brood he saves from starvation at a great green tree in the wilderness.

Lest anyone mistakenly suppose that the pattern of the Three Women is merely a subsidiary of Aarne-Thompson folktale types 550 or 551,[166] I adduce the following Zande tale from the Yambio District in the Sudan, which was noted by Mr. Richard Mambia sometime during the years 1961-1963.[167] No pattern is peculiar to any one *genre* of oral traditional narrative, least of all to any so-called "type" of "folktale." Not every pattern is in every tale, but the same patterns are the organizing principles in oral fable of every type and *genre*. That is so not for any theoretical reason whatsoever, but only because the concrete evidence of actual oral fable shows it to be so wherever fable has been recorded. The Central African story that follows is nominally much too unlike the familiar types of European or Near Eastern folktales to be confused with them; nevertheless one of its central organizing features is the pattern of the Three Women.

> *Two women go fishing together at a time when meat is very scarce. One of them is pregnant. While the women are cutting up their catch, two warriors descend on them from a battle that has been raging nearby. The warriors kill the women, take the fish, and depart; but the pregnant woman's twin children, a boy and a girl, spill out into the water from their dead mother's womb and so survive. They grow to maturity living like fish in the stream.*
>
> *When they have grown to adulthood, the twins move into the deserted houses of the people who were killed in the war at the time of their unnatural birth. Both the twins are extraordinarily beautiful people. A famous trickster named Ture hears of the girl and sends a war party to abduct her for him; his own two wives, Nanzagbe and Nangbafudo, he sends away to live in the houses of his brothers-in-law. The twins destroy Ture's first and second war parties, but the third expedition kills the girl's brother and she agrees to go to Ture with the corpse of her brother. The men cannot lift the cadaver of the dead brother until the girl permits it; it is enormously heavy, or light as a dry leaf, depending upon her will. When she reaches Ture's homestead, he is unable to move from the stool where he is sitting until the girl wills it. The men prepare the cadaver of her brother for cooking, but it will not be cooked until she approves. Later it cannot be eaten until she wills. Then she commands that her brother's bare bones be gathered for her, and wrapping them in leaves, she returns alone to her place in the war-ruined settlement. Ture remains unable to move from his stool, and his two wives return to feed him so that he will not starve to death. The girl meanwhile nurses her brother's dead bones in a pot. On the fifth day they are completely transformed into a handsome young man whom the girl takes for her husband. On the seventh day the newly-wed couple go to visit Ture, and he is released from his stool as they approach. He flees into the bush, terrified now*

of the woman whom he had tried formerly to abduct. Finally the newlyweds depart, and Ture's two wives ridicule him for his lust.

Like the German shepherd woman and the Turkish princess of the netherworld, the two women fishing at the beginning of the Zande story are of no ultimate use to anyone either personally or in the lineage that may descend from them. Two warriors assault these women just as the two elder brothers assaulted the shepherd's wife in the German tale, and just as the water-hoarding dragon assaulted the Turkish princess. But neither the assault on them nor the defense of them is of any lasting value. Ture's two wives, however, are at least temporarily or transiently useful women. They come and go in the tale, rendering mundane womanly services, but contributing no extraordinarily valuable or durable benefits to their male consort. The wonder-working woman is characteristically distinct from all the others. Like the German toad's daughter and the Turkish Khoja girl, she is a compound of virtues unheard of before her advent. Her male consort is a person of little promise indeed until she makes something of him, no matter whether he is a German simpleton, a Turkish youth lost in the underworld and given up for dead, or a Zande pile of dead bones left from a cannibal meal.

A tale of the Cinderella type from Japan will suffice to complete the description of this pattern and demonstrate its pervasiveness both in regard to world geography and the variety of plot-types which it informs.

A mother hates and abuses her daughter's elder step-sister. When all the girls of their village go together to gather chestnuts in the mountains, the elder girl, Komebukuro, is given a harvesting bag with a defective bottom, so that she cannot fill it in time to return home with the other girls. Left alone in the wilderness, she is met by a beautiful little white bird. It gives the girl a new bag, a marvelous wooden flute, and a fine silk dress to wear on special occasions.

The girl returns home with the bird's gifts. Several days later a festival occurs in a neighboring village. The step-mother dresses her own daughter, Awabukuro, and goes with her to the festival, leaving Komebukuro to complete an excessive chore of spinning. But a group of her friends pity her and help her complete the job in time to go to the festival. Komebukuro puts on the bird's silk dress and goes to the neighboring village playing her new flute. Arrived there, she sees Awabukuro and throws things at her. Awabukuro complains of this to her mother, but the mother insists it is not Komebukuro and will not intervene. All return home by separate ways.

A suitor presents himself wanting to marry Komebukuro, but the mother insists that he consider Awabukuro. She outdoes herself preparing Awabukuro for the suitor's approval, but he decides for Komebukuro. Both the mother and Awabukuro then fall into a ditch full of water and become shellfish and snail respectively.[168]

The bad stepmother is a woman who in the end contributes no benefit to anyone. Her line of descent is also useless. Komebukuro's assault on her and her kin at the village festival gains nothing, nor is there any point in putting up a defense against it. Awabukuro's case is different. She is temporarily a serious candidate for the suitor's attention, a transiently interesting woman. But Komebukuro is not to be excelled. The list of her assets makes her a uniquely endowed woman: beautiful white spirit bird as protectress, magic flute, nonpareil silk dress, crowd of friends to help her in her labour, thick smooth head of hair to compete with her step-sister's kinky hair, and seventh, a new husband. Happy the man whose bride is so blessed.

The pattern of the Three Women may, like other patterns, be composed of varying numbers of nominal motifs in each of its generic parts. Thus, the Zande example presents the useless woman as a pair of women fishing, while in Turkish she may appear as a singular princess. But as always, the overlying variations in *name* and *number* are not to be confused with the fundamental pattern. The cohesion and constant generic meanings of the pattern's constituent motifs are its identifying features:

1. Woman useless in herself and in her lineage, subject to assault.

2. Transiently appealing, temporarily useful woman.

3. Woman who is proof against assault and a peerless contributor of lasting benefits to her male consort.

4. THE RESTORATIVE JOURNEY

Another common pattern of oral traditional narrative everywhere involves three kinds of character—a parent or affinal elder who is disabled, a hero (the person who gains or achieves most in the pattern), and an ascendant, non-parental elder—all arranged in the following manner:

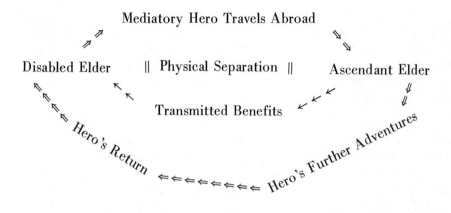

To compensate the first elder's disability, a mediatory younger relative travels as hero across geographic or spatial separation to another elder, who is however not disabled and not the hero's parent. The second, ascendant elder furnishes benefits to the first, disabled one. The hero then returns home across the separation between the two elders, but through a different sequence of events distinct from the transmission of the benefits.

This is the main pattern of such folktales as the classic Grimm No. 97, 'Das Wasser des Lebens,' and more generally, of Aarne-Thompson types 550 and 551. This pattern is however a common denominator also of many other ostensibly unrelated folktale-types, for example 300, 325, 935, and 1525, to name only a few at random.[169] But the paradigm of logic in this oral fabulous pattern is far more revealing about the history of oral narrative than is any of the particular Old World tale-types in which the pattern happens to operate.

The disability of the parental or affinal elder in stories following this pattern is often due to some natural hazard of being an elder: poverty, old age, or sickness, as in Grimm Nos. 6, 60, 69, 71, and 97, to use familiar examples once again. It may also result from a departure by one of the characters from what is understood to be customary or proper behaviour. Thus a father is sometimes disabled in his

parental rôle by a stupid son, or by a prodigy, whose abnormal behaviour the father cannot correct or control. An interesting and familiar example of this form of parental disability is in the ancient Greek
legend of Laios and his son Oidipos.

But sometimes the nature of the elder's disability is more subtle
than in any of the foregoing examples. Consider the case of His Imperial Majesty Bel Beljanin, whose very name bespeaks a perfect, blameless, and holy ruler in the Great Russian tale 'Tri carstva—mednoe,
serebrjanoe i zolotoe,' No. 71b in Afanas'ev's collection (renumbered
No. 129 in Vladimir Propp's standard edition of that classic collection).[170]

Emperor Beljanin has an empress, Nastas'ja of the Golden Tresses,
and three princely sons, Pjotr, Vasilij, and Ivan. A preternatural named
Vixr' (Whirlwind) discovers Nastas'ja in a garden with her suite of fe-
male attendants, and abducts her, thus reducing the imperial family to
only its male members. The emperor grieves for his wife, but does
nothing himself to find and retrieve her. Instead, he waits until his
three sons come of age, when he sets them the task of locating and
bringing home their absent mother.

Marital *ennui* and royal self-indulgence would be an amusing but
wrong explanation of Beljanin's failure to seek his missing wife. In
fact, it is a convention of oral fable that emperors, kings, and other
rulers do not undertake of themselves to restore the losses of persons
or property which alien powers inflict on their realms, but send instead various of their subjects, clients, or debased forms of themselves
(like the Middle English King Orfeo) to do it. Beljanin's strict immobility and dependence on others to mend any breaches of his authority in the Russian story are but the inevitable concomitants of his
rôle as a ruler in fable. Indeed, his immobility is so strict that while
every one of the story's dozen other characters moves from one kingdom to another (or from one social class to another) at least once,
Beljanin will not so much as leave his castle until the very end of the
story, when he finally allows himself to be borne in a golden carriage
over a short distance from his own castle to a new and better one
which his son has built adjoining it. It is as though the sum of all
his subjects' extensive movements were equal to, or could produce,
only a small and undisturbing dislocation for the better in the life
of their sovereign. Moreover, all the events of the story begin and
come to fulfillment in Beljanin's fixed presence, giving him as a motif
the generic import not only of fixity but also of centripetalism in

this nineteenth-century Russian folktale.

The two elder princes, Pjotr and Vasilij, set forth without impediment in quest of their mother. But Ivan is another Benjamin; his father the emperor releases him to join in the search only after Ivan's energetic entreaty. Ivan then travels into a forest where he finds another elder who is not his relative residing in a magnificent court surrounded by various tokens of well-being. This elder provides instruments and counsel which enable Ivan eventually to find his mother and send her home to his father. Leaving the ascendant elder and benefactor, Ivan next meets his brothers encamped with a mighty army on an open plain, as it were midway between his mother and father. He dislodges them from this limbo, and then proceeds to a cave at the foot of a mountain, which is closed with a great iron door. Bursting through the door, Ivan finds a range of mountains inside the cave, and climbs them. On the mountain-tops he finds in succession four empires: one of copper, one of silver, one of gold, and one of glittering jewels. The four realms are possessions of Whirlwind, but he is not present in any of them when Ivan arrives. Instead, Ivan finds four empresses, who tell him that Whirlwind visits them only for reasons of lust at intervals of three months, two months, one month, and once a week, respectively. All beg Ivan to liberate them. The last queen, Whirlwind's favorite and mistress of the jewelled empire, is Ivan's mother. She instructs her son how he may overcome Whirlwind. Ivan is to grasp Whirlwind's battle-mace and cling to it no matter what Whirlwind does to loosen his grip, until Whirlwind is exhausted. Vixr' (Whirlwind) duly appears as a black storm-cloud, flies in at the palace window, and assumes as he touches the earth the form of a handsome youth. Ivan clutches his mace, and Whirlwind flies away with him into the sky, where he successively threatens to eat, crush, and drown Ivan. But Ivan overcomes him in the manner his mother prescribed.

Bel Beljanin's logical opposite is the personified whirlwind—Vixr' —and not only because it was Vixr' who abducted the empress Nastas'ja. Beljanin is immobile, centripetal, and unitary in his rule; he has a single empire and never leaves it. But Whirlwind reigns over four separate, simultaneously subterranean and mountain-top empires and is seldom present in any of them. As his name implies, Vixr''s habit is to roam at large without regard for his own boundaries or anyone else's. He passes freely between the terrestrial and subterranean worlds, and flies through the sky with equal facility. He is a denizen of the whole cosmos, but not a regular citizen anywhere. Moreover, he is unconcerned about the family ties and obligations that govern men; he is polygamous, with a separate wife in each of his four empires, although he is more a transitory, seasonal lover than a proper husband to any of them. Like Ivan's mother Nastas'ja, who is Whirlwind's headwife and empress of his jewel-empire, all of Whirlwind's queens are stolen women and unwilling captives who beseech Ivan to free them and take them back to the terrestrial world whence they came. When the immobile, centripetal Beljanin is bereft of his wife, he remains a widower until he can find the means for a remedy within his own kin and progeny. But Beljanin's opposite, the utterly mobile, centrifugal Whirlwind abducts his several wives whence he pleases and holds them away from their proper homes not by contract or affection but by force. Beljanin is a man and remains one, but Whirlwind is a creature of mixed forms, a shapeshifter who is sometimes man and sometimes elemental wind-storm without tangible being. Physically, morally, socially, and territorially, Whirlwind is a lawless wanderer, a polluted violator who darkens earth and sky where he passes in absolute opposition to Bel Beljanin, the stable, law-abiding, and blameless White Emperor.

The task of mediating between these two personifications of centripetalism at home and centrifugence abroad is a test of manhood and a first stage of initiation for Beljanin's three sons. The mediation is not truly an Hegelian or Straussian reconciliation of binary opposites in a new, superior form of being. The three sons face a dilemma: in order to find their mother and bring her home they must abandon their father's strict fixity and assume at least some of Whirlwind's character. They must like Whirlwind leave home and wander through the terrestrial world, the underworld, and across the mountain-tops without any fixed goal until they discover by luck where their mother is. Then, like Whirlwind, they must ravage her away from her master and carry her off to another kingdom. In order to restore their own family and the integrity of their father's empire, they must at least temporarily assume the unholy role of polluter, violator, and centrifugal power in logical opposition to the character of their pure, immobile, and consequently disabled father. The three princes' dilemma is to be like their authoritarian father, and hence weak, or utterly unlike him, and hence strong. For their father's most essential qualities as a fabulous sovereign—his fixity and centripetalism—are the very qualities which render him helpless against the depredations of his foe the Wind. Those qualities are the disability which he sons must overcome or compensate.

The two elder princes find movement away from their father effortless. On the other hand, they accomplish little by their mobility, and it is not so great in the end as their younger brother's. They remain in the terrestrial world and do not enter the cave nor climb the mountains with their younger brother Ivan (no Vertical Journeys). They make an impressive display of force with their great army, but achieve nothing at all by that; Whirlwind is under no compulsion to come to them and do battle on their terms.

In contrast to his brothers, Ivan feels the full force of his father's centripetalism. The emperor detains him at home and yields only reluctantly to his youngest son's apparent wanderlust. But when at last he is released from home, Ivan forces his way by craft and main strength into Whirlwind's presence and obliges him to accept a contest by seizing his war-mace and threatening to disarm him. Then, having been more centrifugal than his brothers both in escaping his father's detention and in penetrating the distant boundaries of Whirlwind's estate, Ivan suddenly asserts an opposite, centripetal tendency like his father's. He clings unflinching to the Wind's war-mace until the Wind falls to earth unmanned, exhausted, and stationary at last. Then he slays the Wind, laying it to rest permanently. Gathering together all the defeated Wind's women and movable property, Ivan sends them home to his father in the care of his brothers.

As a mediating term between his centripetal father and the centrifugal Whirlwind, Ivan-tsarevič is a study in antithesis. He asserts mobility where immobility is paramount, and fixity where unrestraint rules. The conclusion to be drawn from this piece of antithetical logic seems plain: the contrast between culture (the emperor Beljanin) and nature (the Whirlwind) can by personification in fable be understood entirely within the frame of culture. The opposite of cultural normality as represented in Beljanin is not disorder but only another order, and any dysfunction of normality is an intrusion of one order upon another. Normality may therefore be restored in the same way it is disrupted; Ivan does in kind precisely what his opponent has done and gains the same advantage—an opportunity to impose his order on his opponent. In the final analysis, normality is that which endures, and the most enduring thing in culture is the succession of generations. Through the succession of Bel Beljanin and Prince Ivan, culture can do what nature in the wild state cannot. It can both maintain normality and exploit abnormality, because it possesses both staid fathers and prodigal sons.

The pattern of the Restorative Journey exemplified in this Russian folktale is widespread not only in Slavic oral narrative, but in other ethnic traditions as well, and in the mythologies which those traditions have engendered in the past. A nice analogue to the three male principals of the Russian tale is the ancient Greek set of Zeus Herkeios, Apollo Patroos, and Hermes Psychopompos (or Polytropos). One may understand from this analogy why Hermes' place in the Olympian pantheon was so insecure; he was in regard to his habits of motion the antithesis of Zeus, the primary male authority in the Olympian family. In Slavic tradition, the tragedy of the Russian epic hero Dunai is plainly a consequence of his polytropic nature. He serves his centripetal sovereign Vladimir well, but cannot overcome the innate centrifugence expressed both in his actions and in his name, which is the Slavic name for the Danube River. The Serbo-Croatian epic hero Mujo, another centripetal ruler, and his mobile, often polluted brother Halil, who are discussed elsewhere in this book, are further examples of centripetalism and centrifugence in Slavic oral fable.

But the most immediate application of the contrast between mobility and fixity is in the analysis of preternaturals—creatures of mixed form—for it is the *mixing* of disparate forms and qualities and not merely an *unusual* form that denotes dangerous preternaturals. Consider for a moment more the dragon in Afanas'ev's tale No. 71a (No. 128 in V. Ja. Propp's edition), another variant of the tale of 'The Three Empires—Copper, Silver, and Gold.'[171]

Three brothers seek brides and meet a three-headed dragon who offers them an extraordinary girl if they can move the great stone from the mouth of a tunnel leading into the underworld where she lives. The two eldest cannot, but the youngest, Ivaško Zapečnyj, succeeds, and the dragon kindly helps him descend into the open hole.

Despite his three heads and dracoform appearance, this preternatural is a stationary, non-parental elder and benefactor, the equivalent of the wealthy old man in the woods in the story of Bel Beljanin's son Ivan. The form of dragon is a highly effective device for expressing that he is not the hero's relative, parental or otherwise. Yet he never changes shape, crosses no boundaries, steals nothing, and remains stubbornly posted at the open entrance to the tunnel. Once again, the old lesson of comparative studies in oral fable is brought home. The nominal identities of motifs mean scarcely anything, while what they *do*, how they articulate in constellations with other motifs, and hence what they *mean generically* are all-important. Preternaturals are as preternaturals do, and there is no substitute for sensitive observation of the patterns that govern their activities.

5. THE COSMOGONIC TRIAD

One of the Turkish tales previously cited in connection with the Vertical Journeys illustrates also the pattern of the Cosmogonic Triad. Sukru Dariji's story about 'Shemsi Banı, Padishah [Emperor] of Pidgeons'[161] is about a male person whose name, Shemsi Banı, means "Life-Giving Sun." Both as the sun and as a prince of pidgeons, this wonderful person is a frequenter of the upper, aerial reaches of the world. The refectory where he and his fellow pidgeons regularly dine, however, is at the other extreme of the world's vertical axis, on the bottom of the sea—that is to say, on the lowest level beneath the earth's surface where living creatures may be found in the cosmos. Thus Shemsi Banı is a vertical traveller *par excellence*. Indeed, his proclivity to perpetual travel poses a serious problem of stability as the tale progresses, though it does not in any way hinder his giving of life both to a nubile woman and to her progeny.

A bird flies into a palace and steals a crocheting needle from a princess. Later it finds her in the palace garden and takes away her thimble. As a result the girl sickens, and her father the emperor has a public bath built in the town where the fee for admission is the telling of a tale.

Meanwhile, in a distant land an old beggar woman is travelling about seeking food. She sees a caravan of camels and mules burthened with food and follows it down to the bottom of the sea. There she enters a great chamber together with the animals of the caravan, and finds abundant food, which, however, she is forbidden to eat. Soon hundreds of pidgeons also enter the hall, each being transformed into a handsome young man when it dips its wings in a decorative pool of water. These feast together, then depart from the chamber one by one. Finally only the leader is left. He has the girl's crocheting needle and thimble, and commands the under-sea house and all that is in it to weep for the loveliness of the princess. All weep except the animals of the caravan, which laugh instead. The old woman returns with them to land. Eventually her lone wandering brings her to the emperor's bathhouse, where she pays for her bathing with the tale of her fabulous adventure underneath the sea.

The sick princess takes a lively interest in the old woman's story, and insists upon visiting the underwater palace. The two women go there together, and all the events of the old woman's previous visit recur except that when the crone leaves the sea with the caravan animals, the young princess remains as Shemsi Banı's paramour. He hides her from his pidgeon mess-mates for nine months in the underwater hall, but when she is about to be delivered of a child, he sends her out of the sea to his earthly parents' palace. There, after the birth of their son, Shemsi Banı visits his wife and child in the guise of a bird which temporarily becomes a man when it dips its wings in water. Eventually his wife and parents learn the secret of Shemsi Banı's enchantment, burn his suit of bird feathers on a great pile of pitch pine, and so confine him to human form and human habitats.

Shemsi Banı is a miraculous male person whose primary element is the air. His descents are productive in numerous ways, but his ascents produce nothing useful. His contacts with water uniformly change his shape so as to make him amenable to dealings with women. Whether in the form of a bath-house on land or a pidgeon's palace on the sea-bottom (the nubile girl's bath-house being a house with water in it, and the crone's underwater palace being a house in the water), water is a female asset, and the women of this story are peculiarly aquatic in that they depend in one way or another upon water for all the good things which they obtain (i. e., *food* and *progeny*).

Otherwise the two women are quite dissimilar. One is fertile and wedded in the course of the narrative, the other belongs to an earlier generation and is past reproduction. The old one, however, functions in a way that no one else in the story can. She is a giver of information and other intangible perquisites. When the younger woman is sick and unable either to help herself or to be helped by anyone else, the old crone discovers the location and the fabulous nature of the masculine cure for her ailment. Then, when she has finished her mission to establish the terms and conditions under which new life can arise, the infertile crone disappears from the tale without trace. The marked geographic separation or hiatus between the two women that prevailed at the beginning of the story is thus reaffirmed before the narrative ends.

Of the two women, only the elder is wise; the nubile one has no remembered experience to rely upon and so must obtain guidance from others in all matters except those connected with reproduction and progeny. Consequently the act of story-telling is itself a generic motif in this pattern. Some of the nubile woman's guidance comes from her old female companion, but animals are also peculiarly useful to her. The original of the πότνια θηρῶν, she not only perceives in animals their potential as sources of food or as transportation, but also realizes their fabulous potential for progeny.

The Cosmogonic Triad thus consists of three characters:

1. An unstable, aerial, male fertilizer.

2. An aquatic, fertile female whose procreative destiny devolves upon animals.

3. An infertile female giver of intangible terms and conditions.

To this list of persons must also be added another motif that is generically an indissoluble part of the triadic pattern of cosmogony:

4. A geographic/cosmological separation of the two females.

A modern Greek tale collected in Crete by I. Zographakes[172] displays revealing multiforms of the motifs in the Cosmogonic Triad. Again the primary male character is aerial in nature, full of miraculous powers, and an unstable progenitor whose behaviour is detrimental to family life. *An infertile woman vows to the Sun that if he will let her bear a child she will surrender it to him when it is twelve years old. A girl is born and given the name Maroula. She goes to a spring for water when she is twelve. The Sun observes her beauty and descends in the form of a young man to meet her at the spring. He tells the girl to ask her mother when she will give him what she has promised. The mother instructs Maroula to say that she has forgotten to ask, then lets her return to the spring. There she meets the Sun again, and is given a golden apple to remember him by. Once more the girl asks her mother when she will give the man what she has promised, though Maroula does not understand the purport of the question. The mother answers cryptically, "When he finds it, he may take it," and for a time she keeps Maroula from the spring. When finally she goes to the spring a third time for water, the Sun takes her away to his domain.*

But Maroula is unhappy in the Sun's house, and makes his garden wither through her misery. She conceals her unhappiness from the Sun, who is away from her all day, but one day he turns back in his course to find the girl in tears. He decides to send her home, and summons various animals to ask if they will transport her. First he asks lions (carnivores), then foxes (omnivores), and finally a deer (herbivore), who agrees to carry Maroula safely to her native place. On the way she is detained and threatened by four witches (a mother and three daughters) whom she meets at a well, but she eventually reaches home unscathed through the help of four domestic animals (mouse, cat, dog, and cockerel).

Like her Turkish counterpart, Maroula too by her physical acts transmutes and fixes the form and abode of nothing less than the life-giving Sun himself. Her mother is infertile, but establishes the terms and conditions under which Maroula is reunited with the Sun at the spring. For her part, Maroula is not only nubile, but also has a peculiar power of fertility over plant life, which she makes to wax or wither at will. Yet she has no accumulated wisdom of experience, and must rely on the providence of the other two characters in the Triad for the direction of her life.

Maroula is aquatic in her habits (frequenting springs and wells of water) while her fertile lover the Sun is aerial. The Sun's acts of descent are uniformly productive, while his ascents are useless. He is an unstable progenitor, constantly in motion and insensitive to the needs of family life. His proclivity to motion is the immediate cause of the geographical separation between the two women, which is duly introduced into the tale when Maroula goes away to live in his house. Through her use of animals she is able, however, to compensate for her aerial male progenitor's socially destructive tendencies, and to secure the well-being of the progeny in the story (herself).

Like the tale about Shemsi Banı, this modern Greek fable is cosmogonic inasmuch as it tells how the physical substance and the familiar shapes of a new order arise in the cosmos through the union of an aerial male and a fertile female under the terms and conditions laid down by the third member of the Cosmogonic Triad, an infertile (elder) female.

Fable constructed according to the pattern of the Cosmogonic Triad commonly also contains the motifs of witches and witchcraft.

It is an appropriate nexus in that witchcraft is often expressed in anti-cosmogonic acts that are by the folklorists' familiar Law of Opposites the counterparts of the Cosmogonic Triad's productive actions. So in the case of Shemsi Banı, who is an emperor of pidgeons because he was the victim of a bewitchment in the innocence of his infancy. Maroula similarly meets a demonic hag who would eat her up before the deer takes her safely home. A tale from the Baila of Central Africa (present-day territory of Zambia) describes another attempt at magical negation of the Cosmogonic Triad's productivity.[173]

In primordial time, before the present social separation of men and birds was complete, Blue Jay[174] *sued to marry the daughter of the Sky God. He already had a wife on earth, and at first the Sky God refused to let his daughter descend as Blue Jay's second wife on the grounds that she could not eat the meat of large animals lest she die. But Blue Jay vowed to keep that taboo and so won his marriage-suit.*

He tells his first wife to obey the taboo, but she purposely feeds the meat of a zebra to her rival, feigning that it is the flesh of a tiny gazelle. Consequently the Sky God's daughter dies, is buried, and Blue Jay is called to account in heaven. When he again descends, her father comes too in the shape of a rainstorm and flood to disinter and carry his daughter back to heaven. Blue Jay is destroyed in the storm, and all of him except a few bones that fall to earth remains suspended forever in the aether. This accounts for the characteristic rising-and-falling manner of flight of all his descendants, the blue jays of today.

Blue Jay is obviously an unstable aerial male progenitor who ignores the fundamental social rule of polygamy, according to which multiple wives must be compatible. His ascents all end in futility, but his descents help to introduce new substance and form into the cosmos. Like the Turkish and Greek Sun, his instability and proclivity to vertical motion has the effect of bringing together the disparate elements of heaven and earth with the intent of deriving progeny from the union. The nubile female of the tale is, of course, the Sky God's daughter, who is intensely concerned with animal species, food, forms of transportation, and water. Nevertheless she is an inert figure whose destiny is manipulated by others. The crucial condition of life on earth—that one eats what meat is available regardless of personal predilections—is laid down by the old woman of the story, who has only this and no tangible part in procreating either the intended or the actual (Blue Jay) progeny which is generically required in the pattern of the Cosmogonic Triad.

A Blackfellow tale from aboriginal tradition in Australia also manifests the Cosmogonic Triad:[175] *On a certain day in primordial time, before animals and human society were completely distinct, two 'women,' Gwaineebu and Goomai, were gathering shellfish when suddenly a kangaroo fleeing from hunters hopped into the water near them and became entangled in the water plants. The women kill the kangaroo and hide it so that the hunters will not take it from them. Soon the two hunters, Ooya and Gidgerigar, appear but cannot find their game. The women share their meal of shellfish with the men, but Gwaineebu's small son unceasingly begs for kangaroo meat. Fearful that his nagging will betray their secret to the men, Goomai hits the boy in the face hard enough to draw blood, which stains his chest. The hunters take the hint, however, and slip away to lie in wait until the women produce the dead kangaroo.*

Thinking the men have gone, the women prepare to cook the kangaroo, but the men claim it and will not share it even with Gwaineebu's hungry son. The women retire into a hut where they shut themselves up to incant a great rain- and hail-storm. When the storm strikes, the men plead for shelter, but the women will give them none. Ooya and Gidgerigar perish in the downpour, and are transmuted into two parrots. Their descendants are the two species of parrot now known by the names Ooya and Gidgerigar.

Like the cosmological difference between heaven and earth that separates Blue Jay's two wives in the African story, a great vertical distance also separates the Blackfellow characters Gwaineebu and Goomai. Gwaineebu is the progenetrix, through the lineage of her little son, of the Redbreast species of bird. The injury which Goomai inflicted on Gwaineebu's little boy is of course the ætion of the Redbreast's distinctive plummage. Goomai is for her part, as her Blackfellow name says, a water rat. Both women are obviously aquatic both in their habits (fishing) and in their powers of witchcraft (to destroy their enemies with rain and hail). The transportative, nutritional, and progenerative characteristics of animals are also a special province of the women's concern. But otherwise they are different. Goomai, who has no children, is the old woman who imposes the (intangible) color condition of red breast on her fertile companion's offspring. The pair

of male hunters are also aerial progenitors (of parrot lineages), but
they are unstable travelers who have no proper understanding of familial responsibilities; they accept nourishment from the women, but will
give none in return, not even to an innocent child. The women riposte
with the further social destruction wrought by their weather-witching.
The Cosmogonic Triad of fertile woman, infertile female giver of conditions and (duplicated) unstable aerial progenitor in this Blackfellow
multiform is nevertheless fabulously responsible for the substance and
shape of several distinct species in the present Australian cosmos.

   The industrialized, metropolitan culture of the contemporary
West has not been hospitable to animal tales such as the Baila and
Blackfellow ones I have justed discussed. But like the other fundamental patterns of oral fable, the Cosmogonic Triad is nonetheless well
preserved in those genres of fable which are congenial to modern Western civilization. The Western *genre* of 'joke' or *Witz* affords especially
abundant evidence of traditional fabulous patterns. The micro-cosmo-
gonies of this characteristically Western form of narrative are predicat-
ed no less than their 'tribal' or 'high literary' cousins on the twofold
problem of how to get *food* and *progeny* using the requisite avian,
aquatic, and animal elements: *A bride, who has been given among her
wedding presents a double boiler but no skillet, goes to consult her
mother, a true giver of the conditions and terms of life:*
   "Mother, I need some advice." Not waiting to hear the rest of
   her daughter's question, the mother volunteers: "Of course,
   dear, it's perfectly natural that you should ask. Now tonight,
   when your husband wants to get into bed with you, just remember that men are beasts, and do everything he asks." The bride:
   "Oh, hell, mother, I know all about making love. What I want
   to know is, how do I scramble eggs for breakfast in a double
   boiler?"[176]
The unstable, transitory, familially insensitive character of the
male progenitor is emphasized again in another, versified example:

> A young woman got married at Chester,
> Her mother, she kissed and she blessed her:
>   "This man that you've won
>   Should be just loads of fun;
> Since tea he's kissed me and your sister."[177]

Like many other shibboleths of criticism and interpretation, terms such as 'bawdy' and 'vulgar' may help to define ethnic contexts in which the basic materials of oral fable are used. Thus the pattern of the Cosmogonic Triad may be differently employed in an Anglo-American limerick or 'dirty joke' than it is in the biblical narrative of Creation found in the Old Testament book of Genesis for example, or in the ancient Greek story of creation as told in Hesiod's *Theogony*. But different ethnic interpretations or employments, be they vulgar, bawdy, holy, or divine, in no way alter narrative patterns themselves or their generic meanings.

The Old Testament's account of Creation in Genesis One uses the Cosmogonic Triad in a manner similar to the use of the Four Zones in Dante's *Divine Comedy;* both are literary works that incorporate numerous schemata derived ultimately from oral fable. The great debate about the literal veracity of the biblical Creation which the Scientific Revolution engendered in the West should have taught us at least one thing: all that we or any other people can possibly know about cosmogony is someone's fiction. None of us were there to see it, and the best any of us can do is to surmise by deduction how it must have happened. Disagreement arises only about the principles from which the deduction should proceed. But it is in the innermost nature of all creation that it should consist of the amalgamation or sunderance of things which are not (before creation) ordinarily found amalgamated or sundered. In that sense fiction and cosmogony (or creation of any kind) are and must be identical. One form of fiction or another may be more or less congenial to this or that historical era and its dominant philosophy; thus the ancient biblical tale of Creation gave way in the West in the nineteenth and twentieth centuries to a spate of new cosmogonic fictions or, as they prefer to call them, 'hypotheses' contrived by natural scientists and their popularizers. Biology and astro-physics are the great contemporary hotbeds of cosmogonical fiction, but the essential features of the Cosmogonic Triad have not changed (except in name) even there. The researchers in great modern astrophysical observatories or biochemical research institutes still shape their cosmogonic legends around such central notions as instability, fertility, and "the right conditions" (by which they too mean such things as spatial array or distribution, cyclicity, functional balance between solidity and fluidity, and so forth). It cannot be said that in this sense the personifications in the Cosmogonic Triad of oral fable have ever had any generic meanings very different from those current in the cosmogonic fictions of modern science. Because they too used the Cosmogonic Triad, the ancient Hebrew-speaking authors, compilers, or conflators of the Old Testament Genesis dealt in coin of the same metal as do their modern scientific successors, no matter how different the stamp which they put upon it. But their mintage no less than the serious modern cosmogonists' also bore the motto *ex nihilo nihil.*

The unstable male cosmogone of the biblical Creation in Genesis One is of course *elohim,* the Hebrew 'God,' whose spirit is unmistakably described as both aerial and transient by the participle *merahepet* in the Hebrew text. Some construe that word to mean "hovering"; others see in it a more violent or aimless motion analogous to the action denoted by an English phrase such as "rushing about." Either way, the instability depicted is both *temporal* and atmospheric or *upperworldly.* Together with the unstable, aerial male cosmogone, two grammatically female figures also preexist the first acts of creation to complete the Cosmogonic Triad. They are respectively the fertile progenetrix *'areṣ* (Earth) and the infertile old giver of terms and conditions, *tᵉhom* (Abyss).

> In the beginning of creation, when God made heaven and earth, the earth was without form and void, with darkness over the face of the abyss, and a mighty wind that swept over the face of the waters (*or* the spirit of God that hovered over the face of the water).[178]

In regard to the description of earth as being "without form and void," it may be that the Hebrew words *tōhu wābōhu* ("emptiness and confusion"), which grammatically have masculine gender,[179] should be understood not merely as the *condition* of earth before the work of creation began, but rather as the *thing* (since it is a noun construct) that earth was before it was earth, or out of whose formlessness earth was formed. But feminine earth's functions as one of the Cosmogonic Triad in the subsequent creation show that it is immaterial which comes first, *'areṣ* (earth) or *tōhu wābōhu* (void and disorder). In substance, earth's 'void' or 'emptiness' is the primordial deficiency of all vegetable, animal, or human life, and the 'confusion' or 'formlessness' of the earth proves as the text progresses to be nothing more than feminine earth's condition of indiscriminate mixture with water. Regardless of whether *'areṣ* is merely liberated from its vacancy and muddiness, or should be thought of as gaining its proper identity by virtue of that liberation, earth is the abundantly fertile, aquatically defined female upon whom the unstable aerial male progenitor *elohim* begets the substance and shape of the present cosmos. In perfect accord with the pattern of the Cosmogonic Triad the fecund, wet female *'areṣ* is deeply involved with the kinetic, nutritive, and procreative functions of animal life.

'Areṣ is, however, entirely physical in character, concerned exclusively with matter and the material substance of the new cosmos. She has no remembered wisdom of her own to guide her, and so must be shaped by others. Before her mission can be accomplished, certain intangible terms and conditions must be established, and these are the province of the Cosmogonic Triad's third primordial figure in the Old Testament story of Creation, *tᵉhom*, the 'abyss.' *Tᵉhom's* primal condition is "darkness (over the face of the abyss)," and *elohim's* first creative act is to impose the further intangible conditions of *visibility* and *cyclicity* on the elementary, insubstantive abysmal state:

> God said, 'Let there be light,' and there was light; and God saw that the light was good, and he separated light from darkness.
> He called the light day, and the darkness night. So evening came, and morning came, the first day.

These purely abstract, immaterial modifications of the abysmal darkness set the stage for the substantive creation. True to pattern, once *tᵉhom's* terms (periodic night and day) and conditions (light and dark) have been established, she drops out of the story not to be mentioned again. The fecund pair of male and female, *elohim* and *'areṣ*, are left alone to do their work of begetting and shaping matter. Like the building of shelter to house a new family, *elohim's* first tangible creation is architectural:

> God said, 'Let there be a vault between the waters, to separate water from water.' So God made the vault, and separated the water under the vault from the water above it, and so it was; and God called the vault heaven. Evening came, and morning came, a second day.

The engineering effect of the new vault is to discriminate functionally between solid earth and her aquatic ambient. The aerial progenitor with his typical proclivity to motion moves earth's waters away first along a vertical axis, and then horizontally:

> God said, 'Let the waters under heaven be gathered into one place, so that dry land may appear;' and so it was. God called

the dry land earth, and the gathering of the waters he called seas; and God saw that it was good.

When *elohim*'s work of physical construction is finished, *'areṣ*'s progenerative bearing begins. The aerial male stimulates, and feminine earth produces, abundant vegetation:

> Then God said, 'Let the earth produce fresh growth, let there be on the earth plants bearing seed, fruit-trees bearing fruit each with seed according to its kind.' So it was; the earth yielded fresh growth, plants bearing seed according to their kind and trees bearing fruit each with seed according to its kind. . . .

The intangible condition of visibility and the basic periodicity of night and day have already been established in connection with *tᵉhom*. It is, however, a peculiar kind of night and day, because the segregation of light into the several heavenly bodies of sun, moon, and stars implies a concrete substantiation or *hypostatization* of light, and the substance of the cosmos belongs to *elohim* and *'areṣ*, not *tᵉhom*. So the creation of sun, moon, and stars devolves like all the other shapes, species, and physical matter of the aborning cosmos upon watery earth and her overarching defensive firmament, but *after* the invention of intangible light itself:

> God said, 'Let there be lights in the vault of heaven to separate day from night, and let them serve as signs both for festivals and for seasons and years. Let them also shine in the vault of heaven to give light on earth.' So it was; God made the two great lights, the greater to govern the day and the lesser to govern the night; and with them he made the stars.

The basic vertical rhythm of *elohim*'s creativity continues as he turns his attention next to the animal species of aquatic earth. First he stimulates nether species, then upperworldly ones, and finally earth's spatially intermediate progeny:

> God said, 'Let the waters teem with countless living creatures, and let birds fly above the earth across the vault of heaven.' God then created the great sea-monsters and all living creatures that move and swarm in the waters, according to their kind, and every kind of bird; and God saw that it was good. So he blessed them and said, 'Be fruitful and increase, fill the waters of the seas; and let the birds increase on land.' Evening came, and morning came, a fifth day.

God said, 'Let the earth bring forth living creatures, according to their kind: cattle, reptiles, and wild animals, all according to their kind.' So it was. . . .

Others have observed and commented on the similarity between the biblical Creation and the pagan cosmogony in the first poem of Elias Lönnrot's Finnish *Kalevala*. That similarity resides precisely in the Finnish cosmogony's incorporation of the pattern of the Cosmogonic Triad. Its aerial male cosmogone is the high god Ukko, its giver of terms and conditions (including light and temporal periodicity) is Ukko's brooding goldeneye, and its miraculously fertile, aquatic progenetrix is the so-called 'mother of the water,' parent of the cosmotact Väinamöinen, who is nubile but unwise, being dependent in all her progenerative accomplishments upon the stimulation and deliverance of others.

The ancient Greek story of creation in Hesiod's *Theogony* also reproduces the pattern of the Cosmogonic Triad. There the infertile female giver of intangible terms and conditions comes first:

ἤτοι μὲν πρώτιστα Χάος γένετ'·   116
In truth, Chaos came into being first of all.

The word Χάος is grammatically of neuter gender, but the commentators generally understand the personified deity Chaos as female. She is pure empty space, the epitome of intangibility. Her one and only generative act in Hesiod's cosmogony is strictly parthenogenetic (i.e., self-directed and devoid of any social dependence) and its results are, like Chaos herself, utterly without substance or tangibility.

ἐκ Χάεος δ' Ἔρεβός τε μέλαινά τε Νὺξ ἐγένοντο·   123
Out of Chaos Erebos and gloomy Night were born.

Chaos' offspring are twins as it were, Erebos and Nyx. Erebos is male, and personifies perpetual, unqualified darkness. Nyx or Night is a personification of darkness too, but she is female and carries as Night the implication of another intangible condition, periodicity or cyclical alternation with light. Nyx and her brother Erebos unite incestuously to realize the further condition of light, which is again expressed in the form of a male and female pair, the one invariable and the other periodic, Aither and Hemera. These in turn have no offspring, and so the line of descent from Chaos remains barren of anything but the same intangible terms and conditions that everywhere characterize the

generic motif underlying Chaos in the universal pattern of the Cosmogonic Triad.[199]

Chaos' substantial counterpart in Hesiod's cosmogonic scheme is
the epitome of unthinkingly fertile matter, Gaia or Ge, the Earth. An
unstable and destabilizing male progenitor, Eros, attends the two disparate, substantive and insubstantive females from the very first mention of them in the poetry of the *Theogony*:

> ἤτοι μὲν πρώτιστα Χάος γένετ'· αὐτὰρ ἔπειτα 116
> Γαῖ᾽ εὐρυστερνος, πάντων ἔδος ἀσφαλὲς αἰεὶ
> ἀθανάτων. . .
>
> . . .
>
> ἠδ᾽ Ἔρος, ὅς κάλλιστος ἐν ἀθανάτοισι θεοῖσι,
> λυσιμελής, πάντων τε θεῶν πάντων τ᾽ ἀνθρώπων
> δάμναται ἐν στήθεσσι νόον καὶ ἐπίφρονα βουλήν.[180]

In truth, Chaos came into being first of all; but thereafter
Broad-bosomed Earth, who is the secure dwelling-place
Of all the immortals forever. . .
. . .
And so too came forth Eros, who is goodliest of all the deathless
  gods to look upon,
Who brings melting weakness to the limbs of all gods and men
  alike,
Overruling in their hearts all their wits and wise provisions.

Eros as a personified male "force of generation and reproduction"
(M. L. West)[181] at the very beginning of Hesiod's cosmogony presides
over the period of cosmogonic time during which the aerial male cosmogone Uranos (Heaven) consorts with Gaia. But Uranos' predictable in-
sensitivity to the requirements of orderly family life leads to his cas-
tration, and he is thus made to meet the further typological description of himself as a *transient cosmogone*. His demise as aerial progenitor results directly in the appearance of the personified female force
of generation and reproduction, the goddess Aphrodite, who coinci-
dentally displaces her counterpart Eros as the demiurge of further re-
productivity.

Gaia's first progenerative acts are, like Chaos', parthenogenetic,
but they are all massively material in nature. They proceed vertically
downward; first high Heaven (Uranos) is born, then mountains, and
finally Pontos, the great raging and indivisible sheet of salt sea water.

Thereafter Gaia mates with Uranos. The very first of their numerous material offspring is, like Pontos, a further reinforcement of Gaia's typologically predictable wetness and aquatic attributes, the gentle and tributary Okeanos from whom all of Earth's springs and rivers rise. With Pontos beneath and around her and Okeanos to water her inwardly, wet Gaia subsequently becomes the mother and sanctuary of all kinds and lineages of material beings—kinetic, animal, and vegetable.

EPILOGUE

Some Observations Concerning Method and Rationale

Under the spreading Chestnut tree
I sold you and you sold me.

-George Orwell

V. Propp's supposition about sequence: an illusion
    induced by static inspection of narrative.   *p. 293*

The dynamic principle of agglomeration seen in the
    living practitioners of the Yugoslav tradition.   *p. 297*

The doctrine of 'cultural universals' and functionalism.   *p. 314*

The inalienable conservatism of oral narrative tradition
    sufficiently explains it.   *p. 318*

I f the stories of Creation, Adam in Eden, Moses at the burning
bush, and Samson's misalliances as we have them in the Old Testament are the Word of God (whether literally or metaphorically),
then the force of this book is to suggest that in fact the Word was
Pentecostal from the beginning, and to an equal degree every people
was chosen to receive it. In keeping that gift, all men everywhere have
shared a common destiny as intellectual masters of themselves and
their circumstances, no matter how divergent their disparate material
means and their striving to perfect their different and unique natures
have made them. So long, moreover, as such tales continue to be told
in whatever language, and in some part understood, so long are we
assured that no essential achievement of the intelligence of our distant and anonymous ancestry has been lost. And whether it is in our
stars as a race ever to know any other kind of higher intelligence than
our own, truly no other power of thought would be worth our knowing were it not compatible with that still rather mysterious kind of
thinking longest and most ably expressed among us in traditional oral
fable.

To treat oral narrative tradition in a merely formal manner without thought to the larger duty of comprehension we owe it is to blas-
pheme against the whole history and aspiration of human intelligence
that is expressed in the tradition, if not against God. Still, it is only
in the sum of its fine features that the greater consequence of the
tradition is made manifest.

In its more technical aspect, this study began partly in consequence of certain anomalies which I repeatedly observed in the Parry
Collection whenever I tried to find in its texts evidence of the rule
or 'law' of oral narrative which Vladimir Propp enunciated on the
basis of Russian folktale with the words "posledovatel'nost' funktsij
vsegda odinakova" ("the logical succession of functions is always
identical").

Serious study of oral narrative traditions has always bred the
impulse to segment stories, to reduce them somehow to smaller, more
or less discrete constituent units. To yield to this impulse, as most
critics have, is to view whole narratives as compounds whose various

properties (including meaning) derive from two sources: the sub-narrative constituents or parts of stories on the one hand, and on the other hand the order or organization of those parts by plot, *sujet*, type, etc. Great diversity of opinion has prevailed concerning the identities of the constituent parts and about the varieties and significance of their organization into whole stories, but the fundamental analytical procedure of segmentation is an almost universal practice.

So it was with Vladimir Propp, who called his segments 'functions,' and said that in a substantial sample of Russian folktales he could detect only one 'logical order' or underlying plot. It was this thesis or dictum of Propp's which I found I could not reconcile with the apparent disregard for any sequential plan—either logical or literal—in the mass of metrical and prose tales I knew outside Propp's Russian traditions. My subsequent inspection of the selfsame tales in the original Russian from which Propp had derived his supposed rule of single sequence left me in even greater doubt about both the rule's validity and its worth as a tool of criticism. Having, moreover, a respect for the narratives themselves that compels me to doubt their critics rather than them whenever the two seem not to be in harmony—and particularly so when like Propp the critic was no collector and had never tested his hypothesis against the actuality of living traditional narrators in the act of performance—I came to think that if the freedom of even closely similar tales from a common, uniform order of internal construction which *I* had observed were a reality, that fact might cast light on another phenomenon that had repeatedly puzzled me in my interrogations of live performers in both the Balkans and in Africa. I had found, namely, that every experienced oral traditional *conteur* upon whom I had attempted the experiment could, when told *any* several, randomly chosen motifs or 'functions' from any tale which I knew, surmise not just one but several reasonable facsimiles of it, all differing precisely in regard to the sequence of events, by which the performer would discriminate one tale from another as much as by the changes of names pertaining to the various characters, objects, and events whose similarities otherwise accounted for his multiple response to my suggestion of a single story-line. Were I subsequently to correct the performer with an expanded telling of the one form of the tale that I had drawn upon for my original hints to him, he (or she) would receive it either as a mistaken or an alien tale unless it happened to correspond exactly in regard to sequence with one of his or her usual stories.

This experiment depended of course upon my stripping away the identifying names of heroes, places, and so forth, just as Propp and other segmenters of traditional narrative have regularly done, when I proffered my suggestions of plots and their constituents to actual *conteurs*. Thus I suggested, for example, "the two brothers who found it impossible to live together in the forest, and what happened to them," or "the kingly father who decided to disinherit his son, and what the young man did about it," and so forth. In every such experiment the possibility of changing the sequence of events was essential to the story-tellers' recognition of more than one actual tale implied in a mere plot-sketch of randomly chosen and generalized story-motifs. Moreover, the very names of places, things, and characters in my performers' several alternative responses changed as the sequences changed; thus one set of places, things, and persons was appropriate to the story of a son whose actions led his father to disinherit him, and another set to the story of a son acting in comparable fashion after (or because of) disinheritance. Indeed, the changes of names from one tale to another seemed actually to be the consequence of changes in sequence of motifs which they otherwise shared. Thus was sequence variable, and the fluidity of sequence a source of playful stimulation to my informants. But in stark contrast to that, the names applicable to the several parts of any one sequence belonged firmly to it, and my informants regarded any tampering with those identities as outlandishly ignorant or reprehensibly foolish, or both, because the plot of named characters' stories were the fixed fates of those characters ordained in tradition, and no due regard for established knowledge would allow meddling in this sphere.

Thus Propp's library-bound analysis made narrative motifs perfectly interchangeable because the sequence of functions which they represented were always the same; but my living tellers of tales in Southeastern Europe and in Central and West Africa insisted in the unimpeachable evidence of their actual narrative practice that motifs were isomeric largely, if not exclusively, because their arrangement was different in different tales. Here was a conundrum.

I had arrived at this conundrum by taking as much interest in what actual *conteurs* actually did as in what seemed to be the result of their fabulation once the texts which they delivered had been set down and, as it were, embalmed in writing or in print. This habit of regarding oral fable as a *process* rather than as an accumulation of

static texts and genres (or as some contemporary analysts would prefer to have it, as 'structures') is, I think, indispensable to a right understanding of the subject, and it is a conceptual cornerstone of this book.
So in Africa and the Balkans, I observed that my informants' evident
freedom within tradition to associate certain motifs with a variety of
sequences was yet never so great as to include more than a restricted
portion of any good narrator's repertory. Here, in the scope of the
individual bard's narrative knowledge, was another factor Propp's
analysis did not comprehend. For if, as Propp argued from his experience with static texts, all narrators told essentially the same tale, why
should any story-teller ever care to suppose that he could tell a larger
number of diverse stories as my living informants uniformly did, and
proved they could do, in their process of composing many nominally
distinct tales?

The word Propp used in his native Russian to describe the invariable regularity of sequence in his sample of a hundred folktales was
posledovatel'nost'.[184] There is a certain lexical ambiguity inherent in
the word, for it can mean on the one hand the quality of sequential
order in the most physical sense, and on the other hand it may mean
the internal logic of causation by which one thing in a story gives rise
to another. In regard to the first meaning, Propp himself was in the
conclusion of his work forced to make significant concessions, and in
doing so he fell back heavily upon the second, more philosophical
meaning. But in observing my live informants time and again in the
act of narrative composition, I have come to understand that their
habitual association of certain motifs or 'functions' is due ultimately
neither to the compulsion of any preconceived sequential order nor
to the operation of any fixed causative logic emanating either from
within or from without their narratives. Such associations are, on the
contrary, due entirely to the effect of the tradition, that is, of the
narratives themselves heard and retold countless times, which creates
and continually reaffirms for the *conteur* the propriety of *clustering*
certain kinds of information in his tales, regardless of what he or
anyone else thinks of that information, and regardless of any suppositions about sequential order in it. Neither causative logic nor sequence,
but simply the traditional propriety of *agglomerating* certain information governs the traditional *conteur*'s composition of tales throughout
his repertory.

I find the truth of this understanding affirmed not only in the copious modern evidence of the Parry Collection, but also everywhere in the attestation of traditional oral narrative both in recorded history and in what may be reconstructed or surmised about oral fabulation from prehistory.

This book is devoted mostly to just one example of a motival cluster whose ancient and universal integrity as a process in oral fable ultimately owes nothing, then, to any other social or cultural or philosophical circumstance whatsoever except the tradition itself and its own inherent ideational content. The implication is, of course, that what may be true of a part of tradition may be true of the whole, but I have begun for the sake of manageability with a single cluster of fine details found repeatedly in certain texts of the Parry Collection.

THE DYNAMIC PRINCIPLE OF AGGLOMERATION SEEN IN THE LIVING PRACTITIONERS OF THE YUGOSLAV TRADITION

In July of the year 1935, the great Yugoslav bard Avdo Medjedović sang and dictated for Milman Parry seven long, epic verse narratives with a prodigious combined total of 41,818 decasyllabic verses. The shortest of these was 2,624 verses in length, while the longest came ultimately to 13,331 verses. Medjedović completed five of the seven tales within the month of July, but had by the end of the month sung only the first 6,199 lines of the longest, 13,331-line epic, and so continued it for Parry's phonographic apparatus into August, finishing the additional 7,132 lines on the third day of that month.

The other epic still unfinished at the end of July was "The Captivity of Tale* of Orašac in Ozim," which consisted of 3,738 verses when it was interrupted on 29 July. In August, Medjedović's telling of other tales intervened, however, and Parry was obliged to leave Medjedović's town of Bijelo Polje to return to the United States before Medjedović could finish the story of Tale's imprisonment and rescue in the mythical town of Ozim. Due to force of circumstance, therefore, this one epic comes down to us from Medjedović as an acaudal fragment.

---

* A Serbocroatian hypocoristic modification of the [Turkish] name Tahir; pronounced with two syllables [täle].

Unfinished at 3,738 verses, it is a monumental fragment, especially when one considers that even at that length Medjedović had still not yet brought the party of heroes destined to rescue Tale to the town of Ozim where Tale was captive. Judging from the many similar 'captivity songs' recorded from other Yugoslav epic singers, it is reasonable to suppose that Medjedović's fragment represents not even half the length to which his story would have extended had he finished it.

Within the company of seventy or more major Bosnian heroes whose stories constitute this ethnic tradition, Tale of Orašac is a peculiar figure. Gross incivility, constant poverty, an immunity to delusion often spilling over into clairvoyance, and an indecent predilection for trickery are characteristic of him. Avdo Medjedović gave the following account of his captivity in Ozim and of his friends' undertaking to rescue him: *A company of Bosnian heroes is gathered in Udbina with Mustajbeg of the province of Lika presiding. Among the company are the two brothers, Mujo and Halil Hrnjica, the elder seated with his fellows and the younger, Halil, waiting upon the company as winestewart. All receive Halil's services gratefully except his brother Mujo, who inexplicably repulses him. The head of the assembly asks why, and Mujo replies that not only he but also the entire company should be too pained by the disappearance of their comrade, Tale of Orašac, to take any pleasure in their present leisurely amusement. Nothing, says Mujo, has gone aright with their commonwealth since the day eight years ago when they sent Tale disguised as a beggar to spy upon their enemies in the lands of the hostile empire beyond the Border. From that time until day-before-yesterday, no one has heard anything concerning Tale's fate or whereabouts, whether he is dead or alive. Two days ago, however, Mujo, who has during the time of Tale's absence sustained Tale's numerous family, chanced to see Tale's horse offered for sale in the public market, a sure sign that his family have despaired of his return. Mujo says that he himself bought the horse and has stabled it to keep against the day when some real knowledge about Tale will come to hand.*

All who hear Mujo's speech in the assembly are much saddened by it, and Mujo himself is moved to offer magnificent rewards to any who can bring him news of Tale. Should Tale be a captive, no enemy stronghold would be too formidable nor any place too far for Mujo to go to his rescue, says Mujo; he will, moreover, give his and Halil's maiden sister, a famous beauty, in marriage to the man who reveals

the place of Tale's detention; he will also obtain a high preferment
for that man from their emperor; build him a castle beside, and better
than, Mujo's own; finally, he will give him half his own landed estate
in fee. Hearing Mujo's terrific speech, Halil marvels aloud, protesting
his own complete innocence in the matter of Tale and the injustice
of his brother Mujo's earlier, unprovoked curtness toward him; for,
says Halil, he was but a boy of twelve when Mujo first commissioned
Tale to go a-spying.

At this very moment in their discourse, the assembled Bosnians
observe in the distance a travel-worn foreign courier approaching their
clubhouse. All quail at the sight of the courier, fearing that he brings
a mortal challenge to one of them, for they see that he carries a letter
hanging from the end of an ash-wood stick [the hewn wood of this
story]. In the event it is a letter from the missing Tale, but not addressed as might be expected to the head of the assembly or to Mujo,
but rather to the lowest of the assembly in rank, young Halil. Tale
tells in the letter that he is a prisoner in Ozim, and says that because
he has no confidence in any of the Bosnian dignitaries, he appeals
instead to Halil to rescue him from his foreign captivity. The daughter
of Tale's captor, the king of Ozim, Tale continues, has also promised
herself to Halil in marriage if only he will heed Tale's appeal. The king
of Ozim has proclaimed throughout his kingdom a great horse-racing
contest with both his daughter and the prisoner Tale as prizes in the
sweepstake. Tale implores Halil to beg the loan of Mujo's famous
courser and to bring it to the race in Ozim.

Having heard Halil read this letter, Mujo writes a reply to Tale
saying that after due consultation in the Bosnian assembly, it has been
decided that the journey to Ozim would be hopeless for any of them;
Tale may not therefore expect any expedition by them to rescue him.
Had Tale as originally instructed confined his spying to nearer provinces
the case would be different, writes Mujo, but Ozim is a land from
which no Bosnian ever returns. The letter of reply is dispatched by
the same courier who brought Tale's appeal.

The assembly turns once more to its drinking and pastime, but
now instead of merely serving, Halil also drinks and becomes somewhat drunk. He reproaches Mujo, sarcastically reminding him of the
rich largesse he had promised for news of Tale moments before the
courier's arrival, and of Mujo's boastful promise to go anywhere to
Tale's rescue. Mujo should, says Halil, at least hazard his famous

charger so that he, Halil, may at the risk of no one's life but his own go to the horse-race at Ozim. Mujo says that his hot-blooded younger brother wants to do this not on Tale's account but for the sake of the King of Ozim's daughter; he will not for any reason trust his mighty horse out of his own sight.

Despising Mujo for evidently preferring the horse to both himself and his supposedly dear friend Tale, Halil flings himself out of the assembly and goes homeward, intending there to kill both himself and the disputed horse in the stable. But when he arrives home his mother and sister take his part against his elder brother, and equip him for the journey to Ozim with the horse, which they take responsibility for stealing from Mujo. Mujo too comes home drunk from the assembly just in time for one last violent altercation with Halil as the latter departs riding the coveted white horse.

Alone and with no experience of the world to guide him on so dangerous a journey, Halil now rides away across the Plain of Udbina. Halfway over this plain, he sees a strange warrior waiting and wonders what peril to himself this well-armed stranger may pose so early in his journey. With great relief he learns in the ensuing exchange that the stranger is in fact only a friend in disguise, the older and more experienced hero Osman Tanković, who has heard of Mujo's and Halil's quarrel and decided to go with Halil to Ozim. Osman has reasons of his own for going: both his sister Fatima and his younger brother Ibrahim are, like Tale, also captives in Ozim.

So the two travel together until nightfall obliges them to halt in a wilderness place far from any human dwelling. Here they lead their horses into a dark grove of trees and seat themselves around a small portable table to eat and drink the provisions which they have brought with them to this lonely spot.

The scene is menacingly dark and frought with uncertainty, as much for the two men waiting in the grove as for any other traveller so unlucky as to be benighted in such a place. Medjedović says:

> It was utterly black, a great and deep darkness.
> Along the road huge firs
> Interwove their branches over the ravine.
> Narrow glens and deep pools of darkness extended in all directions.
> Then Halil perceived the sound
> Of a great rumbling in the gorges.[185]

Yet this scene, pregnant as it is with incipient fear, is in fact only

an amplified reprise of Halil's earlier meeting with the other seemingly
menacing but in reality friendly traveller, Osman. So this new apparition of terror also resolves itself into an unexpected helper and friend,
whose eventual value as helper when compared with Osman's is greater
in proportion to the greater threat of his approach:

> "The curse of God upon you, damned mountain of Brešljen,
> You are forever thus full of gloom and murky.
> Tonight the clouds obscure all seeing.
> Before these clouds overcast the sky
> I could at least follow the spoor of Mujo's white horse,
> But now black night has everything more tightly in her grip.　1360
> Neither can I see the white horse's tracks,
> Nor do I myself know the way I ought to go,
> Nor where I am to find young Hrnjica.
> Too late Mujo sent me forth
> To keep his brother safe upon the roads."
> Halil heard, and asked Osman:
> "Brother Osman, can you recognize
> What falcon it is calling in the mountain?"
> Thus said Osman to Halil:
> "It is good fortune, brother, both thine and mine:　　1370
> One of the wise Kurtagići,
> Nušin Kurtagić of Otoka.
> A brother born is a brother true;
> Now you see what care Mujo has had for you,
> Sending Nušin after you
> To guard you prudently in Ozim,
> Both in Ozim and on your way to it
> In every difficult situation.
> But you, Halil, are hereby pledged
> To be obedient to Kurtagić in all things.　　1380
> For by God, handsome Halil,
> There is not in all Bosnia nor on all the Border,
> Dear brother, nor in all the Hungarian lands
> Such another border warrior as is Nušin,
> Nor a stouter champion in battle,
> Nor a better lover,
> Nor any countenance more cheerful
> Than Nušin Kurtagić."[186]

Halil is not, however, the only one in this scene who needs reas-
surance. Cut off until this moment from the goodwill and help of his
politically powerful elder brother Mujo, Halil witnesses with the arrival
of Nušin Kurtagić the simultaneous reunion of himself with the head
of his family and the dispelling of a fearsome uncertainty as to the

character and intent of the stranger approaching in the dark. But
Nušin Kurtagić is until this moment also lost and fearfully uncertain
of what lies ahead in the sightless dark. Halil now delivers Nušin from
his predicament just as Nušin has by his coming delivered Halil:

> Halil called to the worthy Kurtagić:
> "Brother Nušin, dear to me as though thou wert mine own,
> You have not so much lagged behind,
> Nor have you far to seek for Halil.
> Come 'round, my brother, from right to left,
> Here am I and Osman this way."   1395
> He gave thanks, and dismounting,
> Started leftward towards the place where Halil was.
> When he came among the brethren
> He gave greeting and stood beside them.
> Both the lads sprang to their feet then,
> And spreading their arms wide,
> Greeted Nušin Kurtagić with a kiss.
> Halil, taking Nušin by the right hand,
> Seated him at the table already laid with victuals.[187]

The turning of the newcomer withershins is a stock feature of
this scene in the Yugoslav tradition, as is also the unexpected provision
of food ready to eat in so wild a place.

A hundred and twenty kilometres by road eastward from Bijelo
Polje lay the town of Novi Pazar where, one year before his work with
Avdo Medjedović, in July of 1934, Parry obtained by dictation another
text of another captivity narrative from another aged bard, Salih Ugljanin. Ugljanin and Medjedović had never met nor heard each other sing,
but they had similar conventional ideas about the kinds of event that
occurred when famous heroes-to-be went abroad to rescue comrades
from foreign prisons.[188]

*A hero of many legends, Osmanbey of the city of Osek, hears
women mourning before daybreak on bayram, a holiday which should
bring only joy to the town's citizenry. He asks his hundred-year-old
mother for an explanation, and she tells him that twelve years ago
the local military governor, Mustajbey of the Lika, went with a troop
of thirty men on an expedition across the frontier into the neighboring empire. No word has been heard of them since, and it is their wom-
enfolk who are so uncannily lamenting on a holiday morning in Osek.
Osman, who like Halil in Medjedović's story is destined to be a great
hero but who is still only at the beginning of his first heroic adventure*

in this tale, swears that, had he known of Mustajbey's disappearance, nothing could have deterred his going to the very ends of the earth in search of the missing men.

Osmanbey's mother disapproves, but he demands that she give him from her reserves a suitable disguise so that he may now go secretly abroad to look for Mustajbey. He says that unless his mother complies with the demand, he will go forthwith to the stable and there kill both himself and his horse. Yielding in the face of this threat, Osmanbey's mother gives him an alien warrior's clothes as a disguise. On the foreign soldier's cap is emblazoned the name 'Ensign Nicholas of Ċpanur.'

Wearing the foreign uniform, Osmanbey travels over two mountains that are named after two species of hardwood tree (Fagus and Juglans) which presumably grow there: Beech Mountain and Walnut Mountain. Then he comes to a third mountain; it is characterized by fir trees. Here, like Medjedović's novice-hero Halil, Ugljanin's tyro Osmanbey also meets a stranger whom he immediately fears:

> But when he came to Kunar Mountain,
> He made his way down by the whitened trail.
> The scattered firs raised their branches to touch the very heavens.
> When he reached the trail's end,
> He went on by way of a close glen
> Until he noticed an unexpected sound.   150
> Up from below there came a rumbling that set the very ground
>   to quavering.
> The bey was alone, and took fright
> Wondering what monstrous things these were making their way
>   up the mountain.
> So, quickly he slid from his white horse and,
> Turning withershins,
> He hid himself beneath a green fir tree
> Where, taking his medallioned rifle in his hands,
> He waited, trying to imagine who was about to appear.
> No great time had passed
> When a grenadier of lowering mien came into view,   160
> Riding a black horse so spirited it seemed the very jinns
>   possessed it.
> And what a one was the dark grenadier!
> His moustaches reached from shoulder to shoulder
> As though he carried a raven-black calf in his teeth.
> On his breast were spherical pendants hanging free,
> And both parts of his cuirass were of gold.

> About his neck was a collar of gold,
> Two small golden pistols were at his belt,
> And on his hip a golden brand.
> The scabbard glittered with golden dukats.
> He carried a medallion-studded rifle in his hands,
> With four and twenty medals set along it,
> Each weighing half a liter.
> On his right hung his ammunition boxes of gold.
> His black horse gaped as though possessed,   175
> And the darkly glaring grenadier
> Hissed at the top of his voice:
> "Who is it who conceals himself here upon the mountain?"[189]

But this apparition, so terrible in its bearing and so magnificent in its warrior's accoutrements, proves to be not the lethal foe it initially seemed to be. Instead, the ominous stranger is surprisingly benevolent and helpful, and actually promotes the novice's purpose rather than obstructing it. The tyro, however, does nothing, and indeed could do nothing to influence either the stranger's curiously sanguine emotional state nor the sudden shift of fortune whereby an anticipated peril becomes an equally unexpected source of unsought kindness and assistance. Osmanbey's awful grenadier peremptorily commands:

> "Come out from your hiding place onto the roadway,
> Let us not fight, but rather sit down together peaceably,   180
> For no Good can come to us from Evil,
> And without Good there is no profit to anyone."
> When Osman heard these words in his place of hiding
>   underneath the green fir tree,
> He laid hold on the bridle and led forth his white horse.
> The bey stood before him now and wished him godspeed,   185
> And the darkling grenadier returned the wish politely.
> He offered him his hand, and with the handshake
> They two each asked kindly after the other's health.
> The dour grenadier dismounted then,
> And they sat down one beside the other.

As in Medjedović's tale, so also in Ugljanin's: the encounter between strangers in the wilderness beneath green wood coordinates a surprising reversal of expectation with a revelation of true personal identities that were heretofore concealed:

> Then the dour grenadier asked him:
> "My dear ensign, from whence have we the pleasure of your
>   coming?
> From what city or town do you come,
> And by what name are you called?"

The bey replied that he was from the city of Ćpanur,   195
From Ćpanur on the Turkish border,
Ensign Niklas by name.
Then the dour grenadier said to him,
"My dear brother, for shame!
You are no Ensign Niklas,   200
But Osmanbey of Osek himself.
Have you forgotten, poor wretch, when we two swore
    the oath of brotherhood,
For am I not myself, Hasan of Ribnik?"
Then the two of them sprang to their feet,
And spreading their arms, each gave the other the kiss
    of friendship.[190]

Salih Ugljanin's story of the tyro Osmanbey is so like Avdo
Medjedović's account of Halil Hrnjica in so many particulars that one
may regard it as the same tale with only the names of the characters
and other, inanimate details changed. Medjedović expands the number
of characters, assigning to several those same actions which Ugljanin
imposes upon one or two, but the actions of the novice and those
around him remain the same. The same synopsis describes both versions: *A renowned elder hero, notable especially for his skill as a military commander and strategist, has disappeared while on an expedition
deep into enemy territory. Another, younger man who is still a novice
but who is also himself destined to be a famous hero some day, rashly
decides to go in search of the missing elder. Someone boasts that, if
only he had known the plight of the absent elder hero, nothing could
have prevented his searching to the ends of the earth long ere this.
Someone* in loco parentis *also objects to the tyro's undertaking the
mission, but the novice threatens to kill himself and a white horse
unless he is permitted to go and given the trappings he needs for the
journey. Women accordingly supply the requisites, and the novice sets
out under an assumed identity. Beneath a tree or trees in the wilderness on the way, the novice encounters a dire stranger who, however,
unexpectedly offers him gratuitous help and is the occasion or the
subject of a turning withershins. Here strong emotions fluctuate abruptly from one extreme to another, and true identities are laid bare.*

Medjedović's and Ugljanin's tales both belong to a conspicuous
larger category of story in the Yugoslav tradition called the Captivity
Song (*ropstvo* or *sužanjstvo*). Hundreds of texts of this kind have been
collected, and the collections being but a fraction of the tradition,

many thousands of such songs must be assumed to have existed. Not all tell, however, of a novice gone in search of the captive hero. In some, the captive is by other means released to make his own way home. Salih Ugljanin himself sang just such a tale for Milman Parry's recording apparatus on 24 November, 1934, "The Captivity of Ibrahim Djulić." [191]

The Duke of Zadar holds a celebration because he has just captured a Turkish steward. Cast into the Duke's dungeon, the steward finds there a group of thirty other prisoners, Turkish warriors all, who have preceded him into captivity twelve years ago. Among these veteran captives is Djulić Ibrahim, who asks the newcomer for news of home. The steward happens to know Djulić's family, and is able to give him a detailed account of their present lives. Djulić then relates the circumstances of his own captivity, telling the steward how through the importunacy of his comrades-in-arms he had left the bridal chamber to join a military expedition on his very wedding night. His unlucky troop of thirty-two men was the self-same company of unkempt prisoners which the steward now sees before him in the dungeon, for scarcely had the military maneuvre begun when the Duke chanced to encircle and capture the whole troop. This said, Djulić falls to loud wailing.

The uncanny sound of the old prisoner's lament disturbs the Duke's family, who prevail upon the Duke to visit Djulić in the dungeon and either put a ransom on his head or execute him. After hard words and hard bargaining, the Duke at last releases Djulić with the understanding that he, Djulić, will in lieu of ransom betray his fellow countryman Halil Hrnjica (the same hero seen previously as a novice in Medjedović's tale) into the Duke's hands after he has returned to his own land.

So with only his prisoner's weeds, a laissez-passer under the Duke's own hand and seal, an ashwood staff to help him walk (the hewn wood of this story), and an ordinary foot-soldier's sword wherewith to defend himself against hostile man or beast in wilderness places, Djulić is released and sets off homeward. But like Halil Hrnjica, who meets a series of three challenging strangers in Medjedović's tale, or Salih Ugljanin's young hero Osmanbey who crosses three mountains to meet the challenge of the dour grenadier, so too Djulić Ibrahim crosses two mountains without incident but on a third mountain meets three challenges. The first two challengers, who are the Duke's frontier guards,

let him pass on presentation of the Duke's visa, but the third, a certain
Deli Milutin, is a common highwayman who preys upon commerce in
this mountainous territory, and he refuses to honor Djulić's documents.
The scene devolves under and about fir trees:

Djulić passed onward up the mountain,   455
And at the place where his way branched
Into the wide track leading over the mountain,
The swaying firs grew clear up to the sky.
A whooping sound came down to him from the mountain
        height,
And then Deli Milutin emerged,   460
He who had blockaded all four roads
        and stopped all traffic across the border,
Flaying the merchants with his tolls,
Garnering their money and leaving them destitute,
He and his seven or eight henchmen.   465
When Deli Milutin caught sight of Djulić,
He recognized Djulić and shouted at him:
"Hey, Djulić, Turkish ensign,
Do you truly suppose I do not recognize you?
So you have escaped from the Duke's dungeon, have you, 470
And thought to make good your getaway?
But you'll not slip across this mountain, Djulić!"
The adversary called to his seven or eight henchmen:
"Circle 'round and take him!
I'll return him to the Duke,
Who'll give me amnesty
When I've brought him Ensign Djulić." [192]

Djulić responds to this threat as he did to his previous two challengers, presenting the Duke's laissez-passer. But Milutin is an outlaw,
not an agent of the Duke, and he takes no interest in instruments of
legality:

Then Djulić took out his passport:
"Milutin, beware what harm may come to you in this,
And look whose hand and seal have authorized this passport!
The Duke himself has released me from his dungeon,
Setting me free for ransom."
But Milutin would not deign to see the passport,
Because he cared no more for it than he cared for the Devil.
Again he charged his seven or eight henchmen: 485
"Surround this man, and bind his hands!"

The old captive returning home by his own effort receives no
such unearned consideration as did the novice-heroes Halil and Osman-

bey at the hands of their fierce interceptors where fir trees grew in
the wilderness. Djulić finds that he may expect nothing better from
Deli Milutin than the cruelest physical reversal of his hard-won freedom and his hope of returning home. Milutin for his part immutably
expects to victimize Djulić no less than he does every passerby in his
district. But the hearer or reader of these tales soon comes to understand that a meeting of strangers under green wood in the wild regularly upsets their expectations no matter how strong or inevitable
they seem, and apparent fortunes are reversed. Unkempt and wasted
by his years in prison, ill-armed, and outnumbered by Deli Milutin's
band, Djulić Ibrahim appears to be at the mercy of the ruthless outlaw. But the story continues:

> When Djulić saw into what adversity he had fallen,
> He realized that further palaver was useless.
> His hand dropped to his sword-hilt,
> And the sword came singing out of its sheath.   490
> He attacked them then,
> And the eight henchmen pressed in around him.
> Their heads flew off right and left,
> And then he confronted Milutin himself.
> The two of them pursued each other in and out among the
>   fir trees,   495
> And 'round and 'round one green fir,
> Hewing at each other wherever they saw an opening.
> Each hacked at the other as though he were a sapling of fir,
> Until Ensign Djulić brought his man to bay
> And hit him a solid blow.   500
> Thus he beheaded Milutin too
> And stopped to rest
> Beside the broad track over the mountain.
> But then he stripped the arms and apparel from the body
>   of his fallen foe
> And put them on himself.   505

Thus in the end Milutin's expectation of deriving an advantage
for himself from Djulić's misfortune is reversed, and instead Djulić
profits from Milutin's misfortune. Also, the character in the story
who is bent upon a prisoner's return home from a foreign captivity
(in this case the prisoner himself) ultimately secures the help of a
stranger who intercepts him under green trees in the wilderness, just
as in the previous tales about Halil and Osmanbey. The old prisoner
Djulić Ibrahim is obliged to exact that help by violence (as did Sam-

son, who was equally the champion of people under the domination of aliens), whereas the young novices Halil and Osmanbey received it *gratis,* but the result is the same. All these characters go on from their encounters with strangers under green trees with well-disguised identities and improved equipment for contending with the further perils of their journeys.

Expectations upset and reversals of fortune in the Yugoslav tales of heroic captivity are not confined to scenes under fir trees. Whatever their species, the trees are however always green, and their locations mountainous (mountains being in this culture wilderness places *par excellence*). In 1963, another Yugoslav bard in the northern Bosnian town of Cazin (five hundred miles northwest of Novi Pazar) sang for my magnetic tape recorder another epic about another Osmanbey—not the Osmanbey of Osek as in Salih Ugljanin's tale, but rather Osmanbey the lord of Glasinac, another town in Bosnia. In the 1963 tale, Osmanbey is like Ugljanin's Djulić Ibrahim, called away to war on the very day of his wedding. Placed in command of the imperial army, Osmanbey proves himself a brilliant and courageous strategist, but due to treason in the army he is captured by the enemy at the very end of the campaign and not finally released to return home until twenty-one years later. The son whom he had begotten on his wedding-night (the only conjugal night of his life) has during the time of his father's imprisonment grown to maturity, and is himself being wed on the very day of his father's return. As usual in these tales, the liberated captive comes home under cover of an assumed identity, and on the way towards his destination he pauses at a resting-place under a green tree where the unleashing of powerful emotions reverses an expected course of events and inverts fortune.[193]

> So Osmanbey set out towards his native Bosnia.
> Day followed upon day, and inn upon inn,
> Until in the fullness of time   1150
> The bey came to the imperial town of Glasinac
> And a place on the heights above his own manor house of stone,
> A place, my dear brothers, three full hours' journey away,
> Where stood his old apple tree with its ruddy fruit
> And beneath it the well of cool water,
> Where the bey drank his fill.
> "How now, my old apple, bearing your red fruit!
> One and twenty years it is
> Since last I passed this way
> And cooled myself in your shade.   1160

> But when of old I was here at home in my own Glasinac,
> I would on every Friday when I craved the cooling zephyr
>   of your shade
> Ride my horse hither. . ."
> Even as he spoke the sharp report of gunfire broke the calm,
> And when Osmanbey looked that way,
> A troop of horsemen came into view.

The northern Bosnian bard who told this story was geographically much farther distant from both Avdo Medjedović and Salih Ugljanin than those two were from each other. He was also younger than
they by a generation, and composed his tales in a markedly different
dialect according to different prosodic conventions. He put the meeting of strangers under the green tree at the end of his story, not at
the beginning as did Medjedović and Ugljanin. But none of these differences of time, place, language, poetics, or narrative sequence in any
way deflected the Bosnian bard from faithfully reproducing the same
pattern of story found in the two earlier poets' narration. As usual in
a Yugoslav captivity tale, the captive's saviour (either the captive who
has won his own liberty or someone else bent upon redeeming him)
interrupts his journey of redemption to rest or take refuge under
green wood. The natural tranquillity of the green trees' precinct is
disturbed by the unexpected advent of armed men. Strong emotions
then come into play, unanticipated identities are revealed, and apparent destinies are apparently reversed. Thus, like that other returning
captive Djulić Ibrahim in Salih Ugljanin's song, Osmanbey first conceals his true identity beneath the natural disguise of a long-time
prisoner's hapless appearance, and then tells a lying tale in which he
further dissembles who he really is under the assumed name of Ali
Agha Parmaksuz. The name 'Parmaksuz' means 'unfenced'. . .

> A young man mounted on a strawberry horse led the troop,
> And the green banner which he carried whipped about him
>   in the breeze.
> Behind him rode an older man on a white horse;   1170
> In him he recognized his father's brother, Hasan,
>   commander of the troop.
> Osmanbey drew out a cloth
> And spread it on the green grass.
> The prisoner had lain so long in the dungeon
> That his black beard had overgrown his breast,   1175
> The shock of black hair growing on his head tumbled
>   about his shoulders,
> And his fingernails had grown so long that they curved back

upon the palms of his hands like talons.
The bearer of the war-banner approached him and, giving him
    a friendly greeting,
Reined his horse to a halt:
"Sad prisoner, of what city are you a citizen?"   1180
"I come from the imperial town of Kladuša, young man;
Perchance you have heard of Ali Agha Parmaksuz.
I fought under the bey's command at the Seige of Hotin."
The young man gasped, and said to him:
"And do you perhaps know what befell my father there,   1185
My father, Ensign Ibro?
My mother has told me that he
And she had been married but three weeks
When he was called away to fight beside his bey."
"Yes, my son, in faith I do know,   1190
For I saw it happen with my own eyes
When your father lost his life
Beneath Herdelj in icy Moscovy."
The youth threw him a yellow ducat
And dismounted beside the apple tree.   1195
And there unconsolably he mourned and wept.
Next came the commander of the troop, the old man Hasan,
Who also gave a friendly greeting, and said:
"My dear prisoner, who are you, and whence do you come?"
"Old man, I am by birth from imperial Kladuša,
And they call me Ali Agha Parmaksuz.
I fought for the bey at the Seige of Hotin."

So far Osmanbey has lied only about his own identity, telling the
truth about Ensign Ibro's death in the battle of Hotin. But he lies
more, and more cruelly, to his kinsman Hasan:

Then Hasan, commander of the troop, asked him:
"And did you, perhaps, see anything there of my nephew,
My nephew Osmanbey?"   1205
"Your nephew, whom I myself cradled upon this very lap
    at his last hour,
Gave up his soul upon my right knee in the dungeon of
    the King of Moscovy,
And I cast his dead body out through the bars of the window
    into the sea."
The old man got down from his spirited white horse,   1210
And the five hundred others who followed him in the
    wedding procession obeyed his example.
When the bride herself drew near on her white horse,
She too dismounted beside the apple tree.
Then she asked leave of Hasan the commander:

"I should also like to go and speak with the prisoner." 1215
"Go, daughter, and talk with him as much as you please."
She kissed the prisoner's hand, and said:
Poor prisoner, what is your native city?"
"Dear daughter, I am of imperial Kladuša."
"Have you perchance anything to tell 1220
Of my father-in-law, Osmanbey?"
He blushed at that,
And his heart missed a beat,
But he shed no tear, and said:
"Your father-in-law surrendered his soul to God 1225
Upon my lap and knee
In the dungeon of the King of Moscovy."
She screamed when she heard that, and unclasped her
    necklace,
Her necklace of a hundred dukats,
And dropped it before him on his tattered scrap of cloth. 1230
Then she herself fell upon the green grass,
Implored the earth to receive her body,
And praised God for his mercy, would he but take her soul:
"For lo! I am so very miserable."

Osmanbey lies most unconscionably to the nearest of his kin. The cruelty of his deception increases in direct proportion to the intimacy of their involvement in the marriage which he finds taking place on the very day of his return home. He gives his uncle Hasan, who as the eldest surviving male of his family must have authorized the wedding, no small cause for mourning on a day which everyone should reasonably have expected would be one of the happiest in a lifetime. But Osmanbey is not satisfied with this only partial inversion of fortune, and goes on to make those who should be happiest of all, the bride and bridegroom, wish they were dead:

A youth appeared next in the procession, riding a black horse
And leading another, white horse by the bridle.
But when the white horse spied the prisoner,
O Lord, how remarkably it reacted,
For it recognized its own true master,
And leapt for joy the length of two lances straight up
    where it stood. 1240
Childe Mehmedbey spoke from his place astride the black horse,
"Whoa there, o thou white horse of my father!"
And when the lad reached that place he slipped lightly
    out of the saddle
And kissed both the prisoner's hands.
"Poor prisoner, from what city do you come?" 1245

"Dear son, I am a native of imperial Kladuša."
"Do you perchance know ought of my father,
My father Osmanbey?
My mother has told me
How he and she were together as man and wife for only four hours
Ere my father the bey was summoned to serve in the imperial army."
"Your father surrendered his soul to God
Upon my lap and my right knee
In the dungeon of the King of Moscovy."
The lad fell prostrate on the green grass.
"Dear God, pray thee take my soul,
And thou, sweet earth, my corpse."

Thus, in keeping with the immutable (and to the Singer, the entirely unconscious) prescription of the Yugoslav tradition, the inversion of expected fortune is complete, and those who had most thought to be happy are made most miserable in a meeting of ostensible strangers under a green tree. But the tradition of the captivity tale also prescribes that the captive's redeemer will be aided and the captive's return home facilitated by the encounter at the live tree, and so the Bosnian story continues. . .

Now when these things had come to pass, the bride
   put up the purse for a horse-race
From the apple tree to the bey's manor.
So the horses flew away from the starting-line,   1260
And after them followed the rest of the wedding party.
But see you, where Mehmedbey
And the piteous prisoner remained beside the well of water,
The young man spoke: "Come now and ride my father's
   white horse
Home with us to my manor house of white stone."   1265
If only, my brothers, we had been there to see it
   when Osmanbey leapt into the saddle!
For his white horse, turning its head, nipped lovingly
   at his true master's legs,
And sped away to overtake all the other racers.
So Osmanbey came first of them all to his own manor.

The scene under the green tree with its concomitant occurrences is an obligatory part of captivity tales in the Yugoslav epic tradition. As the four examples just given from the story-telling of Medjedović, Ugljanin, and a more recent Bosnian bard show, there is a considerable diversity of expression but a great uniformity of basic pattern in all manifestations of the scene. If it occurred in only one text, or if we could regard all the many texts in which it does occur as somehow just copies of one single story (like versions of a single tale-type in the eyes of the Finnish School, or different editions of the same book in the world of printed narratives) then we might properly dismiss the Green Tree scene as a isolated phenomenon of perhaps some local interest but no systematic or generally explanatory value as regards either the Yugoslav tradition as a whole, or any wider study of oral narrative tradition. That is not however the case. The Green Tree scene has occurred in literally hundreds and thousands of tales in the Yugoslav tradition that are no more "copies" of each other than are the four examples I have cited here. Multiform expressions of the scene like those in Salih Ugljanin's two distinct tales concerning the rescue of Mustajbey and the escape of Djulić Ibrahim, and major sequential displacement of the Green Tree scene as in the Bosnian bard's story of Osmanbey, are the means for making *different* and *new* stories, not just the same story told over again in an oral tradition. To use a biological analogy, we are not dealing here with the phyllology of just one specimen, or of just one species whose individuals have been sighted concurrently at various places in the species' territorial range. The Green Tree scene is rather one element in the overall genetic composition of the Yugoslav oral narrative tradition, and as such it pertains not only to the form but also to the reproductive processes, the evolution, and the ideational adaptability of the tradition.

THE DOCTRINE OF 'CULTURAL UNIVERSALS' AND FUNCTIONALISM

Unlike the historico-geographic school, therefore, we should not be content merely to have recognized and typed four dead specimens from an oral tradition. Nor do I accept that peculiarly modern mutation of Euhemerism that attempts to interpret all recurrent elements in oral fable in terms of 'cultural universals.' According to that doctrine, we should for example see Halil Hrnjica in Medjedović's story as typical of young, inexperienced manhood the world over, which of course needs the help and control of other, more seasoned men (represented by the elder brother, Mujo) to assure its fulfillment in any society. Or again, the marriage of Osmanbey's son Mehmed may be taken as representative of cultural universals in regard to matrimony, as for example the fact that in some sense the marriages or mating of the young are in every society the destiny not only of the marital pair itself but also of their ancestors, whose various interests are as much entrained in a new alliance as those of the bride and bridegroom.

But while such observations may have value as preliminary steps in the investigation of oral fable, they are patently insufficient as explanations of either the Green Tree scene or a thousand other similar *topoi* in a thousand other traditions the world over. For it is absurd to suppose that even figuratively the notion of a soldier-father thought missing in action for fourteen years is somehow integral to the concept of a young nobleman's marriage in Yugoslavia, or that dining with a friend in the woods on a moonless night is an especially good way to secure an angry older brother's help in a reckless enterprise. As always with Euhemeristic arguments, the irreducible element of purely absurd fiction in oral fable remains too large to allow such reductionism any finally explanatory force. And what most of all wants to be explained in the present instance is the fact that the Green Tree scene may serve equally well in the Yugoslav tradition to represent something abstractly essential about both brotherhood *and* marriage.

If not by the Finnish method (because it has not learned that, as in every other science, classification is impossible without and worth no more than the acts of interpretation which inform it), nor yet by Euhemerism (because in trying to make a reality out of every fiction it cannot recognize the reality of fiction), how then can one proceed towards a better explanation of the Green Tree scene (or by implication, any other similar nexus of matter in any oral narrative tradition)?

Others who before me have reacted against the conceptual sterility and mechanistic habits of historico-geographicism have long since devised an alternative ideal of methodology which, though it is not based on any simple form of Euhemerism, does nevertheless depend mainly upon correlating fiction and social reality. Instead of cultural universals, this school rather finds its touchstone of interpretation, its great reality from which the hidden meanings of traditional fiction may be extracted, in cultural idiosyncracies—the web of peculiar, ethnically distinctive ideas and attitudes that are supposedly shared as a philosophically and socially organizing system among (and only among) a given people whose customary fictions may together constitute an oral narrative tradition. Ruth Benedict wrote the manifesto for this school more than forty years ago.

No folktale is generic. It is always the tale of one particular people with one particular livelihood and social organization and religion. The final form that a tale takes in that culture is influenced, often fundamentally, by attitudes and customs that cannot be discovered except with full knowledge of life and behaviour among that people.[194]

Benedict admitted that not all of an oral narrative tradition is necessarily a product or reflection of the present life and behaviour of the people who sustain it. But she found support in other theories of her time for the opinion that what was not a product of the *present* "attitudes and customs" of a people was simply a residue of their outworn *past* attitudes and customs. Either way, oral fable was for her entirely an excretion of some social reality or other, and the more recent the reality, the better:

It has always been obvious to students of every theoretical persuasion that folklore tallied with culture and yet did not tally with it, and the majority of students have agreed upon one convenient explanation of those instances where the two are at odds. Folklore, it is said, reflects not the customs and beliefs of the narrators of the tales, but those of many generations past; cultural survivals of earlier ages are perpetuated in folklore, and these, it is often felt, are the chief reason for the study of oral traditions. Even conditions of barbarism in which fathers are supposed to have eaten their children, and conditions of primal life when man first gained ascendancy over animals, have been said to be embalmed in folklore.[195]

A conservatism that perpetuates long-discarded customs, however, is characteristic of a dead lore rather than a living one, and the great emphasis on the importance of survivals in the interpretation of folklore is evidently due to certain characteristics of oral tradition in Western civilization. European folklore was rescued from the memories of old men and women much as that of the Plains Indians is rescued today. It was recorded by collectors long after its heyday. Grimm's tales [sic] are found to reflect the manners and customs of the feudal age, not contemporary contacts with industrialism or with urban civilization, and the belief has become current that survivals of old customs are perpetuated in folklore through great lapses of time. This, however, is to generalize the senescence of folklore into a law by means of which mythology is elaborately interpreted. Folklore often remains current and can be adequately collected when it is no longer a living trait. North American Indians can almost always relate their folktales long after their aboriginal cultural life is in abeyance, and many valuable bodies of mythology have been collected in dead cultures from old men who learned the stories in their youth. The functioning of myth in culture and the processes of cultural adaptation, however, cannot be adequately studied in these cases. Comparison of variants under such conditions indicates mainly how much or how little different informants have forgotten of a dead culture trait, and such comparison is comparatively unrewarding. . . .

A living folklore, such as that of Zuni, reflects the contemporary interests and judgments of its tellers, and adapts incidents to its own cultural usages. Like any cultural trait, folklore tends, of course, to perpetuate traditional forms, and there is a certain lag in folklore as there is in contemporary statecraft or in morals. But the scope of this conservatism is limited in folklore as in other traits. It is never sufficient to give us license to reconstruct the items of a racial memory; and contemporary attitudes are always to be reckoned with, rather than those that have been superseded in that culture.

The opinion expressed in this manifesto has laid powerful hold on the minds of many Western intellectuals since Ruth Benedict's time, and a numerous school has arisen that is loath to countenance any other interpretative approach to oral narrative traditions. It has become an *a priori* article of faith in that school that such traditions —or the only part of them worth knowing—must necessarily be not only *assets* of the society which harbors them but also ultimately the *inventions* of that society. According to this doctrine, a tradition of oral narrative that is truly "alive" is subject to constant, fundamental re-making as it is 'used' in social intercourse, for it is in the first place only a local cultural elaboration for local social purposes. Thus, all oral traditional fictions in a pristine state are supposedly nothing more than a given people's "formal statements about themselves and their experience."[196]

A good contemporary example of this attitude may be seen in the recently published work by Kenelm Burridge on the Tangu people of New Guinea. Written a generation after Ruth Benedict's credo, Burridge's introductory words nevertheless resonate in such an exact harmony of mind with hers that they might to all intent have been penned at the same moment:

> We turn now to consider Tangu formal statements about themselves and their experience—their myths, folktales, stories, and legends, summed up as 'narratives.' Accepting that the purpose of narratives is to provide a logical model capable of overcoming inconsistencies, we shall see something of the way in which Tangu narratives do this job. Nevertheless while this 'purpose' is entailed in, or emerges from, the analyses that follow, our specific interest is in the experiential content of the narratives. Given that to a large extent narratives are, and must be, 'reflections' of social life, what is of greater concern here is the way in which Tangu use their narratives in their conduct of social relations, and change their narratives in the light of a wider positive experience. Finally, through a conversation between the narratives and other aspects of Tangu culture, we hope to sketch the content of the developing cultural experience in which Tangu are involved.
>
> The general structure of the narratives cannot but be governed by the logic of Tangu social relations. . . .

I have tried to show in this book that the scope of conservatism
is not limited in oral fable as it is in other aspects of culture, and that
the structure of narratives is inherently immune to influence by (yet
always compatible with) the logic of any people's social relations. In
my view it is only a lingering romanticism that clings to the sentimental
wish for "conversation between the narratives and other aspects of . . .
culture" so as to make prodigious conscious philosophers—indeed intellectually awesome Noble Savages—out of living peoples whose alleged
capacity for such sublime conscious intellection is itself a blatant fiction,
forever said to exist and yet forever eluding the best efforts to isolate
and analyze it. We have to do in oral fable with a cultural force far
more potent than either the conscious reasoning of living men or the
vapid mystique of 'racial memory.' Given the great confidence in its
own premise and methods which this school of functionalism has displayed for so many years, I was nevertheless eager at one time to apply
its methods toward explication of such systematic features of the tales
in my own East European and African collections as the Green Tree
scene.

THE INALIENABLE CONSERVATISM OF ORAL NARRATIVE
TRADITION SUFFICIENTLY EXPLAINS IT

In 1966 I reported the inconclusive results of my work along that
line on another part of South Slavic tradition, the ubiquitous tale of
the Two Brothers. Partly because that initial study[197] gave equivocal
results from a functionalist point of view, I was more deliberate and
exhaustive in my search for social usages and social experience in the
South Slavic world that might help to explain the curious, and curiously recurrent, Green Tree scene. For indeed an imposing body of data
is at hand concerning the social attitudes, customs, life, and behaviour
of the Yugoslavs which is quite independent of the oral narrative traditions that have been collected from them. That information is particularly rich for the modern period (nineteenth and twentieth centuries),
but there is an additional priceless advantage for the functionalist who
studies the South Slavs in that their culture is also historically attested
in considerable detail from as early as the Hellenistic Age. Much of
the evidence about Yugoslav social life in the modern period is scientific ethnography and social history, and even the material from previous centuries is often of a similar kind. Because the South Slavs were

throughout their recorded history a subject people first of the Byzantine and later of the Ottoman Empire, or else restlessly disturbed the sensitive peripheries of those and the Austro-Hungarian Empire, their ways of life were of constant interest to others than themselves, and hence much has come down to us about them from the past.

Thus it was all the more perplexing to me that nowhere in all that copious record of the South Slavs and their 'real' (i. e., non-fictitious, non-narrative) social relations or other culture could I find any sound explanation of the Green Tree scene. After more than a decade of dedicated searching for possible social cognates of that persistent narrative element, I have at last been forced to conclude that there just are not any features of social experience or social relations specific to the South Slavic world that (to use Benedict's words) "tally with" the Green Tree scene. Perhaps the fault was in me, but how could even the most inept student fail to find the social 'function' of anything so obvious and essential in the Yugoslav oral tradition as the Green Tree scene, if only it *had* such a function? Remember that no Yugoslav Captivity tale is complete without that scene, and that the Captivity tales abounded in every district of the Slavic Balkans where oral epic was sung—a vast tract embracing hundreds of thousands of square miles and millions of peoples throughout the historical period since Napoleon.

After all that Benedict had said about senescence in folklore, and especially about the "cultural lag" of European traditions in sloughing off the "cultural survivals of earlier ages" that are "embalmed in folklore," I had carefully to consider also that my Green Tree might be just such a survival whose only rationale in real South Slavic social life might belong wholly to some past age. But the cultural history of the South Slavs, available as it is, yielded no such rationale. Here then was the puzzle.

Benedict had said, "Folklore often remains current and can be adequately collected when it is no longer a living trait. . . . A living folklore. . .reflects the contemporary interests and judgments of its tellers, and adapts incidents to its own cultural usages." But what of a folklore that had evidently never been a "living" one in Benedict's sense (yet all the more enduring for that)? And what if—to invert Burridge's dictum—the general structure of the narratives is not governed by the logic of social relations? Or was it really sound thinking to suppose that those things in oral fable that happen not to reflect present social life are on that account merely senescent—outworn reliques of a useless past society just waiting for replacement by something better suited to modern manners and customs? Adopting that way of thinking, would it not be equally logical (and equally wrong) to say, for example, that coniferous trees are a senescent form of plant life because they retain their foliage in winter, past the time when it serves for photosynthesis? Or should we not be obliged to say also that horses and cattle and mankind and indeed every modern form of bird and mammalian life on earth are all senescent creatures because they retain skeletal traits that first arose in the evolutionary adaptation to their environment of the bony fishes? But the truth is that like the bony skeleton oral fable has not only survived but also facilitated thousands of *other* adaptive changes which have not fundamentally changed it, because it already is, as it is, a uniquely necessary and useful structure that requires no basic alteration—much less any replacement—to go on being useful and adaptive indefinitely.

By this course of reasoning I have come to doubt the sufficiency of functionalism to explain what is in oral tradition. For if there are key elements of oral fable that have no communally significant ideational counterparts in the sponsoring society or even in that society's reasonably distant past, then who is to say whether *any* present social value attributable to some part of the tradition was its original value? For what does the present utility of anything in human culture or elsewhere in the evolution of life forms really tell us about that thing's genesis or its residual potential for further applications? And if this is indeed the open question which I believe it is, then the further question presents itself: to what extent do societies ever actually invent, or desire to inherit, or simply act as hosts to oral narrative traditions, and does any of that really determine the uses to which they do or do not put any parts of such a tradition, or what does or does not survive in the tradition?

Needless to say, one cannot even begin to formulate the answers to those questions without interrogating the narrators themselves in an oral tradition. For while it is certainly true that, as Benedict said, every tale "is always the tale of one particular people," it is even truer that at every given moment, every tale is always the tale of the particular storyteller who narrates it. If any discarding, remaking, invention, inheritance, embalming of cultural survivals, 'hosting,' government by the logic of social relations, or statements of positive experience actually take place in an oral narrative tradition, that must happen in the specific practice of individual story-tellers as they ply their personal arts of narrative composition. Such questions are of course notoriously unaddressible to oral traditional fabulators in any direct way, and even such dedicated functionalists as Benedict and Burridge have found it easier to rely upon their own rather than their informants' estimates of what the informants do in practice. Thus, while they give great weight in theory to the oral fabulist as an agent of self-expression for the larger society around him, functionalists have systematically neglected to report actual interrogations of story-tellers that would prove that hypothesis. For this reason too functionalism has often sprung more from a prior dedication in principle to the study of social functions than from any objective evidence that oral fable's *possible correlations* with those functions are also its *causes*.

In the case of the Yugoslav Green Tree scene, I have not been obliged to pursue my investigation of its social function(s) in the absence of the story-tellers' own recorded comments about themselves as agents of narrative tradition. Nor is my reader obliged to do so. Special pains have been taken in the publishing program of the Parry Collection (Texts and Translation series) to issue transcripts of detailed conversations with the informants bearing upon the published texts of their collected narratives. One may thus consult both Salih Ugljanin and Avdo Medjedović, for example, about their own conceptions of themselves as both fabulators and social beings. And here, no less than in other traditions on other continents, the very inability of the pristine oral traditional fabulator to enter into a direct dialogue of critical ideas with a Western investigator of his tradition is itself an important clue about the real relationship between tradition and society. The reader may consult the text of the original conversation for himself either in the original language or in English,[198] but in 1974 I wrote in summary of Avdo Medjedović's own comments upon himself, his narrative art, and his society:

> Another impressive feature of Avdo's talk is the extraordinary irrelevance of chronology throughout his comments on his songs. By the time of this conversation in 1935 he had been singing epos for nearly half a century. Now a man of sixty, he nevertheless made no distinction between the tales which he had learned in his early adolescence and those, like the one in this book, acquired more recently. The persons of many singers whom he had

known and from whom he had learned appear grossly anachron-
ous in his descriptions of them. Some, like his father, were long
dead; others were in their dress, in their customs, or in their
economic habits virtually antediluvian; still others had long since
emigrated away to Asia Minor and so become mere souvenirs of
an unsung, lost former time. Like his own autobiography, Avdo's
shadowy vignettes of their lives are filled with the sense of elap-
sed time, but the lives of the epic songs which he shared with
them lie under no such rule. The tales which he knew from the
men of the past were enduring parts of his *present* mental life,
parts of him one dares despite his sixty years to think even more
secure and less alterable by any accident or effect of time than
even his own mature character. His epic repertory was the one
stable, timeless, and uniformly beneficial component in an unpredictable lifetime of mixed fortune.

To appreciate exactly what the force of oral literary tradition
is and how much more durable it is than other traditions, one
must witness it as it appears here in the life of Avdo Medjedović.
His experience was filled with traditions of many kinds—traditions
of social order, of economic relationships, of political processes,
and so forth. He can and does talk freely about the workings of
such traditions; the very uncertainty about their operation and
durability—their perpetual vulnerability to uncontrollable external influences—makes them good conversational topics. But Avdo's
epic repertory belongs to an entirely different order of culture.
It is the one completely governable and secure traditional scheme
of ideas which he possesses. As such, it is separated from mundane, debatable behavioral traditions by such a complete hiatus
that he does not even possess the logic that might enable him to
enter into dialogue about it. A superbly developed and sufficient
rational system in its own right, the epic tradition was thus well
insulated against ephemeral tampering and banal deflections.
Those who imagine that oral literary traditions are simple functions of the everyday social and economic life in small-group
societies should read Avdo's talk well not only for what he says,
but also for what he does not, and cannot, say.

Medjedović was admittedly the greatest Yugoslav oral poet recorded in more than a hundred years of steady collecting work by many
dozens of collectors all over the Yugoslav territory. But I do not think

he was at all untypical in the insulation of his narrative repertory
against invasions by the various social usages and changes of his lifetime. I think one must reach a similar conclusion from a review of
the corresponding conversations with Salih Ugljanin, a more ordinary
fabulator than Medjedović, or with any of the many other Yugoslav
bards.

The implications of this evident hiatus between contemporary
social awareness and the oral narrative tradition are far-reaching. While
oral traditional fictions do clearly serve society as a fund of organizing
ideas for which that society may find many and varied uses, it does
not follow that the tradition owes anything genetically to the society.
Avdo Medjedović himself perceived models of social organization in
his own stories with respect to both his own family—understanding
and controlling the father-son relationship was a major issue for him
throughout his life—and with respect to the larger complex of mature
male affiliations upon which he perceived that public tranquillity and
prosperity were grounded. But at the same time he did not invent or
construct his tales out of those aspects of contemporary social life.
He got them instead from the bygone generation of other oral poets
who had preceded him in an earlier age with its different social order
and its different cultural concerns, and so on in an infinite regression
into the past. And that was the fundamental fact about the tradition—
that it was *already* so constructed before it came to Medjedović or
Ugljanin or any of the myriad other latter-day Yugoslav oral fabulators
that it could serve their later society in its ever-changing cultural circumstances without topical tampering no less usefully than it had
served earlier societies in earlier ages. The functionalists' postulation
to the contrary is quite literally the intellectual equivalent of Lamarck-
ism in the field of biological genetics.

The effect I describe is not really an unfamiliar one. It is the
same effect whereby the oral traditional poetries of earlier ages preserved in writing have, like Homer's *Iliad* and *Odyssey*, continued to
serve other societies in other times without undergoing any changes
in themselves. Such changes are not necessary. The society where
Homer sang in the Archaic Period in ancient Greece was by any reckoning a radically different one from those which know and value Homer
as literature in this age, and if anything the social value of his tales
has grown rather than diminished. To speak of Homer as a senescent
survival which because of cultural lag we have thus far neglected to

discard is to understand nothing about either society or the narrative tradition, and to preclude the very possibility of such an understanding. The same is true whether we speak of ancient Greek, modern Yugoslav, North American Zuni Indians, Tangu of New Guinea, or any other culture where an oral tradition of fiction is to be found.

Another writer, following T. S. Eliot, has called this effect "the permanent contemporaneity of past works." A tradition so finely wrought and tested in past time as to achieve a 'permanent contemporaneity' must needs be insulated by custom against distortions which, though possibly of momentary use, nevertheless lack the enduring adaptive value that makes a *tradition* worthy of those special skills and energies its conservation demands. At times in many recent human societies, skull bones six inches thick would have had considerable functional utility in mature men, as in times of war, but the genetic tradition of mankind conserves a lighter specification, for it has over long ages proven its greater value in a greater variety of contexts. Similarly, oral fable conserves forms of the greatest proven general adaptive utility, and this conservatism is no less powerful or effective for being unconscious.

As Edward Gibbon remarked long ago, it is an ancient prejudice in Western thought that all *habit* is by nature superstitious and incoherent, while only *conscious reasoning* is enlightened and capable of good results. It is accordingly only the most generous of motives that makes anthropologists in the Western intellectual tradition like Ruth Benedict and Kenelm Burridge want to depict their Zuni Indians, their Tangu, and their other exotic small societies as having a maximal inventive control over their own traditions. Human life is everywhere noble, and the attribution of conscious, reasoning control over their culture ennobles any description of primal social groups to Western minds. But my evidence suggests that, far from being incoherent or stupid, the unconscious, learned habits of oral traditional fabulators may actually be much more efficient and capable of good results than any system of conscious reasoning. No doubt it gratifies a generous sensibility in the Western way of thinking to posit for exotic societies a simpler kind of cultural ownership than we can readily claim for ourselves. It is comforting, and eases the work of description in the absence of good historical information, to think of those societies as both the creators and the outright owners in fee simple of all their manifest cultural assets. They are not really so any more than we.

Contemplating the copious information in the Parry Collection about how recently living Balkan and African oral traditional fabulators have learned their arts, I have often been struck, and in being struck had a feeling uncannily compounded of awe and admiration, how like a parasitized host, or better, a symbiont in zoology a really good oral bard is. Born with a superior facility for rhythmical speech, the storyteller-to-be also displays an exceptional capacity for prolonged mental attention to the enchainment of images in a purely verbal medium at an early age. This combination of ready verbalism and attentiveness renders the subject especially vulnerable towards other storytellers about the time of puberty, when he or she begins consciously to 'collect' stories from accomplished performers. After this period of 'infection' with a variety of tales during the second decade of life, the bard will typically remain interested in learning still other tales throughout his active career, but tends increasingly to assimilate stories that are new to him in terms of his own established habits of narrative composition. In this phase of his career he is highly infectious towards the young of his kind, although he does not ordinarily perform especially for them. Meanwhile others of all ages remain as immune to the contagion of active participation in the tradition as they would if they had actual antibodies in their bloodstreams to protect them against it.

Thus a tradition continues not by any analytical teaching nor by reference to anything outside itself, but solely by the voluntary renewal of storytelling habits from generation to generation in a fraction of a given population. In this way the tradition is scarcely the possession of the whole society, but rather of that fraction that is at puberty mentally vulnerable to its contagion. The *uses* of the material in the tradition may be everyman's, or levitical, or princely, or otherwise distributed and restricted in all manner of socially idiosyncratic ways, but the tradition itself belongs to that limited number whose minds are actually its hosts. Or perhaps it is better, because in time those minds wane and die, to recognize from the outset that in a very real sense it is the tradition that owns its human hosts while they live and practice their storytelling art, moving from mind to mind across the generations as an intangible and invisible but nonetheless living thing in its own right.

But what are the limits, and what has been the history of this peculiar ideational symbiote of man which we call oral narrative tradition? Must we indeed try to traverse a million-year regression of human generations to find its origins, and hence its primal meanings? And if neither cultural universals nor yet the cultural idiosyncracies of the societies that support an oral narrative tradition can be called upon to explain it (while it continues everywhere to explain culture to society), how then is it to be explained. Must we in the absence of reliable external control on our critical procedure (such as the systematic reference of narratives to the rules of social relations) fall back upon a kind of Cartesian subjectivity, already too familiar in conventional literary criticism and in the humanities generally, wherein any man's opinion of what oral tradition means is as good as any other's provided it be clever? The principle of this objection, already raised by Clifford Geertz in regard to Claude Lévi-Strauss's criticism of myth, is a serious one and must be faced.

The problem snaps quickly into focus when it is projected upon a specific element of oral tradition such as the Green Tree scene. Finding no credible rationale or genesis of that basic Yugoslav (and worldwide) narrative element in Yugoslav society past or present, I maintain that it had an inherent ideational value sufficient to assure its indefinite survival in the Yugoslav oral tradition not through any connection with other cultural requisites whether universal or local, but simply in itself. I need make no supposition of my own, however, as to what that value is, nor do I need to draw upon any tentative analogy between the alien Yugoslav story and anything in my own ethnic or national or personal culture to provide a starting-point for interpretation. The ideational value of the Yugoslav Green Tree scene is thus no mere figment of my own mind untested or uncontrollable by means of objective verification. For the Green Tree is not any one single thing; it is rather a multitude of different things or *multiforms* that may be objectively compared one with another, as earlier in this Epilogue I compared just three of its multiforms. So the intrinsic ideational value which I say is the real root of the Green Tree scene's obvious and probably old persistence in Yugoslav tradition need not remain a mystery, nor is there any mystique about the procedure for discovering it: that value is just the common denominator of all the multiforms of the Green Tree scene that have spawned in the innumerable ongoing acts of story-composition that *are* the tradition. In the same way that the traditional *conteur* knows what to tell—through the stability of recurrently exercised habit—in that same way have I gone to seek the meaning of his habit.

Appendix

OGRES AND COSMOTACTS

Further Examples and Notes
on the Two Trees' Pattern

> *An unlucky man, he was once urged by a*
> *clairvoyant to go to Paris where a great*
> *adventure awaited him. He went within a*
> *week, and was killed when a branch of a*
> *tree fell on him.*
>
> — E. Breeze *(South London Press)*

THE COSMOTACTS IN THE ORDER OF THEIR HEWING

IN THE TEXT		IN THE APPENDIX	
Avrom the lumber dealer	p. 36	A Tortoise	p. 331
A Little Thing	p. 38	Kanu the Creator	p. 337
Samson	p. 42	A raffia-cutter	p. 338
A brother youngest of five	p. 58	A banana-thief	p. 338
Mr. Little-Hare	p. 63	A young lord who married a cucumber-girl	p. 339
Adam	p. 72		
Mr. Squeezer	p. 88	Ali the Rose (alias the Naked)	p. 344
Beowulf	p. 90		
A troop of new-born babes	p. 98	Omer Hrnjica	p. 350
A young father	p. 104	Ali Vrhovac	p. 352
A little bird who told	p. 106	Perkunas	p. 358
Kasere, the little dancer	p. 109	The linden's brother	p. 360
Mandu, alias Kalombe	p. 122	A wood-cutter a-courting	p. 362
Moses	p. 143	The Baron of Tearne Wadling	p. 363
The *rex Nemorensis*	p. 156		
Gilgamesh	p. 228	Máel Dúin	p. 379
Djulić Ibrahim	p. 308	Art of Leinster	p. 381
		Ivan Sosnovich (alias John Pineson)	p. 385
		Saint Nicholas	p. 393
		Nicholas the Hermit	p. 395
		King Orfeo	p. 402
		Wurrunna	p. 406
		Nimbamung and Ambwerk	p. 412
		The man who invented agriculture	p. 418
		A handsome hunter-boy	p. 421
		A young man of Salinas	p. 426
		Tečware's brother-in-law	p. 429
		Black Berries	p. 430
		Kasilun	p. 434

The point of this appendix is further to substantiate (without attempting to exhaust) the thesis that the Two Trees are a worldwide pattern in oral fable, and in so doing also to remark those aspects of fable from many places and various ages that to my mind forcibly urge certain methodological preferences in the criticism of oral traditions wherever they occur.

The Awalamba and Bene-Mukuni (Lenje), whose reflexes of the Two Trees' story are discussed in the early chapters of this book, had no monopoly of that story in Africa. It and its cosmotactic hero were known quite generally among Bantu. The Ovimbundu, for example, a people of Angola in West Africa, knew many different tales about cosmotactic characters whose names were the names of animals. The events in such tales belonged to a legendary time when men and beasts lived together in society, before the present laws governing the organization of the world (and the separation of men and animals) entered into force. Those tales told how various animals discovered natural rules of relationship and behaviour, and either obeyed those rules, or if they would not obey, were in some way compelled to withdraw from society and to accept isolation as a distinct animal species. Through their superior intelligence and more nearly human adaptability, some animals were particularly instrumental in expelling others from the fabulous mixed society of men and beasts. The superior animals or *tricksters* could discern the actual limits of their own and other creatures' ability and usefulness better than other animals could, and consequently went about the primordial world both inducing other creatures to overstep natural limits and punishing them when they did so. As elsewhere in Africa, the Hare and the Tortoise were particularly prominent in Umbundu trickster-tales. Although they had no part in creating it, the tricksters of Bantu fable helped to organize and arrange the world as it now is by their discovery and enforcement of natural law. In this way the animal tricksters of Umbundu tales were cosmotactic heroes no different from tricksters in indigenous European, Australian, or American Indian fable. The Umbundu trickster Hare and arch-trickster Tortoise figure in the same

long cycle of cosmotactic adventures that characterizes trickster stories
in oral fable on other continents, and as elsewhere, cosmotactic adventures in Umbundu story-telling entailed the pattern of the Two Trees.

One day Hare said to Hornbill, "Come along with me and let
us visit my wife's family." Hornbill agreed.

After they had walked along the path for some time, Hare
said that he needed to retire to the bush. As Hare was coming
back to the path, he picked up a round stone about the size of
a ball of mush and put it into his food wallet.[93]

The first concern of cosmotactic narrative everywhere is food
and eating, but not simply the conventional acts of food-getting and
ingestion. As in the tales of Adam, Moses, Samson, Beowulf, or Mandu, cosmotactic narrative explores especially those sources of food
and modes of feeding that lie beyond what is ordinarily possible and
permissible. The scatological beginning of this Umbundu tale is a common motif of trickster-story, which often notices the end-products as
much as the initial substances of nutrition. Hare returns from his ex-
cretory excursion with an unacceptable substitute for food, and then
induces the gullible Hornbill to treat real food as though it were a
worthless substitute:

Then when they came to a river, Hare said to Hornbill, "My
mother warned me that to cross a bridge with a ball of mush
in your wallet is unlucky. She said you must throw it into the
stream." When Hare had said this, he took the stone out of his
wallet and threw it into the river. Hornbill took from his wallet
the ball of mush he carried to eat on the road, and threw it into
the stream.

Hare is still the trickster and Hornbill his dupe when they later
stop to rest under a green fruit-tree in the wilderness. It is a place of
unreciprocal feeding and lawless acquisition. Hare pretends to be acting in unison with Hornbill, but actually he seizes every opportunity
to magnify the discrepancy between his own and Hornbill's intelligence and well-being. He does this by concealing the identity of what
it is that he has in his food-pouch:

Farther on they came to a tree bearing an edible fruit. They
sat down under the tree to rest. As they sat resting, Hare opened
his wallet, took out his ball of mush, and began to eat it. Hornbill saw this. He spoke up and said, "What is this! You said,
'Let us throw our balls of mush into the river!'"

Hare said, "Yes, that is so. But since then this ball of mush just cooked itself inside my wallet."

When Hare had finished eating, he called Hornbill's attention to the wild fruit and said, "Let us gather some of these wild plums. But in gathering them, let us gather only the green ones. My mother warned me not to gather red ones, for they bring bad luck." Then they began to gather some of the fruit. Hare moved around to the back of the tree, where he picked the ripe, red plums. Hornbill, as he had been advised by Hare, gathered only green fruit. When they had filled their wallets, they went on once more.

The trickster and his victim go straight on from the green wood to the hewn, but Hornbill lacks the sagacity promptly to lay hold of the hewn wood and use it against his ogreish host when the opportunity presents itself:

As they drew near the village of Hare's wife's family, they sat down under a tree to rest. Hare noticed that there were chips and shavings at the place where they sat down. They started to eat some of their fruit. Hornbill saw Hare eating ripe, red plums and said to him, "Didn't you tell me that we should not pick red ones?"

"Oh yes," said Hare, "I did say that, but these plums ripened in my wallet."

After they had eaten their fruit, Hare said to Hornbill: "At the village ahead, where we are going, they do not have any spoons. When you see them bringing us food, you must come back here to get some of these chips, so that we can eat with them. You will do this instead of my doing it, since we shall need the chips quickly and you have wings which enable you to travel faster than I."

Hornbill agreed to this and said, "That is all right."

Hornbill wants both the ordinary human cunning to save himself inconvenience by picking up the chips of wood when he first sees them, and the traditional knowledge that hewn wood is the first resort in dealing with a food-trickster. Lacking both those human resources of mind—cleverness and traditional knowledge—Hornbill is destined by his own nature to early separation from primordial society. Eventually Hare feeds him (as the ogre in these tales always must), but the cost to Hornbill of accepting the trickster's hospitality is appalling (as usual in this story-pattern):

When they came into the village the people rejoiced to see them and received them in fine style. They were taken to the men's clubhouse, given chairs, and beer was brought for them to drink. Next they were greeted with a formal speech of welcome. Later in the day they were taken to the guesthouse. Near sundown, the hosts were seen bringing them mush and fried chicken.

When Hare saw the food coming, he spoke to Hornbill and said, "Hornbill, remember what I spoke to you about. Now go and get them." While Hornbill was away, Hare ate the mush and the fried fowl that was served with it. When Hornbill returned, Hare gave him some mush served with beans, which had been brought along with the other, saying, "Brother, take this and eat it. I, for my part, shall eat nothing more in this village, for it is an insult to be served food of this sort, of such low quality. I had thought that the mush would be served with meat, but it is not so." Hornbill took the food and ate it, for he was painfully hungry.

Hare's deeds thus far have been tricky, but not yet preternaturally so. Now that element in his character emerges; he is a preternaturally prodigious eater, and he sets about feeding himself as a witch would. Hornbill gets the blame, and the punishment due a witch:

Hare went out in the night, stole a goat, and ate it. He cut a hole in the stomach of the goat, and slipped it over the head of Hornbill. The contents of the stomach were warm and brought a deep sleep over Hornbill. In the morning the owners of the goat came looking for it. They found Hornbill sleeping with the stomach of the goat over his head. They said, "We are looking for a goat. What have you guests to say?"

Hare replied to them: "The old men have said, 'The bull of the herd does not gore his own, for he is their guardian.' " Then the owners of the goat took Hornbill away and killed him.

Hare returned to their village alone. He stayed there for some time.

The arch-trickster who can vanquish an ogre like Hare must adopt the ogre's own techniques of injury. The trickster Hare next invites Tortoise to go with him on a visit to his wife's family's village. But now it is Hare who is undone by stupid, inflexible obedience to a prescribed routine—the same routine that earlier undid Hornbill. Hare puts Tortoise through the same series of deceptions about food which he inflicted on Hornbill, but unlike Hornbill Tortoise is not deceived. Where Hornbill had acted differently or separately from Hare, Tortoise imitates and even anticipates Hare's every move. *On the pretext of relieving himself, Tortoise leaves Hare on the path and picks up a stone the size of a ball of mush. He rejoins Hare, who then does the same thing. Hare again urges throwing their provisions of mush into a river, and both he and Tortoise throw in their stones. When Hare begins to eat mush under the wild fruit-tree, Tortoise questions him and gets the same answers as had Hornbill in that situation. To the astonishment of Hare, Tortoise then begins to eat his own mush. Hare asks how he came by it, and Tortoise gives Hare his own reply—that the ball of mush had cooked itself in his wallet while they walked. Hare again counsels picking only green fruit from the tree, but Tortoise disobeys and imitates Hare, who picks only ripe fruit. The same exchange of questions and answers about the fruit takes place at the site of the hewn wood as earlier transpired about the mush at the fruit-tree. When Hare tells Tortoise to be prepared to return for a chip of wood when their hosts serve them food in the village, Tortoise surreptitiously picks up a chip and carries it with him, sensibly anticipating a future need. Eventually they are served, to Hare's consternation Tortoise produces the chip, and then takes the food directly from the hands of their host rather than from the thieving intermediary Hare. They thus share the meal of mush and fried chicken equally.*

Hare steals another goat that night, but Tortoise places white cowry-shells over his eyes before going to sleep in order to make Hare think that he is awake. Hare sits waiting in the dark for Tortoise to close his eyes so that he may put the goat's stomach over Tortoise's head and so incriminate him, as he had done previously to Hornbill. But like Hornbill Hare himself finally falls asleep holding the stomach. Next morning the villagers find him in this incriminating posture and kill him.

Tortoise understands what Hornbill did not, that to overcome an ogre, one must lay firm hold on hewn wood at the first opportunity, and mete out to the ogre the same offenses which it commits against others. Tortoise triumphs by uniting himself inseparably with Hare in all Hare's strategems. By acting in absolute unison with Hare, he avoids

Hornbill's fate—the separation of himself from society—and achieves instead the segregation of the ogre, Hare.

The green fruit-tree in the wilderness and the hewn chips at the periphery of the village are related to one another in two ways in this Umbundu tale. First, they are logical opposites of each other, the one green and the other dead, the one a resource and the other a social instrument for the Hare and his travelling companions. But the two kinds of wood are also causally related; the one is a remedy for what happens at the other. The chip which Tortoise picks up to use as a spoon is a remedy for the social lawlessness which Hare begins to manifest at the wild fruit-tree. Of these two relationships, the first is generically significant—it helps to define the two generic motifs of trees—but the second, causal relationship is only nominally significant —it pertains only to the Umbundu interpretation of the international story-pattern and does not necessarily have any acceptance or validity whatsoever among other peoples who know the generic story of the two trees equally well in other multiforms. The injured *personae* in the Two Trees' story as others tell it do not necessarily as in Bantu fable hurry out the instant they have been hurt to embrace some piece of hewn wood for its prophylactic and remedial help against the ogre at the green tree. Indeed some perfectly respectable oral traditional story-tellers in other cultures go so far in reinterpreting the causal relationship between the two trees as to make unreciprocal giving or taking of food or other property at the green wood in the wilderness a remedy for the harsh justice of absolute reciprocity at the sign of the hewn wood. Such a local change in the motivation or reason for a particular sequence of motifs has no effect upon the composition of the generic motival cluster, which is not a *fixed sequence* but rather a *freely variable constellation* of motifs. The fixing of motival sequences and assignment of motivations for them are just another form of local, idiosyncratic interpretation of inherited motival material, more elusive perhaps and more a matter of personal or ethnically defined opinions than are the interpretations of fabulous motifs incorporated in a community of religious beliefs. But as generic motifs. neither of the two trees necessarily causes the appearance of the other in any given tale, any more than two atoms of hydrogen necessarily cause the appearance of an atom of oxygen in conjunction with them to constitute a molecule of water. Even the order of the two trees' precedence one before the other in a tale is freely variable. The only invariable fact about their relationship is that they both belong to the same cluster of narrative motifs.

Albert Lord has called the force that keeps such motifs together in tradition the *tension of essences*.[94] This conservative, cohesive tension among the motifs in a given cluster or pattern is partly a matter of inherent logical properties (the two trees are memorable as logical opposites of one another), and partly customary: an oral traditional story-teller narrates them together because that is the way he has always heard them told, and therefore the only right way for him to tell them. But the rationality of causation is not a conservative force comparable to either tradition or the inherent logical properties of the motifs. Great oral traditional narrators (like Homer) may owe much of their reputations to their ability as philosophers—elaborating, inventing, and introducing into their tales various seemly reasons for the traditional courses of events which they narrate. But while such moralism and rationalism is certainly a part of narrative art, it belongs to hermeneutic not strictly narrative tradition, and it must be distinguished from the tension of essences, no matter how appealing or durable a particular story-teller's maxims or causative ordering of events (like Homer's) may be to his own people or to anyone else.

KANU THE CREATOR

Two thousand miles away to the northwest of Umbundu lands in Angola, the Limba people of Sierra Leone, who are not Bantu, knew the story of the Two Trees as well as any people in Central Africa. It was an indigenous part of Limba culture in just as great a profusion of indigenous multiforms as could be found for any other pattern in Limba fable. On the fifteenth of October, 1961, a man named Niaka Dema[95] dictated to a British collector, Ruth Finnegan, a concise cosmotactic tale of disunity and union formed on the pattern of the Two Trees' story. Its *personae* were a curiously disunited group of palm-wine tappers and a great Limba preternatural and trickster named Kanu, who was among other things god of the sky and the supreme deity of the Limba. The tale began with the green food-tree: *Several young men set out to clear undergrowth and tap oil-palms (*Elaeis guineensis*) for palm-wine. While they are aloft in their several trees, Kanu goes from one to another begging the gift of some wine to drink. The young male tappers are disjointed (or as yet un-*

joined) parts of the future human body: hands, hips, neck, head, back, and stomach. All the tappers refuse to give Kanu nourishment except the last, stomach, who entertains him hospitably. Through Stomach Kanu appoints a time for a meeting of all the tappers, and he himself comes to the meeting bearing products of hewn wood wherewith to subdue his ogres—the persons (i.e., parts of the body) who withheld wine from him at their green palm-trees. Using resin, palm-cotton, and ashes, he joins all the previously independent parts of the body together and designates Stomach to be chief and rule them.[96]

A RAFFIA-CUTTER

The same Limba story-teller, Niaka Dema, told Ruth Finnegan another multiform of the Two Trees' story in which the hewn wood came before the green. It too was a tale of hunger and of cosmotactic deeds to benefit the hungry: *A spirit owns a palm-wine tree. While cutting ribs from the fronds of raffia-palms, a man discovers the spirit's tapped oil-palm and steals the wine from it. After he has done this several times, the spirit catches him at it, and generously offers to teach the man, who has not previously known palm-wine, how to clear and tap his own trees. Both the man and the spirit being solitary persons without any families, they become bosom friends. Finally, after the host spirit has taught the man all his art, he demands that his human guest pay him a human child for the teaching. The man protests, but the story-teller omitted to say whether the spirit got his victim or not.*[97] Niaka Dema left the ugly incident of the preter-natural's sudden outrageous demand unresolved, but the conclusion is obvious from the beginning of the tale. The man was already equip-ped with hewn wood before he met the spirit, who first benevolently promoted and then inexplicably violated human interests at the green food-tree.

A BANANA-THIEF

The hewn wood came before the green again in a story told by another Limba man, Dauda Konteh, on the thirteenth of December, 1961: *A pregnant girl longs to eat a banana. The chief of the place owns a banana-tree, but has warned that he will kill any man who takes its fruit unlawfully. The girl's husband nevertheless violates the tree, and the chief does indeed kill him. The young widow moves away to her own family's village, where she bears and raises her child, a daughter.*

When the girl is grown, she returns to her father's village and induces the chief who slew her father to marry her. Left alone with him on the bridal night, she kills him and makes off with all his wealth. Next morning twelve men and boys pursue her on horseback, and one boy overtakes her in the wilderness. When he is about to kill her, she tells him that before she can die he must pick a leaf from the topmost twig of a "huge, tall" kuwunu-tree. He strips and climbs the tree, but the girl mounts his horse and rides away, saying to him that he is a dead man "perched up there on the top twig."[98]

The banana tree is the hewn wood of this tale, because the hungry girl's husband not only takes its fruit but also cuts down the whole tree in the process. It is the chief's domestic stock, and he exacts the price of reciprocity that regularly attends the hewn wood in this story-pattern: the chief kills the man just as the man has killed his tree. But the husband, the lawless violator of the piece, has a tricky, ogreish offspring; like Grendel's dam returning to Heorot to avenge Grendel, his daughter returns to the scene of her father's death where she first entertains and then kills and robs her satiated 'guest,' who has made the mistake of accepting her entertainment on their wedding-night. Then, under the green wood in the wild, she again tricks another victim to death, and thus offsets the dead chief's harsh, unifying rule of strict reciprocity in his village with her own compensatory lawless appropriation of his life and property and the life of his subject at the green *kuwunu*-tree in the wild. Finally, Dauda Konteh gave his tale a cosmotactic coda in the form of an ætion: the events in the story are, said he, the reason why the Limba now have female 'chiefs' (a characteristically Limba social institution).

THE YOUNG LORD WHO MARRIED A CUCUMBER GIRL

Oral fable outside Africa abounds in multiforms of the Two Trees' story; there are examples in any representative collection from any language of the Old World. Warren Walker's and Ahmet Uysal's recently published collection of Anatolian Turkish tales, *Tales Alive in Turkey*,[99] contains several good specimens. In December, 1961, Muharrem Choban, a day laborer forty years of age from a small village in

the *caza* of Chubuk, province of Ankara, told Walker and Uysal a tale
about a beautiful girl born from a cucumber and the young male cosmotact who ultimately married her.[100] The tale begins with a problem
of nutrition: *A young lord offends a witch, who "put a curse upon
him: 'May you become pale and thin,' she said, 'and may you fall in
love with a cucumber girl.'" The curse is realized, and the wan, emaci-
ated young lord sets out with forty mules and forty saddlebags of gold
to find a remedy for his affliction. During his journey he overhears an
old man divining what will befall him:*

> . . .on his travels he is going to find a lion for whom he must
> buy milk; he is going to meet a tiger for whom he must buy
> meat; and finally, he will meet a witch for whom he must buy
> six kilos of chewing gum. Then he will go on and reach a foun-
> tain which has two pipes flowing from it, one pouring out blood
> and the other, pus. He must say to the fountain, 'What nice wa-
> ter you have,' and as he says this, he must scoop up three hand-
> fuls and drink it. After this he will go on, and then he will come
> to a large pine tree from which he will knock a chip with his axe.
> This chip he must take to the giants he will meet next. When he
> comes to the giants he must wait until they are asleep. If their
> eyes are closed, that will mean that they are awake; but if their
> eyes are open, then they will be asleep. When he is sure that
> they are asleep, he must go past the giants to a giantess who
> guards three cucumbers. To her he must give the pine chip and
> all the gold that he has in his saddlebags, and for this, he will
> receive the three cucumbers. If he cuts open these cucumbers
> in a waterless place, three girls will jump from them but they
> will soon die of thirst. If he cuts them in a place where water
> is available, the three girls will live, and then this young man
> will be saved from his trouble.

Like Niaka Dema's polymorphic cosmotact in the Limba story
of the two trees, the young Turkish hewer and subduer of ogres also
cuts material from a tree in order to gain his object, an edible bride
(a clever preternatural expression of the equation which I have alluded
to before as a regular concomitant of the Two Trees' story: food $\cong$
progeny). From this point the tale moves on quickly to the unhewn
green wood: *The young man does as the old diviner indicated that
he should, and obtains the three cucumbers. He wastes the first two*

*experimenting in dry places to see whether they really contain girls.
But he saves the third until he arrives at a fountain on the outskirts
of his own town. When he opens the last cucumber, a surpassingly
beautiful maiden springs forth crying for water. He plunges her into
the fountain, and when she is properly wetted, they two agree to
marry. But she commands him to leave her at the fountain for an
interval of forty days and nights while he celebrates his betrothal
in the town, and then to return to her. Meanwhile she will await
him in the top of a poplar tree that grows over the fountain.*

The expected contest between trickster and arch-trickster at the
green wood now ensues: *An ugly serving-woman comes to draw water
from the fountain and sees the image of the girl in the poplar tree
reflected in the water. Thinking that it is her own reflection, she becomes vain and refuses to be a servant any longer. Eventually she
learns that the image in the water is not her own, and begs the girl
atop the poplar to raise her into the tree-top too. She offers to be
the girl's foster-mother and groom her, and the cucumber-girl speaks
to the poplar, which bends at her bidding and raises the ugly woman.
Masking her evil design in the guise of friendly intimacy, the woman
then tricks the cucumber-girl so as to make her fall out of the poplar,
and substitutes herself in marriage with the young lord when he returns to the tree at the appointed time. But a sesame plant springs
up at the place where the cucumber-girl fell; the bridegroom notices
it, plucks it, and wears it on his hat as a cockade.*

The ugly woman, the original habituée of the green poplar, is of
course the ogress of the tale. First she helps and then in a sudden reversal tries to destroy her 'guest,' the cucumber-girl, who has come
from a distant place to the fountain which the ugly woman frequents
each day, drawing water there for the sustenance of herself and the
people whom she serves. Although she is a foreigner, the cucumber-
girl comes to the fountain and takes water from it without the least
thought of reciprocal exchange or payment to the regular denizen of
the place. Nor does the ogress insist on reciprocity; on the contrary,
she offers her friendship and help gratis to the cucumber-girl. But the
ugly woman's ogreish capacity for capricious change from a helpful
to an injurious attitude is revealed even before she has learned the
true identity of the beautiful image in the water; seeing the reflection,
she capriciously decides to cease serving those whom she has daily
served 'til then. This monstrous quality is emphasized again in her

alternately benevolent and malevolent dealings with the cucumber-girl.

The hewn pine-tree enters the tale at a time when the young lord has separated himself from his own people, and when he is about to face dangers that would certainly prevent his ever being reunited with them were it not for the mysterious help of the pine-chip. The poplar at the fountain has just the opposite effect. It and the preter-natural girl who commands it intervene in the young lord's career at a time when he is about to reenter his own town with the fabulous bride whom he has sought and won at great jeopardy in a strange and far place. But no sooner has the girl hospitably announced her willing-ness to marry the young lord than she incongruously refuses to enter his town and be united with him in marriage. Then, even after he has lost her and married the substitute bride instead, she continues to interfere in his affairs, causing various of his people and his property to be detached from him until finally she, the arch-trickster, defeats the tricky, ogreish substitute bride and detaches her from the man whom she, the cucumber-girl, is still destined to marry. Imitating the original ogress and trickster, the cucumber-girl performs one unset-tling, disuniting act after another until she has perfected an ideal un-ion. And like her husband-to-be, she too turns to hewn wood in her paradoxical quest for union through acts of segregation. Even more than did Pygmalion's bride, the cucumber-girl ultimately owes her very existence in human form to her future husband's hewing, for he causes her to be wrought from plant material not once but twice: *After she has become pregnant, the substitute bride urges her husband to destroy his cockade of sesame stalk. He throws it into the fire, but two pidgeons emerge from the flames as it burns and fly away into the garden. There they incant charms to cause him bad luck. The sub-stitute bride demands that the pidgeons be caught and cooked for her to eat. Her husband complies, but where he sheds their blood a pop-lar springs up, beside the threshold of the house. Each night the tree raps on the roof until it is cut down for wood to make the new-born child's crib. An elderly serving-woman picks up one of the chips from the carpenter's work and takes it home with her. There the chip be-comes the girl again, and she induces the old woman to quit her mas-ter's service. Famine comes to the land, and the young lord has his stable of horses farmed out to be fed by others while the famine lasts. All die except one feeble beast placed with the old woman, which sur-*

*vives and becomes a splendid mount because the cucumber-girl can
cause fresh green grass to grow for it to eat wherever she steps. She
walks back and forth feeding it until the famine passes. When the
young lord comes to retrieve his horse, the girl reveals her identity
to him; he destroys the substitute bride and her children, marries the
girl, and they live together contentedly thereafter.*

Each multiform of a pattern in oral narrative tradition has a
large but variable number of the set of generic motifs belonging to
that pattern. While each multiform reproduces most of the motifs,
no motif is necessarily reproduced in every multiform which may
happen to be told in a given language. Like any biological process,
story-telling is not always perfectly efficient in the use of its inherited
means. In any population some individuals are born imperfectly formed; similarly, even the best of oral traditional story-tellers sometimes
botch a performance, and less capable narrators will misconstruct
theirs in proportion to their lesser facility. Still, tales told in oral
tradition seldom lack more than one or two of their generic members
even when they are badly done. If they lack more than that they are
not tales. Most of the complexity in the relationship of one multiform to another is not due to any truncation of basic pattern, but
to differences in the choice of nominal motifs to represent the generic features of a pattern, and in the sequential arrangement of the
nominal motifs so chosen.

In African fable, for example, personal powers of shape-shifting
like those of the Turkish cucumber-girl are frequently more evident
at the beginning of the Two Trees' story in the person of the first
ogre or trickster than in the person of the arch-trickster and ogre-
tamer. The particular changes of shape through which the cucumber-
girl passes—cucumber, woman, sesame-stalk, pidgeons, poplar, and
woman again—are more or less unique features of Muharrem Choban's
Turkish tale, at least in relation to other tales of the same pattern in
African for instance, or Chinese, or Australian, or American Indian
fable. Those changes of shape immediately give the cucumber-girl the
same preterhuman stamp that so often marks the untamed trickster
at the green tree in indigenous African fable, who is also frequently
a good shape-shifter. But shape-shifting in both the Turkish and African multiforms of *this* story-pattern (as distinct from the generic significance of shape-shifting in *other* patterns) is a matter of concealing
identity—a regular generic component of the Two Trees' story wher-

ever it is told. The ogre at the green tree is frequently the first to conceal his real nature in African multiforms, with his nemesis the archtrickster joining in and winning the game of hide-and-seek later on. The African arch-trickster and ogre-tamer is better at concealments than his untamed opponent, just as the cucumber-girl hides her identity better and more often than the ugly woman who competes with her. But the difference between the Turkish and African multiforms is only a matter of names and sequences. The cucumber-girl emerges from the cucumber and hides herself again in the foliage of the poplar beside the fountain before her ugly ogress even comes into the tale, yet the ugly serving-woman is herself no less preternatural and no less a skillful concealer of her identity for that. Muharrem Choban mentioned time and again as he told his tale how like a witch the ugly woman was, and he connected her twice with pots, which are usual instruments and, together with ugliness, identifying attributes of Turkish witches—patently preterhuman beings. This ugly Turkish witch furthermore overcomes and deposes the cucumber-girl by a typical witch's wile—discovering and assaulting her fair rival's 'vital spot.' So she too is preternatural, and if she is less so than the cucumber-girl, that is perfectly consistent with the pattern of the Two Trees' story. Her cunning assumption of the cucumber-girl's identity is just as respectable a piece of trickery with the same results as any African trickster's deceit in a tale of two trees, and the cucumber-girl outdoes her guile with the same stunning display of impenetrable disguise and adaptability that the best arch-tricksters in African fable can devise. The tale's the same; only the names and the sequences have been changed to protect the ethnic identity and the particular cultural interests of Muharrem Choban and his people on the one hand, or the various African narrators and their peoples on the other. . . .

GOL ALIJA

Two male contestants at the green tree displace the females of the Turkish tale in an oral epic multiform of the Two Trees' story from Novi Pazar in Yugoslavia. The American collector Milman Parry recorded the tale there from an old, bi-lingual (Serbo-Croatian and Albanian) story-teller named Salih Ugljanin in 1934. Salih told the tale in Serbo-Croatian; it was nominally about an orphan and recluse named Ali, who abandoned society after two serious personal misfortunes

and went to live as a voluntary exile in the wilderness:[101] *Ali and his
sister were orphaned when they were young, and then a band of bor-
der-raiders plundered the district where they lived, kidnapped his sister, and took her away to parts unknown. Alone and embittered, Ali
withdrew to live in an icy cave on a high mountain. There, like the
English Robin Hood, he began to form a company of bandits and
highwaymen. Later, he provided his band with a flock of a thousand
sheep, which he put in charge of one of his companions, Ibro Hurem-
ović, as chief shepherd.*

This was not exactly a temple-flock, nor was Ibro exactly the
guardian of cattle depicted on ancient Mesopotamian seals (cf. Figures
53 and 54). Yet the flock and its fabulous shepherd suggested to Salih
a doorway with a banded stock set upright before it just as surely as
if Salih had known the iconography derived from the story of the
Two Trees in ancient Mesopotamia. But of course his knowledge was
better than that—he knew the traditional Two Trees' story itself in
its South Slavic reflex: *Immediately he had formed the flock, Ali had
a fir-tree that stood before the door of his cave covered with gold-
plate, and bound the bole of the tree with three heavy bands of gold.
Beneath it he constructed a fountain of gold and silver, and then proclaimed the whole mountain a fane, forbidding even the birds of the
air to trespass over it in their flight. This strict interdiction endured
for twelve years, until a train of events began in Istanbul that was
fated to end Ali's seclusion and the inviolability of his mountain sanctuary.*

Ali's gilt pillar is the epicenter of his all-male, bandit society on
the mountain, signifying its unity and self-sufficiency. As hewn wood,
it is a traditional symbol of concentricity, but it is not suited to denote separation like the segregation of Ali and his forty thieves from
the rest of mankind. A green tree in a wild place is required for that
signification, and Salih supplied one at the proper moment in his tale:
*The sultan in Istanbul hears that a certain Christian king has a unique-
ly lovely daughter named Nastasija, and he determines to have her. He
dispatches orders to one of his Moslem vassals in Bosnia to go to the
neighboring Christian kingdom and capture the girl, or forfeit his own
head. The vassal thinks himself unable to carry out so risky a venture,
and decides instead to send from his retinue a certain rogue named
Radovan to go and enlist the help of the bandit-chief Ali. Radovan
must therefore travel onto Ali's interdicted mountain at the jeopardy*

*of his own life. This he does, until he emerges above a clearing on the
mountain and sees there Ali's wondrous shepherd Ibro with a golden
rifle on his shoulder and dressed "all in silver and pure gold." The
shepherd's twelve dogs spy the emissary Radovan and set on him,
whereupon*

> Radovan fled up a green fir tree
> 'Til he found a perch on the branches of the fir.

Fir trees are a commonplace image in Serbo-Croatian oral epic
tradition, but the description and circumstances of the two in Salih's
tale are extraordinary. The gilding of the dry fir that stands before
the entrance to Ali's lair is highly unusual, and the golden shepherd
who frightens Radovan like a guardian seraph at the green fir is equally peculiar. The events which next occur beneath the two trees set
them even farther apart not only from the common imagery of this
tradition, but also from each other: *Alerted by his dogs, Ibro the shepherd approaches and looks into the branches of the tree, where he sees
Radovan. He takes his golden rifle from his shoulder with a lethally
threatening gesture, and calls to Radovan to ask him who he is and
why he trespasses on the forbidden mountain. Radovan is saved from
death by a happy accident. He recognizes Ibro, a friend from the past,
and appeals to their former friendship. Ibro's threatening attitude
changes suddenly to one of warm welcome when Radovan identifies
himself. The interloper descends then from the branches of the fir, but
he is so overwhelmed by hunger that he collapses at Ibro's feet. The
shepherd feeds him white bread gratis and so revives him.*

Albert Lord, the editor and translator of Milman Parry's collection from Novi Pazar, remarked in a note to this story: "It is not
clear what the function of the theme of hunger and bread is. It has
not been foreshadowed, nor does it have any importance in any later
action."[102] Seen as motifs in the international story of the Two Trees,
Radovan's hunger and Ibro's bread are obviously the usual hunger of
the cosmotact and his people, and the usual nourishment which a preternatural person offers to the cosmotact at the sign of the green tree
in the wilderness. But whereas the sense of these two motifs is perfectly apparent in the larger context of Old-World fable as a whole,
it was anything but obvious within the confines of Serbo-Croatian
oral epic tradition, even to a man who knew that tradition so exceptionally well as did Albert Lord. Here again is an instance where comparative analysis of oral fable on an international scale penetrates its

local meaning better than local, ethnically delimited study can do, because informed comparative analysis can discriminate between the basic elements of fable and the idiosyncracies of particular cultures to a degree which studies confined to this or that language or region cannot emulate.

In modern Yugoslavia the two trees did not individually or as a pair carry anything like the heavy charge of symbolic meaning which they had for various Bantu peoples in modern Africa. Yet the story was just as prominent in South Slavic as in Bantu tradition, and like other Yugoslav singers of tales in this century, Salih Ugljanin faithfully maintained the Two Trees' pattern with all its constituent motifs in his repertory, even though neither he nor any cult among his people attached any special, extra-narrative importance to any part of the pattern. As local reflexes of the story's generic motifs, Radovan's hunger, Ibro's bread, and each of the other elements in Salih's multiform of the Two Trees' story had a germinal meaning—its meaning in the story-pattern. On some other cultural soil with favorable social, economic, religious, and other circumstances, any of those motifs might have struck root and grown into a great and locally potent symbol. But that was not the fate of the motifs in the story of the Two Trees in Yugoslavia; the rationale for Salih's use of them was neither more nor less than that they were traditional in the basic pattern of his tale. With his usual acuity, Lord puts us onto the right course toward understanding Radovan's encounter with Ibro, a superficially unmotivated piece of Salih's tale, by pointing out that its significance is self-contained, inherent in the story itself, and not to be found in Salih's or anyone else's opinion (or lack of opinion) about it.

Salih's business as an oral narrative poet was not to rationalize or explain the elements of his stories in any sense, not even to the extent of making the elements necessarily cohere as he told them. His obligation was rather to reproduce all the motifs in the patterns of the tales he knew as fully and as exactly as he could. A meticulous adherence to the traditional pattern of a story was far more important both to him and to his listeners than anything he or they might happen to think about the story in the way of explanation or philosophy. Explanatory and philosophical musings come and go, but unless a tale is well and truly told—a good re-creation of what has been told before in the tradition—there would be nothing to muse about or to explain, because oral fable cannot exist without retelling. So the fact of Radovan's collapse from hunger at the green fir mattered to Salih vastly more than *why* he was hungry, or why he collapsed at just that moment in Ibro's presence. Nor did it matter whether Radovan's hunger and Ibro's feeding 'contributed' anything at all to the subsequent 'development' of the tale; tradition dictated only the inclusion of those motifs, not their motivation in any given way. When Salih had finished telling of Radovan's hunger and how Ibro fed him, he had obeyed perfectly that part of his mandate from tradition; he had well and truly reproduced several requisite motifs of the Two Trees' story. The others followed in turn.

After he has eaten Ibro's bread, Radovan asks by what route he may reach Ali's cave, and Ibro begins to tell him: "'Go this way,' he said, 'from right to left, and you will find a dry-branched fir-tree.'"

The 'tension of essences' drew Salih's mind swiftly on from the green tree to a dry one, because in oral fable where the one is the other must surely follow. Only the identity of the trees as firs and the widdershins direction of the tension between them betray Salih's Yugoslav and European milieu. But Salih had yielded to the force of association between the Two Trees a bit too soon; he began to narrate the dry wood with its attendant constellation of motifs before he had completed the circle of motifs that cluster about the green wood. He had omitted one important motif in particular. The preterhuman denizen of the green tree in the wilderness is regularly the keeper of a hitherto inaccessible source of wealth and well-being: e.g., the Lamba father-in-law's fabulous cáches of food; the riches in Grendel's underwater lair; the Mukuni Rain-Lord's boundless stores of precious water; Jehovah's Promised Land flowing with milk and honey; and so forth. Salih had made Ibro give a simple meal to Radovan, but had not yet linked Ibro as the preternatural denizen of the green tree with the requisite treasure of unexploited food, womanhood, or wealth (wealth being the imperishable means of buying the more basic but perishable commodities of food and progeny). Responding to this piece of unfinished pattern, Salih did what the Lenje narrators of *Kapepe* did in comparable situations. He returned to complete the unfinished part of the pattern through a progression. Ibro continues his directions to Radovan:

> Pass by the dry-branched fir tree, and you will find another
> great fir where the bandit's sheep are grazing. There a thousand
> sheep are grazing, all in the shade beneath that green fir. Pass on

to the height beyond, where you will come upon a cloth spread from the fir to the door of the cave; beneath that fir there is another, dry and encased in gold plate, with three hoops of gold about it. . . .

Thus Salih created a twofold progression with four members:

Green Fir	Dry Fir	Green Fir	Dry Fir
of ordinary size; site of a man's entertainment by a preternatural	undecorated; designates the way to site of shelter for Ali's animals	of gigantic size; site of a preternatural's hoard	richly decorated; designates the way to site of shelter for Ali's men

The field of a thousand herbivores feeding under the canopy of Ali's enormous green fir is so forcefully reminiscent of ancient Aegean and Mesopotamian iconography (cf. Figures 23-25 and 59-62 in the main text) that it almost seems Salih must have known and consciously imitated ancient art as he composed his tale in Serbo-Croatian. But that is simply impossible. The same is true also of Ali's wonderful door-pillar. The only alternative conclusion seems to be that oral fable is ultimately a more conservative medium of imagery than even graven stone or gold. By 1934 the iconographic traditions of the ancient Aegean and Mesopotamia had so long ago died out that they might as well have belonged to another planet, and there is no reason to think that they were ever known in Salih's region of the Balkans anyway. Yet in that year Salih Ugljanin still knew the green tree as the feeding and resting place of gentle herbivores, and the upright hewn stock marking the gateway of a sanctuary, as surely as if he had himself heard those motifs woven together in the pattern of the Two Trees' story from some long-dead Sumerian or Minoan teller of tales. A tradition of oral fable is in this way a veritable time machine, affording those like Salih Ugljanin who have achieved the intellectual discipline required to operate it a facility of cultural communication over prodigious spans of time.

With the two trees now doubly established in his tale, Salih went on to elaborate the cosmotactic adventure that must accompany them: *Radovan takes the way indicated to him by Ibro the shepherd and eventually comes to the dry fir before Ali's cave. There beside his gilt coven-tree Ali agrees to go to Korman for the beautiful girl Nastasija, and makes a last will and testament against the chance that he may not return alive from so hazardous an expedition into the lands of a traditional enemy. In the will Ali apportions his accumulated treasure to his forty companions and to Radovan according to their former service and friendship to him.* This act of positive, benevolent reciprocity completed at the place of the hewn wood, Ali proceeds to Korman, where his mission is one of negative reciprocity, i.e., retribution and vengeance: *In Korman Ali finds his lost sister and recaptures her; then he captures the King's daughter, Nastasija, and plunders the King's treasury, even as in Ali's youth the King of Korman had plundered Ali's wealth and female kin.* Thus Ali metes out to the ogre King of Korman the same abuse which he and his people had earlier suffered at the hands of that ogre. The cosmotactic denouement (in its characteristically South Slavic form) follows: *Coming home from Korman, Ali dissolves his band of forty thieves, marries Nastasija (who is happy to marry him), and returns to live in a normal, sociable manner as a respected citizen in his native community.* Thus Ali discharges the cosmo-tactic mission which Radovan transferred to him from the more exalted officers of the empire, and so finally sets aright the disorders of a world which he did not create.

OMER HRNJICA

Salih had numerous other multiforms of the Two Trees' story in his repertory of tales. Some of these are discussed in the Introduction to this book; another concerned the Dioskouroi of the Moslem epic tradition in Serbo-Croatian, Mujo and Halil Hrnjica, and Mujo's son Omer who once fought off a marauding band of Hungarians from the cover of dry wood. . . .[103]

A group of thirty maidens led by an especially attractive, nubile young woman named Mejra Bojičić goes to reap a field of ripe wheat. The field lies in an exposed position on the Hungarian border, and so Mejra's brother Ali with thirty-two comrades-in-arms accompanies the girls to keep watch over them while they work. Mujo Hrnjica hears of the reaping-party, and sends his twelve-year-old son Omer to work beside Mejra for the sport of it. Omer goes, carrying his uncle Halil's flint-lock rifle:

> Beneath a dry fir Omer put off his clothes and laid down his arms, then took up a steel scythe and began to cut beside Mejra. So together they reaped the fine wheat.

Omer and Mejra are famous lovers in South Slavic lyric and bal-
ladic tradition. By making them reap together in the wheatfield, Salih
succinctly established the requisite equation of food and potential progeny, and then moved on to a scene of ogre-taming and retribution at
the dry tree:

No sooner had they found the rhythm of their work than the
mountain resounded and the Prince of Zadar appeared with his
thousand fiends. Ali and his men were fast asleep in the deep
shade, and so the Prince captured and bound them, and took
them away as prisoners onto the mountain. Then the Prince
caught sight of the girls in the wheat, and commanded his troop:
"Forward, dirty Magyars! Let us seize the Turks' girls where they
are reaping the fine wheat!" They rushed headlong down the
mountain toward the girls. But the Sirdar's son Omer threw
down his steel scythe, reached for his far-sounding rifle, and
fought from behind the dry fir. There he slew two and twenty
of the enemy.

Omer bears all the usual traits of the cutting, ogre-slaying, cosmotactic hero whom one expects to find acting out the routine of vengeance at the dry wood. Even the kind of fire-arm he fights with, his
uncle's elaborately mounted and inlaid Turkish *cevherdar* bespeaks the
wielder of the hewn wood in contrast to his dangerously but less po-
tently armed Christian ogres, the Prince of Zadar and his Hungarian
troop, who wound Omer with a much less elegant, crudely hafted
weapon, the *şeşhane,* a kind of long rifle.

But Omer in turn was wounded with fierce wounds, two of them
inflicted by the enemies' long rifles. Yet he did not cry out, nor
did the mountain echo with his complaint. He only took Mejra
Bojičić and fled with her up the mountain 'til he came to a green
fir. There beneath the green fir he sat down, and Mejra took him
in her lap. He cried then, and the whole mountain echoed the
sound.

So Omer escapes from the strict reciprocity of giving and taking
blow for blow with an uncivilized enemy whom he prevents from lawlessly taking away his food and his women at the dry tree to the gratuitous sanctuary of the green tree. There in the shade of the green
wood the two herbivores (wheat-eaters) Omer and Mejra rest, while
Mejra gently entertains the wounded Omer. It is a scene of great ten-
derness given and received without thought of price or exchange. Yet

it is also a scene frought with mortal danger (as the locality of the green wood must be), because Omer is badly wounded and the listener must wonder as do Mujo and Halil later in the tale whether Omer will survive or die. Uncertainty and lack of measure or rule permeate every event here at the green tree in the wilderness, even Mejra's effort to summon help:

> Then Omer said to Mejra, "Oh, Mejra, Bojičić's sister! Take my uncle's flint-lock and load it. Aim it toward Kladuša and fire it, that my uncle and the Sirdar may hear it and help me this day!" Mejra loaded the piece, but her woman's hand did not know the right measure and she filled it too full of powder. When she took aim at the town of Kladuša and put fire to the flint-lock it exploded and the whole mountain groaned. Mujo's glass windows trembled from the shock.

ALI VRHOVAC

Salih Ugljanin's knowledge of the Two Trees' story was not exceptional among singers of epic tales in Serbo-Croatian, even though his choice and concatenations of nominal motifs were sometimes startlingly unusual. Milman Parry's collecting in northern Bosnia, at the opposite extreme from Novi Pazar in the geographic range of Serb-Croatian oral epos in 1934, produced several multiforms of the story. A young singer named Ćamil Kulenović sang one of those multiforms for Parry's recording apparatus in the town of Bihać. Situated in the Bosanska Krajina, Bihać was some two hundred miles distant from Novi Pazar, separated from it by very mountainous terrain over the whole distance, and was demographically quite distinct from Novi Pazar and its province of the Sandžak. The degree of nominal dissimilarity between Salih Ugljanin's multiforms and Ćamil Kulenović's was proportionately great, but the story of the Two Trees was nevertheless the same story in Bihać as it was in Novi Pazar.

Ćamil's tale, Parry text No. 1976,[104] went as follows: *Mustapha, governor of a Moslem border province called the Lika, sits in his council-chamber surrounded by his liegemen. But one of his men, Ali Vrhovac, is absent. Tattered and burnt from battle, one of Ali's Christian servants enters the council-chamber and announces that a traditional Christian enemy of the Lika named Captain Gal has attacked Ali's demesne at Vrhovi with a corps of militia and taken Ali and his lady prisoners. He accuses Mustapha of betraying Ali to Captain Gal for a carriage-load of ducats. Mustapha's other liegemen are disposed to believe this allegation, and one by one they leave in anger to go and verify the facts of the matter for themselves.*

Left alone with only an ensign to attend him, Mustapha also decides to go to Vrhovi, but his horse will not move from the place where he mounts it in his own courtyard. He exchanges horses with his ensign, but the same thing happens again. Then a wood-nymph calls to Mustapha from a mountain to the south to tell him that he has been falsely accused, and that the false accusation is the cause of his immobility. He may not move until he is cleared of it. She describes to Mustapha how at Vrhovi his doubting liegemen have one by one fought their way into the camp of Captain Gal's marauding troop, and while fighting have shouted to the captive Ali their question whether he was betrayed into captivity. When Ali has vindicated Mustapha to all seventy of them, Mustapha's horse is released from its mystical paralysis, and Mustapha rides with his ensign to Vrhovi. There he sees the carnage left behind by Captain Gal's force as it fought and withdrew toward its own territory beyond the frontier. Ćamil's verses 720-723 describe Mustapha's sighting of the enemy:

> Kroz Vrhove protišće goluba.
> Pa on krenu sentu Velebitu,
> Do bunara i starca jablana
> Đe je dundar Gale Kapetana.

> He pressed his dove-grey horse on through Vrhovi,
> And turned then toward the frontier on Mount Velebit,
> Toward the well and agèd apple-tree
> Where Captain Gal's horde was gathered.

Pursuing Captain Gal's rapacious troop, Mustapha's liegemen have overtaken and engaged it beside a well where stands a living tree. Mustapha and his ensign join in the fray too, but the fighting is useless and they soon retreat; the disunited Moslems are unprepared for the sustained, organized battle which they would have to fight in order to free Ali from the Captain's superior force. Each of the Moslems has charged into the ranks of the enemy separately and without any concerted plan of attack. Ill-equipped, leaderless, and divided among themselves, they can do nothing effective to stop Captain Gal's lawless taking of their comrade Ali's person and chattels, nor can they make him pay a proper price in blood for his looting and mayhem at Vrhovi.

One by one Mustapha's men emerge from the melée beaten and wounded. Each comes separately to Mustapha to beg his forgiveness for their former disrespect in doubting his honour. Without a word of reproach to any of them, Mustapha receives each of the seventy gently and forgivingly, and confers his blessing on each with the words:

> Halal tebi od meneka bilo,
> Baš ko mliko od tvoje matere.

> My benediction be upon you; freely given,
> May it nourish you like your mother's milk.

Thus Camil's green fruit-tree at the well in no-man's land fulfills its prescribed function as a focus of disunity, suddenly alternating peril and kindness, and emotionally motivated, unreciprocal dealings between both friends and enemies. The motif of feeding appears on cue, if only in a simile, and the motif of hidden and discovered identity is present too in the enigma of whether Mustapha, the duly appointed regent of the Lika, is really his people's defender or betrayer.

Having described the Moslem disaster at the green tree, Camil moved quickly on to the antidotal hewn wood. It was a rod of fir: *Hurt and disheartened, the Moslems break off the skirmish and return to their homes, while Captain Gal withdraws with his captives and booty to his own lands across Mount Velebit.*

The Moslems recuperate from their wounds for two months. Then a Moslem spy discovers and reports to Mustapha the whereabouts and condition of the prisoner Ali Vrhovac. In the words of the spy:

> I was there and saw with my own eyes,   1015
> Oh my bey Mustapha, chief of all the Lika!
> I saw my brother bound
> In the courtyard of the Prince of Novi.
> Across his knees he held a stake of fir,
> And he wore nothing but breeches and a thin shirt,
> Bare-headed and barefoot.
> The stake was pointed with a steel tip;
> His hands were bound,
> And heavy shackles on his legs.

The Christians mean to execute Ali Vrhovac by impaling him of the stake which they have made him hold.[105] It is, of course, a great error on their part to have equipped him with an instrument

Meridies.

Fig. 67. Detail of a prospect of Papa (Hungary) in: Georg Braun von Hogenberg, *Civitates orbis terrarum*, Bruxelles, 1618. A modern Balkan devolution of the retributive use of hewn wood.

of hewn wood (no matter how much they intend it to his harm) because it introduces reciprocity into the tale. The nearer the Christians
come to executing Ali on the stake, the nearer the Moslems come to
their moment of revenge for the injuries they have suffered. The Christians' reported abuse of Ali infuriates Mustapha, who sets about relieving his captive subject by imitating Captain Gal's method of border-
raiding and certain other Christian habits: *Mustapha gathers a troop of
fighting men to raid the Prince of Novi's demesne where Ali is held
prisoner. Mustapha's wounded liegemen have recovered and are eager
to unite in this expedition under his command. The entire Moslem
troop dresses in Christian disguises and proceeds into the Christians'
country. There on the road they meet a contingent of Christians that
is taking Ali to the church which they intend should be his place of
execution. Ali carries on his shoulder the stake for his own impalement.*[106] One of the Moslems, a famous blasphemer who is now disguised as a Christian priest (thus imitating the ogres who from the
Moslem point of view were most typical of Christendom), insinuates
himself into the executional procession on the pretext of securing
Ali's conversion to Christianity so as mockingly to absolve him of his
sins before death. The rest of the Moslems, still disguised as lay Christians, join the procession as though to witness the execution.

*The procession reaches the church, where the stake is fixed up-
right in the ground before the church door. When the blasphemous
rites of conversion and absolution are finished, the executioners raise
Ali to impale him on the stake. This is the signal to the Moslems to
throw off their disguises and attack the Christians. They rout the
Christians and free Ali, who himself kills Captain Gal by cutting him
in two through the waist. The Moslems loot the district and return
to their own lands laden with booty.*

By united action, close imitation of the original ogre Captain
Gal, and well-timed concealment and revelation of their identity,
Camil's Moslem heroes rejoin Ali, their cutter and bearer of hewn
wood, to their own community and return enriched to their own
country. Camil Kulenović told the story of the Two Trees fully and
well, though he was a young story-teller of still only moderate accomplishment.

The most able singer of epos whom Milman Parry found in the
Balkans, and the man who sang the longest tales ever collected in a

Slavic language, was a Montenegrin peasant farmer, butcher, and long-time soldier named Avdo Medjedović, from the district of Bijelo Polje. The difference in ability between the two epic bards Ćamil and Avdo was not directly correlated with either the wholeness nor the scope which they gave to the pattern of the Two Trees in their tales. Excellence in storytelling is a matter of performance, not of what is performed. Avdo did what many Yugoslav singers of epic did when he incorporated the two trees with almost telegraphic brevity in the last six verses of *The Wedding of Smailagić Meho,* an epic tale which in his performance in 1935 had a grand total of 12,311 verses.[107] The final six verses with the two trees in them were part of a benediction that was the customary ending of an epic performance in the Serbo-Croatian tradition. In it the story-teller wished pleasure and comfort upon his listeners: pleasure from his narration, and comfort from the hand of God (Christian or Moslem). The eight lines of Avdo's benediction were composed stichically, but arranged in four periods of two verses each, or four logical (though not rhythmic) couplets.

> Od mene Vi malo razgovora,
> A od Boga dugo i široko.   12305
> Vita jelo, pouzdigni grane,
> Svoj gospodi da su zdravo glave!
> Zelen bore, pomogni nam Bože;
> Amin, Bože, hoće ako Bog da.
> Po sad doba da se veselimo,
> Veselimo i pesme pevamo.[108]

I give you for my part a little conversation,
But longevity and magnanimity come from God.
Lift thy branches, oh thou pliant fir,
That all my lords may have good health and clear understanding!
And thou, green pine, help us, oh Lord!
So shall it be, if God wills; amen.
Now in this time let us be merry,   12310
Merry with singing of songs.

The subjects of the first three couplets are explicitly men and God, alternating antiphonally from verse to verse in the first couplet, and from couplet to couplet thereafter. The subjects of the final, fourth couplet are again a complementary pair, human happiness and epic narration; this time a pair of human and divine properties rather than the beings themselves are referred to, since epic narration is here understood as the corpus of orally imparted traditional knowledge about God's ordination and guidance of human affairs. The two trees in the second and third couplets respectively are (dry) fir and green pine. Like Salih Ugljanin's pillar of fir and Ćamil Kulenović's fir stake, Avdo's fir also belongs to a context of human needs and human purpose as distinct from the green pine with its context of God's inscrutable, preterhuman will. Schematically stated, the substance of the eight verses is as follows:

verse 12304	The bard's power of benefaction
verse 12305	Divine power of benefaction
verses 12306-7	Apparent human needs and human instruments
verses 12308-9	Inscrutable divine purpose and divine instruments
verse 12310	Present human pleasure
verse 12311	Past doings of men and preternaturals

PERKUNAS

Highly condensed references to the Two Trees' story like the terminal verses of Avdo Medjedović's epic tale are typical of oral lyric poetry in Europe. Indeed, references to narrative patterns in lieu of narration are so typical of European oral lyrics that one may justifiably call the lyric a *referential* genre of oral poetry. The archaic tradition of *dainos* in Lithuanian, for example, abounds in references to all sorts of stories, including the story of the Two Trees. The *daina* quoted in the translation below tells, for instance, of interference at a wedding by the Lithuanian sky-god and preterhuman hewer, Perkunas. The poem begins with reference to a procedure for getting preternatural progeny (an attempted exogamic marriage of a tree with a star) and ends with an allusion to the holiday (St. John's Day) that heralded the beginning of harvest (i.e., the getting of vegetable food) in the annual cycle of traditional peasant agrarian economy in Lithuania. The action belongs to a mythic time when the present order of the cosmos had not yet been established (stars might still contemplate marriage with trees); Perkunas cosmotactically hews down the would-be bridegroom to prevent such a monstrous alliance. The question stated and answered in the subsequent dialogue of the piece is how to coordinate marriage (i.e., wearing the white bridal gown) with food-getting by cultivation and cutting (with wooden-hafted tools) rather than by dependence on the green oak (bearer of wild nuts). Two high authorities, male (Perkunas) and female (the sun), collaborate to make the bereft bride give up the green wood and reconcile herself to the hewn:

> Morning star lauded her wedding,
> but Perkunas rode through the gate,
> struck, felled the green oak.

> —The oaken blood welled out,
> splotched my spotless gown,
> spattered my wreath.

> Sun's daughter wept
> for three years as she gathered
> together leaves that had withered.

> —Where, O Mother mine,
> shall I wash clean the gown?
> Where wash the blood away?

> —Young one, daughter, child,
> go to that still pool
> where the nine streams flow.

> —Where, O Mother mine,
> shall I dry out my clothes?
> Where in the wind dry them?

> —Young one, daughter, child,
> in that still garden
> where the nine roses bloom.

> —When, O Mother mine,
> shall I put on the gown?
> Walk out in the white gown?

> —Young one, daughter, child,
> on that miracle day
> of nine suns white above.[109]

This imaginary Lithuanian bride's acquiescent reaction to the death of a transgressive lover is diametrically opposite to that of her Limba sister in Dauda Konteh's tale "The Man Killed for a Banana" cited and discussed above. The main *personae* of the Limba tale and the Lithuanian *daina* are the same: husband, supreme male authority who kills the husband, mother, and daughter. But the Limba women's response to the same situation was all remorseless vengefulness, and the avenging woman moved away from the hewn tree to the green

one, exactly counter to the submissive Lithuanian women's progress
from green to hewn. Limba and Lithuanian poets arranged the motival pieces of this story-pattern in different sequences and supplied the
personae with different motivation for their acts, yet the same generic
pattern of narrative informed them both.

The Lithuanian sky-god, hewer, and cosmotactic hero Perkunas
regularly cuts down transgressive bridegrooms in the *dainos*. The green
oak's transgression was in attempting preternatural exogamy—choosing
for his bride a star, a female of the wrong genus. Elsewhere the transgression is incest (morning star being daughter of the sun in this mythology, as seen in the preceding poem):

> The mood wedded the sun
> in the first springtime.
>
> The sun rose in the dawn,
> the moon abandoned her,
>
> wandered alone, afar,
> and loved the morning star.
>
> Angered, Perkunas thundered
> and cleft him with a sword:
>
> —How could you dare to love
> the daystar, drift away
> in the night alone, and stray?[110]

THE LINDEN'S BROTHER

The sudden reversal of fortune at the green oak in the first of
these Lithuanian poems (from the happiness of wedding to the sad-
ness of funeral) is echoed polymorphically in another *daina* where
the green tree is the lime or linden (Tilia). Here the reversal is between
safe passage and lethal obstruction. A clump of lindens in the wilderness first permits the safe movement of its human visitors, and then
suddenly, gratuitously obstructs and causes the death of one of them:

> Three lime trees in a swamp,
> all growing from one stump.
>
> Among these limes by the stream
> three maidens wandering came.

> The boughs two sisters seized
> and in between them squeezed.
>
> But the last was unable to
> and fell into the flow.

True to their motival type, the wild lindens separate friends and relatives: the girl drowns. After the green wood has thus killed her, the water conceals her whereabouts :

> Her the current carried
> towards the Nieman wide.
>
> Her the Nieman did not want
> and to the Rusne sent.
>
> Her the Rusne did not want
> and to its estuary sent.

To supply the antidotal hewn wood, the drowned girl grows into another linden on the shore. A male hewer finds her tree, and although he cannot restore her to life, he discovers her hidden identity and reunites her with her own people as fully as he can by carving a flute from the wood of her tree:

> There into a lime tree green
> she grew with branches nine.
>
> Her brother came a flute
> to cut from a lime shoot.
>
> —My flute plays beautifully,
> its voice speaks mournfully.
>
> But his mother said to him:
> —That voice is not from the lime;
>
> that's the soul of my daughter
> swimming upon the water.[111]

The oak was male and the linden female in the symbolism of the *dainos*. Both were sometimes green and sometimes hewn. The following lyric describes the two together in the wild, unhewn state. Predictably, the scene is one of free giving and taking in an emotionally motivated exchange, without any reckoning or enforcement of price or recompense. It is, in short, a love-scene:

> The oak, the linden,

both green and both fair,
stand by the road together.
Branches incline within each other,
leaves interweave in air.[112]

Boy stands, girl stands,
both of them young and fair,
in their clasped hands together.
Their shoulders lean one to the other,
rings of betrothal given.[113]

A WOOD-CUTTER A-COURTING

Marriage is the subject of many *dainos,* but of course there was more to marriage in agrarian peasant Lithuania than merely the impulsive, gratuitous sharing between two lovers. In real life, autumn was the most expedient season for the culmination of courtship in marriage, after harvest and before the rigour and relative confinement of winter. Then the parties to a marriage—the prospective bride, bridegroom, and especially their respective kin—would meticulously calculate the reciprocal gains and losses that might result from a proposed match, including in their reckoning estimates and bargains about such things as bride-price and dowry. *Sub arbore vivo* was a good place for the budding of love in summer, but the right location for counting assets and actually contracting marriage as a matter of public interest and family alliance was *sub arbore utili.* The industrious hewer had the best prospects of union, and could best unite his family with another by marriage:

—O thou oak tree,
tree so green,
why this autumn
art not green?

—How this autumn
should I be green?
I heard coming
woodcutters twain.

Many a branch
the first one lopped off
and my summit
the second chopped off.

...From this tree's branches
I'll make a bed.
I'll bend a cradling
from this tree's head.

I myself will lay me
on that same bed,
and in the cradling
I'll swing a maid,

half the day through
till breakfast tide.
Oh *chuchia, lulia,*
my very own bride![114]

Hewn wood was unifying even when it was anonymous. It might not prevent or nullify misfortune, but it could assure reunion in even the most tragical circumstances. 'Tending the steeds of God' was a common metaphor for male death in the Lithuanian *dainos,* and a wooden plank could be a footway where the toll imposed for passage between the world of the living and the dead was terribly high:

Sister went for water
With the newest pails
And silken bucket chains.

Cold was the running stream
But not frozen over,
And the plank icy.

And from the glazed plank
She slipped down and down
To the bottom of the earth,
To the land of the sea.

There she found her brother
Tending the steeds of God,
Plaiting their silken manes.[115]

THE BARON OF TEARNE WADLING

Arboreal motifs are very prominent in the written records of oral traditions in eastern Europe because more of oral tradition has been recorded there than in any part of central or western Europe (or anywhere else in the world for that matter). But that fact represents nothing more than historical accident. It particularly indicates nothing about the true range or pervasion of the Two Trees' story in European fable either now or in the past. The Two Trees belong as much to earlier British balladry, for example, as to the more recently recorded Lithuanian *dainos* or oral epos in Serbo-Croatian.

Popular balladry in Britain was sometimes concisely lyrical like Lithuanian *dainos,* and sometimes expansively narrative like oral epic poetry in the Balkans. In other words, some traditional ballads of Britain were whole tales told in song, while others were only sung allusions or embellishments to narrative more in the nature of ritual[116] elaboration on storytelling than actual story itself. But the Two Trees were familiar in both the narrative and lyrical kinds of British ballad. One early and decidedly narrative ballad preserved in a document from the seventeenth century, "The Marriage of Sir Gawaine" in Bishop Percy's Folio Manuscript, relates King Arthur's adventure with two victims of a witch. One of the victims was a certain 'Baron of Tearne Wadling,' and the other was that baron's sister, whom the ballad[117] describes but does not name.

King Arthur and all his barons except the one bewitched at Tearne Wadling gather at Arthur's capital in Carleile (modern Carlisle) to celebrate Christmas together. But sometime between Christmas Day and New Year's Day Arthur goes up from Carlisle into Inglewood Forest and arrives alone at the place Tearne Wadling (modern Tarn Wadling), which is situated on a considerable height above Carlisle in the Pennine Mountains of Cumberland. There the Baron of Tearne Wadling blocks Arthur's way and will not let him pass unless Arthur can defeat him in a fight, or else pay a 'ransom' for the right of passage through the baron's demesne. The 'ransom' is to answer a hard riddle: what thing does a woman most desire in all the world? Arthur chooses not to fight and returns to Carlisle to ponder the riddle. Later he learns the right answer from an unnaturally ugly woman whom he meets alone on a deserted moor. She is sister to the lone Baron of Tearne Wadling, and like her brother she too lives isolated from the rest of mankind. She ultimately reveals that both she and the baron are in the power of an unnamed witch, who has so cursed him with churlishness and her with ugliness that neither may lead normal, sociable lives—not even with each other—until someone will liberate them from the alienating bondage of the witch's enchantment. Arthur subdues the fierce baron with the information gotten from the baron's sister: the thing a woman most desires in all the world is to have her own will. Then Arthur's cousin Gawaine undertakes to marry the ugly hag, and by betrothing her despite her ugliness undoes the witch's curse; she becomes his beautiful and gracious bride.

This British ballad is superficially quite unlike the other multiforms of the Two Trees' story which have been considered here thus far. Certainly it is different—and distinctively British—in such aspects as its metrical form and its nominally Arthurian motifs. But as narrative it begins in the same way as Camil Kulenović's Yugoslav tale about Mustapha and Ali Vrhovac, i.e., with a gathering of liegemen around their ruler:

> Kinge Arthur liues in merry Carleile,
>> & seemely is to see,
> & there he hath with him Qqueene Gene*ver*,
>> *that* bride soe bright of blee.
>
> And there he hath with Queene Genever,
>> *that* bride soe bright in bower,
> & all his barons about him stoode
>> *that* were both stiffe and stowre.
>
> The King kept a royall Christmasse
>> of mirth & great honor,
> . . .[118]

All Arthur's barons 'about him stoode' at Carleile—all, that is, save one, the Baron of Tearne Wadling, whom a witch had by her enchantment captured and alienated from all his own people. Similarly in Kulenović's Yugoslav tale, all Mustapha's liegemen attended their chief's assembly at Udbina except Ali Vrhovac, who stayed away because he had fallen into an alien captivity at the hands of his and his people's ancient enemy, Captain Gal.

Moreover, both Mustapha's assembly at Udbina and Arthur's at Carleile end with an uncanny forcible restraint upon the movement of the presiding chief; the absent, captive liegeman is the cause of the chief's temporary immobility in both tales. Thus, news of the captivity of Ali Vrhovac terminated the gathering at the seat of Mustapha's authority in Udbina, and on account of Ali an uncanny spiritual force for a time prevented Mustapha's making his lone journey by way of Ali's demesne at Vrhovi. Similarly, after the assembly of barons at

Carleile Arthur attempts to pass by way of his captive baron's demesne at Tearne Wadling, but the uncanny power of the witch expressed in the baron's unaccountable churlishness prevents Arthur's passage.

Even the geography which Mustapha and Arthur traverse between their respective capitals and their captive liegemen's demesnes is strikingly similar. In Serbo-Croatian, the place-name "Vrhovi" from which Ali's name "Vrhovac" is derived, means 'summits,' or by extension 'village or inhabited place on the heights.' "Vrhovi" is too common a toponym to be exactly identified in modern Yugoslav topography. But the nymph who calls to Mustapha from her vantage in the mountains (verse 546 *ff.*) to explain to him why he is immobilized says that she has seen the mayhem at Vrhovi from atop Mazinac, a mountain peak southeast of Udbina. By itself, the English word 'tarn' is also a common toponym, and it also signifies a high place; it means 'small lake in the mountains.' One knows which tarn is meant in the English ballad by the additional designation 'Wadling,' which like Mazinac is a true place-name and not merely a descriptive term comparable to 'tarn' or 'Vrhovi.' The peak called Mazinac in the Yugoslav tale rises above the modern village of Mazin, which lies amidst a number of spectacular high mountains (Jasenov Vrh, Milićev Vrh, Kremen, etc.) southeast of Udbina in the Yugoslav province of the Lika. John Britton and Edward Brayley describe the mountains of Cumberland, the setting for King Arthur's journey, in a gazetteer printed in the year 1802:

> The MOUNTAINS of Cumberland are exceedingly numerous, and many of them of immense elevation, and singular structure. They enter into the composition of almost every view; and either by their sublime heights, their romantic forms, the dignified grandeur of their aspects, the immensity of the rocky masses that compose them, or the wild, awful, and imposing majesty of their appearance, are well calculated to give birth to interesting emotions.[119]

To reach Tarn Wadling from Carlisle, Arthur must have gone southeastward into Inglewood Forest and along the Vale of Eden, climbing as he went a perpendicular rise of somewhat more than two hundred meters to Tarn Wadling. Britton and Brayley provide a description of the place:

> . . .*Tarn-wadling* spreads its waters on a naked and barren common, about one mile west from the river Eden, at Armathwaite, above

which it rises 600 feet perpendicular. It covers about 100 acres, and is much frequented by wild fowl: the carp it produces are extremely fine.[120]

Daniel and Samuel Lysons tell more in their gazetteer of 1816 about the military potential of Tarn Wadling:

> Near Aiketgate is a small lake or tarn called Tarn Wadling, covering about 100 acres of land, belonging to Mr. Milbourne. On a lofty eminence near this tarn were, some time ago, the remains of a fortress, called Castle Hewen, thus spoken of by Leland: "In the forest of Ynglewood, about six miles from Carluel, appere ruines of a castle call'd Castel Lewen." The neighbouring tenants pay a yearly rent to Mr. Milbourne as lord of the manor, called Castle Hewen rent.[121]

If one supposes, as surely one must, that Arthur's isolated and estranged baron held (however fictitiously) such a fortress and rents at Tarn Wadling as those which Leland and the Lysons knew, then he was indeed a proper feudal analogue of Ćamil Kulenović's Moslem hero, Alaga of Vrhovi.

Tarn Wadling had changed greatly by 1895:

> Watling Tarn, which covered about 100 acres, has been filled up and converted into grazing land. The living is a vicarage in the diocese of Carlisle. . . .[122]

But the previous existence of the fortress at Tarn Wadling was not forgotten as late as 1932, although its exact location was by then a trifle obscure:

> Tarn Wadling, an old lake basin, now drained, Cumberland, under Blaze Fell, 2½ m. SE. High Hesket. An ancient castle stood in it.[123]

Like Carlisle in the British province of Cumberland, Udbina in the Yugoslav province of the Lika also lies in the southeast quarter of a broad plain (Krbavsko polje). And like King Arthur ascending six hundred feet and more along his way southeastward from Carlisle to Tarn Wadling, Mustapha too must have set out southeastward into the mountains surrounding the present village of Mazin, ascending as he went to a height not less than two hundred meters above Udbina (840 meters above sea-level) in order to reach Vrhovi-beneath-Mazinac. So Arthur and Mustapha are both detained by a weird spiritual power during a journey of the same compass-bearing and geographic character that takes each of them through an inhabited but unsuccessfully de-

fended place in high country that is the demesne of a baron in alien
captivity. Arthur tells his knight Gawaine how the detached and isolated baron at Tearne Wadling stopped his progress:

> "... .when I came to tearne wadling,
>   a bold barron there I fand,
> with a great club vpon his backe,
>   standing stiffe and strong;
>
> "And he asked me wether I wold fight,
>   or from him I shold begone,
> or else I must him a ransome pay
> verse 39   & soe depart him from.[124]

This hindrance to the ruler's movement must be put down by
answering a paradoxical question correctly; both Mustapha's and
Arthur's very right to rule and the continuation of their government
depend upon a discovery and public declaration of the correct answer.
The question in both cases is a matter of identity. Is Mustapha really
the champion of his people, or a traitor? In King Arthur's case, the
immediate question is a riddle about the nature and rights of women,
but Arthur's manner of obtaining the answer to the riddle kindles the
same suspicion about him which Mustapha's men entertained about
their chief; namely, that he was willing to give his own loyal liegemen
and kin into an alien captivity in order to gain a personal advantage
for himself. Arthur tells Gawaine the riddle which the Baron of Tearne
Wadling has set as his ransom:

> "To fight with him I saw noe cause,
>   methought it was not meet,
> for he was stiffe and strong with-all,
>   his strokes were nothing sweete;
>
> "Therefor this is my ransome, Gawaine,
>   I ought to him to pay,
> I must come againe, as I am sworne,
> verse 47   vpon the New yeers day.
>
> 48   "And I must bring him word what thing it is
> 13   that a woman most desire.
> 14   'this shalbe thy ransome, Arthur,' he sayes,
> 15   'for Ile haue noe other hier.' "[125]

Like Ali Vrhovac with the steel-tipped stake of execution on his shoulder, Arthur's baron at Tearne Wadling is also a carrier of hewn wood 'with a great club upon his backe.' Predictably therefore, Ali's and the baron's missions are the same: to test the power and resolution of their respective lords, and thereby cause them to set right certain disorders in a world which neither they nor their lords have created. As usual, the cosmotactic heroes' hewn wood signifies reciprocity and payment, and the unification of diverse natures in common cause. The baron's imposition of ransom is accordingly just the kind of act that should be expected, for it establishes at one stroke a perfectly reciprocal relationship of mutual rights and duties between the baron and Arthur. To ransom himself from the baron, Arthur must produce the answer to a riddle that will simultaneously ransom the baron from the witch. That done, the baron must release Arthur, as Arthur has released him. So both Ali Vrhovac and the Baron of Tearne Wadling require ransom from their lords to break their captors' power over them and their kinfolk, and their respective rulers Arthur and Mustapha must either redeem them or forfeit their own sovereignty. Thus the plight of captive liegemen reciprocates with the plight of their lawful rulers at the sign of the hewn wood, because Ali and the Baron of Tearne Wadling make the liberation of themselves and their kin the price which Mustapha and Arthur must pay to retain their own sovereign freedoms.

Not finding among his own people the means to pay that price and so escape the predicament which he shares reciprocally with the captive baron, Arthur leaves Carleile alone to go and meet a monster under green wood in the wilderness, just as the Yugoslav Mustapha went alone at the equivalent moment of his career to meet Captain Gal at the live apple-tree in no-man's land. The remedy for inequity or hardship experienced at the one tree is an opposite experience at the other:

> Then king Arthur drest him for to ryde
> in one soe rich array
> toward the fore-said Tearne wadling,
> that he might keepe his day.

> And as he rode over a more,
> he see a lady where shee sate
> betwixt an oke and a greene hollen:
> she was cladd in red scarlett.

> Then there as shold haue stood her mouth,
> > then there was sett her eye,
> the other was in her forhead fast
> > the way that she might see.
>
> Her nose was crooked and turnd outward,
> > her mouth stood foule a-wry;
> a worse formed lady than shee was,
> > neuer man saw with his eye.[126]

verse 64

This preternaturally hideous female monster whom Arthur meets under green wood frightens him speechless. But then she suddenly and unexpectedly offers him gratis precisely that bit of help which he so desperately needed and could not find among his own people—the knowledge and the willingness to answer the lone baron's hard riddle:

> To halch vpon him, King Arthur,
> > this lady was full faine,
> but King Arthur had forgott his lesson,
> > what he shold say againe.
>
> "What knight art thou," the lady sayd,
> > "that will not speak to me?
> Of me be thou nothing dismayd
> > tho I be vgly to see;
>
> "for I have halched you curteouslye,
> > and you will not me againe,
> yett I may happen Sir Knight," shee said,
> > "to ease thee of thy paine."[127]

verse 76

The reciprocity between rulers and their captive subjects that is established at the sign of the hewn wood in this British and European tale is a manifold and paradoxical thing. The rulers may ransom and release themselves from impediment only by ransoming and releasing their subjects from alien and alienating captors. But before the ruler can ransom his captive subjects, he must himself be ransomed by others of his subjects who remain in his dominion. The Yugoslav hero Mustapha must free Ali Vrhovac from the power of Captain Gal, but he may not even challenge Captain Gal until his other liegemen have liberated him from their suspicion of his complicity in Ali's misfortune. Mustapha is thus utterly dependent upon his liegemen for all his power, even the ability physically to move which their

displeasure and doubt of his virtue can take from him with all the
sudden unpredictability of hasty anger and rash distrust.

So the sovereign's capacity to aid any one of his subjects is entirely contingent upon the sum of his subjects' willingness to aid him.
Yet the liegemen's aid to their chief is not the same as his to them.
He is bound by a strict and manifold reciprocity in his exchange with
them, but their contributions to him are strictly gratuitous. A true and
favorable answer to the paradoxical question about Mustapha's character as governor of his people—is he their defender or their predator?—
is indispensable to him, but it cannot come from Mustapha himself,
who is powerless to exact it from his liegemen. Only they in his absence can obtain it for him at great, gratuitous cost to themselves in
the disorganized and disastrous fighting with Captain Gal at the old
apple-tree in no-man's land. Similarly, the burden of ransoming Arthur
from the Baron of Tearne Wadling falls upon Arthur's cousin Gawaine
and others of his knights, for only through their self-sacrifice can Arthur ransom the witch's captives and so ransom himself. Arthur has no
right to demand such a sacrifice of his men, and although it seems for
a moment that he will demand it, in the end he does not, nor does
his monstrous host at the green tree demand that he do so. But the
proper place for gratuitous self-sacrifice of Arthur's supporters is, of
course, under the green wood in the wilderness, and there Arthur ini-
tiates their donation. Caught up in the spirit of gratuitous giving and
taking that always envelopes the precincts of the green wood in fable,
Arthur gratuitously volunteers to give away his own cousin and loyal
knight Gawaine to the preternatural hag whom he has met in the wild
between an oak and a green holly. Arthur speaks to the hag, reward-
ing her unsolicited and unforeseen offer of help with an equally unsolicited but extravagant counter-offer, disproportionately generous
considering that he does not yet even know what help she can give
him:

> "Giue thou ease me, lady," he said,
>   "or help me any thing,
> Thou shalt have gentle Gawaine, my cozen,
>   & marry him with a ring."[128]

Unlike Arthur and the baron, who at the sign of the baron's
great club speak to one another only of ransom and constraint, Arthur
and the hag say nothing of price or retribution. To be sure, there is a
residual implication of *quid pro quo* in the mutuality of their gift-giv-

ing, for if the hag will donate to Arthur her priceless knowledge about
the paramount desire of women, he will give her the priceless Sir Gawain to be her husband. This residual reciprocity is plainly signalled
in the arboreal motifs of the tale by the hag's location "betwixt an
oke and a green hollen" where she talks alone with Arthur. It is December when their meeting occurs, and in this season of the year the
oak, which naturally appears as though dead, presents a striking contrast to the evergreen holly. This is also the prime season, as any British cottager might know, for working such wood as oak into tools,
weapons, furniture, or other useful forms. So long as a residual implication of price persists in the relationship between the interlocutors
of the tale, so long too the *implication* of hewn wood persists in their
arboreal surroundings. The hag's position between oak and holly is
the vegetable equivalent of her attitude toward Arthur, which is generous without apparent expectation of reward although she is desperately in need of reward and in the end receives it. The hag and her two
trees are thus intermediate in a progression from the pure compulsion
of Arthur's dealings with the baron (at the sign of the baron's club)
to a pure gratuity yet to come in the unfolding of the Two Trees'
pattern in this English multiform.

Arthur's dealings with the churlish baron seem at the beginning
to be the main business of this ballad tale, and his interlude with the
hag seems only a means to the resolution of that strictly male business.
But in the event the utilization of the hag turns out to be the main
business, and Arthur's two meetings with the baron are only a means
to the establishment of a firm tie between her and Arthur's court.
This shift of emphasis in the abstract ideas of the story is also signalled by the progression from hewn to green wood with its epicenter
in the scene where the hag sits between oak and holly.

Although Arthur's meetings with the bewitched baron and his
sister are both characterized by acts of exchange, the kindly gratuity
of the exchange between man and woman at the greenwood is sharp-
ly differentiated from the strict contractual obligation between man
and man that prevails under the menace of the dissident baron's hewn
club at Tarn Wadling. The effect of the contract between king and
baron is politically far-reaching if short-lived; oppositely, Arthur's pact
with the hag is socially rather than politically far-reaching, and long-
lived by virtue of its marital implication. The real force of the pact
with the baron lies in the baron's riddle: what does a woman most

desire? In effect, Arthur has agreed that only the man who knows most about the gratification of female desires will enjoy the ultimate gratification of being king. When Arthur makes a further pact with the loathely lady to ally himself with her by marriage in return for her aid against the baron, he unwittingly makes his contest with the baron a competition between affinal male kin, because unbeknown to him the hag between the oak and the holly is the baron's sister, and he has pledged his consanguinous kinsman Gawaine to be her husband.

When Arthur first meets the lonely baron with the great club at Tarn Wadling, only the baron is a desperate man, isolated from any and all society of other men by the witch's curse upon him. At the conclusion of their meeting, both the baron and Arthur are desperate, the one to escape isolation, and the other to keep himself at the center of congregation as the incumbent upon the throne. When later Arthur and the hag meet between the two live trees, exactly the same arrangement of desperation prevails initially, both the interlocutors being desperate; the only difference is that the hag and her trees take the place of the baron and his club. But the outcome of this male-female encounter is just the opposite of what emerges from the male meeting. Arthur leaves the hag assured of his continued kingship (whether he knows it or not), while she remains alone in the wilderness with no means of escape from her predicament in view. She tells Arthur the answer to the baron's riddle, and Arthur carries the answer to his second meeting with the baron, who now quickly assumes the rôle of hewer with all its political implications.

> And when he came to the tearne wadling
>   the baron there cold he finde,
> with a great weapon on his backe,
>   standing stiffe and stronge.
>
> And then he tooke king Arthurs letters in his hands
>   & away he cold them fling,
> & then he puld out a good browne sword,
>   & cryd himselfe a King.
>
> And he sayd, "I have thee & thy land, Arthur,
>   to doe as it pleaseth me,
> for this is not thy ransome sure,
>   therfore yeeld thee to me."

And then bespoke him Noble Arthur,
  & bad him hold his hand,
"& giue me leaue to speake my mind
  in defence of all my land."

He said "as I came over a More,
  I see a lady where shee sate
betweene an oke & a green hollen;
  shee was clad in red scarlett;

"And she says 'a woman will haue her will,
  & this is all her cheef desire':
doe me right, as thou art a baron of sckill,
  this is they ransome & all thy hyer."

He sayes "an early vengeance light on her!
  she walkes on yonder more;
it was my sister that told thee this;
  & she is a misshappen hore![129]

Deserved or not, the baron's aspersion on the woman's sexual
fidelity reminds one again of Samson's women in the Old Testament
Book of Judges, who were all of a kind with Delilah. And like the
Philistines in the legend of Samson, Arthur's bad baron thinks burning
the proper way to treat a consanguinous kinswoman who has brought
disaster upon him at the hands of her affinal kinsman:

"But heer Ile make mine avow to god
  to doe her an euill turne,
for an euer I may thate fowle theefe get,
  in a fyer I will her burne."[130]

Arthur is not so prompt in meeting again with the loathly lady
as he was in keeping his appointment with her brother. She must wait
till spring for her second encounter with the king. But when finally he
does go to see her, an entire retinue of his liegemen goes with him.
The male contest between Arthur and the baron having now been
settled, motifs of weaponry, scenes of rift and hewing, and the strict
calculation of values given and received give way to motifs of natural
growth, scenes of social consolidation, and the unpredictable consequences of impulsive behaviour. The foul lady correspondingly moves
from her ambiguous position "betweene an oke and a green hollen"
to an unambiguous posture directly "vnderneath a greene holly tree."
In that location she is decisively the monster under green wood that

first threatens its visitors, then suddenly changes and bestows on them
an uncanny bounty. Like others of her kind, she is also a physical
shape-shifter:

> Sir Lancelott & Sir Steven bold
>   they rode with them that day,
> and the formost of the company
>   there rode the steward Kay
>
> Soe did Sir Banier and Sir Bore
>   Sir Garrett with them soe gay,
> soe did Sir Tristeram that gentle knight,
>   to the forrest fresh and gay.
>
> And when he came to the greene forrest,
>   vnderneath a greene holly tree
> their sate that lady in red scarlet
>   that vnseemly was to see.
>
> Sir Kay beheld this Ladys face
>   & looked vppon her smire,
> "whosoeuer kisses this lady," he sayes,
>   "of his kisse he stands in feare."
>
> Sir Kay beheld the lady againe,
>   & looked vpon her snout,
> "whosoeuer kisses this lady," he saies,
>   "of his kisse he stands in doubt."
>
> "Peace cozen Kay," then said Sir Gawaine,
>   "amend thee of thy life;
> for there is a knight amongst vs all
>   that must marry her to his wife."
>
> "What! wedd her to wiffe!" then said Sir Kay,
>   "in the diuells name anon,
> gett me a wiffe where-ere I may,
>   for I had rather be shaine!"
>
> Then some tooke vp their hawkes in hast,
>   & some tooke vp their hounds,
> & some sware they wold not marry her
>   for Citty nor for towne.[131]

But the lady undergoes the sudden transformation expected of monsters at the green wood, and shows herself in the form of a lovely maiden. The only question remaining is how permanently to stabilize the desirable part of her. . .

Then shee said "choose thee, gentle Gawaine,
    truth as I doe say,
wether thou wilt haue me in this liknesse
    in the night or else in the day."

And then bespake him Gentle Gawaine,
    which was soe mild of Moode,
sayes, "well I know what I wold say,
    god grant it may be good!

To haue thee fowle in the night
    when I with thee shold play;
yet I had rather, if I might,
    haue thee fowle in the day."

"What! when Lords goe with ther seires," shee said,
    both to the Ale & wine;
alas! then I must hyde my selfe,
    I must not goe withinne."

And then bespake him gentle gawaine,
    said, "Lady, thats but a skill;
And because thou art my owne lady,
    thou shalt haue all thy will."

Then she said, "blessed be thou gentle Gawain,
    this day that I thee see,
for as thou see me att this time,
    from hencforth I wilbe:

"My father was an old knight,
    & yett it chanced soe
that he marryed a younge lady
    that brought me to this woe.

Shee witched me, being a faire young Lady,
    to the greene forrest to dwell,
& there I must walke in womans liknesse,
    Most like a feend of hell."[132]

The proof of the pudding is in the eating, and beauty in a woman

is a matter of taste. Sir Kay, the lady's erstwhile worst critic, savours
the maiden and pronounces the flavour good:

> "Come kisse her, Brother Kay," then said Sir Gawaine,
> "& amend thé of thy liffe;
> I sweare this is the same lady
> *that* I marryed to my wiffe."

> Sir Kay kissed that lady bright,
> standing vpon his ffeete;
> he swore, as he was trew knight,
> the spice was neuer soe sweete.[133]

As with most of her kind in oral fable, the twin ideas of edibility
and physical attractiveness [food ≅ progeny] characterize perfection in
this Cinderella-like lady. Kay continues his praise of her:

> "Well, Cozen Gawaine," sayes Sir Kay,
> "thy chance is fallen arright,
> for thou hast gotten one of the fairest maids
> I euer saw with my sight."[134]

CÚ CHULAINN AND MÁEL DÚIN

The Two Trees are old in the oral poetic traditions of Western
Europe. Outside of Britain, they appear for example in such early
traditional tales as the Irish "Wasting Sickness of Cú Chulainn" *(Serg-lige Con Culainn),* a story from before a. D. 1100 that is preserved in
Old Irish in a composite manuscript of mostly narrative content, the
Lebor na hUidre. One multiform of the Two Trees occurs in this instance as a mere vignette embellishing a long and stately tale; the
manner of their deployment in this Irish example is in fact highly
reminiscent of the similar vignette of fir tree and pine which the
modern Balkan bard Avdo Medjedović used to close his grand epic
of *The Wedding of Smailagić Meho* in 1935. The trees are, however,
introduced in the midst rather than at the end of the Irish story:

*The great hero Cú Chulainn sickens when an otherworldly lady
named Fann puts an enchantment upon him. An ogress at one moment, Fann is Cú Chulainn's gratuitous benefactress the next, for having made him sick, she then entices him with promises of sensuous
pleasure to her marvelous demesne at the place called Mag Mell. Before
accepting her invitation, Cú Chulainn distrustfully sends his chariot-
driver Lóeg to see whether Mag Mell is really what its Irish name says*

it is, a 'Plain of Delights.' Lóeg obediently visits the place and returns to give Cú Chulainn a description of its splendours in verse. Among these, a certain mast-like tree (crann) standing at the boundary of Fann's temenos or fane is notable for the metaphors Lóeg uses to describe its particular beauty. They are the very coin of conventional fungible value and exchange, the precious metals silver and gold:

> A-tā crand i ndorus liss
> (nī hétig cocetul friss),
>   crand airgit ris tatin grían
>   (cosmail fri hór a roníam).[135]

> There is a tree before the enclosure
> (to sing in unison with it is not unpleasant),
>   a silver tree upon which the sun shines
>   (its brilliance is as that of gold).[136]

Were it possible to take any part of this tree's glitter literally, it would be a perfect Irish multiform of the ancient Near Eastern and Mediterranean hewn and banded posts standing at doors and gateways.

The contrasting green wood follows promptly in the very next verse of Lóeg's report. As though to give appropriate scope to the requisite munificence of the living wood, not one but an entire grove of sixty fruiting green trees appear. Unlike the infertile, lone tree that precedes it, the grove requires no human acts of reciprocity such as singing in unison with it to realize its full utility. Although the first tree makes a fine display suggestive of wealth, it does not gratuitously bestow that wealth on men; the grove however gives up its largesse unconditionally and without stint. And finally, whereas the former tree suggested fungible value and exchange, the green grove's bounty is in a strictly unfungible form. Lóeg tells his master Cú Chulainn:

> A-tāt and tri fichit crand
> (comraic nād chomraic a mbarr);
>   bíatar tri chét do cach crund
>   do mes ilarda imlum.

> There are sixty trees there
> (their branches almost meet);
>   three hundred are fed from every tree
>   with abundant huskless mast.[137]

Elsewhere in the writings that survive from the same era of traditional Irish story-telling, the Two Trees figure more familiarly as the warp-beams sustaining a considerable web of narrative rather than as mere self-contained vignettes. The so-called Yellow Book of Lecan (*Leabar Buidhe Leacain*), a putatively fourteenth-century manuscript, preserves a long tale entitled "The Voyage of Máel Dúin" *(Immram curaig Máele Dúin)* which is full of paired trees. Although the manuscript is younger, the tale of Máel Dúin's voyage itself belongs to the same era as does the "Wasting Sickness of Cú Chulainn;" indeed, most of the story about Máel Dúin was originally also in the same manuscript, the *Lebor na hUidre,* that contained the tale about Cú Chulainn. A single pair of examples will suffice to show the presence of the Two Trees with their usual generic meanings in the "Voyage of Máel Dúin;" any reader of the "Voyage" will find himself travelling with Máel Dúin through a veritable forest of motifs which have arisen in this tale from the seed of the Two Trees' pattern.[138]

Máel Dúin is the son of a nun by rape. Fostered by a kindly queen who is the nun's friend, he grows to become a mighty warrior who excels all his peers in games of strength. They insult him for his doubtful parentage, and he goes away to his father's estate. There he is insulted again for negligence of his duty to avenge the previous violent death of his father. He decides on a sea voyage with a retinue of other young braves to carry out his vendetta obligation. Argonaut-like, Máel Dúin and his men sail from one wondrous land to another in their quest after his father's killers. Their twelfth landfall is an island where the principles of the hewn wood reign:

Early in the morning of the third day thereafter they saw another island and a brazen fence over its middle which divided the island in two and they saw big flocks of sheep therein: a white flock on this side of the fence and a black flock on the other side, and a big man separating the flocks. Whenever he threw a white sheep over the fence to the black sheep it became black at once. Whenever the black sheep were put over the fence to the far side to the white ones they became white at once. They were adread at seeing that.

'It would be well for us,' Máel Dúin said, 'to throw our sticks onto the island. If they change colour we shall change [as well] if we go into it.'

They threw rods with black bark onto the side where the white sheep were and they became white at once, and they threw white rods onto the side where the black sheep were and they became black at once.

'We were wise to make that test,' said Máel Dúin. 'Our colour would not be better than the colour of the rods.' They retreated again although they were worn-out, tired, fearful, and although they were famished and hungry.[139]

This island is ruled by an absolute law of exchange. We see no consumption of the animal wealth represented by the two flocks of sheep; the man standing at the fence is wholly absorbed in acts of managerial severance and government, not exploitation. He neither gives nor takes anything without immediately evident compensatory consequences. The voyagers who observe him at work would be happy to appropriate some of his wealth to their own use, but they can do so only at the prohibitively high price of submitting to the law which he serves and becoming themselves indistinguishable in hue from whichever flock they might exploit. It is a vivid representation of the principle that a buyer must in the nature of purchase give something of himself in exchange for what he buys. The island is a place perfectly divided where nothing can change sides or change hands without a corresponding, completely predictable addition or subtraction to itself. Appropriately, it is the voyagers' own sticks of cut wood that prove to them the inexorability of the laws of separation and compensation. Despite their fear and disappointment, it is a place of fundamental civility which Máel Dúin and his men leave behind at their departure from this island.

Their twenty-third landfall brings them to a place of diametrically opposite character, though it may be contested whether it is correct to call it a "landfall." They approach this new place vertically rather than horizontally, and instead of fearing some obstacle to a desired landing as they did at the island of black and white sheep, this time they fear lest there be no way to avoid plunging to a landing which they do *not* desire.

Thereafter they came into another sea like a cloud and it seemed to them that it would not support themselves nor the boat. Then they saw under the sea below them ornamented forts and a lovely country and they saw a big, awful, monstrous animal in a high tree and a drove of herds and flocks round about the tree and an armed man near the tree with shield, spear and sword. When he saw that big animal that was in the tree he went at once in flight from there. The animal stretched forth its neck out of the tree and set its jaws into the back of the largest ox of the herd and dragged it with him into the tree and devoured it at once in the twinkling of an eye. The flocks and the herdsman fled away at once. When Máel Dúin and his crew saw that, equally great terror and fear took hold of them for they supposed that they could not pass without falling down through it because of its thinness like mist.[140]

Despite its evident prosperity, the strange netherworld which the voyagers have passed over is a wilderness, not a place of civilization. Here there is no simple sorting of animal wealth, but an unopposed, lawless, violent consumption of it by the familiar ogre at the green tree. A cosmotactic hewer is at hand with his instruments of division and severance—sword, spear, and shield—but unlike his counterpart on the tranquil island of the black and white sheep, this one does not exercise his divisory skills and implements to protect his animals against uncompensated appropriation. Like the Garden of Eden, this 'lovely country' too is one from which all are ultimately obliged to depart in fear by the capricious lawlessness of the monster at the green tree. It is a land without established and enforced rules of fair exchange to make it habitable.

ART OF LEINSTER

A congener of such voyaging heroes in other traditions as Odysseus and Asdiwal, Máel Dúin is also a precursor of modern folktale heroes in Irish like Art, the fabulous King of Leinster, who also has his share of dealings with the Two Trees. A tale recorded in county Kerry in 1946 from a seventy-six year-old man named Muiris Conner is a case in point.[141]

An only son conceived after many years of his parents' barrenness, Art determines when he is grown that he will marry exogamously rather than among his own people. When he is advised where in foreign lands he can find the most beautiful bride, he sets out on a voyage to her land. There he is given lodging by a kindly old man who explains to him the hideous price which the girl, the daughter of the king in that land, has set upon herself. She will marry no one except a man able to bring her "the head of a warrior in the eastern world;" those who fail forfeit their own heads when they return to her empty-handed. She has impaled her collection of heads on iron spikes stuck in the wall of her father's castle, and all but one of the spikes now has the head of an unfortunate suitor on it.

Outraged by the girl's exorbitant price, the cosmotact approaches hewn wood intent upon curtailing her monstrous tax on unmarried manhood:

When he had eaten his breakfast, Art went toward the king's castle. He walked around, looking at the wall and the heads and the castle. His blood was rising at what the old man had told him. At last he went up to the challenge pole and put all the strength he had and he hadn't into the blow he gave it with the palm of his hand. The king felt the castle shake as well as the chair he was sitting on.

"Heavens! that's the heaviest blow that has been struck on that challenge pole since it was erected," said he. "Whoever struck it must be a terrible strong man, the blow he gave it. I thought I felt the chair shaking under me."

He sent out a messenger to see what the man outside wanted.[142]

The challenge pole, a mast-like post set in the earth outside the wall of the girl's *temenos,* designates a zone suited to bargaining and the enforcement of rules, but not for gratuitous kindness. There is no free entertainment for Art at the hewn wood:

The messenger asked Art what was troubling him.

"I want the king's daughter or fight," said Art.

The messenger returned to the king.

"What does he want?" asked the king.

"He wants your daughter or fight."

". . .Go out to him and tell him he'll get his answer before long."

The messenger went out, and Art waited. It wasn't long until the king and queen and their daughter went out to him, and if they did, none of them invited him in for a bite or a sup or worried whether it was long or short since he had eaten. The daughter told him that it wasn't fighting or quarreling she wanted but the head of the warrior from the eastern world, that she would marry only the man who could do that and that the man who failed to bring it would have his head cut off.[143]

Cosmotact that he is, Art insists upon a clean separation between the procedures of enmity and those of courtship. He declares himself ready to enforce the distinction:

"And do you imagine that I'm so foolish as to come back to you to have my head cut off, if I don't have the warrior's head for you?" asked Art. "If I return at all without the head, I'll come, not to have my head cut off, but to challenge you to fight."

Faith, that answer from Art took the edge off her grandeur and haughtiness.[144]

The price of severing the girl socially from her parents—taking her away as a wife to live in her husband's land— is an act of physical severance: beheading the warrior of the eastern world. Once this system of price and reciprocity has been established at the sign of the hewn wood, Art is ready to resume his voyage toward the predictable encounter under green wood. So he comes to another foreign land where another helpful old man directs him to the live tree and a proper monster who is gentle and fierce by turns:

Art went toward the tree and stabbed the warrior in the leg with his sword. He rose up and asked Art what he wanted.

"I want your head in a fair fight," said Art.

"'Tis the devil's own work that ye are all coming for my head," said the warrior. "Here I am, interfering with nobody nor going to make trouble for ye. Why are ye all after my head?"

"We have nothing at all against you," said Art. "A young woman's *geasa* [spells] are the cause of it all."

"I'll be ready for you in a minute," said the warrior.

He rose up and got ready for the fight. Any man who wished to see a hard struggle should have watched Art and the warrior fighting. The frightening thing was that, so well trained were they both, neither of them could get in a blow at the other. Fiery sparks flew from their swords. Late in the day, when both were tiring a little, Art struck a powerful blow with all his might and turned the warrior about so that he fell on his back on the ground.

"I'll have your head now," said Art.

"Take it and welcome," said the warrior. "Only for being able to take it, you wouldn't get it. Neither would I get yours, if I weren't able. Take it now."[145]

The cosmotactic hewer does his prescribed work of cutting, but no property obtained from a denizen of the green wood is a secure possession:

Art drew a great blow at the warrior and struck him on the neck, cutting off his head. He took the head in his hand and was going toward the tree, when three grey crows flew over him, as if they were trying to snatch the head from him. Art became afraid that they would peck out his eyes, so he threw the head on the fence, in order to pick up a stone to throw at them. When he raised his head again with the stone in his hand both the warrior's head and the crows had vanished.[146]

The district of the live tree is a zone of lawlessness, a lawlessness expressed in this case in the person of the monster who will not obey the usual law of life and death. Art goes to the green wood again on the morrow and finds the weird warrior alive and whole, just as he had been the morning of the previous day. Again they fight, and again Art beheads him, but still Art has not learned that he must shun the green tree in order for any of his accomplishments to be final:

> With a strong blow, Art cut off his head and took it up in his hand. He was going toward the tree when he met four men, who were carrying a coffin.
>
> "Where are ye making for, good men?" asked Art.
>
> "We're burying a headless body," said one of them.
>
> "A headless body," cried Art. "Show it to me."[147]

Just as, on the previous day, the impulsive acquisitiveness of the three crows robbed Art of his prize, so on this day his own impulsive generosity nullifies the profit he has realized from a day of violence:

> "We will and welcome," said the men, laying down the coffin.
>
> When Art saw the headless body, "That's as fine a warrior as my eyes have ever seen," said he. "If this head which I have here fits him, he won't have to be buried without a head."
>
> He put the head on the lifeless body and it fitted exactly. The next moment, the coffin, the body, and the four men had vanished from sight.[148]

Unpredictable concealments and discoveries characterize the precinct of this Irish tree no less than its counterparts in other traditions of oral fable the world over. Only the *manner* of the hiding and disclosure are peculiar to the tradition in county Kerry. Art returns from the green tree to the old man who has been his host in this strange country:

> They spent a long part of the night talking, and next morning, when they had eaten their breakfast, the old man said, "I knew well, Art, that you were like your father. It was I who took the warrior's head from you during the past two days to see what kind of man you were. I have the head here in my room, and I will give it to you now."[149]

IVAN SOSNOVICH

From the Mediterranean to Ireland, to the Karelian shore of the White Sea in the Soviet Union, the pattern of the Two Trees is current wherever oral narrative tradition has persisted in modern Europe. Shortly before the Second World War, an outstanding *conteur* named Matvey Mixailovich Korguyev from the village of Keret' in Karelia dictated to the Russian collector A. N. Nechayev a fabulous tale about a hero who was personally a piece of hewn wood. Like Art of Leinster, this hero too came into the world because of a barren marriage:[150]

An aged couple have no children. The man cuts a piece of pine wood in the forest and carves it into the likeness of a boy. His old wife rocks the wooden image in a cradle for three years, whereupon it comes to life, walks, talks, and names itself Ivan Sosnovich (John Pineson). At the moment of the boy's animation, the old wife is preparing to take dinner to her husband, who is away plowing in the fields. The new-"born" boy volunteers to do this chore as his first act in life, and so goes food in hand to meet his foster-father. The old man invites the lad to eat with him, but he refuses, preferring instead to continue the plowing while his father rests. In this he fails, because he is too prodigiously strong to work harmoniously with the mare that pulls the plow. It is his first and last attempt to succeed as a grower of plant food. Eventually he releases the mare to graze while his father sleeps in the afternoon.

When the foster-father awakens, he sends the boy to fetch the mare home. The lad finds that a wolf has killed the mare and is eating it. When the wolf threatens to eat him too, John Pineson slays it with his bare hands. He then reports to his foster-parent that though their mare is dead, the wolf will prey no more on the livestock of others. Arriving home, the man recounts the boy's exploits to his old wife with the comment that whereas they had hoped in getting John to gain a provider for their old age, he probably will not remain long in their house.

The next day John asks his father to have the blacksmithy make an axe for him weighing 1,800 lbs. When it is ready, the boy must himself bring it home from the forge since it is too heavy for the blacksmith to deliver. Only then for the first time does John consent to take a meal at his foster-parents' table, saying that when the meal is finished he will go to cut wood in the forest with his new axe.

*The amount of wood which he is able to cut in a day is exactly proportionate to the weight of his axe. For each Russian measure of weight in the axe-head (*pood, = 36 lbs.*) John cuts one Russian cord of wood (*sazhen', = 2.13 meters*). At the end of the first day, he complains that the axe is too light, and orders another twice as heavy— one hundred pood—to be made ready for his next day's work. For the third day he requires one of a hundred and fifty pood—5,400 lbs. At the end of the third day he takes all three axes back to the smithy, saying that he will need them no more. The smiths are now to forge for him a war mace equal to the combined weight of the three discarded axes, three hundred pood (*10,800 lbs.*). At the third attempt, the smiths satisfy John, who pays them for this work the richest fee they have ever received. Next he tells his foster-parents that he is going to leave them, and that they must not expect to see him ever again. He gives them plenty of money to last through their old age in addition to the huge surplus of wood which he cut in the forest during his hewing phase. No explanation is given as to where John got the money to pay the smithy and his foster-parents, but in the Russian peasant context, the source is obvious. Cut wood was, and is still in many parts of Eastern Europe, a prime source of cash in peasant economy.*

Taking leave permanently of his foster-parents, John Pineson also undergoes a fundamental change of character. *Carrying his enormous war mace, John sets out on an aimless journey. Eventually he comes to a pair of great live oaks with an old man standing between them. From time to time this ancient knocks the two trees against each other for sport. John greets him in a 'run' of formulaic, commonplace folk-tale diction:*

—Zdravstvuj, bogatyr' Dubinja!

—Zdravstvuj, zdravstvuj, dobroj chelovek. Njet, ne jest' ja bogatyr' Dubinja. Vot Ivan Sosnovits' volka ubil, vsja zemlja drozhala, vot eto bogatyr'!

—Nu, dak vot ja i jest' Ivan Sosnovits'.

—Voz'mi menja, brat, soboj.

—A kuda?

—Kuda golova nesjot.

—Nu, pojdjom.

"Hail, Sir Oakman!"

"Hail! Hail, good man. But I am not he who should be called

'sir.' He truly is Sir Knight who slew the wolf, when the very
earth trembled, Sir John Pineson!"

"Truly it is I, John Pineson, who am here before you now."

"Then take me with you, brother."

"But where shall we go?"

"Whithersoever your fancy leads you."

"Let us be off, then."

They come to a third person who stands between two mountains,
from time to time knocking them together for sport. His name is
Gorynja, "man of the mountain(s)." When he has joined the footloose
band, it proceeds until it reaches a wide river. Between the river's
banks a great mustachioed fellow named Usynja (Mustachio) provides
a ferry-service for travellers, transporting them over the water on his
mustaches. He too leaves his place to join John Pineson's wandering
band.

They come to a large and prosperous farmstead, but find no one
at home. Entering the kitchen, John tells Oakman to slaughter and
roast for their dinner five of the oxen from the herd in the farmyard
while he and the other members of the band explore the neighborhood. During their absence Oakman begins to feel apprehensive. Soon
a little old man appears with overgrown fingernails and a beard grown
down to his elbows. This ancient pulls behind him forty wagonloads
of hay. When he reaches the farmyard, he releases the cattle that are
penned there so that they may drink, and counts them as they go out
at the gate. Finding the herd short five head, the old man discovers
Oakman in the kitchen and beats him ferociously. For all his prodigious strength, Oakman is helpless against the weird ancient and runs
away to hide outside under a corner of the house. When he recovers,
Oakman goes back into the house, which is once again deserted, and
finds that his cooking fire has gone out. After rekindling it, he lies
down on a bed to rest. There his comrades find him when they return.
They ask him why he does not join them in eating the dinner which
is now ready. Oakman replies that the smoke from the cooking fire
has given him a headache, so that he prefers to remain in bed.

On the following two days, first Mountainman and then Mustachio are left to do the cooking. The same events occur as previously,
except that at each meal the band complains of too little to eat. So
instead of five, seven oxen are butchered the second day and ten the
third day. None of the band tells his comrades who have not yet stay-

ed behind to cook that he has been attacked by the vicious old man.

On the fourth day John Pineson is to be the cook. He slaughters twelve oxen, and when the old man appears, he tears out the old curmudgeon's beard, whereupon nothing remains of the ancient except his head. This John nails to the wall in another room of the house for his comrades to see when they return at the end of the day. But while they are inspecting it, it pulls free of the nails and rolls away out-of-doors. John pursues it with his mace, but before he can catch and smash it, it escapes down a hole into the underworld.

John divines that the monstrous head has gone into the netherworld to raise an army wherewith to attack them. He tells his band that one of them must go below to prevent that. The others refuse, so Pineson himself must go. They slaughter all the remaining cattle to make a strap of leather long enough for his descent into the deep hole.

In the netherworld, John meets successively three maidens, each of whom is engaged in embroidering. They are a princess, a queen, and an empress, respectively. At each pull of their threads one, two, and three armed soldiers leap out of their needlework. Promising them marriage in the world above, Pineson induces them to throw their embroidery frames into the fire. Then he kills the old man, who in the netherworld reappears as a giant recovering from the wounds which John had earlier inflicted on him with hammer and nails.

John's three companions, who have remained at the upper mouth of the hole into the underworld, pull up the princess, queen, and empress on the leather strap by which Pineson had descended. But when John's turn comes to be hauled up out of the earth there are only enough women for the three companions to marry; so, fearing lest he will be the only one left single, Oakman cuts the leathern strap and abandons Pineson to an uncertain fate below. There John wanders until he comes to an open plain with a great pine growing green at its center. A fine herd of cattle graze peacefully beneath the pine, unattended by any herdsman. Disconsolate, Pineson sits beneath the green pine, when from its crown he hears the voices of unfledged eaglets calling for him to rescue them. Their mother has been too long away from the nest, and they are starving. Pineson butchers one of the nearby herd of cattle to feed the eaglets. They warn him to hide behind the tree when their mother returns for fear she might kill him for their dinner. When she does return, the eaglets recount Pineson's kind-

ness to her, whereupon he reveals himself and she offers him her services. He asks to be flown home to his own country. She requires a
supply of water and meat for the journey; he slaughters forty more
of the neighboring herd for this provision. But during the flight, the
eagle consumes all of the meat before reaching their destination; Pineson is obliged to cut away the calves of his own legs and feed this
filthy meal to her to sustain her until they land. When it is time for
him to dismount from the eagle's back, he complains that his damaged
legs will no longer support him. The eagle regurgitates his calves, which
adhere to his legs and grow back in place at once. Subsequently, Pineson finds his three erstwhile companions dead, marries exogamously,
and inherits his father-in-law's kingdom.

As a traditional intellectual experiment, the advent or 'birth' of
John Pineson is a remarkably successful fiction. It is a true fiction of
sundered reality (for in this sense all good fictions are true). It disin-
tegrates the real-life event of birth into its basic conceptual components, permitting each component to be considered and analyzed in
its pure state unqualified by the impingement of all the other elements
which together make up the complex idea of any actual birth in the
real world. Unlike a real, uterine child, Pineson comes into the world
by well separated, sequential stages. First his 'mother' suggests to his
'father' how the boy can be brought into being, relying upon the authority of a tradition of womanly knowledge for proof that the suggested process will work. Then, in an entirely separate event, the old man
forms the physical person of the boy. Only when he has done and
finished his work does the woman get possession of the still lifeless
form. The father's part in the process is one of pure motion: going
to and from the forest, hewing, and carving. In this respect, his (pro-)
creative activity is indistinguishable from the economic activity that
sustains him and his wife. Going to and from the forest and the fields
and executing the appropriate skilled movements in those locations
are the very essence of a male peasant agriculturalist's life.

Appropriately then, the wooden child's mother continues to 'rear'
him once his form is complete by subjecting him to unremitting motion
in the cradle for three full years. Thus from the moment he is cut from
the tree, John Pineson is kept continuously moving; that, says the
story, is the fundamental characteristic of human life as contrasted
with the life of trees or other vegetables, which though alive, are incapable of automobility. In this manner the attention bestowed on

him first by his father and then by his mother is a true education in the essentials of living. It is, of course, an education which may benefit the attentive hearer of the tale even more than it does the somewhat wooden hero.

Three years from conception is a reasonable elapse of time between the begetting of a real child and its first discharge of small social duties; in this regard Pineson is not different from any normal uterine Russian peasant boy. What is different about him is the fictitious conflation of his first movement (physical) with his first act (sympathetic) of economic and social contribution.

Just as human life differs from arboreal life by its mobility, so too hewn wood differs in its utility from green wood by its detachment and capacity to be moved. Reared for three years with the lesson of motion constantly upon him, Pineson finally adopts that trait, learning as it were simultaneously to be both hewn and human. And consequently, from the moment of his coming to life (that is, from the moment he achieves automobility) he is a veritable bundle of reciprocities. His very first thought is to compensate the parents who by their movements have brought him into the world. So he spares his mother, who for three years has kept his cradle in continuous motion, the necessity of moving her husband's dinner to a distant field. Similarly he attempts to move on behalf of and instead of his father, assuming the hard labor of moving the plow in the heavy moist earth of spring.

But once he has been divorced from the immobility and natural increase of the green, John Pineson cannot return to it. He fails immediately in his one and only attempt to lead the life of a peasant agriculturalist. He cannot plow, for his movements are too powerful. Nor can he sit still merely waiting for vegetable processes to do their work for him: he puts the mare to graze, but the earth's uncompensated donation of green, growing food to the mare fails to yield any benefit in his presence. Indeed, every kind of gratuity fails where this hewn wooden youth goes, especially free benefits or entertainment. He refuses to share the dinner which his father gratuitously offers him after he has brought it to the field, and then similarly refuses to let the predatory wolf feed gratuitously on either himself or his father's dead mare. Keenly defensive of property rights, John is a true cosmotact, who enforces the compensatory laws of civilization not only for his own good but also for the good of a larger polity. He kills the wolf when it has killed his parents' mare, not because it has also threatened him, but in order that, as Korguyev makes him say,

Bol'she uzh on ni u kogo kobyl jis' ne budet.

Never again will it consume the mares of other men.

No less than those other, more familiar cosmotacts, Samson, Beowulf, or Art of Leinster, Pineson has enormous strength in his bare hands, for bare-handed he destroys the wolf. Being himself an implement hewn of wood, he needs no other. In time he accomplishes other feats greater than this, but this is the one by which he later remains forever aphoristically famous among the men of distant and alien lands.

John's foster-father realizes from the incident of the wolf that though he and his wife had hoped through getting Pineson to provide for their old age, the boy is too talented a cosmotact to remain long in their house. But since provision for their declining years is the price of his very existence, Pineson cannot in his nature fail to pay it, even if he does not choose either to live or to marry among his own people. The question of whether the debt is fungible never even arises, for his sense of reciprocity is so strong that he manages to repay his parents in exactly the same coin that bought his being. They gave him his material existence by an act of hewing, and he in turn provides for the material needs of their existence by more hewing. So the hewn child becomes the hewing adult. Only after he has acquired his first axe does he consent to eat for the first time at his parents' table (where they further provide for the material needs of his existence), but even then, eating is only an act of preparation for labour in his parents' interest.

Having hewn for them as earlier they hewed for him, John Pineson is free to leave home. His first step in that direction is to exchange his axes for a mace. His sense of exactitude in exchange is unfailing; the mace is exactly the combined weight of the three discarded axes, and the fee which he pays to the smiths is far greater than any they have been paid before, just as the mace which they have forged for him is far greater than anything they have forged before. Not until he has actually left home does Pineson's meticulous sense of reciprocity begin to fade. He is, of course, outward bound toward green wood, which he reaches through a two-stage progression.

Himself a hewn conifer, Pineson progresses toward a live conifer of his own genus by way of green deciduous wood—the two great oaks

between which the first of his travelling companions, Dubinja (Oakman), stands. In the zone of these deciduous green trees, compensatory and law-abiding relationships cease; Pineson's companions all
imitate Oakman, who enlists gratuitously and follows aimlessly in
Pineson's wandering band. Together, the four lawless travellers prey
mercilessly on the unprotected herd of gentle herbivores in the weird
old farmer's farmyard, without ever a thought of compensation. While
Pineson and the unhewn Oakman consort, friend does nothing to fore-
warn friend about mutual jeopardy, and the old man who at one moment carelessly nourishes his visitors from his penned herd at the next
moment beats them unconscious in an impulsive display of violence.
In the netherworld, Pineson's relations with the old man degenerate
further into open warfare and bride-theft with no form of trickery or
exploitation barred and no form of recompense even suggested. And
when finally the old man is dead and the brides-to-be have been taken
from him without compensation (as earlier his cattle were taken without compensation), the number of nubile women does not reciprocate
with the number of men to be married. It is logical (in the logic of
the Two Trees' pattern) that Dubinja, the first companion who impulsively befriended Pineson, is now the one who impulsively abandons
him. Dubinja owes his bride and his hope of marriage to Pineson, but
coming as he does unhewn from between the two green oaks where
Pineson originally found him, he is an unreciprocating monster of in-
gratitude. Bereft of friends, desolate of resources, and abandoned in
the deserted netherworld, Pineson continues his aimless wandering
toward a final encounter with monstrous uncertainties at the last and
most fabulous of this tale's green trees. It is a great green pine, and
in its precinct a great herd of gentle, unresisting herbivores grazes.
Contradicting this fine resource of unexploited nourishment, the unfledged carnivore eaglets starve, unable to predict when or whether
their mother will return to the nest to feed them. Hiding himself behind the tree, Pineson duly reveals himself again, as the pattern of
the tale of the Two Trees requires, when the elder eagle does appear.
The demand she unforeseeably makes (eating his flesh) after gratuitously lending her fabulous aerial mobility to Pineson's escape from the
netherworld is the negation of his equally but differently fabulous
mobility: she eats the calves from his legs, leaving him unable even
to stand upright, much less to move of his own accord. But then, in
a sudden reversal, the eagle restores his flesh as quickly and as unexpectedly as she had taken it. And whereas early in this tale Pineson's

hewing other wood among his own people at home seemed to unite him with them but in the event only led to his separation from them, so his hewing of himself in the presence of the alien eagle seems at first to result in his inability to separate himself from her, but in the event leads to reunion with his own kind, the emperor's daughter to whom he is betrothed.

The Russian-speaking Finn Korguyev on the shore of the White Sea beneath the Arctic Circle and the Bantu Mwana Mbirika in Central Africa did not need in any way to know each other's tales for each to reproduce exactly the same array of narrative around the Two Trees. Their common teacher, the poetic tradition in their own language, assured far more effectively than they or any historic intermediaries between them could consciously have done that they would tell the same tale in their unrelated idioms. The notion of migratory narrative is simply extraneous to such cases as these. And so I maintain it has always been since fabulous narration became established in human custom, because that which is narrated in oral tradition is inseparable from the act of narrating. It is the traditional process of making a tale, with its firm and universal rules about the association of certain images and generic ideas that determines the likeness of geographically distant narrative specimens, not any vague "wandering" of isolated motifs or supposedly discrete tale-types.

SAINT NICHOLAS

Multiforms of the Two Trees' pattern with the motifs of bees and honey are also common in modern Russian fable. One particular nominal motif of person was usual in such Russian tales—the popular Saint Nicholas. Sometimes he is the honey-trickster, and sometimes an alter-ego of other tricksters. A tiny text recorded in the district of Perm in the last century contains, for example, the whole pattern:[151] *An inveterate burglar is one day observed in the act of stealing and flees from that city, whence a posse pursues him into a nearby forest. He traverses the forest, but is still being chased when he reaches its farthest limit. Before him lies an open steppe many miles wide; there, he realizes, his pursuers can easily see him at a distance and run him down. Terrified, he suddenly begins to pray to Saint Nicholas to have mercy on his sinful soul and conceal him. He offers in return for this kindness to dedicate a ten-kopeck candle to the saint at the first opportunity.*

Suddenly a middle-aged male figure (the saint) materializes, makes the thief repeat his supplication, and hears his confession. Then he points to the rotting carcass of a dead head of livestock lying nearby, and recommends that the thief conceal himself in it. This he does, despite the terrible stench. The posse arrives, looks about, sees no one, and departs empty-handed. The thief emerges from his place of concealment in the dead beast to see the saint taking a comb from a honey tree a little way off. Nicholas tells the thief that because he is an odious sinner, the stench from his thief's candle would stink in the saintly nostrils no less than the carcass did to the thief when he hid in it. Never again, says Nicholas, will divinity respond to any wrongdoer who prays for remission of the earthly consequences of his crime. This said, Nicholas vanishes.

This example of the Two Trees is so brief and obvious that it scarcely needs any comment. The living forest dominates the first part of the tale, accompanied by the usual violent absence of recompense; the thief who flees to the greenwood neither repays his victims for their losses nor do they succeed in exacting civilized penalties for his constant disregard of property rights. Thievery, the burglar's erstwhile source of bounty for which he paid nothing, suddenly becomes in the greenwood the source of mortal danger to him. Here in the wood the thief hides himself, and here too the saint surprisingly reveals himself to the thief not once but twice. The verdant wood, which had seemed the place of the thief's certain and permanent separation from the rest of mankind, nevertheless turns out to be the scene of his social salvation, for the saint sends him back to civilization with the express commission to tell other men about divinity's future policy toward the supplications of transgressors.

In the present legend of Saint Nicholas there is also the usual contest between tricksters at the bee-tree. The saint effectively tricks the thief's pursuers by concealing the fugitive in the dead carcass. But the thief is the arch-trickster who in the end tricks even the trickster for despite the saint's edict about future saintly morality in such matters, the thief still gets clean away with both his own freedom *and* the stolen goods.

Setting the limits of transgression, Nicholas is obviously the cosmotact, as he is also the hewer of the piece. Once he has severed divinity from the future access of such unworthy men as the thief, never again in the Orthodox cosmos shall the twain meet. The saint's dilemma is also obvious, contingent as it often is for the cosmotact in this pattern upon the mixed stinging and sweetness of the bees and their honey. Nicholas was in popular Russian Orthodox hagiography the saint preeminently responsible for such aspects of civilization as property rights, legacies, social hierarchy, equitable distribution of wealth, duties of the young toward their elders, and so forth. Yet like any other saint, he is sensitive to the appeals of those who need divine help in matters within his saintly jurisdiction. In an affair concerning property, such as the predicament in which the thief finds himself, Nicholas is plainly the saint to whom a supplicant should turn no matter what the merit of his appeal. Nicholas's dilemma is how to reconcile his responsibility to protect property rights with saintly mercy toward a devoted client. If he resolves the dilemma badly, it can only be said that so he usually does, as the following tale about him, given below, will further show.

NICHOLAS THE HERMIT

Compromise, engendered by the familiar dilemma-motif in the Two Trees' pattern, goes everywhere that Saint Nicholas goes, no less in European oral fable than in European Christmas custom with its ubiquitous clogs and evergreens. Even tales too licentious to be printed in 'serious' books show the full paradigm:[152] *The young wife of an old peasant secretly takes a lover. The husband discovers it and tells his wife that he has learned the whereabouts of saintly Nicholas the Hermit, who has the power to grant anything asked of him. Next day he seats himself in the forest in the hollow trunk of a live pine and waits, pretending to be Nicholas. Soon his wife arrives with a basket of dainties for the hermit. Not recognizing her disguised husband, she begs the false Nicholas to grant that her old husband may be struck blind. The masquerader declares that it shall be so and sends the woman home.*
When he has eaten up the dainties, the old man cuts a heavy stick and taps his way home with it, feigning that he has suddenly fallen blind. That evening the woman boldly receives her lover, giving him delicacies to eat and telling him that they now have nothing to fear from the old man, who she supposes cannot see. While the lover is rapaciously eating, the faithless wife leaves the room for a moment to fetch a lubricant sauce lest he choke. While she is gone, the husband shoots his cuckolder dead with an arrow, then stuffs the victim's

mouth full of food to conceal the real cause of death and make it ap-
pear that he has suffocated by eating too greedily.

    Returning to find her lover dead, the wife hides the corpse under
the stairs where her "blind" husband will not come into contact with
it, then she goes to bed. Deprived of her lover, she shamelessly invites
her old husband into bed with her, but he refuses. During the night
he cries out as though in a nightmare that he has seen the lover's body
under the stairs, but she reassures him that he is only dreaming. Later
he drags the corpse to the house of a wealthy peasant, where he poses
it as though it were in the act of stealing honey from one of that
man's casks. Duped, the man cudgels the body on the head, and sup-
poses he has killed it. The old trickster then springs out from a corner
where he has hidden himself and accuses the "murderer," who pays
him richly to dispose of the body. This the old man does by mount-
ing it on the back of the village priest's horse as though it were a
horse-thief. When the priest tries to stop the supposed thief, the horse
bolts and knocks the corpse's head against a rafter so that it again ap-
pears freshly killed. Again the trickster blackmails his dupe, and final-
ly buries the corpse.

    Once more the scene at the live pine in the greenwood is one of
seemingly benevolent, mutual service and donation that is destined,
however, to change suddenly and violently into lethal lawlessness. The
cozy three-part unity of husband, wife, and lover that seems to develop at the verdant wood in reality holds the promise of dissolution for
all the bonds that hold them together: husband~lover, lover~wife,
and even husband~wife, for not even the successful and successfully
concealed murder of his young rival is enough to make the old man
accept his wife's offer of her bed.

    As usual, the green pine presides over a zone where free nourish-
ment is given and received. It is in sharp contrast to the young lover's
mortally costly eating in the cuckold's house after the old man has
hewn for himself the thick walking-stick, the emblem of his feigned
blindness. Between this hewn staff and the stable rafter that finally
dispatches the cuckolder out of the tale, retribution and price are the
whole burden of the story once hewn wood has been introduced into
it.

    The old man's tricks with his dead rival's corpse are firmly in the
tradition of the honey-trickster, as the use of the honey-cask motif
plainly implies. There are, indeed, exactly seven distinct contests in

the trickery of concealment and discovery in this tale, echoing again
the numerical cadence found so often in the trickery of the Two Tree's
pattern the world over:

1. Wife and lover conceal their illicit affair, but the cuckold
   discovers it.
2. The husband claims to discover the whereabouts of the
   preternatural Nicholas, and successfully conceals himself
   from his wife in that guise.
3. The husband hides his ability to see from both his wife and
   her lover; they reveal to him their respective kinds of
   greediness.
4. The husband conceals how he killed the lover; the wife discovers the (supposed) cause of his death.
5. The wife conceals her lover's corpse under the stairs; her
   husband taunts her with his discovery of it.
6. The murderous husband conceals the death of his victim
   by posing him as a live thief; then he reveals himself
   from his hiding place and "discovers" the supposed murder of the thief by the wealthy peasant.
7. The husband conceals the prior death of his victim by
   posing him as a live horse-thief, then discovers the "murder" of the thief by the village priest.

The historic-geographic or "Finnish" school of folktale scholarship would have us believe that such features of traditional fabulous
narrative as the Two Trees are like populations of ferns, toadstools,
birds, insects, or other plant and animal species, and that they have
relatively recent histories of adaptation and evolution which can be
traced like those of biological forms through comparative analysis of
the fossils which they have left on the territories they now occupy,
or formerly occupied. But tales neither flower, fly, swim, nor creep
upon the earth; they live in the minds of men, and *only* in the mind.
We have, furthermore, no evidence whatsoever of any specific evolutionary change in human intellect since the very earliest arguable attestation of any matter stemming from fabulous narrative tradition.
It may be (though it has nowhere yet been generally proven to be)
of some peculiar local interest to specialists in Russian cultural history, for example, to know whether, or how frequently, the green
tree is represented as a pine in Russian traditional oral fable. In other
words, the contexts and distribution of the pine as a *nominal* motif

at a given moment in this or that particular ethnic tradition may be of some interest in a local sense. But such things can hardly be of very great interest even locally in the absence of a rather better understanding of the universal *necessity* of individual fictional motifs than is now widely available.

Of course not every pine in Russian oral fable belongs necessarily to the pattern of the Two Trees. But every pine and every other motif in that tradition (or in any other) does belong to *some* generic pattern, and the generic patterns are in no way derivative from nor contingent upon the specifically modern Russian body of fabulous tradition, nor yet upon any of its specific ethnic precursors within historic times. Patterns and their constituent generic motifs are, on the contrary, the concrete universals of oral fabulous tradition wherever it is found. They are not any such diffuse, abstract categories as are for example Jungian archetypes, Freudian *ego* and *id*, Straussian binary pairs, or Proppian 'moves,' which dissolve away into pure philosophical vapour in the face of every determined attempt to isolate them in specific texts from specific story-tellers. Rather, generic motifs are just such specific, easily recognizable, concrete facts of individual tales as the green wood and the hewn. Nothing is gained by flogging Russian, Irish, ancient Minoan, or any other single evident tradition for an original explanation of these basic elements in fable. Yet nothing fundamental—nothing that lies deeper than the very surface of any worthwhile traditional oral tale—can be understood about fable without a thorough knowledge of patterns, their constituent generic motifs, and the principles of their articulation one with another. That is because without these very concrete and isolable patterns there simply is not, nor could there be, any such thing as traditional oral story-telling anywhere in the world. Without the web of generic motifs that constitutes it, there could not be any such thing as "true fiction" that is memorable and repeated in poetic modes of speech wherever oral narration is a tradition. The universal tradition of story-telling is universal because each of its constituent elements belongs to a universal genus, and its genera are universal because the intellectual analysis of reality that inheres in them is superior to that in any idiosyncratic description of perceived actuality which any one individual could independently render from the fund of his own personal culture at any one time in any civilization. For this reason one must dismiss the perennial, presumptive opinion that oral fables of any *genre* must "have

. . .their diffusion from one definite point of our planet."* The notion
that every tale in oral tradition must once, however long ago, have
had a single author continues as an *a priori* proposition to grip the
minds of even well-informed scholars in our own time, whose prag-
matic experience of fabulous narrative should have led them induc-
tively to the opposite opinion; so, for example, Claude Lévi-Strauss
in the concluding chapter of his four-volume study, *Mythologiques:*
". . .tout mythe doit, en dernier ressort, prendre son origine dans une
création individuelle. . . .chacun [récit] ait été imaginé et narré une
première fois par un individu particulier."† And together with the
baseless 'theory of single authorship' one must discard also the kind
of narrative analysis that grew out of it in nineteenth-century European learning. It is a terrible and dangerous folly to butcher anything
so universally valuable to the intellect as traditional oral fiction in the
compulsively uncomprehending way in which one habitually sees it
dismembered by the institutionalized motif- and type-indices of the
Finnish School.

According to an opinion widespread among contemporary social
scientists, it is only the local, ethnic use of cultural material that gives
it its importance. But if one puts aside the sentimental attachment to
strange peoples and the romantic inclination to geographic or temporal exoticism that have so powerfully motivated many anthropological
and sociological ethnographers in the modern era, it is hard to escape
the conclusion that what is best and most worthy of outside notice in
the life of local ethnic groups is precisely the ingenious and determined
efforts of some of their members to sustain a cultural tradition that
transcends themselves. Oral fable is and always has been such a tradition.

Social scientists as a class have been interested in the characteristic *uses* to which the peoples they study put this or that element
of oral fabulous tradition—if, indeed, they pay any attention to that
aspect of culture at all. It is entirely understandable, even inevitable,
that such an approach has sometimes helped its followers gain insight
into the workings of particular societies, but rarely yielded more than
an occasional fleeting glimpse of the fundamentals of oral narrative

---

* Written in 1929 by Alexander H. Krappe in *The Science of Folklore*, New York
(W.W. Norton & Co.), 1964, p. 70.

† C. Lévi-Strauss, *L'Homme nu*, Paris (Librairie Plon), 1971, p. 560.

tradition itself. In their own way, many humanists who are authorities on narrative have also neither known nor cared to know very much about the fundamental constituents of narrative traditions. This scholar is a classicist intent upon particular ancient civilizations, while that one is a mediaevalist, who is absorbed, let us say, in the culture of western Europe in the twelfth century; similarly, this one knows best the relics of ancient Akkadian civilization, while that one studies modern novels. Unlike social scientists, such humanists concern themselves little with the actual uses to which their subject peoples have put the stuff of story in their several epochs, for often little or no certain information about that survives from either recently deceased or long-dead civilizations. Instead, humanists of this kind often fasten upon such issues as 'motivation' and *genre* to guide them toward a better understanding of fable. They make a great thing of distinguishing between epic and romance, hagiography and legend, ballad and folktale, and so forth. If they can discern, for example, that among a certain people in a certain period of history, 'romance'was mystical and epic mundane, they may feel satisfied that they have understood something basic about that people's reasons for storytelling, and hence something basic about the stories themselves. To them, nothing is more revealing about narrative than the rationalizations of it which they can extract from the documents of a given time and place. But while this too may result in valuable contributions to understanding the 'spirit' or distinctive idiosyncrasies of various peoples in their own times, in truth it adds little to understanding the basic categories of oral fabulous tradition, which like intellect itself have always been available to reason and *adaptation* but never to any essential *alteration* by the terms of particular civilizations. So in the ancient Near East the tale of the Two Trees was sometimes part of the myth of the state, or part of cosmology; in modern Irish it may be pure once-upon-a-time fairy tale; in Africa or in the Balkans, it is epic; in Russia, hagiography and bawdy story; in twelfth-century western Europe it was allegorical romance, and in twentieth-century Australian blackfellows' culture it was legend pertinent to witchcraft and sorcery. The *uses* and the *reasons* for fable are as infinitely variable as the intellectual activities to which men have, and may yet, apply themselves. But the basic *content* of oral fabulous narrative was long ago in prehistory refined to such a superb degree of adaptability that it does not need, any more than the human minds which continually learn and recompose it need, any fundamental modification to suit it specially to a particular cultural application. The critics call us to marvel at one ethnic application after another, but the real marvel, and the one most essentially in need of explication, is the almost incredible tenacity and universality of narrative patterns and their generic components in oral narrative everywhere.

I do not mean to denigrate the services of the many scholars who throughout the history of western learning, and especially during the last two centuries, have observed and studied various parts of the universal fabulous tradition. They have been cautious because the state of knowledge required them to be; they have known securely only what their personal command of languages has permitted them to know, and under that hard regimen all cultures seem ethnically delimited. Thus, the Celticist inclined to comparative studies might within his certain competence go no farther afield from Britain than to Ireland, to Normandy, or *vice versa*. In time, the Indo-Europeanist, relying on the foundation of knowledge amassed in many ethnic fields akin to Celtic or Germanic or Greek, might venture speculatively to range over so vast a tract as the territory from Ireland to as far away as India. But not even in this century has the Europeanist of any kind consorted comfortably with information about autochthonous cultures in such remotely distant zones of civilization as East Asia, sub-Saharan Africa, aboriginal Australia, or the Americas; nor have the scholarly authorities on those regions felt any impulse more strongly than the desire to protect the understanding of their fields from the misapplication of alien conceptions, especially those of Europeanists.

But times have changed, the state of learning has changed, and so must we who study narrative. Today even authorities on different aspects of the same ethnic civilization rely upon one another for subsidiary knowledge of their own specialties. We can therefore at least allow authorities on other cultures to tell us in their editions what tales they have found there. In reality, there is in the late twentieth century no longer any absolute dearth of dependable information about oral narrative traditions in far places, such as formerly prevented an accurate appraisal of elements continuous from one zone to another in the spectrum of the world's ethnic civilizations and continents. Scholarly caution is a necessary trammel, but refusal seriously to examine what previous generations of careful scholars and collectors have laid before our very eyes would be inexcusable. And if we do examine their data carefully, then we must reckon for all that it implies with the plain fact that there is no generic difference, for instance, in the *narrative* content of an allegorical Middle English metrical romance and a blackfellow tale from an aboriginal Australian culture.

KING ORFEO

Let us consider, for example, the so-called Breton Lay of King Orfeo, a twelfth-century tale consisting in its surviving written form of·six hundred and four rhymed verses, which many will admit is not only a traditional story but also probably derived at no great remove from oral story-telling (though few would at present argue that the extant text is oral). It tells of a King Orfeo, who like his ancient namesake Orpheus lost his wife and set out to win her back from another world. But the medieval King Orfeo of Middle English is not exactly the classical Orpheus; he is successful in winning back his wife as Orpheus was not, and he is a manipulator of hewn wood, while his wife, Queen Meroudys, is a victim of the preternatural at the green wood:[153]

Dame Meroudys falls asleep one spring morning under a fruit tree in an orchard. When she awakens in the afternoon she is seized with a fit of madness, tearing her hair and rending her cheeks with her fingernails. Taken home to her chamber, she recovers enough to explain to her husband the king that she has had a vision whilst sleeping under the green tree. In her dream a fairy prince has abducted her, shown her his rich castle and estate, and commanded her that she must, whether she please or not, meet him again next day under the same tree, when he will carry her away to his country to remain with him and his court permanently.

King Orfeo accompanies his wife to the green tree in the orchard to dispute his fairy rival's claim on Meroudys; nevertheless, she is spirited away at the appointed hour. To remedy the gratuitous injury inflicted on him by the preternatural at the green wood, Orfeo turns to the hewn. Voluntarily he exiles himself from his own domain, taking with him only two articles, both artifacts wrought of wood:

> 230 A staff to hym he gan take—
> He had nether gowne ne hode,
> Schert, ne non other gode,
> Bot an harpe he toke, algate—
>
> A staff he did take with him—
> Neither gown nor hood,

Nor shirt, nor yet any other thing,
But only his harp, which he did also take—

Orfeo proceeds to the application of his hewn wooden implements by way of a second tree that is also green. Like the Lamba Mr. Squeezer in Central African fable, the Middle English hero too recovers his abducted kin by travelling to the wilderness with wood hewn to musical utility:

   In a tre that was holow,
270 There was hys haule, evyn an morow.
   When the wether was feyre and bryght,
   He toke hys herpe anon ryght;
   And mydys the wodde he sett hym dounne,
   And temperyd hys herpe wyth a mery sounne,
   And harpyd after hys awne wylle—
   Over all aboute it was full schylle.

In a tree that was hollow,
There was his abode-hall morning and evening.
When the weather was fair and bright
He took up his harp, tuned aright,
And in the midst of the woods he sat him down
To play his harp with a merry sound,
And he harped the tunes that pleased him best
While round about the sound rang out.

All the beasts of the wild gather to listen tamely, and eventually the retinue of the fairy king appears too. Orfeo sees Meroudys among them, and resolves to follow her. Again the means to assertion of his right and the recovery of his lawfully wedded queen are the two articles of hewn wood:

345 He toke a staff as he spake,
   And threw an herpe at hys bake.

As he spoke he took up his staff
And slung the harp upon his back.

The exile comes to the fairy castle and gains admission as a minstrel to entertain the king. There among various other horrors he sees Meroudys lying under her tree. He harps for the fairy king and craves Meroudys as his fee; the king donates her to him. When he returns with her to his own domain, his harp is the token whereby his steward recognizes and reinstates Orfeo as king after the ten years of his absence.

From the very beginning of this medieval western European romance it is apparent that the hero has a skill to use hewn wood for every encounter and mishap that may befall him and his dame in the presence of green trees. Verse 34 of the text tells us in so many words that no man was ever Orfeo's equal in manipulating the harp:

> So gode herper never non was.

Against the great acquired skill which the man Orfeo has earned by dint of learning and long practice, the woman Meroudys and her several female companions soon juxtapose green wood with its implication of unearned, natural increase:

> 49 It befelle in the begyning of May,
> When foules syng on every sprey,
> And blossom spring on every boughe
> . . .
> Than the quen, Dame Meroudys,
> Toke wyth hyr ladys off grete price,
> And went in a undryn-tyde   [forenoon]
> 55 To ply hyr in an horcherd syde.

The rest of the narrative is simply an account of how Orfeo, handling his artifacts of wrought wood, step by step imitatively counters and vanquishes the lawless violence and caprice of the green wood's precinct.

First dame Meroudys goes mad beneath a fruit tree in the orchard where she has gone to amuse herself. Then, in her report to Orfeo of what befell her there, she introduces the green tree into the poem for the second time and discloses how she beheld the person of her abductor beneath it. Next, the same fruit tree is revisited for the third time, when Meroudys departs on her journey to fairy land.

Orfeo responds to these three occurrences of green wood with his staff and harp. In an act of calculated madness of his own, he tells his steward (who thinks the resolution insane) that he is abdicating his throne in order to go naked into a self-imposed exile in the wilderness; this said, he picks up staff and harp and departs. Then, countering the green tree where Meroudys saw her abductor, Orfeo harps to behold her, the victim of the abduction. Next, he reposts to the green tree that was Meroudys' point of departure on her jour-

ney to fairy-land with his second taking-up of staff and harp as he
departs on his own journey to the same fairy-land.

The fourth instance of green wood in this Middle English metrical romance is the hollow tree in the wilderness where Orfeo lodges
for ten years. It is both the place and the token of the undeserved
separation from his wife. To this too he has a hewn antidote: once
in the fairy palace, he puts his harp to work to earn a deserved reunion with his wife. While he harps, she lies silent under the fifth
green tree, which marks her restoration by the elphin king's *donation*
of her to renewed queenship in her own country. Correspondingly,
Orfeo's harp finally betokens his restoration *by right* to kingship in
his own land. The entire romance is a bilateral web of Orfeo's hewn
artifacts and Meroudys' live trees in six successive permutations:

1. His harp ~ her green bough.
2. Fruit tree of her madness ~ staff and harp of his madness.
3. Fruit tree with male abductor revealed ~ harp with female
   victim revealed.
4. Fruit tree of her journey to fairy-land ~ staff and harp of
   his journey to fairy-land.
5. Tree as the place of his undeserved separation from his wife
   ~ harp as instrument of his deserved reunion with his
   wife.
6. Tree of her restoration by donation ~ harp of his restoration
   by right.

Christian moralists, scholastics, and modern medievalists alike have
already at one time and another attributed all manner of esoteric meanings to this medieval tale, and will no doubt continue in the future to
do so. It is even conceivable that some such speculations as present-day
humanists lavish on hypothetical motivations, allegory, and refinements
of moral intent for such tales as this did occasionally also occur to the
minds of some individuals who lived in the age when the story of King
Orfeo was current. But unless one is for some reason dedicated to attempting to relive (or improve upon) the cultural life of the Late Middle Ages in England and western France, there is no compelling reason
to linger over the hermeneutic peculiarities of the previous scholarship
on this Breton lay. For there is one central fact that governs the primary meaning of this tale, and any secondary local significance it may
have had must be a refinement or elaboration consistent with that
fact. The fact is that the metrical romance of King Orfeo is construc-

ted on the pattern of the Two Trees, and the generic meanings of that pattern govern any local significance that might reasonably have been attached to it either in its own age or later. Meroudys' green trees are about donations and uncompensated exploitation, lawlessness and unpredictability, monstrosity, concealment, and ultimate separation; Orfeo's hewn wood is inversely about rights and compensation, equity and dependability, measure, discovery, and ultimate reunion. Local, esoteric interpretation may ring any changes it will upon these generic meanings, but so long as the tale endures those generic meanings remain its inviolable principles. The only way to overturn or abjure them is to disintegrate the pattern and destroy the tale itself.

WURRUNNA

An enlightened contemporary medievalist, Morton Bloomfield, has said, "The wide distribution of folktale motifs argues for a lengthy time of diffusion, . . .yet the ubiquity and universality of motifs argue against this explanation in all cases. The presence of motifs in America and Australia tends to prove an earlier period of unity."[154] If one discriminates, as experience teaches that one must, between the local ethnic names given to motifs and the underlying genera to which they belong, then not only generic motifs but also their categorical meanings are seen to belong to an "earlier period of unity." The aboriginal Australian story-teller has different names for his stock of universal motifs, and arranges them in as diverse a variety of sequences as any of his European, African, or Asian counterparts do. Yet *no* temporal or spatial disjunction in the telling has any effect on the primary meanings of the Two Trees' pattern; the Australian is as much a continuator of the common fabulous tradition as any other *conteur*. The text of the following tale from New South Wales[155] is of no less doubtful orality than the text of *Kyng Orfew*, but the tale itself is no less certainly a traditional fable.

A hunter named Wurrunna returns to his people's campsite tired and hungry at the end of a day's unsuccessful hunt. He asks his mother for prepared grain food, but her supply is exhausted; when he asks others in the place for raw cereal to prepare for himself, they refuse him. Enraged, he takes up his weapons and departs to seek a better society elsewhere.

He comes first in his journey to a monstrous old man who is cutting wild honey from standing wood. The man has no eyes, but

sees well through his nose, as do all his tribe. He is gratuitously kind,
giving Wurrunna as much honey as he can eat and hospitably inviting
him to stay with his people. But the weird figure makes Wurrunna feel
uneasy, so he quietly slips away to continue his journey.

Next he comes to a large lagoon where he drinks and lies down
to sleep for the night. When he awakens in the morning, only a large
dry plain lies where the lagoon was the previous evening. While he is
puzzling over this, a heavy storm begins to rise, and he hurries away
until he comes to a pile of cut bark lying on the ground ready for
use in making a shelter. He cuts a few poles and sets up a framework
to support the sheets of bark, but when he lifts the first sheet to put
it in place, he discovers under it an utterly terrifying creature who
shouts its name at him with such an appalling voice that he drops the
bark and flees headlong into the wilderness.

He flees until he reaches a great river and can go no farther.
There he encounters a flock of wingless birds (emus) just emerging
from the river, and decides to kill one for food. He climbs a tree and
conceals himself there to ambush the birds. He spears one of them as
they pass the tree, and descends to collect his prey, but when he
reaches it he finds that he has killed a man around whose dead body
the rest of the tribe are angrily gathered. Again Wurrunna flees in
stark terror.

Thinking only of the danger behind him, he goes forward headlong until he stumbles into a strange camp which he has not seen until he is in it. There seven girls, whose name is Maya-mayi, are living
alone. They receive Wurrunna hospitably, feeding him and allowing
him to share their campsite that night. The next morning he pretends
to depart, but hides nearby to watch the seven girls' movements in
hopes of catching one alone and capturing her for his wife.

The girls leave their camp to forage for food with their digging
sticks in hand. After they have found a supply, they lay their sticks
aside and sit down to eat. Wurrunna steals two of the sticks and
again conceals himself. When they have eaten, five of the girls find
their sticks and go back to their camp; the other two Wurrunna captures while they are searching for their sticks.

The two girls live contentedly with Wurrunna for some weeks.
Then one day he orders them to cut bark from two green pines nearby to use as kindling for a fire. They protest that if they do so he
will see them no more, but he insists. When they attempt to cut the
pines, the trees begin to stretch upward carrying the two girls with

them skyward. Soon the tops of the trees touch the heavens and the two girls disappear there forever.

If after the manner of Edmund Leach one probes this native Australian tale for its philosophical message, such a message will not be far to seek. But it will require the utmost degree of informed percipience to determine wherein that message is characteristically blackfellow, and the task will be truly hopeless unless one can first determine what part of the tale's philosophical system transcends blackfellow culture and is simply a consequence of the universal tradition of story-telling. It may be questionable whether, if one is already sufficiently informed about blackfellow culture to discriminate properly in that way, there is any particular utility in a purely ethnocentric study of blackfellow tales. Possibly the only sure value to be gotten from the study of any one people's multiforms of oral traditional fable is the same value that the *conteur* and his hearers derive— the enlargement of one's own intellectual experience of human potential. There is value of that sort for any educated man or woman in the knowledge that an Australian blackfellow *conteur* in this century expressed the rules of property and price in the same motival system that an unknown twelfth-century Breton poet used to construct the tale of Kyng Orfeo. Like Orfeo, Wurrunna too has his implements of hewn wood whereby to dispel illusions and secure benefits. Like Orfeo's, each set of Wurrunna's hewn implements is matched with greenwood haunted by preternatural monsters. Both are tales of a cosmotact voluntarily exiled to overcome the intractability of women.

The tale of Wurrunna begins with a scene of pure reciprocity. An empty-handed male hunter, he has no meat to offer in exchange for vegetable food, and finds the female gatherers of plant food in his camp equally as empty-handed as he. True to pattern, he thereupon lays hands on the hewn wood of his weapons, and departs. His impulsive anger takes him, with equal fidelity to pattern, to standing wood which a preternatural monster frequents. This alien monster, simultaneously threatening and benevolent, gives him nourishment with a liberal generosity exactly opposite to the unyielding meanness of Wurrunna's own people. But like the yield of the green *ympe tre* in *Kyng Orfeo,* the yield of the successive green trees in Wurrunna's adventures also steadily diminishes until finally the last manifestation of the live wood presides over restoration of abducted women.

Fleeing from the equally untenable extremes of his own weaponry (with its social implications) at home and the bee-tree in an alien land, Wurrunna comes next to the monstrous bark-backed creature whom he at first mistakes for cut wood, but who in fact is a kind of horizontal green wood. Cutting poles for a shelter, Wurrunna comes close to earning a new campsite for himself in this place, but makes the mistake of trying to appropriate unearned property in the form of the supposedly pre-cut bark. Under that bark skin lurks a howling monster who suddenly snatches away the same unearned bounty which a moment before he had seemed to offer for the taking. As surely as the fairy king taught Orfeo while he moved from tree to tree to earn a civilized domesticity by reliance on the just practice of his own skills, so surely do Wurrunna's monsters of the wilderness teach him the same lesson.

The next incident in Wurrunna's adventures finds him again involved with a standing tree. He conceals himself in its canopy to spear a passing wingless game-bird. His trees are becoming as it were progressively 'greener,' involving progressively more and farther-reaching forms of the fabulous green tree's usual motival satellites. Thus Wurrunna's tree of ambush has the remarkable power to make the man hiding in its canopy himself a monster who reaches out of the tree's foliage to kill a gentle creature grazing in its precinct. This tree is a place whose illusion is the interchangeability of wingless bipedals. It is also a less hewn green tree than either of its two precursors in the tale.

The bee-tree being cut by the old man who saw through his nose gave at least one meal's worth of unnegated benefit to Wurrunna. The bark-like skin on the back of the howling bark-monster had the appearance of having been hewn, but in the event was green and yielded nothing. The third live tree, where Wurrunna hides to kill the emu, has worse results: it almost yields a meal after Wurrunna's monstrous if unwitting slaying of his own kind, but then in a sudden reversal it is the scene where Wurrunna's own life is threatened by the dead man's tribe, who pose the specifically human danger of vendetta. The illusion fostered by this tree not only disappoints its visitor, but threatens to pursue him and take away even that barest minimum of well-being which the visitor brought with him when he first approached the tree: the mere satisfaction of still being alive. The actual imposition of the duty among men to pay a life for a life is of course made not while Wurrunna is in the green treetop, but rather when he descends to follow his hewn wooden spear to the place where his kill lies.

The final set of hewn wood and green follows immediately in the story. Fleeing the supposed pursuit of the dead bipedal's avengers, Wurrunna finds himself in the camp of the seven girls. They live in an orderly and civilized way, by means of the digging sticks which they use to earn the vegetable food that sustains them. Who possesses the sticks possesses the women, or so it seems, and Wurrunna claims a pair of each. But they are the cruelest illusion of all, for though they seem to belong to the world of the hewn, they have a special relationship with the evergreen pine. The Maya-mayi are in fact the monstrous denizens of the ultimate green wood in the story, and are, like the conifers' everlasting colour, themselves immortal.

Having left the cruel society of his own people where the hunter must buy all he obtains with reciprocal contributions to the welfare of others, Wurrunna living with his two captured Maya-mayi brides seems to have achieved by lawlessness and rapine that more perfect society which he had set forth in anger to seek. But the hewn wood, which in the form of the girl's digging sticks seems at last to have worked its proper magic of social unification, is in the event a mere trifle when set against the awful power of the pine. No price in the means of man to pay can buy the permanent company of the two immortal women who, when the illusion of Wurrunna's purchase upon them and their immortality is dispelled by the act of their hewing, rise into the sky to become everlasting stars in the Pleiades. He is not expelled or barred from his Eden when his women violate its forbidden green tree; it simply departs to a place whither he cannot follow. Finally stripped of every illusion that he can obtain something for nothing, Wurrunna is left alone in the wilderness with no alternative but to go back, as ultimately he does, to his own people, there to play the civilized game of equitable give-and-take according to the established rules.

One cannot rationally say that Wurrunna's four sets of hewn and verdant wood are any less nor differently instructive than King Orfeo's five sets. The cultures to which the two multiforms of the story are addressed have different idioms, and by appropriate nominal adaptation of the generic trees the same tale speaks equally well to both cultures. The *ympe tre* that stands now in Orfeo's orchard, now in the fairy king's palace, is neither more nor less marvelous than the green pine which instead of dying grows when it is hewn until finally it can carry away a female passenger from one realm to another. It is not more nor less marvelous, just differently named in the descriptive idiom of the one culture and the other. But tradition seems to go to almost any length to protect the traditional generic identity of its motifs, no matter how multiform the process of renaming and redescription makes them from one ethnic culture to another. Consider again the Middle English *ympe tre* and the Australian blackfellows' pine that grows the better for being hewn. The precise meaning in Middle English of the word *ympe* or *impe* is 'a grafted scion;' thus the ultimate green tree of the Breton lay is also a tree that grows the better for being hewn. No wood is greener than that whose growth cutting improves. The modern English professor's customary contempt for the assumedly foolish, 'animistic' wonders of 'primitive' folktales is in no way justified. Western folklorists and mythographers have arguably too long been foolish and intellectually primitive believers in the outward appearance of things, but oral traditional fable is not. Not even the best of the favorite, canonical literature in the college and university curricula of the West will give up its real secrets until we learn to take oral traditional fable seriously.

So Wurrunna's lesson is what Orfeo's was before him. It concerns the nature and acquisition of property; his artifacts of hewn wood, for all their seeming impotence before his exile, yield progressively more and more as he gains experience with them during his time of trials in the wilderness. Inversely and proportionately, the gratuitous donations and seizures of property at green wood yield a smaller and smaller balance of profit. And just as King Orfeo learned to give up material comforts in order to possess his woman, Wurrunna learns that having material comforts means giving up the company of women. In the final analysis, the hewn wood triumphs and the law of price prevails in both the blackfellow and Middle English forms of the story.

WURRUNNA'S TREES

HEWN	*GREEN*
1. Weapons (yield nothing)	1. Bee-tree (yields a meal)
2. Poles (almost yield shelter)	2. Bark-backed monster (yields stationary horror)

3. Spear (almost yields a meal)	3. Tree of ambush (yields bereavement and terror of pursuit)
4. Digging sticks (temporarily yield wives)	4. Pine (yields bereavement that precludes pursuit)*

NIMBAMUNG AND AMBWERK

Far from being a novelty of aboriginal Australian fable, the Two Trees are pandemic in Pacific Oceania. While its distance from the Asian mainland has for many suggested about Australia an ultimate degree of cultural remoteness and isolation, in fact its aboriginal people and their oral fable display great likeness to pre-Bantu strata in Central and South Africa. In many ways the most nearly ideal antipodes of our planet have proven to be in Melanesia, where, as in New Guinea, the more mountainous and heavily forested terrain has harbored a cultural isolation even more notable than that of the Australian continent. Kenelm Burridge, though he was looking for anything but generic patterns, nevertheless could not collect oral fable among the Tangu of northeastern New Guinea without meeting the Two Trees at every turn.† The story of Nimbamung, whose native narrator Burridge does not identify, is a representative example.

---

* This tale is governed by both the Two Trees' and the honey-trickster's pattern. Illusions, deceptions, and terrifying discoveries begin when Wurrunna meets the ancient honey-hewer, and progressively expand in fabulosity. There are seven contests of concealment; Wurrunna begins successfully to conceal himself in the fourth contest.

(1) Honey-gatherer conceals eyes in nose, yet sees Wurrunna.

(2) Wurrunna finds a lagoon in the evening; it conceals itself overnight.

(3) Bark-backed monster conceals itself under semblance of bark; Wurrunna discovers it while attempting to hide from storm.

(4) Wurrunna hides in a tree-top, and alien men hide in the semblance of emus; Wurrunna discovers their true identity.

(5) Wurrunna finds seven girls, hides himself from them.

(6) Wurrunna hides two digging sticks; girls find Wurrunna.

(7) Two pines conceal girls in heaven; Wurrunna discovers them in act of departure.

† Reported in: Kenelm Burridge, *Tangu Traditions*, Oxford [Clarendon Press], 1969, Part Two, "Mythology." The tale of Nimbamung is given on pages 225-228.

Once upon a time there was a blind man called Nimbamung who lived alone with his dog. One evening, as he was thinking of collecting some tree grubs on the morrow, he hafted a stone axe-blade, not taking to his pallet until he was satisfied with the balance.

Next morning, taking bow and arrows and the newly hafted axe, he set off into the forest to look for tree grubs, his dog showing him the way. They found a right good tree where tree grubs should be and, ripping away the bark with his axe, Nimbamung started to flick the grubs into the bamboo barrel he had brought with him.

Now Ambwerk happened to be close by at the time. He heard the old fellow at his work and he thought he would see what was happening. So, creeping through the undergrowth, he hid himself at the edge of the clearing. Who was this man? he wondered. Why was he behaving so strangely?

Ambwerk waited for a while, watching closely. Suddenly he understood. The fellow must be blind!

Stepping carefully so as not to make a noise, Ambwerk eased his way through the clearing and started to scuffle Nimbamung's grubs into a barrel of his own. . . .

'Out of my way! Leave my grubs alone!' Nimbamung scolded, thinking his dog was stealing the grubs.

Ambwerk stayed with Nimbamung the whole day long, filling his barrels with the grubs which Nimbamung and his dog had found. Afterwards, he followed Nimbamung to his home.

The fellow took a strange trail, eventually stopping in front of a *wamunga* shrub. Creeping close, Ambwerk waited to see what would happen.

Nimbamung blew his spittle over the bush and uttered a spell: the leaves of the *wamunga* shrub parted to reveal an open door leading into a hole in the ground.

Ambwerk memorized the spell. Then, as the dog led the way down, Ambwerk followed close behind, leaving Nimbamung to bring up the rear and shut the shrubbery door.

Obviously we have to do here with a Tangu multiform of the Russian Saint Nicholas, and with a progression rather than a simple set of green and hewn wood. First Nimbamung hafts an axe (hewing in preparation for hewing). The function of the axe is to *discover* a hidden bounty of food, and it is opposed in this to the grub-tree, where Ambwerk *conceals* himself (to be entertained) in the company of the blind hunter and his animal companion. The wooden-hafted axe, seemingly an instrument of separation (to separate the food from the green tree) in the event brings about a new and unexpected social unity, summoning by its blows upon the food-tree the trickster Ambwerk to join the reclusive Nimbamung. And obversely, the grub-tree which seems at first to preside over a new social unification (Nimbamung + Ambwerk) in reality betokens instead an intolerable sequestration (Ambwerk and Nimbamung with his hidden treasure of foodstuffs from the rest of hungry Tangu).

The second set in the progression of woods exceeds the scope of the first set in its signification. Bamboo barrels (hewn) and *wamunga* shrub (green) each first conceal and then reveal the whereabouts of hidden food and men. The bamboo barrels that Ambwerk (and later also his younger brother Tuman) uses to purloin Nimbamung's grubs seem to connote a division in the society of three which together exploits them as food, but the scene among the water-barrels in Nimbamung's house subsequently restores that unity. Conversely, those who pass the barrier of the *wamunga* bush with Nimbamung seem to be joining with him, but in fact are separated from the larger society of human-kind and the normal rules of conduct that obtain in it, for social union with Nimbamung is impossible for any kind of true human, be he wise (Ambwerk) or foolish (Tuman).

The fabulosity of the green and hewn wood expands still further in the third set of the progression. The fabulous fruit trees (verdant) around Nimbamung's house and household of hewn wood are themselves polymorphic clusters of the green and hewn principles.

> Down inside the hole, Ambwerk saw they had come on a beautiful *mwenk* [homestead]. Coconuts a-plenty grew around the perimeter, areca-nuts hung in thick clusters, the bananas were bending with fruit. Ambwerk started to help himself. And Nimbamung, hearing the sounds of eating and thinking again it was his dog, scolded the animal, shouting to it to stop.

> Inside Nimbamung's house quantities of meat hung from the rafters, and a large heap of yams was piled on the floorboards. Ambwerk set to on the meat.

> Nimbamung took a small yam, scraped it clean, cut it into small pieces and put them into his stew-pot. Ambwerk followed

suit—with a large yam, a hunk of wallaby meat, and some saltwood. He took a coconut, scraped out the meat and mixed the
latter with coconut milk. Ambwerk did himself proud, eating
hugely, very quickly, while Nimbamung, eating slowly, cursed
the dog which he thought was eating all his food.

They slept.

Next morning, Nimbamung rose early to go hunting. Ambwerk
slept on. When he awoke he gorged himself on all the good food
that was there, collected as much as he could carry and, remem-
bering the spell, opened the shrubbery door and set off for home.

The second of two brothers now repeats all the adventures of
the first, except that by failing to observe the necessary reciprocity
with Nimbamung's dog at the sign of Nimbamung's hewn wood, he
meets with the unwise hunter's bad end: instead of eating, he is himself eaten. The formerly bountiful provider is suddenly lethally inim-
ical.

Arrived back at his village, Ambwerk showed his younger brother all the food he had stolen, hanging his spoils from the rafters.

'Where did you get all that food?' asked Tuman.

Ambwerk told Tuman all about Nimbamung, that he was blind,
what a lot of food he had, and how easy it was to rob him.
Tuman was excited. 'I'll go along tomorrow!' he exclaimed. 'I'll
go and collect as much as I can and bring it back here!'

But Ambwerk had not finished. 'Mind now', he cautioned.
'When the old fellow opens the door you must get in after the
dog and before he does—he shuts the door behind him. When
you get into his *mwenk,* eat as much as you like—but leave his
dog alone. Let the dog eat as much as it wants.'

Next morning, Tuman went off into the forest to look for
Nimbamung. He found him where Ambwerk had said he would
be, and he did as Ambwerk had told him to do. He filled his
own barrels with grubs while Nimbamung, cursing his dog, shovel-
led pith and rotting bark into his own. He followed the old man
to the *wamunga* shrub, crept close as the fellow blew his spittle
over the shrub and uttered the spell, then darted in ahead of
him, following the dog down into the *mwenk.*

There it was, just as Ambwerk had told him. He picked some
bananas.

'Stop eating my food!' Nimbamung shouted crossly. 'Get out

of it, there!' Still he thought it was his dog. Grumbling and scolding, he put a pot on the fire, sliced a small yam, and threw the pieces into the pot.

Tuman followed suit with a large yam, some saltwood, and grubs. The water bubbled merrily, the food was cooked, and Tuman ate fast and furiously while Nimbamung, groping blindly, eating little, muttered and swore at his dog.

Then, as often may happen, Nimbamung's dog nosed its way into Tuman's food. He hit it on the snout. The dog yelped.

'What's that?' Nimbamung roared. 'Who hit my dog?' he raged, rising to his feet and taking down his adze. 'Who is in here eating my food?'

Tuman fled to the back of the hut and hid himself behind a pile of water barrels. And Nimbamung, stumbling blindly, thrusting and swinging his adze, crashed against the pile of barrels as he brought the weapon down in a wild overhand stroke. . . .

Tuman could do nothing. The blade struck him between the eyes and he fell lifeless to the floor.

Nimbamung carved the corpse, cooked the flesh, and ate it. Head and bones he hung under the porch of his house.

The third set of verdant and hewn wood in this cosmotactic tale —Nimbamung's fruit trees and wooden house—is ultimately enclosed within a fourth and last set. The *wamunga* shrub, earlier Nimbamung's device for concealment and exclusion of other men from his private Eden, now becomes Ambwerk's road sign pointing the way to speedy discovery and invasion of it by the whole troop of his and Tuman's fellow villagers. Via the green *wamunga* they come with their hewn spears to devastate Nimbamung's house and orchard. The hewn wood that unites the greatest number (the spears) prevails over all other, and imposes universal unity; while the *wamunga,* once the portal leading to a place of effortless repletion and bliss, suddenly and unexpectedly becomes for those who dwell within the portal to their death and annihilation:

After five days of waiting, Ambwerk knew that something had gone awry with his brother. So, taking his bow and arrows, he went to the *wamunga* shrub, blew his spittle over it, and uttered the spell. The door opened and he went down into Nimbamung's *mwenk.* He saw the bones hanging on the porch, he recognized the head.

Ambwerk returned to his village at once. He selected a large pig and placed it on the *pekas* [plaza] in front of his house. Then he fetched bunches of areca-nuts and placed them beside the pig. All the men of the village gathered round to hear what was afoot.

Ambwerk told them about Nimbamung and what had happened to Tuman. Something would have to be done.

Next day, then, the villagers shouldered their spears and set off for Nimbamung's home. Ambwerk uttered the spell and blew his spittle over the *wamunga* shrub. The door opened and the party trooped down to the *mwenk*.

Ambwerk was first with his spear, thrusting it deep into Nimbamung's side. Then each of the others followed Ambwerk's example, turn by turn, until all had had a share in the killing. They killed Nimbamung's dog too, packed all the meat and food-stuffs they could carry into string bags, and then piled faggots around the outside of Nimbamung's house.

When the pyre was ready, they placed Nimbamung and his dog on the top and set it alight. They waited there until house, man, and dog had been entirely consumed, burnt in the flames. Then they returned to their village.

Being a tale of Two Trees with the food-trickster as cosmotact, this Tangu multiform contains the expected seven contests of conceal-ment and discovery grouped about the hewn and verdant wood. The first three sets of wood belong to Ambwerk; the same three are ex-perienced again by Tuman in imitation of his elder brother, but the fourth set is Ambwerk's alone, giving the total of seven:

Ambwerk	Tuman	Ambwerk
1. Nimbamung's axe/ grub tree	4. Nimbamung's axe/grub tree	7. *wamunga* bush as point of access/ villagers' spears
2. bamboo barrels/ *wamunga* as device of concealment	5. bamboo barrels/ *wamunga* as device of concealment	
3. Nimbamung's food-trees/wooden house	6. Nimbamung's food-trees/wooden house	

Morton Bloomfield, our enlightened modern critic, tells us "the presence of motifs in America and Australia tends to prove an earlier period of unity" than that which might be required for a less ancient process of mere 'diffusion.'[154] Acting upon his suggestion, and having looked into the outback of Australia as well as the remoter parts of Oceania, we should before leaving the Two Trees satisfy ourselves also that they have some plausibly pre-Columbian currency in the Western Hemisphere. In fact the positive evidence for this proposition is so overwhelmingly plentiful that the best proof of it I can suggest is only to have the reader of this book look into the pages of any *bona fide* published collection from native American sources. To introduce any one text as evidence here, as I now do, is a gross slight to the evidential authority of hundreds of other books less theoretical than this where good texts of Amerindian oral traditions have been published.

THE MAN WHO INVENTED AGRICULTURE

Four Jicarilla Apache men in northern New Mexico gave the American collector Morris Opler a major corpus of their traditional oral fable during the years 1934 and 1935. It is not recorded in the published results which of the four—Cevero Caramillo, John Chopari, Alasco Tisnado, or Juan Julian—told Opler the following tale:[156] *A man is left destitute by gambling losses in the hoop and pole game. He obtains an axe and finds a spruce tree near a river, which he attempts to cut down on three successive days. At sunset of each day the tree is almost felled, but he finds it whole again each morning. On the fourth day a preternatural called Black Hactcin frightens the man, asking what he is doing to the preternatural's tree. The man tells him he wants a length of log sufficient to hide himself in, and Black Hactcin then cuts down his own tree, hews the required section of trunk, and replants the leafy upper portion. This springs instantly to life and grows as before.*

Woodpeckers help the man hollow the hewn trunk, then he pays them and the preternatural for their labour. He rolls the finished log to the river, creeps inside, and spiders with the help of a swallow seal the entrance into the log with mud and web. Floating downstream inside the log, the man is stopped four times and required to pay toll for the continuation of his journey downriver inside the hollowed log.

Finally he lands in a fertile country, where he lays out a garden. Using a pointed stick, he plants the seeds of all useful vegetables. They mature in twelve days. Next he observes the flickering of a light on the opposite bank of the river on each of three successive nights, but

*cannot find the firesite on the morrow. On the fourth night he sets
a forked stick in the ground to help him divine the exact place of the
fire, and next morning he finds the young woman whose fire he has
been observing each night. Then he finds a cicada among the leaves of
a green tree and obtains from it a flute to use in wooing the woman.*

The cosmotact of this piece is the Jicarilla Apaches' mythic inventor of gardening. He is also the principal hewer of the piece, for although he sub-contracts for all the effectual carving and woodchopping
that is done in the story about him, he alone among all the story's
characters is the designer of civilization who understands the uses of
hewn wood. For each occurrence of green wood, he obtains a corresponding artifact of dry wood wrought to a civilizing purpose.

Initially impoverished by the exactly predetermined forfeits that
are the price of gambling at the (hewn) hoop and pole game, the man
retreats from the hardship imposed by the hewn wooden artifacts of
that game to the refuge of the green spruce in the wilderness. No wood
is greener than that which grows the better for being cut; four times
the hewer cuts, and each time finds the spruce as whole as if it were
not the same tree. Then in the midst of his fourth attempt he is frightened by a preternatural who at first seems to threaten him, but who
suddenly makes instead a gratuitous donation of the desired tree-trunk.
Typically of this pattern, the wood of the tree itself is free, but the
man must pay a price for the hewing; in this case, it is a fee of ritual
cornflowers explicitly described in the story as the preternatural's
wages for labour rendered.

The effect of hewing the spruce is to make the bole of the tree
mobile. Once it is cut away, it can move as few things can, both ter-
restrially and aquatically—that is, both by rolling over the ground and
by floating in the water. Its instrumentality is thus two-fold. In both
ways it is drastically different from the green top that remains behind,
replanted by the hand of the preternatural to root itself again in the
same place where formerly it had stood.

But the hewn log is no less a thing of recurrent stages than the
green tree from which it comes. The difference is that the stages of
live wood are invariably only the recurrence of new growth, while
hewing may add wholly new forms of civilized value to dead wood.
Once the Apache man's log has achieved *mobility*, it remains to be
hewn further in a way that will render it also *portative*. The woodpeckers hollow it so that the man can ride inside and share its aquatic

mobility.

Four times the green wood is hewn only to retain its verdure, and four times the man manipulates wood that is surely dead. After the sectioning and hollowing of the log for mobility and portage, the man comes into a new land where he is a self-made exile. Planting stick in hand, he plants the seeds of an Eden-like garden. Then, after using the single-pointed cut wood of his planting stick to encourage plant reproduction and the growth of *food,* the man obtains a double-pointed, forked stick to locate a nubile woman and encourage human reproduction, or the growth of *progeny.* For whereas new plant life may spring from a single seed, humans must be paired like the forked stick to reproduce their kind.

Thus for each of four green trees that uniformly keep their verdure, the Jicarilla Apache hero has four pieces of hewn wood, each yielding a different benefit according to the virtue of its proper form. Only when the pattern of the Two Trees has thus been fulfilled does the Jicarilla story-teller move on to tell of the courtship that develops between the newly discovered woman and the exiled man, between the musical cicada's green tree and hewn flute.[157]

A reader unaccustomed to the ways of oral narrative tradition may find the constancy of patterns implausible. There is really nothing like it in Western literature. The more schooled and learned the reader, the more deeply suspicious he is likely to be, and the quicker to call eccentric anyone who insists upon the critical importance of constant patterns. Common readers of 'uneducated' literary tastes usually find constancy of pattern appealing in fiction, but bookish men with modernistic and *avant-garde* predilections are good at communicating their distrust and dislike of it. Have not the great authors of Western literary tradition achieved their greatness by avoiding repetition?

And yet oral tradition does not simply repeat itself. Its bearers throughout the world continually reconstruct it according to patterns that have been proven the most potent vehicles of meaning over periods of time and diversities of culture that dwarf the duration and scope of any literary tradition in the world. The resultant pervasive resonance of each ethnic oral tradition with every genre of oral fable in other ethnic traditions is an achievement for which written literature is both far too young and technically ill-suited. The literary bushel is bad measure for oral fable.

A HANDSOME HUNTER-BOY

On the basis of her experience as a collector of 'myth' from the Zuni pueblo in the southwestern United States, Ruth Benedict has written so forcefully about the ethnic idiosyncracy of oral fable that one dare not pass over her collection when trying to ascertain the generic features which American Indian folklore shares with that of peoples elsewhere.* One distinctively Zuni story in her collection was *The Hunter Transformed into Coyote.* The version of this Zuni pueblo tale which she collected and published was, she said, "particularly satisfactory from the point of view of the Zuni story teller." It gave satisfaction because, as she commented, much of its content occurred also in other Zuni stories, and because the arrangement of that content in her version gave especial scope to elaboration of narrative incidents that were well-known and widely liked among Indians of the Zuni pueblo. The familiarity and ready acceptability of her version's content to the Zuni mind marked it as typically Zuni folklore to Benedict's way of thinking:

> The *Transformation into Coyote* is a favorite Zuni incident and enters into a number of plots. It is the conclusion of Deer Boy, in three of the four Zuni versions. . . ; it is the conclusion of a tale of the despised child who gains a patron in Coyote and becomes a great hunter. . ., and in this [version] it is the initial incident of a contest with a false friend. The present version is particularly satisfactory from the point of view of the Zuni story teller because it gives opportunity for developing the theme of the hunter's revenge upon his false friend, a theme implied in the incident but not possible to develop when the incident is used as a conclusion. In the present tale, on the other hand, the revenge upon the false friend becomes the climax. . . . The hunter's life with the hospitable Spider Woman and her grandchild, the pursuit by Toothed Vagina Woman, and the *Killed by co-habitation* are introduced as experiences of the hunter's exile from human intercourse, and he obtains the power of Echo Man to turn his enemy into a like impersonation, a favorite incident.†

But whereas Ruth Benedict discerned in such Zuni tales as this the quintessence of Zuni taste and Zuni-ness, we must discern in the Zuni *Hunter Transformed into Coyote* the essence of its broader humanity, the international and prehistoric narrative pattern (among others) of

———————————

* See above, pages 315-317 et seq., in the present volume.

† Ruth Benedict, *Zuni Mythology*, vol. 2, New York (Columbia University Press), 1935, pps. 110-121, and notes, pps. 285-286.

the Two Trees and the food-trickster that unite it absolutely with the ancient and universal human tradition of oral fable. For in the final analysis, even ethnic uniqueness and the incommensurability of every distinct people's distinctive way of life with any other is itself a fiction in oral tradition conveyed by ancient and universal patterns of fable no different in kind from the Two Trees or the other fabulous patterns treated in this book. The names, the sequences, and the motives in Ruth Benedict's favorite Zuni story are incontestibly Zuni, but the tale itself is the one, familiar to all mankind, about hunger and food, concealment and discovery, donation and price, unity and rift, reversal of fortune, trickster and arch-trickster, the green wood and the hewn. . . .

Two hunters, the one consanguinously and the other fictively related to the same girl, go hunting together, but their ostensible shared purpose of obtaining food from the wild is soon displaced by a deep rivalry in acts of transformation, hiding, and disclosure. Emotional impetuosity, gratuity, and a specious unity that is soon shattered develop as usual under a standing tree:

> The people were living at Matsaka. The hunter was handsome and his father was loved by all the people. He had a close friend. One day they went hunting. The handsome boy went to his brother's house. His (friend's) sister was making cornmeal mush balls. His brother said, "Sister, is our lunch ready?" "Yes." She rolled the mush balls in the boy's blanket. The boy said to his friend, "I am ready now, brother." They went to the south to Slit Rocks and separated to hunt for rabbits. The handsome boy killed eight and returned first to the meeting place. He fell asleep waiting for his friend. The witch boy killed only three. He came back and saw his friend asleep under the tree with eight rabbits. He said to himself, "I wish I had your rabbits. When you wake up I will ask you to give me three of your catch." He touched the boy. "Did you come?" "Yes. I think people at home will be waiting for us." They ate their mush balls. The witch boy said, "Brother, how did you kill so many?" "My eyes are straight." "Give me three. I am ashamed to go in and let the people see that I have three and you have eight." The handsome boy made no answer. He got up and laid one of his rabbits beside the witch boy's three. Immediately he started for home. He was angry. When they reached the pueblo the hunter did not stop in his friend's house. The witch boy thought to himself, "I was jealous when he killed so many rabbits but I will not think of that any more." He took his rabbit blanket and threw it about him and went to his friend's house. The hunters' father and mother received him kindly. The witch boy said, "Shall we hunt again tomorrow?" "Yes." "Come to my house tomorrow." "Yes." "We shall go to sleep now so that we shall be fresh in the morning." The boy went to his own house.

To alleviate the inequity of portion at the green tree in the wilderness, the witch boy next day adopts a strategem with hewn (cedar and yucca) wood. Formerly a bosom friend, witch boy suddenly and stealthily becomes the handsome hunter's enemy in an unexpected reversal of fortune. His enmity is expressed in a seemingly kindly act of largesse (helping the handsome hunter to a prodigiously bountiful catch of game); but the apparent benevolence conceals an actual malevolence, and instead of being the hunter (or eater), the handsome youth finds himself the hunted (in instant jeopardy of being eaten by other, animal hunters) while he himself goes destitute of anything fit to eat:

> As soon as he had eaten his morning meal the hunter went to his friend's house. They went again to Slit Rocks but a little to the east. They separated to hunt. The witch boy bewitched his friend so that he caught nothing. The witch boy also killed nothing. They returned at lunch time and ate their mush balls. The witch boy said, "I know what we can do so that we may kill many rabbits easily." "What is that?" "I shall teach you." The witch boy tore a cedar branch and tied it into a hoop with yucca fibre. He hilled up the dirt and set the hoop upright. "I shall teach you, my brother. This is the way we kill rabbits easily." The witch boy ran through the hoop and immediately he was a coyote. He returned and ran through the hoop again. Immediately he was a person once more. "See what we shall do. There is no danger. When you run through the hoop again you become a person immediately." "I see." The hunter ran through the hoop and was transformed into a coyote, and the witch boy also. They went hunting. The hunter killed eighteen rabbits and the witch boy killed ten and they brought them to the tree. The witch boy said, "I am going a little to the west and I shall call you." When his friend was out of sight the witch boy went back to the hoop and took his own shape again. He tore up the hoop and scattered the branches about. He took all the rabbits they had both killed and started for home. "Ha, you've got what you deserved. You hurt my feelings yesterday. Today they are healed." When he reached his own house he took up eight rabbits and said to his sister, "My sister, take these rabbits to my brother's father. His son went to hunt with the Kakima people. He will be back in ten days." His sister took them to the hunter's house. The father and mother of the hunter greeted her and made her sit down. She said, "My brother has gone to hunt with the Kakima people. My (own) brother brought these rabbits home to you for him." The father and mother mourned and said, "Poor child, he has to hunt with other people's lunches. He hasn't any of his own."
>
> When Coyote was hungry he came to the place where he had jumped through the hoop. He saw the branches scattered about. All the rabbits were gone. He knew what had happened. He saw the witch boy's tracks going back to the pueblo. It began to get dark. He lay under the tree. "I wish there were somebody around here. I shall go to find somebody." His

heart was thumping. He ran till he was close to the pueblo. The dogs smell-
ed him and chased him. He ran all the way back to Slit Rocks and lay down.
He was tired. In the morning he was starved and thirsty. He ate worms and
beetles. . . .

The witch boy's timely destruction of the cedar and yucca hoop
temporarily arrests the reciprocal effect by which he should experience
the same injury he has devised unjustly to punish the friend of whom
he is jealous. But the reciprocity persists nonetheless, and is only so
much the more devastating for being delayed. Furthermore, another
ritual contraption of cedar and yucca is a vehicle of the penalty when
it is finally visited upon the wrongdoer. The wronged innocent returns
from exile to reestablishment of himself, however, and to a civilized
revenge against the food-trickster, through not one but a series of
hewn woods.

Coyote takes refuge at Vulva Spring on Corn Mountain. There
Little Spider discovers him and reveals his whereabouts to Spider
Grandmother. She uses her stirring stick (hewn) to remove Coyote's
skin and so restore the handsome boy to his proper human form. She
also donates her (deceased) husband's bow and arrow (hewn) to him,
and he goes with Little Spider to hunt birds at Vulva Spring. Little
Spider is frightened and hides while the handsome hunter shoots blue-
birds for dinner, but emerges when the killing is over.

Next day the boy attempts more ambitious game—antelope—and
proceeds alone beyond the springs on Corn Mountain to Peach Or-
chard (green). There, from behind a small tree (green), he shoots a
first antelope. But portage of the kill is difficult and delays him until
with the help of a yucca headband (hewn) he is able to carry it to his
foster-home with the Spiders.

Again he hunts antelope on Corn Mountain, but as he is about to
shoulder his second kill he notices blood falling onto (rather than from)
the meat. Looking up, he sees Toothed Vagina Woman above him in a
pinyon tree (green), whence she is dropping her menstrual discharge
onto his game. She demands sexual intercourse with him, but he flees
through seven ritual performances in seven different settlements until
late at night he reaches Goat Man, who subdues the female monster.
Next day the hunter returns to Grandmother Spider unharmed.

She sends the hunter to fetch home to her the previous day's kill
of antelope. Then she constructs a rack (hewn) consisting of a long
cedar pole (which the hunter supplies) with cross bars of cedar attach-
ed by means of yucca fiber. On this the hunter carries the copious

jerked meat from his last kill of antelope home to his native place at Matsaka. On the way he obtains a baton from Grandfather Echo, and this he uses after his return home to transform his old rival the witch boy permanently into a kachina (spirit being), Echo Man. As part of the ritual whereby Echo Man is irreversibly banished from living Zuni society to dwell in Kachina Village, the whole population make prayer-sticks (hewn) from willow wands tied with yucca fiber.

Thus in the end the hewn wood accomplishes its task as the instrument of civilized equity and reciprocity. As the witch boy used it to punish the great hunter by exiling him to that capacity alone (to be in the form of Coyote nothing else but a hunting creature), so reciprocally the handsome hunter uses it to punish a great usurper of the property of others by banishment to that function alone (to be in the form of Echo Man nothing else but a usurper of others' voices and utterance). A proper cosmotact, by means of the hewn wood the handsome hunter finally metes out to the ogre of his story the same injury that ogre had theretofore inflicted on others; or, as the Zuni *conteur* himself said all the people of Matsaka had said, ' "He started it and now it has happened to him. He has got what he wished to do to other people.' "

The seven-fold contest of concealments and disclosures is also reproduced in this Zuni tale. While he is outward-bound—moving away from his native place at Matsaka towards ever increasing perils and expandingly fabulous monsters—the handsome hunter moves always within the contrast between green and hewn wood. His homeward journey, however, is attended only by hewn wood:

Handsome Hunter Outward-bound

1. *Green tree:* yes
   Contestants: witch boy and handsome hunter
   Hewn wood: hoop of cedar and yucca fiber

2. *Green tree:* yes
   Contestants: Coyote and the Spiders
   Hewn wood: stirring stick

3. *Green tree:* Peach Orchard
   Contestants: hunter and antelope
   Hewn wood: Spider's bow and arrow

4. *Green tree:* pinyon tree
   Contestants: hunter and Toothed Vagina Woman
   Hewn wood: yucca headband (instrument of portage)

Handsome Hunter Homeward-bound

5. *Green tree:* none
   Contestants: returning hunter and the Zuni community
   Hewn wood: venison pole of cedar and yucca (instrument of portage)

6. *Green tree:* none
   Contestants: returned hunter and witch boy
   Hewn wood: Echo Man's baton

7. *Green tree:* none
   Contestants: witch boy (as Echo Man) and the Zuni community
   Hewn wood: prayersticks (willow and yucca)

A YOUNG MAN OF SALINAS

Lest anyone suppose that in the New World the Two Trees are a pattern only in North American Indian fable, it should be witnessed elsewhere in the Western Hemisphere too. The Zinacantecos in the Mexican province of Chiapas are claimed by some to be the modern continuators of many traits that have persisted in Mayan Indian culture since pre-Columbian times. One of their oral fables collected by Robert M. Laughlin in the 1960s provides an obvious Central American multiform of our arboreal pattern. The Zinacantecos' principal English-speaking ethnographer, Evon Vogt, has described the story in these words[158]:

This tale describes the events that led to the construction of the Catholic chapel in the hamlet of Salinas (?Ats'am), commonly called "Salinitas" in this myth. The three sisters that have now become important saints in Zinacantan Center, Ixtapa and Salinas each had to have their "homes" built. The eldest sister is the Virgen del Rosario in the church of San Lorenzo in Zinacantan Center; the middle sister is the Virgin in Ixtapa (a municipio that borders Zinacantan on the west). This left the youngest sister without a house until she persuaded the young Zinacanteco who was out working his small field to assemble his relatives and build a small "cow house" (an old type of Zinacanteco house) for her across the river from the present chapel in Salinas. It seems the ground was soggy on this side of the river and there were floods. So the people built a better house for her on dry ground across the river and installed the hollowed-out log on top of the salt well behind the chapel. The myth weaves together the three settlements

involved in the salt industry that has been important for the Zinacantecos
since before the Conquest.

*The Holy Mother of Salinas meets a lone young man in an un-
inhabited place and suggests that she would like to settle in that district. She asks him to meet her again in fifteen days to tell her whether he and the other men of his hamlet will donate their labour to
build her a house there. He agrees to the proposed meeting, but asks
where exactly he should expect to find her when they rendezvous.
She tells him that she will be the preternatural at a green tree which
bears herbaceous food and will make a gift to men of a hitherto unexploited bounty:*

> "I'm coming here to sit beneath the avocado *[tree]*,
> Here, beneath the avocado,
> There I'll come to sit,
> Ah, but you understand,
> If they want,
> I will bring something."

*Her gift is the merchantable salt of the salt-well now at Salinas. Once
the men of the hamlet have received this donation, however, the rule
of gratuity and the green tree are to cease. They are to exact a recompense for their salt in their civilized commerce with other people.
Hewn wood and its generic meaning of compensation are accordingly
invoked in the preternatural's next words to her human messenger:*

> "I want them to make the hollowed-out log for our salt,
> Our salt will be born,
> You will prepare our salt, you understand,
> You will look for your money,
> You look for your half *reales*."

*The preternatural lady of the green avocado tree explains that she is
being separated from the society of her sisters, but that her severance
from them can be the occasion of a new unity centered on her chapel
at Salinas. All that is needed is a spirit of gratuitous hospitality toward
her when she next appears under her verdant tree:*

> "I am the youngest sister,
> My older sister is the one in Hteklum,
> My younger sister is in Ixtapa," she said.
> "My older sister is content now,
> She is living there now,

> She has her house now,
> Her house is already built,
> But the men there accepted her command,
> . . .
> Now I would like,
> I want my house too,
> If you will be so very kind,
> If you will build my house."

Like all her kind, this denizen of green wood also seems capable of unlooked-for largesse at one moment and a lethal threat at the next. She is an absolute mistress of concealments and revelations, mazing the minds of mortals. When she has finished her speech to the man who met her alone in the wilderness, she vanishes from sight:

> You see, that's just the way he was spoken to,
> Just like that;
> The boy didn't see where the woman went;
> "Ah, was it a real person,
> Was it a person who told me she wanted a house,
> Couldn't it have been some dirty business,
> Something casting sickness on me,
> If I were to die of this," said the man.
> "Ah, I guess I'll go chat first with my mother and my
>   father,
> See what they tell me,
> If it's a caster of sickness [a witch],
> If they tell me it's something bad,
> Then certainly it's terrible,
> It isn't good at all," said the awful boy. [sic]

Time and again the Zinacanteco *conteur* reiterated the antiphony of green wood and hewn. When the preternatural lady returned to keep her appointment with the people of Salinas,

> Then she landed under the avocado, leaning against it;
> Our Holy Mother jumped out
> When her house was flooded, it seems,
> Now there is made one hollow log now;
> Long ago the hollow log.

The hewn log is the occasion of civilized communal life in Zinacantan just as elsewhere, and music is contingent on it no less than

for King Orfeo or the mythic Jicarilla Apache inventor of gardening.
Here too music is played for the lady of the green tree:

> They made a new hollow log here on this side,
> For there they took out the salt water,
> It is soggy on the other side of the river,
> So it passed over here to this side of the river,
> So now there is a hollow log there till now;
> They hold a fiesta,
> There is the Fiesta of the Rosary,
> The musicians enter, descend, whatever they do,
> Again and again;
> There is a fiesta,
> For that is what our Holy Mother wants.

THE BROTHER-IN-LAW OF TEČWARE

The Apinayé, a native Amazonian people of Brazil, had a tale
about a preternatural named Tečware which the Brazilian collector
Curt Nimuendajú noted in the 1930s.[159] It is a good brief example of
the Two Trees in native South American fable, and it is about a mortal contest of deception between two affinally related males.

*Tečware, whose name means "sharpened-leg," went with his
brother-in-law to the woods to hunt. While they are resting by their
fire at night, Tečware thrusts his leg into the fire and burns off his
foot. He throws the charred foot at a piquy tree, then wakens his
sleeping relative and sends him to collect the fruit which he says has
just fallen from the tree so that they can roast and eat it. The brother-
in-law looks for the fruit in vain; meanwhile Tečware whittles his shin-
bone to a sharp point. In the morning he attempts to stab his brother-
in-law to death with his sharpened leg bone, but the latter escapes to
the village where he reports the incident to his fellow citizens.*

*Tečware stealthily invades the village and kills sleeping men on
subsequent nights. The survivors paint a log from the trunk of a mamohy tree to give it the appearance of a man; Tečware attacks it at
night but the sharp point of his leg-bone sticks in the hewn wood
preventing his escape, and the citizens beat him to death. They behead
the corpse, but the head is still alive and gets away into the woods. It
begins to kill people in broad daylight. The villagers trap the head in
a pitfall, cudgel it to death with clubs, and bury it deep so that it will
not murder again. A mangaba tree rises from the grave.*

The preternatural's green piquy tree in the wilderness seems by night to offer its mortal visitor a gratuitous bounty of herbaceous food, but by day it is the scene of a sudden, unexpected, and nearly successful attempt on his life. Contrastingly, the hewn mamohy log set up to give the appearance of a man in the middle of the village is a calculated implement of civilization devised to impose the law of retribution on a murderous ogre who is heedless of the boundary between a civilized precinct and his own lawless zone of wilderness. Himself suspiciously like green wood (which grows the better for being hewn), Tečware at the fruiting piquy tree is immune to the law that levies an unalterable price of pain and crippling upon any ordinary man who might willfully or otherwise burn his foot to the bone. But Tečware at the hewn mamohy log pays the civilized price of death for his own acts of murder.

Again as though he were himself a thing of live wood, Tečware when his head is hewn off only grows stronger and more terrible for the cutting. Now he does not even keep to the concealment of night, but reveals himself to commit his gratuitous murders in broad daylight. When the villagers armed with clubs seek him in the green woods, he darts among them untouched by their attempts to hit him and so stop his vicious mobility. Only when they return to the civilized precinct of their roadways and dig pitfalls along the edges of the roads are the villagers successful, for only when he attempts to cross out of the wild and invades the roads is Tečware finally laid low under the blows of men manipulating wooden cudgels. Yet even then the mangaba tree rises green over the place where he is confined in the earth.

AHZUAK

In conclusion to this Appendix, it must also be observed that the want of forests or of real trees in nature has nowhere diminished the force or plenitude of the Two Trees' pattern in oral fable. No people on earth is without *knowledge* of live trees and hewn wood, no matter how devoid of real wood their immediate surroundings may be, or have become. The valley of the Kobuk River in northern Alaska, emptying (when it is not frozen solid) into the lower Chukchi Sea north of the Bering Straits, lies entirely in tundra. The Eskimo native to the valley of the Kobuk accordingly had less choice as to their nominal motifs of trees than did the Tangu in New Guinea or the Apinayé in the Amazonian rain-forest, where trees of multitudinous species are still more firmly in possession of the land than man is. Thus any standing wood frequented by a preternatural in Eskimo fable is likely to be some variety of *Salicaceae,* while wood for hafts and other hewn artifacts comes mostly (and plentifully enough) from the sea as driftwood.

An Eskimo man named Ohyahock told Clark Garber the following tale, which Garber gave the title "The Lost Sons of the Kobuk."[182]

Far up toward the headwaters of the Kobuk River, many sleeps from the ocean, there lived a man and wife who had one child, a little son. Near them lived a man who had neither wife nor child. At the time of this story, the little boy was about eight winters old. Being the only son and only child in the little colony, he was greatly loved by his father and mother and all the other people of the village. If no more children came to them, they would at least have one son to place offerings on their graves when they should go beyond this world to the "Land of Happiness." When the little boy was about ten winters old, his proud father made him a small kayak, an exact model of the one he used for hunting seal . With the help of their kindly neighbor, the little boy was taught how to balance himself in it and paddle the little kayak swiftly over the water. His neighbor, who thought no less of the little boy than his own parents, made him a small spear like the one his father used for seal. Thereafter the little boy hunted ducks and geese on the lakes and river, and was very proud when he brought his game home and added it to the family larder.

Some winters later, when the little boy had grown to be a young man, he had in his heart a longing to see the world beyond and there to seek adventures. One day, while hunting seal in the river, he decided to see what kind of country lay beyond the limits of his hunting ground. Following the river toward its source, he came to a place where a tall clump of willows grew along the river bank. He drew to the shore and pulled his kayak up on the beach just far enough that it would not drift away, but would still be at hand in case of sudden need. Near the willows he found a well-beaten trail. Curious to know where it would lead him, he followed it until he came around a sharp bend. There in the dense growth of willows he suddenly disappeared and was never to see his people again.

The Eskimo hunter's dilemma in dealing with the mysterious preternatural at the green tree is as for his counterparts everywhere, how to be a predator without becoming prey. To accomplish this he must excel as manipulator of hewn artifacts—in this Eskimo tale, the wooden-framed kayak and wooden-hafted hunting spear. Two other sons go to their weird fates the same way as the first, making a total of three victims before the hero is born who will have the requisite skill. Ohyahock did not even bother to name the three sons who were slain, but the fourth and fifth sons merited naming. The fourth did not go to the green wood at all, but remained as provider of manipulatable hewn wood to the fifth son. Having both the advantage of his strong, stay-at-home elder brother's support (cultural superiority) and an innately greater skill and strength of his own (natural superiority), the fifth brother is destined to be the ogre-slayer. A proper cosmotact, he metes out to the ogres of his story the same injury they have inflicted previously on his people:

. . .The fourth son, who had been given the name of *Oakpone*, blood in a poke, was an unusually large and strong boy. When he was only eight winters old, he begged his father to make him a kayak so that he might hunt ducks and geese on the lakes and river. His father, mindful of the loss of his first three sons, did not want to make his fourth son a kayak in which he might meet the same fate. But Oakpone would give his father no rest. He begged so persistently that his father finally agreed to build the much-desired kayak.

The fifth son to be born to these parents was called *Ahzuak*, black berries. He was only two winters younger than the fourth son. When he became old enough to hunt, his brother, the fourth son, wanted him to have a kayak so they could go hunting together. His skill with the kayak and the spear was much greater than the skill of his brothers before him. His father had refused to build a kayak for him because he did not want to loose his two remaining sons at the same time. Ahzuak secretly practiced with his brother's kayak and weapons so that he might soon go in search of his three lost brothers.

Early one morning, Ahzuak took the kayak belonging to his brother Oakpone and paddled swiftly up the river. As his strong arms paddled him farther and farther from home, he wondered why his three older brothers had never returned. So much did he think upon this problem that he finally decided to follow the river and search for them. Far up the river, he came upon some strange and terrible animals. He tried to evade them but they attacked and tried to kill him. But Ahzuak's great skill with the spear saved his life. After battling with the monsters all day long he finally succeeded in killing them. Then he thought that these terrible animals must have killed his three brothers so he continued to hunt them and killed all he could find.

After several more sleeps, he came to the trail through the willows. When he had followed this trail for some distance, he came upon three kayaks hidden in the brush. They looked just like his own kayak, so he knew that his father had made them and that they belonged to his three lost brothers. Seeing that his brothers must have taken this trail he cautiously followed it through the overhanging willows. At length he came to a large and strange looking *innie*. Suspecting that his brothers had met foul play here, he stealthily entered the place. Resting on the floor of the *innie* and leaning against the wall, he saw the heads of his brothers. But they did not speak to him because their heads had been severed from their bodies. Strangely there seemed to be life in their eyes. They tried to warn him to leave the *innie* as quickly as possible. They seemed to tell him, that danger lurked within the walls of this place. Ahzuak had but one purpose in his mind. That was to find his lost brothers, so he gave no heed to the warning. As he came farther into the *innie,* he saw an old woman, who was unusually large, sitting in a corner. To the woman Ahzuak said, "you are the evil one who has killed all my brothers."

"Yes, yes," replied the old woman. "One has been waiting a long time for the meat of a young hunter. One will kill you and place your head beside the heads of your brothers," said the evil old woman as she began to crawl toward Ahzuak.

Ahzuak was ready and waiting for this move. With a powerful thrust of his spear, he drove it through the evil one's body killing her. Then out of fear that some strange magic might overcome him, he quietly withdrew from the evil place and stealthily followed the trail through the willows. He found his kayak lying on the beach where he had left it. But before placing his kayak in the water, he brought the kayaks of his three brothers from the brush and tied them fast behind his own. Soon he was gliding swiftly toward home towing the kayaks of his three lost brothers behind him.

With the river current in his favor, he reached the village of his people in the middle of the following night. Straight to the *cosegy* he went. There he sounded the alarm on the big ceremonial drum calling all the people together. At length all the people were assembled and then Ahzuak, with much pride, recounted his experiences and adventure. Thereafter the people could hunt far up the river without fear of the man-eating monsters and the evil old witch-woman who had killed and eaten all young hunters passing her way.

KASILUN

For my last example of the Two Trees, I turn once again to Mesopotamia, where the virtually total destruction of arboreal life by man and the flooding rivers was already complete before the beginning of history—and of all places on this planet history is there most ancient. The following tale is from Arab tradition in Baghdad in the third decade of the twentieth century.[183] The stick *Al Madhūna* with its power to enforce civilized reciprocity (robbing the cannibal robbers) and the reversals of fortune between mutually self-concealing human guest (cosmotact) and preternatural hosts at the coppice of green trees are typologically so pure and obvious that they need after the previous discussion in this Appendix no comment beyond the bare evidence of the tale itself.

There was once an industrious woman who earned a living for herself and her family by carding cotton. Her husband earned nothing, for he was a lazy lout who did nothing but sleep in the courtyard of the house, and never went without. All that he did was to clamour for food, and if his wife did not bring it to him, he would beat her with his thick stick, which he kept greased with fat stolen from her kitchen. This stick he called *Al Madhūna*, 'the Greased One', and if she dared to reproach him for his laziness, he would reply 'Bring me the Greased One', and as he was powerful and strong she quickly stopped her scolding and ran off lest she should be beaten.

One day when she was in the market, she told a friend of her troubles, and complained that her husband had become an intolerable burden.

The friend was a wise woman, and said to her, 'Endure his laziness no longer! When he has left the house, lock the door and refuse to let him enter until he comes with money in his hand!'

The cotton-carder said, 'How shall that be, seeing that he never leaves the house. He never leaves our courtyard, faith, the whole day he sleeps!'

Said the old woman, 'Has he a favorite dish, my sister?'

Said the cotton-carder, 'He is very fond of pācha.'

Said the old woman, 'He is a dog, the son of a dog, and like the dogs must be led by the nose. Cook some pācha and throw it outside the door and entice him into the street, and then close the door upon him.'

The cotton-carder followed the advice of her wise friend and bought some pācha, which she cooked very succulently. When it was ready, she scattered a little in the courtyard near the corner where her husband slept, and the rest outside the door of the house.

Then she shook him, and while he was yawning and still half asleep, she cried, '*Ya* Kasilun [Lazy-Bones]! See! In the night it has rained pacha!'

He rubbed his eyes and took up the pacha and began to eat.

'Leave this here,' cried his wife, 'Go outside, there is abundance there, and if we don't get it, the neighbours will eat it!'

So he ran to the door, and while the stupid fellow was still gathering up the pacha and cramming it into his mouth, his wife closed the door upon him and bolted it.

'Hey wife,' cried Kasilun, 'I have picked up pacha enough—come and get the rest. Open the door, I want to go to sleep again.'

'No, not I!' replied the cotton-carder from within the door. 'I will not open to you until you return, as a man should, with money in your pocket!'

'Bring me the Greased One!' shouted Kasilun in a great rage, and when she threw him the stick from a window, he rattled at the door and made such a noise that the neighbours gathered to laugh at him. At last, mad with anger, he set off, all bareheaded as he was, and walked far into the desert.

At nightfall, when he was far from Baghdad, he saw a fire, and as he was cold and hungry, he went towards it. Round the fire were sitting seven 'afarit [demons], and upon the fire a pot was boiling. Now 'afarit are addicted to human flesh, and when they saw Kasilun approaching, they said, 'Here is good fortune! This man will make us a meal tomorrow!'

As for Kasilun, when he saw the pot and smelt the hot meat, he was very pleased, for he had eaten nothing since the pacha that morning; so, approaching them, he wished them peace. They gave him the salutation, and invited him to join them.

Said he, 'I will eat with pleasure, for since it rained pacha this morning, I have not eaten a crumb!' and so saying, he dipped his frozen fingers in the pot and drawing out the lamb that seethed therein, he tore it in half, and devoured it.

After he had eaten he fell asleep, and the 'afarit, seeing how fat and big he was, decided to kill him next day so that they would have fresh meat to last them for some time.

The next morning they roused him and said, 'We are going to kill meat soon; go, take this water-skin and fill it with water and return to us so that we can fill the pot ready for the boiling.'

'This will never do,' thought Kasilun when he saw the big skin that they gave him to fill. 'They will make a water-carrier of me!' So when he reached the river, he bent as if he were filling it, but in reality he put his lips to it and blew until it was swollen with air and appeared full to the brim, Then, tying it, he began to return with the skin on his shoulders. The 'afarit expected to see him bowed under the weight of the water, but lo! he walked as if the skin were but a feather. When he was near their tents, however, he sat down, and putting his mouth to the skin, he made as though he were emptying it, and did so until the skin was deflated.

'What sort of man is this?' said the 'afarit. 'He drinks more at a draught than an ordinary man in a week!'

They went up to him, and when he saw them, he said that he had drunk the water and was still thirsty, and would go down and refill the skin.

'We will send one of our number,' said the 'afarit. 'But as you are a strong fellow, we will send you to get the wood to make fire for the pot.'

'Where shall I find the wood?' asked Kasilun.

'There is a coppice of trees at a little distance from here. One of us will show you were it is.'

'This is very bad,' thought Kasilun, 'they are making a beast of burden of me!' and he asked for a very long rope. When they had reached the coppice, he said to the 'afrit who had accompanied him, 'Take this end of the rope and walk around the coppice and come back with it here.'

'Why must I do that?' asked the 'afrit, but Kasilun insisted, and as the 'afrit was afraid of the strength of a man who could drink a water-skin at a draught, he did what was required of him. Then Kasilun tied the two ends of the rope and bent his back.

'Now we have tied the wood together,' said he, 'hoist it on my back!'

'How can I hoist living trees!' cried the 'afrit.

'That is nothing,' said Kasilun. 'I shall do the real work when I carry it back! Hoist the wood on my back and be quick about it!'

'But,' said the 'afrit, 'we only want a few faggots!'

Then Kasilun pretended to be very angry. 'What is this?' he said. 'You refuse to hoist a few light trees on to my back? Am I to do all the work? Then I refuse to carry them at all!'

He went back to the camp and told his story as if he were in the utmost indignation.

The 'afarit became more than ever afraid of him when they heard he had wanted to carry the coppice on his back, and made up their minds to kill him in the night when he was asleep, lest he should prove too much for them.

So that night they took him to their house, and pretending to welcome him, they put him into the best room.

'There is something in this,' thought Kasilun, who had become suspicious of their intentions, and, when night came, instead of sleeping beneath the fur mantle which they gave him to cast over himself, he went and hid in the oven, from which hiding-place he contrived to overhear his hosts discussing their plot of killing him.

As soon as he understood plainly their intention, he went back to the room, arranged the fur mantle over some carpets so that it had the appearance of a sleeping man, and hid himself in another part of the house. At midnight, the 'afarit came with daggers and sticks and attacked the heap all at once, and went out making sure that their guest was dead.

In the morning, Kasilun greeted them as if nothing had happened, and told them that he had been a little disturbed by mosquito-bites during the night, but that towards morning he had slept soundly.

The 'afarit then resolved on a fresh attempt to kill him. They had in their house a cupboard lined with scimitars, which closed upon the victim when a button was touched without. But Kasilun overheard their plan from his hiding-place in the oven, and made up his mind that they should die in their own trap. The next day they led him to the door of the cupboard and told him that if he went in, he would find gold and treasure, which would be his from henceforth.

'I am a big man,' said Kasilun, 'and I could not get into the cupboard.'

The 'afarit assured him that he could. 'Why,' said they, 'it would hold six of us!'

'I will believe that when I see it,' said Kasilun.

So in they went, and when they were safely inside, he pressed the button and the knives closed and killed them.

There was only one 'afrit left, and Kasilun began to think that as he had disposed of the others so easily, he need not fear him. Indeed the case was entirely otherwise, as the 'afrit came to him and implored him to save his life, saying that if he did so he would show him where his brothers had kept their treasure, for it had been their practice to rob caravans in the desert and take possession of the goods of their victims after they had killed and eaten them.

Kasilun filled a large sack with the stolen gold, and told the 'afrit to carry it, for he was going back to his home. Thus they set off together; Kasilun clad in the rich robes which he had found amongst the stolen goods, and the 'afrit walking behind him like his servant with the sack of gold on his shoulders.

'Life in the desert does not suit me,' said Kasilun to the 'afrit. "There is too much hard work there! One is better off in a town.'

At nightfall he came to his house in the city, knocked at the door, and bade his wife open, telling her that he had returned bringing her some money.

Though she could scarcely believe him, the cotton-carder opened the door.

'Here is a guest, wife,' said Kasilun; 'and here is a sack of gold. Make us a good meal, for I have hardly had a bite since I went away.'

The cotton-carder prepared a sumptuous meal and they spent three days in feasting and music.

At the end of the three days the 'afrit said to Kasilun, 'I want to have a furwa [a skin cloak or coat with the hair inside] made, for it is cold.'

Said Kasilun, 'Go to Hasan the tailor, he will make you a furwa.'

The 'afrit went and gave the order to the tailor, but each time the 'afrit went to see if the furwa was ready, the tailor answered 'Tomorrow!' At last the 'afrit went to Kasilun and said, 'The tailor will not make the furwa that I need for my journey.'

Kasilun said to the 'afrit, 'Tell him you are the guest of Kasilun, and that he must hurry with the work.'

The 'afrit went to the tailor and said, 'I am the guest of Kasilun, and you must hurry to finish the furwa!'

The tailor knew Kasilun as a good-for-nothing and lazy man, and when the 'afrit said this, he began to laugh in the 'afrit's face, saying, 'I am not afraid of Kasilun! He is always asleep! Come, we will go together, and will talk to him in his own house!'

So the tailor and the 'afrit went together to Kasilun's house, and the tailor knocked at the door and calling to Kasilun bade him open the door as he was not afraid of him. When Kasilun heard, he roared out to his wife, 'Wife, bring me the Greased One!' And the tailor had his hand on the door to open it, the 'afrit being beside him. When the 'afrit heard Kasilun call for his stick, however, he pulled the tailor back in fear, and Kasilun coming out and seizing the tailor by the other hand, the tailor was torn in two pieces, and the 'afrit took one half and ran away in mortal fear and never came back!

Notes

1 Erwin Panofsky, "The History of Art as a Humanistic Discipline," in: *The Meaning of the Humanities*, T. M. Greene, ed., Princeton (Princeton University Press) 1940, 92-94.

2 Jerome R. Mintz, *Legends of the Hasidim*, Chicago (Chicago University Press) 1968. 389-390.

3 This entire tale is in: Clement M. Doke, *Lamba Folk-Lore*, New York (American Folk-Lore Society) 1927, pps. 192-201.

4 This is the Lamba word meaning: 'persons of Lamba ethnic identity.' The singular is *Umulamba*.

5 This is the Lamba word meaning: 'a person of Lamba ethnic identity.'

6 Doke, *Lamba Folk-Lore*, p. 193.

7 Unless otherwise noted, all quotations from the Bible appearing in this book are drawn from the Jerusalem Bible. I do not, however, share the opinion of the Jerusalem Bible's editors that "the story of Samson supposes the existence of an historical personage. . . " Other evidence than the story itself may suppose that, but the evidence of the international tale pattern as adduced in this book strongly argues to my mind the superfluity of any supposition about real historical persons not only in connection with Samson but also in connection with the several other Old Testament characters whose tales follow the same fabulous patterns as his.

8 Doke, *Lamba Folk-Lore*, p. 195.

9 Ibid., p. xiii.

10 This is the Lamba name for their own country.

11 Doke, 304-305.

12 Ibid., 126-131.

13 Ibid., 34-39.

14 Ibid., 140-143.

15 As particular frequenters of human and animal bodies, food, carrion, and excrement, the flies would of course be most likely to gather in large numbers to 'eat' rather than to be eaten, thus sharing in their own way in the essential paradox peculiar to the generic motif of Chilubwelubwe's tree.

16 Doke, 8-11.

17 Fr. Klaeber, ed., *Beowulf and the Fight at Finnsburg*, Boston (D. C. Heath and Company) 1950. 51-52.

18 Ibid., 53.

19 Ibid., 57-58.

20 Ibid., 61.

21 Ibid., 58-59.

22 Chicago (University of Chicago Press) 1962.

23 London (Kegan Paul, Trench, Trubner & Co.) 1921.

24 Julius Torrend, *Specimens*, 85 ff.

25 Photographed by the author in Kangaba, Mali, 1969.

26 Torrend, 9-14.

27 Ibid., 24-28.

28 Julius Torrend, *Specimens*, 40-46.
29 Ibid., 97-145.
30 Daniel Biebuyck and Kahombo C. Mateene, *The Mwindo Epic*, Berkeley and Los Angeles (University of California Press) 1969.
31 Torrend adopted the convenient practice of dividing such long tales as "Kapepe" into sections according to the tunes of the songs specific to each.
32 Torrend, 145.
33 For more information about this tree in Central African fable, see Doke, *Lamba Folk-Lore*, 39 ff., and the *Zambesi Mission Record* for the year 1907, number 35, page 142.
34 Victor W(itter) Turner, "Symbols in Ndembu Ritual," in: *Closed Systems and Open Minds: The Limits of Naivety in Social Anthropology*, edited by Max Gluckman, Chicago (Aldine Publishing Company) 1964. 20-51.
35 Ibid., 26.
36 James George Frazer, *The Magic Art and the Evolution of Kings*, London (MacMillan and Company) 1911, vol. I, 8-9.
37 Ibid., 11.
38 Ibid., 21.
39 The italics are mine.
40 This translation is from *The New English Bible*.
41 It is immaterial whether Paul or anyone else in particular wrote what we read in the Epistle to Timothy. The point is that it had the force of religious dictate down through the ages of Christian history, not so much to the detriment of actual storytelling, which is simply irrepressible in man, but to the great detriment of analytical knowledge about oral fable, which could not be concertedly studied in an open, organized manner wherever and so long as the Pauline doctrine held sway.
42 J. G. Frazer, *The Magic Art and the Evolution of Kings*, vol. 2, 7-96.
43 In the *Journal of Hellenic Studies*, vol. 21, 1901, pps. 99-204.
44 Arthur J(ohn) Evans, "Mycenaean Tree and Pillar Cult," p. 106.
45 Ibid., 145.
46 Ibid., 186.
47 Ibid., 163-164.
48 Ibid., 156-157.
49 Ibid., 164.
50 Evans had not yet adopted the term 'Minoan' to differentiate his own archaeological discoveries of Bronze-Age civilization on Crete from the remains of the somewhat later Bronze-Age civilization on the Greek mainland which is now properly designated 'Mycenaean.'
51 Henri Frankfort, *Cylinder Seals: A Documentary Essay on the Arts and Religion of the Ancient Near East*, London (MacMillan and Co.) 1939, pps. 107 and 181.
52 Edith Porada and Briggs Buchanan, *Corpus of Ancient Near Eastern Seals in North American Collections: The Collection of the Pierpont Morgan Library*, New York (Pantheon Books, Inc.) 1948, vol. 1, p. 89.

53   Ibid., 92.
54   Ibid., 92.
55   Ibid., 83.
56   Ibid., 71.
57   Ibid., 68-69.
58   Ibid., 67.
59   Frankfort, *Cylinder Seals*, 205-206.
60   Ibid., 206-207.
61   Ibid., 189.
62   Porada and Buchanan, *Corpus of Seals*, 67.
63   Ibid., 21-22.
64   Frankfort, 126-127.
65   James B. Pritchard, ed., *Ancient Near Eastern Texts Relating to the Old Testament*, Princeton (Princeton University Press) 1969, p. 85.
66   Frankfort, pps. 15 and 28.
67   Ibid., 30-38.
68   Ibid., 19.
69   Pritchard, *Ancient Texts*, 73.
70   Ibid., 73.
71   Ibid., 73-74.
72   Ibid., 75.
73   Ibid., 74.
74   Ibid., 78.
75   Ibid., 76.
76   Ibid., 79.
77   I have followed the translator's suggestion in Pritchard, *Ancient Texts*, page 82, that the cedar is singular, and have altered the translation accordingly.
78   Pritchard, 82.
79   Ibid., 83.
80   Ibid., 83.
81   Ibid., 85.
82   Ibid., 88.
83   Ibid., 88.
84   Ibid., 97.
85   Chicago (Chicago University Press) 1970.
86   Grahame Clark, *World Prehistory: An Outline*, Oxford (Oxford University Press) 1962, pps. 16-17.
87   Evans, "Mycenaean Tree and Pillar Cult," pps. 201-203.
88   In *Sovetskaya ètnografiya*, nos. 1-2, Leningrad (Akademiya nauk) 1934, pps. 128-150.
89   See for example "Aschenputtel," No. 21 in: Jacob and Wilhelm Grimm, *Kinder- und Hausmärchen*, Munich (Winkler-verlag) 1949.
90   See for example "Von dem Machandelboom," No. 47 in Grimm, op. cit.
91   Leningrad (Leningrad University Press) 1946.
92   Leningrad (Leningrad University Press) 1955.

93 This tale is entitled "Hare, Hornbill and Tortoise," and is in: Merlin En-
nis, *Umbundu: Folk Tales from Angola*, Boston (Beacon Press) 1962,
pages 295-299.

94 See Albert B. Lord, *The Singer of Tales*, Cambridge (Harvard University
Press) 1960, page 97.

95 Ruth Finnegan, *Limba Stories and Story-Telling*, Oxford (Clarendon
Press) 1967, page 254.

96 Ibid., pages 254-257.

97 Ibid., pages 257-259.

98 Ibid., pages 137-140.

99 Cambridge (Harvard University Press) 1966.

100 Walker and Uysal, *Tales Alive in Turkey*, pages 64-71.

101 "Ženidba hajduk Golalije," No. 11 in: *Serbocroatian Heroic Songs*, collected and edited by Milman Parry and Albert Bates Lord, vol. 2, Belgrade and Cambridge (Serbian Academy of Sciences and Harvard University Press) 1953, pages 107-116.

102 Ibid., vol. 1, 1954, page 372.

103 Ibid., vol. 2, pages 149-157.

104 Unpublished text in the Milman Parry Collection.

105 See Figure 67 on page 355 for a visual representation of this method of
execution, which was one of the more appalling retributive uses of the
hewn wood in actual custom in the Levant. A complete verbal description of such an execution is in the modern Yugoslav author Ivo Andrić's
novel *Na Drini ćuprija* [The Bridge on the Drina] (see for example his
Sabrana dela [Collected Works], vol. 1, Belgrade, 1965, pages 44-52).

106 From Ali's lap to his shoulder, the stake is moved in its first two ap-
pearances in the story in a manner external to Ali's body that corresponds exactly to the points of entry, exit, and direction which his
executioners would give to the stake in the eventual act of spitting him
as prescribed by this method of execution.

107 Published in: *Serbo-Croatian Heroic Songs*, collected by Milman Parry
(Albert B. Lord and David E. Bynum, eds.) vol. 4, Cambridge (Center
for the Study of Oral Literature) 1974.

108 Ibid., page 386.

109 Algirdas Landsbergis and Clark Mills, eds., *The Green Linden: Selected
Lithuanian Folksongs*, New York (Voyages Press) 1964, pages 36-37.

110 Ibid., page 27.

111 Ibid., pages 30-31.

112 A common motif of ballad in the English-speaking world, the so-called
'Lovers' Knot' of sympathetic plants employs the image of the green
wood with affective connotations, e.g.:

> Lord Thomas was buried without kirk-wa,
> Fair Annet within the quiere,
> And o the tane thair grew a birk,
> The other a bonny briere.

> And ay they grew, and ay they threw,
>> As they wad faine be neare;
> And by this ye may ken right weil
>> They were twa luvers deare.

(Stanzas 29 and 30 of variant A, No. 73 in: Francis James Child, *The English and Scottish Popular Ballads*, Boston, 1882-1898.)

113 Landsbergis and Mills, *The Green Linden*, page 51.
114 Ibid., pages 68-69.
115 Ibid., pages 31-32.
116 Ritual or customary, that is, inasmuch as great numbers of such recorded 'lyrical' songs pertain in some way to seasonal (calendary) or personal festivals, customs, and rites.
117 Thomas Percy, *Reliques of Ancient English Poetry*, vol. 3, 1794, pages 350-358, and: John W. Hales and Frederick J. Furnivall, eds., *Bishop Percy's Folio Manuscript*, vol. 1, London, 1867, pages 103-118.
118 Hales and Furnivall, *Percy's Manuscript*, pages 105-106.
119 John Britton and Edward Wedlake Brayley, *The Beauties of England and Wales*, vol. 3, London, 1802, pages 51-52.
120 Ibid., page 51.
121 Daniel and Samuel Lysons, *Magna Brittania*, vol. 4 (Cumberland) London, 1816, page 112.
122 J. H. F. Brabner, ed., *The Comprehensive Gazeteer of England and Wales*, vol. 3, London, n. d. (received in Harvard College Library in July, 1895) page 133.
123 John Bartholomew, *The Survey Gazeteer of the British Isles*, eighth edition, Edinburgh, 1932, page 662.
124 Hales and Furnivall, *Percy's Manuscript*, page 108.
125 Ibid., 107-108.
126 Ibid., 109.
127 Ibid., 110.
128 Ibid., 110.
129 Ibid., 111-112.
130 Ibid., 112.
131 Ibid., 112-113.
132 Ibid., 115-116.
133 Ibid., 117-118.
134 Ibid., 118.
135 Gerard Murphy, *Early Irish Lyrics*, Oxford (Clarendon Press) 1956, page 108.
136 Ibid., page 109.
137 Ibid., 108-109.
138 Hans P. A. Oskamp, *The Voyage of Máel Dúin*, Groningen (Wolters-Noordhoff Publishing) 1970.
139 Ibid., 125
140 Ibid., 144-147.
141 Sean O'Sullivan, *Folktales of Ireland*, Chicago (University of Chicago Press) 1966, pages 97-117; 266.

142 Ibid., 100-101.
143 Ibid., 101.
144 Ibid., 101.
145 Ibid., 104.
146 Ibid., 104.
147 Ibid., 105.
148 Ibid., 106.
149 Ibid., 106.
150 A. N. Nechaev, *Skazki M. M. Korgueva*, Petrozavodsk (Karelian State Publishers) 1939, pps. 277-297.
151 A. N. Afanas'ev, *Narodnye russkie skazki*, volume 3, Moscow (State Publishers of Fine Literature) 1957, page 270.
152 A. N. Afanas'ev, *Russkie zavetnye skazki*, Valaam, Year of the Devil's Murk, pages 166-170.
153 Thomas C. Rumble, ed., *The Breton Lays in Middle English*, Detroit (Wayne State University Press) 1965, pages 207-226.
154 Morton W. Bloomfield, *Essays and Explorations*, Cambridge (Harvard University Press) 1970, page 113.
155 "Maya-mayi the Seven Sisters," in: *Australian Legendary Tales*, collected by K. Langloh Parker, edited by H. Drake-Brockman, New York (The Viking Press) 1966, pages 148-154.
156 Morris Edward Opler, *Myths and Tales of the Jicarilla Apache Indians*, New York (American Folk-Lore Society *Memoirs*, volume 31) 1938, pages xviii-xix; 210-213.
157 Ibid., pages 213-215.
158 Evon Z. Vogt, *Zinacantan: A Maya Community in the Highlands of Chiapas*, Cambridge (Harvard University Press) 1969, pages 319-326.
159 Curt Nimuendajú, *The Apinayé*, Washington (Catholic University of America, Anthropological Series No. 8) 1939, pages 175-177.
160 Warren S. Walker and Ahmet E. Uysal, *Tales Alive in Turkey*, Cambridge (Harvard University Press) 1966, pages 10-24; 259.
161 Ibid., pages104-111; 272-273.
162 Ibid., pages 34-54; 264.
163 Grimm, *Kinder- und Hausmärchen*, No. 1. I know the unreliability of this collection as a record of oral fable. The reader may, as I have, want to consult Johannes Bolte and Georg Polivka, *Anmerkungen zu den Kinder- und Hausmärchen der Brüder Grimm*, second edition, volumes 1-3, Hildesheim (Georg Olms) 1963, to verify the traditionality of the multiforms in Grimm of those particular motifs, patterns, and themes which I have discussed in this book. My use of certain material from the Grimms' collection should thus not be interpreted as an uncritical endorsement of the entire collection as authentic oral fable, which it is not.
164 Ibid., No. 16.
165 Ibid., No. 63.
166 Antti Aarne and Stith Thompson, *The Types of the Folktale: A Classification and Bibliography*, second edition, Helsinki (Finnish Academy of Sciences) 1961. Pages 195-197.

167 Edward E. Evans-Pritchard, ed., *The Zande Trickster*, Oxford (Clarendon Press) 1967, pages 17; 100-106.

168 Fanny Hagin Mayer, tr., *Japanese Folk Tales: A Revised Selection by Kunio Yanagita*, Taipei (The Orient Cultural Service) 1972, pages 85-87.

169 Aarne and Thompson, *Types of the Folktale*, pages 88-90; 113-114; 331; 431-436.

170 Afanas'ev, *Narodnye russkie skazki*, volume 1, pages 231-239.

171 Ibid., pages 228-230.

172 Georgios A. Megas, ed., *Folktales of Greece*, Chicago (University of Chicago Press) 1970, pages 113-119.

173 Edwin William Smith and Andrew Murray Dale, *The Ila-speaking Peoples of Northern Rhodesia*, volume 2, London, 1920, pages 347-348.

174 This name in Ila is *Chikambwe*.

175 Parker and Drake-Brockman, *Australian Legendary Tales*, pages 221-225.

176 Quoted with minor differences also by George Legman in his *Rationale of the Dirty Joke: An Analysis of Sexual Humor*, New York (Grove Press) 1968, page 447.

177 Found in: Legman, *Rationale*, page 449.

178 The English translation quoted throughout my discussion of Genesis One is from *The New English Bible*.

179 I am very grateful to Mrs. Susan Niditch-Doran for her kind, expert advice concerning the grammatical and lexical characteristics of the Hebrew words cited in this discussion.

180 Here and elsewhere I use the text of the *Theogony* edited by Friedrich Solmsen in *Hesiodi: Theogonia; Opera et Dies; Scutum*, Oxford (Clarendon Press) 1970.

181 M. L. West, *Hesiod: Theogony*, Oxford (Clarendon Press) 1966, 195-196.

182 Clark M. Garber, *Stories and Legends of the Bering Strait Eskimos*, Boston (The Christopher Publishing House) 1940, pages 160-164. For additional examples of the Two Trees in Eskimo traditions see also: D. Jenness, *Report of the Canadian Arctic Expedition 1913-18, Volume XIII: Eskimo Folk-Lore*, Ottawa (F. C. Acland, Printer to the King's Most Excellent Majesty) 1924, pages 49A-52A; 53A-56A.

183 E. S. Stevens, *Folk-Tales of 'Iraq*, London, 1931, pages 224-230.

184 V. Ja. Propp, *Morfologija skazki*, second edition, Moscow (Nauka) 1969, pages 25-28.

185 Parry text 12428, verses 1348-1353:
        Karamanluk je, i tmuša velika.
        Pokraj puta prevelike jele
        Preko klanca preplešu grane.
        Tijesni klanci, dugi karamani,
        Dok se Halku dade poslušati:
        Tutanj velik ide uz bogaze.

186 Further in Parry text 12428:
        I iz glasa viče serhatlija:
        "Bog te kleo, Brešljen gora kleta,   1355

Vazda li si tmušna i mrčana.
Noćaš nema vida od oblaka.
Doklen vida od oblaka,
Sve nahodah traga od djogata,
A sad više steže pomrčina.   1360
Nit' ja vidim traga djogatova,
Niti znadem kudar ću hoditi,
Ni sad dje ću Hrnjičića naći.
Dockan me je opravijo Mujo
Da mu brata putovima čuvam."
Halil čuje, a pita Osmana:
"Moj Osmane, poznaješ li, brate,
Koji soko u planini viče?"
Osman 'vako besjedi Halilu:
"Sreća, brate, i moja i tvoja.   1370
Ono mudra Kurtagića glava,
Od Otoke Kurtagić Nušina.
Nema brata dok ne rodi majka.
Vidiš što se potrudijo Mujo,
Te za tobom spremijo Nušina,
Da te mudro u Ozimu čuva,
U Ozimu i do tamo džadom,
Na svakome mestu tijesnome.
Tek, Halile, amanet ti težak,
Nemoj, što ne'š slušat' Kurtagića.   1380
Valah bilah, goješan Halile,
U svoj Bosni ni u svoj Krajini,
Mili brate, ni Undjurovini,
Ka Nušina serhatlije nema,
Ni u boju boljega gazije,
Ni na srcu Tak'og ljubavnika,
I njegova lica nasmijana,
Ka Nušina Kurtagića nema."

187   Further in Parry Text 12428:

Halil zovnu gazi Kurtagića:
"Nuško, brate ka od moje majke,   1390
Njesi, brate, mlogo ostanuo,
Nit' ćeš mlogo Hrnjičića tražit'.
Z desna, brate, na lijevo zadji,
Evo mene i Osmana amo."
Kad je Nušin čuo za Halila,
'Blagoš' reče, odsjede dorina,
Na lijevo kod Halila zadje.
Kad je doš'o medju pobratime,
Selam dade, pa pokraj njih stade.
Oba momka na noge skočiše,   1400

    A bijele ruke raširiše,
    S Kurtagićem Nuškom poljubiše.
    Halil Nuška za desnicu ruku
    Za gotovu sofru posadijo.

188 "Haso od Ribnika izbavi Mustajbega," Nos. 18 and 19 in: *Serbocroatian Heroic Songs*, collected and edited by Milman Parry and Albert Bates Lord, volume 2, Belgrade and Cambridge (Serbian Academy of Sciences and Harvard University Press) 1953, pages 158-184.

189 Ibid., pages 173-174.

190 Ibid., page 174.

191 Ibid., pages 55-98.

192 Ibid., page 60.

193 Unpublished text in the Milman Parry Collection. Consult volume 6 of *Serbocroatian Heroic Songs.*

194 Ruth Benedict, *Zuni Mythology*, volume 1, New York (Columbia University Press) 1935, page xiii.

195 Ibid., pages xiii-xiv.

196 Kenelm Burridge, *Tangu Traditions; A Study of the Way of Life, Mythology, and Developing Experience of a New Guinea People*, Oxford (Clarendon Press) 1969, page 195.

197 David E. Bynum, "Kult dvaju junaka u kulturnoj istoriji Balkana," in: *Anali Filološkog fakulteta* 4, Belgrade, 1964, pages 65-73 (English summary on page 73).

198 David E. Bynum, ed., *Serbocroatian Heroic Songs Collected by Milman Parry*, volume 4, Cambridge (Center for the Study of Oral Literature) 1974, pages xx-xxii.

Grandville

Index

Aarne, Antti, 26.
Aarne-Thompson folktale-types, 267, 271.
Abraham, 145-146.
Acacia, 146, 244.
Adam, see Genesis.
Aegean, see Evans, Arthur J.
Afanas'ev, A[leksandr] N[ikolaevich], 248-249, 272.
Affinal rivalry, 45, 50.
Affinity, see affinal rivalry.
Ali Agha Parmaksuz, lying tale of, 310-311.
Al Madhuna ('The Greased One'), 434 ff.
Anglo-Saxon, 8-13.
Anli, Mehmet (Turkish narrator), 261.
Anu, see Gilgamesh.
Apache, Jicarilla, 418 ff; 429.
Aphrodite, 212, 289.
Apinaye, 429, 430.
Apollo, 195, 276.
'Areş (earth in Genesis), see Genesis.
Aricia, see Frazer, James G.
Ark, Tabernacle, and Alter, see Moses.
Art[hur] of Leinster, 381-384, 385, 391.
Arthur, King, 365-374.
Asdiwal, 381.
Awabukuro, see Komebukuro.

Baobab (Adansonia digitata), 128-131, 133, 135, 136.
Baron of Tearne Wadling, see Tearne Wadling.
Banana-thief (Limba tale), 338-339.
Bees [see also Honey], 39-42 (in a grass-stalk); 51, 60, 90, 393.
Bel Beljanin, Emperor (character in Russian tale), 272-276.
Benedict, Ruth, 315-317, 319, 421.
Bene-Mukuni (Lenje), tales of, 98-146.
Benson, L. D., see Anglo-Saxon.
Beowulf, 8, 12, 13, 90-96, 107-108, 190, 332, 391.
Bettelheim, Bruno, 21, 23.
Bible, 165.
Bird (tattling), 106-109.
Bishop Percy's Folio Manuscript, 364.
Blind Padishah (Turkish tale), 259-260.
Blood-wood tree [see also Kalombe], 110, 113, 149.
Bloomfield, Morton, 406, 417.
Blue-Jay (character in Ila tale), 281-282.
Boetticher, Carl W., 171-172, 180.
Bronze age, see Evans, Arthur J.
Buchanan, Briggs, 195, 201, 206.

Buffalo (bush), 46 ff.
Bull of Heaven, see Gilgamesh.
Burridge, Kenelm, 317, 319, 412.

Cambridge University, see Smith, W. Robertson.
Campbell, Joseph, 21.
Captain Gal (character in Serbocroatian oral epic), 352-354, 365, 371.
Captivity Song (in Serbocroatian oral epos), 305-306, 319.
Coyote, transformation of, 421 ff.
Cazin (town in northern Bosnia), 309.
Cedar Forest, see Gilgamesh.
Centrifugence, 272-275, 276.
Centripetalism, 272-275.
Chante fable (African), 98, 109, 122-123.
Chaos, see Theogony.
Chiapas (province of Mexico), see Zinacanteco(s).
Child, Francis J., 30,31.
Chilubwelubwe, see Shichinongomunuma.
Chipwampwilu, 153.
Choban, Muharrem (Turkish narrator), 339, 344.
Christ and Satan, 8.
Christmas, 364, 395.
Cinderella, 25, 269.
Clark, Grahame, 242.
Concealments and discoveries [see also Seven Contests], 413-414.
Conflation (of real facts), 41, 51, 52.
Conner, Muiris (Irish narrator), 381.
Consanguinity, 50.
Cosmogone, 161.
Cosmotact, 162n (defined); 228, 238, 288, 346, 349-350, 358, 360, 381, 382, 383, 391, 394, 419, 434.
Creation, Biblical, see Genesis.
Crete, Cretan(s), see Evans, Arthur J.
Cu Chulainn, 377-379.
Cucumber-girl (character in Turkish tale), 339-344.

Dainos (Lithuanian oral poetry), 358-363, 364.
Dante Alighieri (use of Four Zones pattern), 265.
Dariji, Sukru (Turkish narrator), 259-260, 266.
Darwin, Charles, 157, 160.
Delilah, 44, 374.

Dema, Niaka (Limba narrator), 337, 338, 340.
Diana, *see* Nemi, Vale of.
Divina Comedia, see Dante.
Djulić Ibrahim (character in Serbocroatian oral epic), 306-310, 314.
Doctrine of Survivals, 244.
Doke, Clement (collector in Africa), 38, 41, 52, 53, 57, 58, 63, 69, 88, 98.
Double ax, *see* Zeus.
Douglas, Mary, 23.
Dragon, 276-277.
Drum(s), 115-117, 124-125, 132, 143, 239.
Dryopithecine, 257.
Dunai (character in Russian oral epic), 276.

Echo Man (character in Zuni tale), 421 ff.
Eden, Garden of, 72, 86-88, 381, 410, 420.
Eliot, T. S., 324.
Elohim (God in Biblical Genesis), *see* Genesis.
Emphatic repetition, 49, 103-104.
Enclosure of trees, 165-170.
Endogamy, 42.
Enkidu, *see* Gilgamesh.
Erech (=Uruk, q.v.).
Eros, *see* Theogony.
Eskimo, 430.
Essential idea(s), 3, 13-18.
Euhemerism, 315.
Euphorbia ('milk-tree'), 110-112, 145-154.
Evans, Arthur John, 165-247, 248.
Exogamy, 42, 43, 45, 58, 59, 60, 66, 68, 358, 360.

Fabulosity, 45, 250.
Fabulosity, expanding, 48.
Fall of Man, 72-78, 97.
Fann, 377.
Father-in-law, *see* "What a Little Thing Did."
Faulkner, William, 30.
Fiction, 38-41, 284.
Fig, 168, 190.
Finnegan, Ruth (collector of folktales), 337, 338.
Finnish School, *see* historico-geographic method.
Firth, R(aymond), 23.
Flood, story of, 118-119.
Food, paradox of, 70.
Food and progeny, 103, 115, 146, 154, 278, 283, 340, 420.
Food-trickster, 154, 333, 422.
Frankfort, Henri, 203, 206, 209, 214, 227.

Frazer, James George, 156-165, 203, 206, 231, 248, 250, 252.
Freud, S(igmund), 21.
Frog Prince, the (German tale), 261-262.
Fromm, Erich, 21.

Gaia (=Ge), character in Hesiod's *Theogony*, 289-290.
Geertz, Clifford, 23, 24, 326.
Generic meaning(s), 77-81.
Genesis, Biblical (Books 1-3), 284-288.
Gibbon, Edward, 324.
Gidgerigar (character in Australian tale), 282.
Gilgamesh, 192-193, 209-211, 214, 228-239, 264.
"Going-right-away," (flute in Lamba tale), *see* "Sons of Squeezer."
Golden Bough, the, see Frazer, James G.
Goomai (character in Australian tale), 282.
Greased One, the, *see* Al-Madhuna.
Great-mind theory, 257-258.
Green Tree Scene, 314-315, 318-319, 321, 326.
Grendel (and Grendel's dam), *see* Beowulf.
Grimm, Jacob, 20, 26.
Grimms' *Kinder- und Hausmärchen*, 30, 249, 251, 261, 262, 265, 271.
Gwaineebu (character in Australian tale), 282.

Hactcin, Black (character in Jicarilla Apache tale), 418.
Halil Hrnjica (character in Serbocroatian oral epic), 276, 298-302, 303, 305, 306, 308, 309, 350, 352.
Hare (character in Umbundu tale), 331-336.
Heaven, *see* Theogony
Helen, 120-121, 149.
Heorot (*see also* Beowulf), 339.
Herbivores, 181, 182, 189, 202, 216, 220-226, 349, 351.
Hermes, 276.
Hesiod, *see* Theogony.
'High' or sky-god, 190, 195, 240, 281, 358, 360.
Historico-geographic method (Finnish School), 20, 25, 27, 314-315, 397, 399.
History, 36.
Homer, 3, 5, 11, 12; 180, 323-324, 337.
Hominidae, 242.
Honey, 39; in Samson's lion, 43-45; in grass-stalk, 39-41; 71; 46, 47-49, 57, 64-65, 71, 393-394, 396, 406-407.
Honey-guide (*inguni*-bird), 57-60, 66.

Honey-trickster (*see also* Food-trickster), 49-51, 63, 65, 66, 68, 114, 393, 396.
Hornbill (character in Umbundu tale), 331-334.
"How Can I Silence Katubi?" (Lenje tale), *see* Katubi.
Hrothgar, *see* Beowulf.
Humbaba (=Huwawa), *see* Gilgamesh.
Hypaethral enclosures (sanctuaries), 165-168.

Ibro the shepherd (character in Serbocroat oral epic), 346--349.
Inanna, *see* Ishtar.
Isaac, *see* Abraham.
Ishtar, *see* Gilgamesh.
Ivan Tsarevič (character in Russian tale), 272-276.

Judges, Old Testament Book of, *see* Samson.
Jung, C(arl) G(ustav), 21.
Juniper-Tree (German tale), 246.

Ka-labi, 98.
Kalevala, 288.
Kalombe, 122-124, 332.
Kapepe (Lenje tale), 122-146, 151-152, 348.
Kasere, *see* "What Do You Mean, Block of Wood?"
Katubi (Lenje tale of), 104-106.
Kay, Sir, 375, 377.
Khoja girl (character in Turkish tale), 266-267.
King Orfeo (Middle English lay of), 263-264, 272; 402-406, 408-409, 410, 411, 429.
Kluckhohn, Clyde, 23.
Knossos, *see* Evans, Arthur J.
Kobuk River (Alaska), 430.
Komebukuro (character in Japanese tale), 269-270.
Konteh, Dauda (Limba narrator), 338, 359.
Korguyev, Matvey Mixailovich (Russian narrator), 385, 391, 393.
Korman (mythical city in Serbocroatian oral epos), 349-350.
Kulenović, Camil, (Yugoslav epic singer) 352, 354, 356, 358, 365.

Lancelot(t), Sir, 375.

Leach, Edmund, 23, 408.
Lebor na hUidre (Irish), 377, 379.
"Let the Big Drum Roll" (Lenje tale), 106-109, 246.
Lévi-Strauss, Claude, 22, 23, 326, 399.
Limba (people of Sierra Leone), 337-339.
Linden, 240, 360-362.
(Mr.) Little-Hare and What Ate Wulambe (Lamba tale), 63, 67, 70, 75.
Little Thing (son-in-law in Lamba tale), *see* "What a Little Thing Did."
Lóeg, 377-378.
Lord, Albert B(ates), 79, 337, 346.

Máel Dúin, The Voyage of, 379-381.
Mag Mell, 377-378.
Magoun, Francis P., *see* Anglo-Saxon.
Mambia, Richard (Zande narrator), 267.
Man and the Ogre, Lamba story of, 69, 72, 75, 86-88.
Mandu, *see* Kalombe.
Mannhardt, Wilhelm, 161.
Marduk, 195, 198.
Maroula (character in Modern Greek tale), 279-281.
"Marriage of Sir Gawaine," 364-377.
Maya-mayi (characters in Australian tale), 407, 410.
Medjedović, Avdo (Yugoslav epic singer), 16, 297-298, 302, 303, 304, 305, 306, 310, 313, 314, 321-323, 357, 358, 377.
Meroudys, *see* King Orfeo.
Milk-tree, *see* Euphorbia.
Milutin (character in Serbocroatian oral epic), 307-308.
Minoan(s), *see* Evans, Arthur J.
Monsters (defined), 41.
Moses, 143-146, 185, 190, 244, 332.
Moslem ritual (at Tečino selo in Macedonia), 245.
"Mother, Come Back" (Lenje tale), 98-103.
Motifs ('nominal' and 'generic'), 77-81 et passim.
Mountainman (character in Russian tale), 387 ff.
Moya's fig, *see* Katubi.
Mudyi-tree (Diplorrhyncus mossambicensis), *see* Turner, Victor W.
Mujo Hrnjica (character in Serbocroatian oral epic), 276, 298-301, 350, 352.
Mukula-tree (Blood-wood tree), *see* Turner, Victor W.
Mulombe (Blood-wood tree), 149.
Multiformity, 65-66, 250, 314, 326.
Mumba (Mukuni narrator), 109-122, 132, 133.

Mustachio (character in Russian tale), 387 ff.

Mustapha [Mustajbey] of the Lika (character in Serbocroatian oral epic), 302-303, 352-356, 365.

Mwana Mbirika (Mukuni narrator), 393; *see also* Kapepe.

Mwana Rumina (Mukuni narrator), 133.

Mycenae, Mycenaean(s), *see* Evans, Arthur J.

Nabu, 195.

Nastasija (character in Serbocroatian oral epic), 345, 349-350.

Nastas'ja (character in Russian tale), 272-274.

Ndembu (people of Central Africa), *see* Turner, Victor W.

"Near-at-hand" (flute in Lamba tale), *see* "Sons of Squeezer."

Nemi, Vale of, *see* Frazer, James G.

Nimuendajú, Curt (Brazilian collector), 429.

Nkang'a, see Turner, Victor W.

Nkula, see Turner, Victor W.

Noble savage(s), 318.

Nušin Kurtagić (character in Serbocroatian oral epic), 301-302.

Nyx (Night), *see Theogony*.

Oak, 190, 240, 358-359, 361-362, 372.

Oak of Mamre, *see* Abraham.

Oakman (character in Russian tale), 387 ff.

Oakpone (character in Eskimo tale), 432.

Odysseus, 381.

Oedipus (Oidipos), 24, 25, 272.

Ogre-with-the-big-pot-at-the-back, *see* Shichinongomunuma.

Ohyahock (Eskimo narrator), 431, 432.

Okeanos, *see Theogony*.

Old English, *see* Anglo-Saxon.

Omer and Mejra (Serbocroatian oral traditions of), 350-352.

Omer Hrnjica, 350-352.

One-hopelessly-lost, *see* Shichinongomunuma.

Ooya (character in Australian tale), 282.

Opler, Morris (American collector), 418.

Oral Theory, 5, 8n.

Oratorio, 123.

Orpheus, *see* King Orfeo.

Osman Tanković (character in Serbocroatian oral epic), 300-302.

Osmanbey of Glasinac (character in Serbocroatian oral epic), 309-314.

Osmanbey of Osek (character in Serbocroatian oral epic), 302, 305, 306, 307-308, 309.

Ovid, *see* Pygmalion.

Ovimbundu (people of Angola), 331.

Ozim (mythical town in Serbocroatian oral epic), 297-301.

Panofsky, Erwin (parable of a dog), 36, 38, 52-53.

Parmaksuz, *see* Ali Agha Parmaksuz.

Parry, Milman, 3-19; 302, 306, 344, 352, 356.

Parry Collection, 3, 13, 297, 321, 325.

Parry Test, 5-12, 15.

Paul, Saint, 19, 159-160, 246.

Pauline doctrine, *see* Paul, Saint.

Perkunas, 358-360.

Pestle, mortar and, *see* "Mother, Come Back."

Piaget, J(ean), 21.

Pictorial art (as means of narration), 227.

Pineson, John (character in Russian tale), 385-393.

Plain narrative, definition of, 37-40, 52-53, 59.

Plane tree, 190.

Pontos, *see Theogony*.

Porada, Edith, 195, 201, 206.

Progeny, *see* Food and Progeny.

Propp, Vladimir Jakovlevich, 26, 246-254, 272, 293-296.

Punting poles, *see* Gilgamesh.

Pygmalion, 110.

Quinn, Esther Casier, 97.

Radin, Paul, 21.

Radovan (character in Serbocroatian oral epic), 346, 348, 349-350.

Rain-Lord (character in Lenje tale), 125 ff; 185, 348.

Rebbe, see Z., the *shohet*, story of.

Referential poetry, 358.

Rex Nemorensis, 157, 162.

Riddle of Samson, *see* Samson.

Riddling, 43, 45.

Robin Hood, 345.

Rood-tree, 97.

Salinas, Virgin of, 426-429.

Samson, legend of, 42-52, 58, 59, 63, 64,

66, 67, 72, 75-76, 106, 119-120, 185, 308-309, 332, 374, 391.
Seth, quest of, 97.
Seven contests (concealments and discoveries), 51, 59, 60-63, 119, 397, 412, 417, 425-426.
Shakespeare, William, 31.
Shamash, *see* Gilgamesh.
Shemsi Bani, Emperor of the Pidgeons (Turkish tale), 260, 277-278, 281.
Shichinongomunuma and Chilubwelubwe, Lamba story of, 58-64, 67, 70-71, 75.
Smith, Sidney, 203.
Smith, W. Robertson, 160.
Snake's Three Leaves, The (German Tale), 262-263.
Son-in-law, *see* "What a Little Thing Did."
"Sons of Squeezer and Mr. Water-Lizard, The Story of" (Lamba tale), 88-90, 92-97.
Spider Woman (character in Zuni tale), 421 ff.
Spurge, *see* Euphorbia.
Squeezer, Mr., 403; *see also* "Sons of Squeezer, etc."
Steeds of God, 363.
St. John's Day, 358.
Story-pattern (defined), 79, 259.
Story-telling, social custom of, 52-53; 79, 86, 325, 343, 398.
Sudan, 267.
Sunderance (and conflation of real facts), 41.
Symbol(s), definition of, 80.
Szasz, Thomas, 21.

Tale of Orašac (character in Serbocroatian oral epic), 297-300.
Tangu (people of New Guinea), 24, 317, 324, 412, 430.
Tearne (Tarn) Wadling, 363-373.
Tečino selo, 245
Tečware (character in Amazonian Indian tale), 264, 429-430.
Tᵉhom (abyss in Biblical Genesis), *see* Genesis.
Tension of essences, 337, 348.
Textkritik, 20.
Theme(s), defined, 79.
Theogony, 284, 288-290.
Thompson, Stith, 26.
Thorn tree, 135-139, 247-248.
The Three Empires—Bronze, Silver, and Gold (Russian tale), 272, 276.
The Three Feathers (German tale), 265-266.

Timnah, Vineyards of, *see* Samson.
Tohu wabohu, 285.
Toothed Vagina Woman (character in Zuni tale), 421 ff.
Torrend, Julius (collector in Africa), 98.
Tortoise (character in Umbundu tale), 334-336.
Tree of wisdom, *see* Fall of Man.
Trickster (*see also under* Honey), 331 ff.; 341, 343, 393, 394, 396, 414, 422.
Troop of new-born babes (*see also* Umbilical child), 99-100.
Troy Saga, 120-122.
Tsimshin, 23.
Tuman (character in Tangu tale), 414 ff.
Ture (character in Zande tale), 268-269.
Turner, Victor W(itter), 23, 149-156, 163, 236, 253.
Two brothers, tale of, 295, 318, 415.
Two Trees, 29, 140-142, 145, 146, 151-152, 217, 220, 238, 242-244, 254, 257-259, 331, 332, 336, 337, 340, 343, 344, 345, 346, 347, 348, 350, 352, 358, 364, 365, 372, 377, 378, 381, 392, 393, 394, 395, 397, 398, 400, 406, 412, 417, 418, 422, 426, 430, 434,

Ugljanin, Salih (Yugoslav epic singer), 13-18, 302, 305, 306, 310, 313, 314, 321, 323, 344, 347-349, 352, 358.
Umbilical child, *see* Katubi.
Umbundu, *see* Ovimbundu.
Unity, 88 ff.
Uranos (Heaven), *see Theogony*.
Uruk, *see* Gilgamesh.
Ut(a)napishtim, *see* Gilgamesh.
Uysal, Ahmet (Turkish folktale collector), 339.

Väinamöinen, 288.
Vansina, Jan, 23.
Variation, emphasis by means of, 86.
Vixr' (character in Russian tale), 272-275.
Vogt, Evon, 426.
"Voyage of Máel Dúin, The," *see* Máel Dúin.
Vrhovi (place name in Serbocroatian oral epic), 352, 353, 366.

Wakalulu, *see* Little Hare
Walker, Warren (folktale collector in Turkey), 339.
Wanga (tree), *see* "What a Little Thing Did."
Water of Life (German tale), 271.

Water-Lizard, *see* Sons of Squeezer.
Wedding of Smailagić Meho, The, 357, 377.
"What a Little Thing Did," Lamba story of, 38-42; 45-53; 57, 58, 66, 67, 71, 75.
"What Do You Mean, Block of Wood?" (Lenje tale), 109-122.
Whirlwind (character in Russian tale), *see* Vixr'.
Willow (*Salicaceae*), 240, 431, 433.
Witch, 91, 151, 344, 364, 365, 423-424.
Withershins (widdershins), turning, 302, 348.
Witz (narrative genre), 283.
Women, Three (pattern in fable), 265 ff.
Word of God, 293.
Wudu (wynleasne; wyrthum faest), see Beowulf.
Wulombe, *see* Little Hare.

Yellow Book of Lecan (Irish), 379.
ympe tree [*see also* King Orfeo], 408, 410, 411.
Young father, *see* Katubi.

Z., the *shohet* (ritual butcher), story of, 36-37.
Zapečnyj, Ivaško (character in Russian tale), 276-278.
Zeus, 190, 195, 240, 276.
Zinacanteco(s), 426-429.
Zuni, 317, 324, 421-426.